PUBLISHING HOUSE

151 Howe Street, Victoria BC Canada V8V 4K5

For information and bulk orders, please contact:
info@agiopublishing.com *or go to* www.agiopublishing.com

Luck was my Companion
ISBN   978-1-897435-09-0 (trade paperback)
       978-1-897435-10-6 (electronic edition)

Printed on acid-free paper that includes no fibre from old growth forests. Agio Publishing House is a socially responsible company, measuring success on a triple-bottom-line basis.

10   9   8   7   6   5   4   3   2   1

DEDICATION

To my daughter Susan and my sister Caroline,
without whose help and encouragement
this book would never have been written.

ACKNOWLEDGEMENTS

Special thanks to the late Angus Baxter, a well-known genealogist from Toronto, for his many years of generous help with family research, and to the staff of the Salvation Army in London, England.

Thanks also to Agio Publishing House for publishing my story, and to Bruce and Marsha Batchelor for their expert assistance.

Pictures of the Battle for Omaha Beach by kind permission of the U.S. Army Center of Military History.

Pictures of the Malta Convoy of August 1942, codenamed Pedestal, by kind permission of the Imperial War Museum. [HU043689 on page 221; GM001426 on page 230 left; GM001505 on page 230 right; GM001483 on page 231]

TABLE OF CONTENTS

CHAPTER 1

CHILDHOOD DAYS

The signing of the Armistice between Victor and Vanquished, on the eleventh of November 1918, brought an end to the First World War. With the remnants of the German Mediterranean fleet trapped in the Sea of Marmara, ships of Britain's Royal Navy patrolled the area, to stop them escaping under cover of darkness.

In June of 1919, five months after my birth, my father, Edward Rutley Pocock Marshall, Warrant Officer aboard *H.M.S. Wildfire*, was sent out to Salonika on a two-year commission of duty, to keep the peace between the warring factions in Greece and Turkey.

Not wishing to be known as a grass-widow, my mother formed an association with John Brandon, a stoker from the nearby naval station at Chatham. I was six months old at the time and things were moving along smoothly until July of 1921, when the inevitable happened. Mother found herself with child. I became a burden to her, so she took me to St George's Cathedral, London, and had me baptized into the Catholic faith. On the sixth of December that year, I was taken by a person unknown to the seaside town of Littlehampton in the County of Sussex on England's southern shores, and handed over to nuns of the Franciscan order at St Joseph's Convent.

There in the open doorway of a large grey-stone building, the elderly gentleman patted me on the head, before handing me over to an old lady dressed in black. Closing the door behind her, she carried me up a flight of stairs and put me in a cot, where I was left to cry myself to sleep. I was five years of age before realizing the place where I lived was a convent named St Joseph's, where children were cared for by nuns of the Franciscan Order.

My father, Edward Rutley Pocock Marshall, as a young man.

Built in the early nineteenth century, the convent was situated on the outskirts of Littlehampton. The building lay back off the road hidden from prying eyes by tall privet hedges, surrounded by six-foot high spiked railings. A safety measure we were led to believe, to stop undesirables from breaking in.

Looking out on a world the nuns viewed as evil, a life size statue of St Joseph guarding his flock stood amid a lawn of green edged with a profusion of colourful flowers. This appeared to be the only bright spot in a cold and forbidding establishment, the only home many orphaned girls and boys were ever to know.

Entering the convent one passes through an oak panelled door, along a heavily carpeted passage leading to a spacious office, where the Mother Superior received her visitors. Overlooking the front of the building, at ground level, is the children's nursery where I spent my early years, cared for by young girls referred to as novices. This period of my life was reasonably happy, as I recall, although at times an occasional cry of distress was heard when a child was smacked for wetting the bed. The unfortunate infant then had to stand at the bedside, with a wet sheet over his head.

Rising at seven each morning, the four- and five-year-olds were shepherded downstairs to the bathroom to wash their faces and brush their teeth, before dressing themselves. Then, under the ever-watchful eye of a member of the nursery staff, they were ushered into the dining-room for breakfast. Seated round a large table, each child was given a bowl of porridge with ample helpings of milk. As soon as the meal had finished they were taken into a classroom adjacent to the nursery and were taught lessons in the three R's.

Infants aged two to three were left in the playroom under the supervision of a young novice, until it was time for their mid-day meal. After lunch, the four- and five-year-olds were allowed out to play until four-thirty, when the final meal of the day was served. This was followed by evening prayers with all present singing the well rehearsed hymn *Star of the Sea*, before being packed off to bed.

As with all Catholic run schools, convents, and such-like institutions, prayers are said morning and night, come Hell or high water. So it was woe betide any child caught misbehaving during the service, which many of us were guilty of through sheer boredom. A dig in the back of the neck from the nun in charge, was enough to make you sit up and pay attention. Sunday was taken up with morning mass in the convent chapel said by resident priest Father Morrisey, followed by benediction in the evening.

At aged four, I left the children's nursery and moved in with boys from five to nine in the convent proper where the living quarters were dark and austere, with high ceilings and bare walls that took time to get accustomed to. When I discovered orphaned children at St Joseph's were shown neither love nor kindness, life lost its joyous feeling. The nuns in charge of us came from Ireland, and were strict disciplinarians. Moving around in crepe-soled slippers and dark grey habits that swept the floor, they watched a child's every move. Were it not for the clacking of their rosary beads as they moved along, you were never aware of their presence, as they sneaked up behind you like black ghosts.

Meals were served in the refectory, a large room with polished wood floor, where tables and forms provided seating for forty boys. In one corner of the room a large pot-bellied stove surrounded by a high wire guard gave little enough warmth in the winter, when the nun in charge saw fit to light it. There was no such thing as central heating at the convent in the nineteen twenties and early thirties, and as a result many children suffered with chilblains each winter. My sleeping quarters were up a flight of winding stairs leading to two dormitories, the lower dormitory for five- to nine-year-olds, and the upper for ten- to fourteen-year-olds. A door in the rear wall of each room used only in an emergency, opened out onto a fire escape leading down to the boys' playground.

At the age of seven I attended St Catherine's, the local school, in the town of Littlehampton, to which we were escorted by the nun in charge. Each school day I would walk half a mile back and forth to school with the rest of the boys, returning to the convent at the end of the day. While attending St Catherine's, I could not help noticing a vast difference between children shut away in the convent, and those who lived in town. At the end of each day the parents of children living in town arrived at the school, to take them home. The only home I knew was the convent, where everyone called the superior, Mother.

Throughout the many years I spent at the convent, often referred to as the house of horrors, the nuns, in whose care I was entrusted, never tired of reminding me I was an orphan. This I believed to be true until reaching the age of ten, when a parcel addressed to me arrived for Christmas of 1929. This set me wondering if they were telling me the truth, more especially since I received a postcard at the end of January 1930, wishing me a happy birthday. Enclosed was a postal order to the value of one shilling, which I was allowed to spend one penny a week on sweets. The name of the sender of these gifts, that continued to arrive until I left the convent, remained a mystery.

Sleeping in a large dormitory with twenty other children, who to me were perfect strangers, was rather frightening until I got to know them, and the strange nicknames they were given. With my surname being Brandon, they called me Brandy for short. It was at this particular period my life at the convent was to change quite dramatically, and from that day forward I learnt the real meaning of fear.

Come winter and summer we were sent to bed at six o'clock,

and with the light fading as the summer petered out, gas lamps in the dormitory were lit. Then on dark winter nights after the lights were put out I had to listen to ghost stories told by Dusty Millar, one of the fourteen-year-old boys. He would scare the daylights out of me with his tales of ugly witches on broomsticks flying off to haunted castles, where in dark dungeons they kept weird monsters and werewolves who ate people. Hearing this, I would hide beneath the blankets too terrified to move, until falling asleep exhausted.

One night I awoke with a start to see two figures dressed in white wandering around the dormitory, and thinking they were ghosts, I dared not move until they had gone. At six o'clock next morning my friend Paddy Ryan who slept in the bed next to me, removed the blankets covering my head, and whispered, "Sister's shouting for everyone to get up, Brandy, so you'd better hurry."

I was still in shock and sat there, staring at him.

"What's the matter, Brandy?" he asked. "You look as if you've seen a ghost."

"Yes, I have. I saw them last night, Paddy," I mumbled.

"You've been dreaming," he chuckled. "Dusty Millar's ghost stories must have given you the creeps."

"But I'm telling you, Paddy, I saw them," I insisted.

"Aw c'mon, Brandy, you're having me on," he laughed. "Nobody believes in ghosts any more."

"But there were two of them, Paddy," I protested. "They were dressed in long white gowns, and crept around the dormitory."

"I suppose you heard them telling jokes to each other," said Podgy Barnes, who'd been listening.

"What d'you mean, Podge, did you see them, too?" I asked.

"No, I didn't, you daft idiot, they were the two nuns in charge of our dormitory you saw last night," he said. "If they hear a noise after lights out, they come from their cubicle, and look around the dormitory to see if anyone is out of bed."

"Oh gosh," I said. "They frightened the blooming life out of me."

I was just getting used to my new surroundings when one of our favourite nuns left the convent, to go on retreat. Only to be replaced by Sister Rose, a real old tyrant who at a stroke altered the routine and comparatively easy going life we had become used to. Her strict code of discipline upset the peace and tranquillity of our daily lives. In its place a feeling of mistrust developed between ourselves and the convent staff, where none previously existed.

Like most nuns who came from Ireland, she was tall, pale of face and wiry, with piercing grey eyes. A sharp pointed nose set in a face thin and gaunt, resembled something chiselled out of granite. At times her nose would drip like a tap, prompting the boys to christen her, Dewdrop. It was a nickname whispered behind her back with derision by many of her charges who had good reason to loathe and fear her, as someone incapable of showing the tiniest spark of love or kindness. She would remain tight-lipped, aloof, and outwardly calm, until a child dared disobey her. Then without warning her attitude would change and the cruel streak in her make-up would come to the fore.

At the time, I was no more than knee-high to a grasshopper, a timid little boy just out of the nursery. I did, however, try to put on a brave face, even though I was scared to death of her. I well remember her first morning in charge and the way she strode into the dining-room to stand before us and gaze down on everyone, like some giant colossus. Her entrance had the immediate effect of stopping the usual hum of everyday chatter among children seated at the breakfast table. In the deathly silence that followed, you could hear a pin drop as those hawkish eyes swept around the room, causing everyone to fidget uncomfortably.

"You will all sit still and pay attention to what I have to say!" she screamed, and in a voice like thunder, said, "From now on, silence will be observed in the dining-room during meals."

Pressing home a demand for obedience from every child, she leaned forward menacingly like a vulture about to attack its prey, and warned, "Any child caught misbehaving will be severely dealt with."

An eerie silence prevailed on a hushed dining-room for several minutes with no one daring to move, until she turned on her heel to leave. Then, as if in a gesture of defiance, a peal of laughter erupted from the rear of the dining-room, causing all heads to turn in alarm. Turning around, she stood facing us, and in a voice both loud and authoritative, demanded, "Everyone will face the front immediately."

With cat-like strides she strode to the rear of the dining-room, where the culprit was sitting. Her arm snaked out with lightning speed to seize a boy by the ear, lifting him from his seat. Seething with anger she dragged the unfortunate lad in front of a stunned assembly and ordered him to face the wall, saying, "I'll deal with you later, my boy."

From that moment on I lived in dread of this nun who had just taken charge of us, after seeing how she caused the boy to suffer. Blood was seen to ooze from a bruised and badly swollen lobe on his left ear, where Sister Rose had dug her nails into it. Then, as he turned to look in my direction, I recognized him as the boy who befriended me when I left the nursery section. He was my pal, Paddy Ryan, whom they'd nicknamed Smiler. A sturdily-built lad of eight with a mop of red hair, a podgy nose, and a pair of laughing Irish eyes. He obviously had taken an instant dislike to Sister Rose, and the harsh discipline she introduced.

Paddy and I were told we had no parents, and were often reminded by certain nuns we were orphans. Why these so-called holy people would choose to treat us with contempt, I could never understand. On the other hand, children at the convent who had parents and were allowed home for their winter and summer holidays, never suffered the sort of punishment metered out to orphans, fearing they'd upset the doting parents.

Breakfast on this particular morning was a solemn affair, eaten in absolute silence. No child dared utter a word while sitting at the table, for fear of bringing the wrath of Sister Rose down upon their heads. Then as soon as the meal finished everyone except Paddy Ryan who waited to be punished was ordered to leave the dining-room, and file out into the playground.

Collecting our hats and coats from the cloakroom we were told to remain in the playground until the nun on duty was ready to take us to school in Littlehampton.

Moving within earshot of an open dining-room window I stood with a group of seven boys listening to the swishing of Sister Rose's cane, as it whistled through the air. There were seven of us, Bully Bromwich, Dipper Dykes, Haystack Jones, Podgy Barnes, Squeaker Smith, Lofty Towers and myself, counting each stroke of the cane she gave Paddy.

"He's getting six of the best," said Podgy Barnes.

"He won't feel a blooming thing," chorused Lofty Towers, a skinny lad also nicknamed the Pipe Cleaner. "He's sure to have a book stuffed down the back of his pants."

"Oh! I wouldn't want to be in his shoes," moaned cross-eyed Squeaker Smith, the snitch. "She's got arms like a big Irish navvy."

Huddled together underneath an open window of the refectory we heard Smiler's anguished howl of pain from inside the dining-room. Startled by Smiler's sudden scream for mercy, Podgy Barnes stood on tip-toe and peeped through the window to see what was going on, only to recoil with shock by what he'd seen.

Ashen-faced and visibly shaken, Podgy gasped, "Cor blimey, they've ripped Paddy's trousers off, and his bum's red raw."

Turning to cross-eyed Smith the Squeaker, Podgy sneered, "It's your fault, you little runt, you were supposed to hide old Dewdrop's cane."

It was at this point Smiler's agonized cries subsided to no more than a whimper, then all was quiet.

"D'you think he's alright, Brandy?" Lofty asked, a tremor of fear in his voice as he spoke.

"I'll take a peep inside but you'll have to watch out for the sister on playground duty, so she doesn't catch me," I warned.

A hurried glance through the dining-room window sent a shiver down my spine. Sister Rose nicknamed Dewdrop had the sleeves of her nun's habit rolled up above the elbows, revealing a pair of forearms an Irish navvy would indeed have been proud of. All the while she was swishing the cane back and forth in a threatening manner over a whimpering Smiler, as he struggled to put his trousers on. Beads of perspiration glistened on Dewdrop's forehead, but the granite-like face, having turned from grey to red as a result of her exertion, showed not the slightest trace of emotion.

Fearing I'd be caught by the nun on duty, I quickly moved away from the window when the warning bell rang out, reminding everyone it was time we were off to school.

"Let's go," shouted Podgy Barnes, and off they ran with me in hot pursuit, struggling to put my hat and coat on as I ran toward the convent gates. There I joined up with the rest of the boys for our daily trek to St Catherine's.

.   .   .

School was the happiest part of my childhood. I looked upon it as a haven of safety, free from the everyday fear I lived with at St Joseph's Convent. Each school day I looked forward to a few precious hours of freedom, to mix and enjoy a little fun and laughter with children from Littlehampton. One such occasion I recall was the day my town friend Paul Engle received a clockwork submarine for his birthday, and brought it to school to show his friends.

Proud as a peacock, Paul lifted the toy submarine from its box and held it aloft for his pals to see. "Let's take it to the boating pond this afternoon instead of going to cricket practice," they chorused. "We don't have to let teacher know."

Without bothering to ask the head teacher for permission we hurried to the huge boating pond, where children of all ages sailed their model yachts. Taking the submarine from its box, Paul wound up the tiny mechanism and placed it in the water. Surging forward, the toy submarine gathered speed as it circled the pond, much to the delight of all. This was a toy the convent boys had never set eyes on before.

"Gosh, that's smashing," said Lofty, dancing with delight.

"Wind it up again, Paul?" pleaded Haystack Jones.

A jolly good idea came the response from all the lads present except Podgy Barnes, who as usual did not agree. "Submarines are supposed to go under water, so why can't yours?" he moaned.

It was at this point Gerald Bromwhich the school bully butted in and said, "Why don't you leave him alone, Podgy, it's his birthday present, not yours. Maybe we should chuck you in the pond instead of the submarine," he laughed. "You need a good ducking."

Podgy stood quietly by as Paul wound up the tiny engine of his toy submarine. He dare not utter a word in protest until Bully Bromwhich, who scared him to death, was out of earshot. Only then did Podgy whisper in Paul's ear, "Tilt the rudder so we can watch it dive."

Doing as Podgy asked, Paul placed his submarine back in the water and looked somewhat apprehensive, as it circled the pond to slowly disappear beneath the murky waters. When the submarine failed to reappear, Paul feared it was trapped on some object below the surface, and a gasp of alarm escaped the lad. All this while the submarine's tiny propeller continued to churn up the water causing a muddy patch to appear on the surface. Seeing this, Paul's look of horror quickly turned to tears, as Podgy taunted him.

"The blooming thing's been torpedoed," he hollered, breaking into a fit of laughter.

The loss of Paul's birthday present upset everyone except Podgy Barnes who carried on laughing, until Bully Bromwhich reappeared. Hearing what had happened to the boy's submarine, he walloped Barnes round the ear. The noise attracted the attention of Spit on the Baton, the town policeman, who happened to be passing by on his beat.

"What's the matter, sonny?" he asked Paul, who stood at the edge of the pond, crying.

"I've lost me submarine, mister," Paul wailed.

"You've done what, lad?" said the policeman, puzzled by the boy's remark.

Removing his helmet the policeman wiped a stream of perspiration running down his fat red face and scratching his ginger mop, remarked, "Did you say you'd lost a submarine, son?"

The mystified policeman looked around, and seeing no sign of it, asked the boy, "So where is it then?"

Pointing to the muddy water in the pond, Paul sobbed, "It's somewhere down there, mister, stuck in the mud."

With a considerable effort, the portly constable loosened his uniform jacket, and bent his huge torso over the edge of the pond. Scanning the muddy waters and seeing nothing, he turned to face the lad and sternly declared, "'Ere, are you 'aving me on, son?"

"Oh no, sir!" cried Paul through his tears. "It was my birthday present."

"It must be stuck in the blinking mud down here," groaned Squeaker Smith, "'cause I can't see anything."

"That's because you're cross-eyed, you daft bat," sneered Lofty.

It was then pint-sized Dipper Dykes pointed an accusing finger at Podgy Barnes, and hollered, "He's to blame! It was him who told Paul to make it dive underneath the water. I heard him, the big fat slob."

Dykes didn't wait to hear the fat boy threatening to punch his face in and took to his heels, with Podgy in hot pursuit. Seeing the huge figure of Spit on the Baton, the village policeman, peering into the pond looking for Paul's missing submarine, Dykes sought refuge behind him. When looking round to find Podgy within an arm's length of him, he collided with the policeman. A stifled cry of alarm escaped the boy's lips, and with a loud splash the pair fell head first into the pond. A column of water shot high in the air, as together they disappeared beneath the muddy surface.

Dykes was the first to pop up from the murky depths to discharge a mouthful of muddy water, and draw in great gulps of fresh air. But there was no sign of Spit on the Baton other than a stream of bubbles rising from below the surface, marking the spot where he'd disappeared.

Then like some prehistoric monster from bygone days, he suddenly re-appeared from the deep. Making huffing and puffing noises like a wounded walrus he waded to the edge of the pond, and prepared to clamber out. Seeing young Dykes in the water nearby trying to scramble out of the pond, he seized him by the scruff of the neck, and shaking the frightened lad as if he were a rag doll, said, "Now then, my lad, what's your blooming game?"

"It weren't me, mister," pleaded the boy. "I was pushed in by Podgy Barnes. He's standing over there, mister," said Dykes, pointing to a group of boys at the edge of the pond.

But he might as well have tried looking for the proverbial needle in the haystack because Podgy Barnes was nowhere in sight, having long since disappeared from the scene. Letting the frightened lad go, the policeman warned him to be more careful in future, whereupon young Dykes quickly took to his heels. He was long out of sight by the time the wet and bedraggled policeman returned to the local police station, to make his report.

Meanwhile, Dykes arrived back at school soaked to the skin, and was told by his form teacher to report to Miss Malone the head mistress, nicknamed 'Molly' by all her pupils.

Differing in many ways from other teachers at St. Catherine's, Miss Malone was a buxom lady with arms like the branches of a young oak tree, or as one of her pupils was heard to remark, "Cor, she's built to withstand the force of an earthquake."

Waiting outside the head teacher's study, young Dykes shivered convulsively, more in fear of having to face the wrath of Miss Malone, than from the wet clothes he stood in. Then in answer to his timid knock on her door, she replied in her usual authoritative voice, "Come in."

With a feeling akin to terror, the boy's hand shook like a leaf as he slowly inched his way forward to touch the door handle, causing it to rattle.

Irritated by the noise, the head teacher shouted, "I said come in whoever you are. Or are you deaf?"

Plucking up courage, a somewhat shaken Dykes once again took hold of the door handle, and gently pushed it open. Stepping inside he stood in awe of the enormous figure of Miss Malone, staring at him from behind her desk. He was lost for words, too frightened to speak.

"Well, aren't you going to close the door behind you?" she growled, peering at him over horn-rimmed reading glasses.

Dykes appeared nervous and unable to move. He simply stood rooted to the spot like the fly trapped in the spider's web, waiting for the head teacher to devour him. With a supreme effort he forced himself forward and with mechanical step pushed Miss Malone's study door shut, then waited for her to pronounce sentence on him.

Removing her glasses, Miss Malone placed them on the desk in front of her. Then, easing her huge body off the high-backed chair on which she sat, she approached the boy in a threatening manner. Towering head and shoulders above the petrified Dykes, she thundered, "And what in heavens name have you been up to, my lad?"

While the head teacher watched muddy water from the boy's sodden clothing drip onto the polished floor of her study, she waited for Dykes to explain what had happened to him.

"Sorry, miss," a tearful Dykes stammered. "It weren't my fault, I was pushed in by Podgy Barnes."

"Pushed in where?" she asked.

"'Twas at the boat pond, miss," said Dykes, gesticulating with his hands, trying to explain to an irate head teacher how he had come to be in such a mess.

"And what, may I ask, were you doing at the boat pond," she replied, "when you were supposed to be at cricket practice?"

There was nothing he could say in response to her question, and chose to remain silent. This seemed to irritate the head teacher who simply lost patience with the boy and ushered a wet and dishevelled Dykes out of her study. Rebuking him as he left, she warned, "You had better go and get yourself cleaned up. I will find out who was responsible for this later."

As the bell rang out for their afternoon break, children in class seven were told to remain at their desks, while the head teacher lectured them. Deploring their unruly behaviour, Miss Malone reprimanded whoever was responsible for disobeying orders, and declared, "All games will be cancelled until further notice."

Turning to Podgy Barnes, whom she ordered to face the wall, she hissed, "You, my boy, will also remain in class during playtime, as an extra punishment for your part in this dreadful incident."

No sooner had she left the classroom, Bully Bromwhich, a keen sports enthusiast who loved his game of cricket, objected to the head teacher's decision. Pointing an accusing finger at Paul Engle, he shouted, "You're to blame for this. Did you have to bring that blooming submarine of yours to school, you stupid idiot?"

Then shaking his fist at the boy in a threatening manner, he scared the daylights out of the lad. It was at this point my pal Paddy Ryan and I stepped forward to protect our friend, and told Bully Bromwhich to leave him alone.

"It's Podgy Barnes you should be speaking to," we told him. "He's the one who got us into this mess."

Bully Bromwhich simply shrugged his shoulders as if to say "who cares," and wandered off, in search of the missing Barnes.

It had come as something of a shock to Bromwhich when the head teacher decided to cancel all games until further notice, so he planned to get even with her. But, one way or another, he now faced the prospect of extra lessons in class on subjects that bored him to death, instead of playing his afternoon game of cricket.

Seeing the head teacher standing at the school gates when they arrived next morning, prompted latecomers to hurry to their respective classrooms, to avoid being marked absent. Children in class seven sat quietly at their desks that morning waiting for the head teacher, who had yet to arrive. Yesterday's episode at the boating pond appeared to have been forgotten by everyone in class seven except Bully Bromwhich, who told his pals he had a surprise in store for Miss Malone.

"She's late," said Bromwhich irritably. "I wonder where the old windbag's got to?"

"Probably looking to see if anyone is on the loo," said Paddy, with a derisive chuckle.

"She must have fallen in," joked Lofty.

The animated chatter ceased abruptly, as the door leading from the head teacher's study into class seven, swung open. Framed in the doorway was the awesome figure of Miss Malone who, like some feudal baron, looked down on their subjects before going into battle. Taking stock of her surroundings, the piercing blue eyes swept the classroom looking for absentees. Evidently satisfied she had the attention of her entire class, she addressed them in her usual authoritarian voice, "Good morning, children."

As one, the class responded with the well-rehearsed greeting, "Good morning, miss."

Then in a voice that echoed through the rafters, she said, "Each child will answer their name, as I call the register."

Bully Bromwhich, sitting with his pals at the rear of the class, was getting impatient, and muttered under his breath, "Why doesn't she hurry up and sit down to read the blooming register?"

Watching her every move, he rubbed his hands together gleefully, as with purposeful steps she now strode toward her desk. Bully could hardly wait to see her fall into the trap he'd set for her, and a feeling of satisfaction welled up within him.

For such a large person she appeared to move with consummate ease as she squeezed her huge body between desk and high chair. Then, placing one foot on the bottom rung of the chair, she hoisted herself up and gingerly lowered her considerable posterior into position, on the seat below. As her broad beam touched the chair, an agonized howl of pain escaped her lips. For one of such ample girth it was simply amazing to see her leap from the chair with the speed and agility of a scalded cat, hurtling across the classroom. With a sickening thud she bounced off the opposite wall to land in a crumpled heap on the floor, and lay prostate. Were it not for her ample bosom heaving up and down like the roaring tide she might have been mistaken for dead, for there appeared to be no other sign of life in her.

Suddenly the inert figure moved, as she fought to catch her breath. Her hand moved ever so slowly down to her posterior, to remove the object lodged in her backside. Seeing a large drawing pin in the palm of the teacher's hand, the children burst into fits of laughter, reverberating around the classroom. In a gesture of mock sympathy, Podgy

Barnes asked the head teacher, "Will you be needing a stretcher, miss?"

"That's enough from you, my boy," snarled Molly Malone, wincing with pain. "We can do without your sarcastic wit, thank you."

The boy's saucy remark caused a ripple of muted laughter among the children, who appeared to be enjoying the head teacher's fall from grace. Grimacing with pain she staggered to her feet, and faced the class. Her ghostly white face quickly turned a bright crimson as the children, treating the incident as a joke, laughed at her. In an effort to regain control she moved with determined step, to confront the assembly.

Hands on hips and legs astride, like some Sergeant Major on parade, she stood there studying the face of each child in turn, looking for some sign of guilt. Finding none she limped over to her desk and taking out a heavy stick she used as a punishment cane, brought it down with a resounding whack on the desk top. The noise startled her pupils who sat in hushed silence while she began to lecture them, and warned, "Whoever is responsible for this outrageous behaviour will own up now," then adding, "The culprit will be found I can assure you."

There was no response, and with a look of disgust at the silent class, she hobbled from the room, saying, "You have two minutes to make up your minds and, if on my return the culprit has not come forward, you will all be severely punished."

No sooner had the head mistress left the room, children started accusing one another of placing the drawing pin on the head teacher's chair. No one dared ask Bully Bromwhich if he was responsible for Miss Malone's untimely exit, as he sat watching them squabbling among themselves. Satisfied his secret was safe he sat gloating, thinking he'd got away with it.

Hidden away in one corner of the classroom, Squeaker Smith was whispering in the shell-like ear of Kathleen Byrne, a shortsighted girl with long black hair, Squeaker Smith's only friend at school, and like him, an informer. Neither was trusted by the boys and girls at St Joseph's and although Smith was not a friend of Bully Bromwhich, he must have overheard Bully telling his pals he'd put the drawing pin on the head teacher's chair, and decided to tell the girl.

Before any of Bully's friends could warn the Squeaker not to snitch, the classroom door opened and in the silence that followed, they watched their teacher limp across the room to her desk. Carefully examining the seat of her chair, she gently massaged her rear end with the palm of her hand before easing herself into place. Then taking stock of her silent classroom, she declared, "Well, have you made up your minds yet?"

Hardly had the words been spoken when a hand was raised, at the back of the class.

"You there with your hand up, come out here!" cried Miss Malone, a look of triumph on her face.

Then, as if by some prearranged signal, every pupil in class seven turned to stare at the informer who as we fully expected was none other than Kathleen Byrne. Ignoring whispered insults and threats to her person from Gerald Bromwhich's friends, she strode toward the head teacher, who smiled with satisfaction as the girl approached her desk.

"Come along now, I'm not going to bite you," Miss Malone reassured the girl. "Tell me, do you know who the culprit is?"

Without further prompting from the head teacher, she spluttered, "Please, miss, it was Gerald Bromwhich," and turned to point an accusing finger at the boy.

Squeaker Smith's face had by now turned a deathly shade of white and Bully Bromwhich's pals threatened, "We'll get you for this, Squeaker."

Wincing with pain, the head teacher rose from her chair and limped to the back of the classroom, where Bully Bromwhich sat at his desk in stunned silence.

"So it was you, my fine bully boy, who put the drawing pin on my chair," she sneered and, seizing the terrified lad by the scruff of the neck, dragged him from his desk to a corner of the classroom.

"Face the wall, my lad. I'll deal with you later," she said.

As the bell for morning break rang out, the pupils in class seven put away their books and filed out into the playground, leaving Gerald Bromwhich to be dealt with by the head mistress. Out in the playground the sound of children's voices at play was suddenly hushed by a high pitched squeal of pain from Bully Bromwhich, as Miss Malone walloped him with the cane, much to the delight of many boys and girls who lived in town, and were scared stiff of the bully. Now it was his turn to receive a taste of his own medicine from the head teacher.

An atmosphere of fair play continued to exist between convent and town children in spite of disagreements, and as time moved on we learned to value each other's friendship.

Some of the happiest moments in our young lives were spent at school with our town friends strolling through the Sussex countryside, or along the beach in Littlehampton, albeit with the company of a nun in charge. We at least were away from the daily routine of the convent. This helped bond a spirit of comradeship between orphans at the convent who were few in number and town children, vowing we'd stick together through thick and thin, come what may.

CHAPTER 2

A FRIGHTENING EXPERIENCE

Mid-summer of 1931 saw a dramatic change in the lives of or-phaned boys at St Joseph's, when Sisters Clare and Vincent were given leave from the convent to go on retreat, a time nuns must spend in prayer and silent meditation. This kind and caring couple, who on occasion scolded children for misbehaving, would never raise their hand to chastise any child, and treated the orphan children as human beings. The others regarded us as worthless creatures.

Shortly after they left, Sisters Anthony and Magdelen arrived to be greeted like old friends by Sister Rose. As evening shadows closed in, the ten- to fourteen-year-old boys were sent to their dormitory and told to stand by their beds. Minutes later the new arrivals entered the room and approaching each bed, looked the boy up and down, as if they were inspecting cattle at the market. Seeing one or two beds were not made as they would have liked, Lofty Towers, the boy nearest them, was reprimanded.

"Why didn't you make your bed before you had your breakfast this morning?" they asked.

His response was to shrug his shoulders as if to say, why should

I. This appeared to upset Sister Anthony, the smaller of the two, who screeched, "Haven't you a tongue in your head, boy?"

Then, reminding everyone they were now in charge, she said, "My name is Sister Anthony," and, introducing her partner as Sister Magdelen, demanded obedience from all present.

For a moment there was a hushed silence, and rather foolishly I asked, "Why did you choose the name of Mary Magdelen, sister? The Bible says she was a wicked woman."

Sister Magdelen's face turned deathly white as she approached me, and hissed, "What is your name, boy?"

Shaking like a leaf, I stammered, "My name is Ronald Brandon sister. I didn't mean any harm."

Obviously not the type to forgive easily, she simply brushed aside my protests, saying, "How dare you speak to me in that manner. I'll remember you for this. Now be off with you, and watch your tongue in future."

For a moment, I was rooted to the spot with fear but then hurried off to the far end of the dormitory, where the rest of the boys had gathered. Past experience served to warn me this episode would not go unpunished. Retribution would surely follow.

Sister Anthony, the smaller of the two in stature, had fiery red hair and the look of an angel with blue eyes that bored into your very soul, from behind gold-rimmed spectacles. Given to strutting around the dormitory like a ballerina with her nun's habit pinned up at the back, she became a target for much banter among boys who nicknamed her 'The Peacock.'

Her companion, Sister Magdelen, was twice her size and solidly built, with exceptionally large hands and a ruddy complexion that set her face aglow. Her deep-set grey eyes followed your every movement. The boy's nicknamed her 'Shino,' because the carbolic soap she used to wash herself with each morning made her face glisten in the morning sun. Her strength was such that a well-aimed clout round the ear from her ham-sized fist, was like a charge of electricity shooting through your body.

"You're for it now, Brandy," whispered Lofty, as Sisters Magdelen and Anthony turned to leave our dormitory.

"They're sure to be on the warpath, so you'd better watch out. Just look at the big one, she's built like a blooming battleship."

I knew I was in hot water and feared what might happen to me, but it was too late for regrets. Nothing could alter the awkward situation I now found myself in, and no amount of apologies would appease Sister Magdelen who would, I feared, punish me in her own good time for an unfortunate slip of the tongue. Little did I realize an unguarded moment on my part would give her the opportunity she had been waiting for, sooner than I anticipated. It was therefore with a sense of foreboding I faced the summer of 1931, realizing I would be under the watchful eyes of Sister Magdelen.

It was the end of our school term at St Catherine's and excited town children looked forward to their summer holidays. Back at St Joseph's convent most boys, waiting to go home, were busy packing their clothes away before their parents arrived to take them off. Waving goodbye through the window of the refectory as they left, I stood with other orphan children who were few in number, and tried to imagine what it was like to have a mother to care for me. All too soon, my daydream was rudely interrupted by Sister Rose, hollering, "How many times have I told you boys to keep away from the windows? They are images of the devil!"

What could we say? Orders had to be obeyed or we would all suffer the consequences. Discipline at the convent was maintained at all times, even during holiday periods. It was up to each of us so-called waifs and strays, a name tagged on to us by the nuns, to stick together at all costs.

During the long hot summer days that followed, we were taken for walks down country lanes with alternate visits to the stony beaches of Littlchampton, or along the sandy shores of the nearby village of Climping. While strolling along the beach in search of hidden treasure, one often unearthed a golf ball, the result of a wayward drive off the eighteenth tee on the nearby golf course. If perchance you managed to slip past the eagle eye of the nun in charge without being seen, the finder would be suitably rewarded when returning the ball to a club member. Sometimes a penny or two was given to the lucky boy, depending on the generosity of the golfer in question.

At a loss for something better to do, there were occasions when I would nestle down amid the sand dunes 'neath a warm midday sun, and watch cotton wool clouds go drifting by. Or maybe I'd be content to listen to the cry of sea birds wheeling overhead or the sound of an incoming tide, as it crashed on the shore. Sometimes I would lie there daydreaming and imagine I was a castaway on some desert island, listening to the cry of seagulls on the wing high overhead as warm ocean breezes caressed me, only to have my dream rudely shattered by the sister in charge.

Echoing back and forth across a wide expanse of empty beach, the raucous voice of Sister Anthony could be heard, hollering, "Come along there, Brandon, hurry up and get yourself dressed. We have to make ready to return to the convent!"

I was in no hurry to go back to that house of horrors and purposely took my time to slip my shoes on before joining up with the rest of the boys. Then, as was the usual practise, the nun in charge that day made a hurried check of all present, and found Haystack Jones and Paddy Ryan were missing. Ordering all present to remain seated, she crept down to the water's edge in time to catch Jones unaware. Just as Sister Anthony arrived on the scene, Jones was caught throwing the green bottle he'd picked up on the beach, into the sea.

As it landed with a splash in the surf, Sister Anthony shouted, "What are you doing there, Jones?"

His face turned as green as the bottle he'd thrown in the sea, as he stuttered, "'Er, nothing Sister, we were just having a laugh."

"Well, let's find out what's so amusing, shall we?" she sneered, a hint of sarcasm in her voice. "You can fetch that bottle you've just thrown in the water for a start, and bring it here to me."

Stripping down to his underwear, Jones waded into the chilly waters of the English Channel, to retrieve the bottle. A foaming sea swirling around his lanky frame almost knocked him off his feet, as he grabbed hold of it. Then, lifting it clear of the water, he turned it

upside down and shook it vigorously in a desperate effort to dislodge
its contents, but to no avail. A piece of paper, on which he'd written a
message, refused to budge.

"You can bring whatever it is you have there to me, Jones!" she
barked, as she watched him.

Jones's face had turned a deep shade of green, like the bottle he
was holding, as he approached Sister Anthony, and handed her the
wet piece of paper he'd taken from it.

"What's this you've written on here?" she said, as she opened the
wet paper and read the message the boy had written.

Sister Anthony's eyes narrowed and the pallid face turned a shade
of crimson as she faced the boy, and hissed, "Did you write this,
Jones?"

"It was only done for a joke, sister," pleaded the terror stricken
boy.

Pausing long enough to catch her breath, she threatened him,
"Just you wait until I get you back to the convent, my lad."

Fearing what might befall him as they neared the convent, Jones
was far from happy as he passed through the huge iron gates on that
summer's afternoon. The message he'd placed in the bottle, intended
as no more than a practical joke, had somehow backfired on him.
Instead of floating away toward the French Coast, as his pal Paddy
Ryan suggested it would, the bottle had drifted back ashore and now
lay in the hands of the last person on earth he would have ever wished
to receive it.

Realizing he had as much chance as a snowball in Hell of escaping the punishment laying in store for him, he prepared himself
for the worst. It was late afternoon when Haystack Jones faced the
wrath of Sisters Rose and Magdelen, the fearsome pair nicknamed
Dewdrop and Shino. Warning the boy he would burn in the fires of
Hell for writing such a blasphemous poem, Sister Magdelen seized
hold of him and, in one swift move, tore his trousers off. Holding the
frightened lad down in a vice-like grip across a wooden bench, she
allowed Sister Rose to beat him unmercifully, on his bare backside,
with the cane.

Each stroke wielded with immense power from the muscular arm of Sister Rose left huge red welts across the boy's bare buttocks, extracting cries for mercy from the terrified lad. His pleas were in vain, as Sister Rose's arm swung relentlessly up and down with hammer like force. Hearing the boy's agonized screams echoing across the playground, I ran to the refectory window to see what was happening, and signalled my friends to join me.

"Let's have a look," said Podgy Barnes, as Paddy Ryan and Bully Bromwich joined us beneath the refectory window, to peep inside.

A tremor of fear swept through the four of us, as we stood and watched them thrashing our friend Haystack Jones, well aware that, if we were caught, we'd be accused of spying on them and receive the same punishment. Luckily for all of us, we were able to stay out of sight from prying eyes for, had we not witnessed this horrific spectacle, we would never have believed nuns would carry out such an inhuman act. This was surely an instance when the teachings of the good book were tossed aside by people who should have known better. How could they treat children, placed in their care, with such barbaric cruelty, and call themselves Christians. Had they never read a passage in the Bible in which the Lord said, 'Suffer little children come unto me, and I will comfort you'?

I can not recall a time, during the ten long years I spent at St. Joseph's, when a spark of love or kindness was shown to an orphan child by many of these so-called charitable people. Having taken holy orders, there were among them certain nuns who seemed to derive some form of sadistic pleasure in punishing orphan children, without the slightest provocation, often referring to the old adage, 'the sins of the parents shall be visited on the children.'

Shepherded into the refectory for our evening meal, we saw Haystack Jones standing in one corner of the room shivering with fright, his tear-stained face pressed up against the wall. Anyone witnessing this act of barbarity (for there is no other way I can describe it) would not forget it in a hurry. As we prepared for bed that night, an air of sadness pervaded our dormitory knowing the same could happen to any one of us. There was little we could do to help him or let the nuns in charge know how we despised and feared them, whereas the town folk thought they were angels who could do no wrong. To us orphans they were nothing more than disciples of the devil.

Soon after lights out that night, I said to my friend Paddy Ryan, who slept in the bed next to me, "What did Haystack Jones write on the note he put in the bottle, Paddy?"

There was a slight pause, then I heard the sound of his muffled laughter, as he whispered, "D'you really want to know, Brandy?"

"Yes," I said, "let's hear it, Paddy, but you'll have to hurry before old Shino comes around again."

Listening to Paddy recite, word for word, the poem Haystack Jones put in the bottle, caused a chill to run down my spine. To Sister Anthony, this was nothing short of blasphemy, that went as follows,

Hail glorious St Patrick came down one day
And sat at our table munching away,
Like Oliver Twist, he asked for some more
So they kicked old St Paddy right out the door.

"You're kidding," I whispered, as he finished. "He wouldn't dare write anything like that, you're having me on."

"No, it's the truth, Brandy. I don't know where he heard it. Must have been from one of the town kids at school, I reckon."

"Blimey, it's no wonder old Dewdrop went bonkers. We'll have to keep out of her way for a while, Paddy."

Our whispered goodnights were said none too soon, as the door of the dormitory slid open on well-oiled hinges, and the ghostly figure of Shino, on her nightly rounds, appeared in the doorway. Holding a lighted candle aloft, as she moved from one bed to the next, her silhouette cast an ominous shadow on the wall opposite. As she approached my bed, I slipped beneath the blankets and, closing my eyes, lay perfectly still, as though fast asleep.

My heart beat ten to the dozen as her slippered feet crept ever closer, she hesitated a moment before bending over me and I heard the sound of her heavy breathing. A slight tug at my bedclothes was enough to remove the covers from my head, allowing the cool night air to caress my face. The sound of her heavy breathing grew louder as, once again, she bent over me and, in the light of her flickering candle, stood for a while studying my face.

Assuming I was fast asleep, she shuffled away, leaving me to ponder over the day's events. Uppermost in my mind, I recalled the terrible thrashing Haystack Jones received at the hands of two of these so-called god-fearing people.

Such was the measure of the boy's discomfort next morning. He had great difficulty sitting at the meal table, with the rest of the boys, in the days to come. The huge red and blue welts across his buttocks slowly faded with the passing weeks, as did the pain, but the memory of the brutal punishment he received would, no doubt, linger on. It would remain an episode in the young boy's life he would never forget, leaving him scarred emotionally, if not physically.

Time, as always, the great healer, allowed our orphan friend Haystack Jones to recover from the shock of the savage beating, as the final weeks of our summer holidays drew to a close. With the forecast of a warm sunny day for our mystery trip to an unknown destination on the morrow, excitement ran at fever pitch among boys in the upper dormitory, as night fell.

In the fading light of a summer's evening, a gas lamp flickered in the darkened street outside, casting eerie shadows across a now silent dormitory. Whispered conversations among boys at the far end of the room having long since subsided, I lay listening to my friend Paddy Ryan, in the bed next to me, snoring his head off.

Finding sleep impossible, I sat up in bed and, tucking my knees under my chin, allowed my mind to wander at will. Where, I kept asking myself, would our mystery tour on the morrow take us?

Deeply engrossed with thoughts of my own, I failed to hear the furtive tread of slippered feet moving up the stairs, until it was too late. Alerted by a noise on the stairs leading into our dormitory, I slid beneath the bedclothes and feigning sleep, I watched with bated breath as the door slowly swung open.

Through half-closed eyes I saw the shadowy figure of Sister

Magdelen, in the open doorway, a lighted candle in her hand. The wraith-like figure of Sister Anthony who, like an ominous black cloud, accompanied her wherever she went, stood behind her. Seeing the ghostly pair dressed in white night attire coming toward me, I was scared out of my wits as they approached my bed, fearing what might happen to me. Keeping my eyes tightly closed I lay motionless until Sister Magdelen placed her lighted candle close to my face, causing me to recoil in fright from its searing flame.

"Why are you awake at this late hour?" she hissed. "You needn't pretend you were asleep, Sister Anthony and I saw you sitting up in bed."

In the light of her candle I shrank in terror, as the face of Sister Magdelen leered down at me.

"It's too hot for me to sleep, sister," I stammered nervously.

"Oh! is it?" she mocked. Then turning to her ever-present shadow Sister Anthony, she sneered, "Did you hear that Sister, he can't sleep? We'll have to give him something to encourage him then, won't we?" she replied.

There was a rustle of garments as they rolled up their sleeves before snuffing out the candle and, in that darkened room, their hands reached out and seized hold of me. Lifting me bodily from the bed, they bundled me unceremoniously down the stairs to the bathroom below, where a bath of cold water had been prepared beforehand by Sister Magdelen. In a trice they tore off my night clothes, leaving me as naked as the day I was born. Then tossing me into the bath, one took hold of my arms and the other my legs, and proceeded to duck me up and down in the cold water.

My frenzied cries for mercy were stifled with a wet flannel Sister Magdelen repeatedly pressed against my mouth, to deaden the noise. Any attempt on my part to break free from their clutches proved useless, against such brute force. Every time I opened my mouth to snatch a mouthful of fresh air, my head was thrust beneath the water, banging my body against the side of the bath in the process. I felt I was going to die. When the bathroom started to cartwheel around me, suddenly the ducking stopped.

Only then was it possible for me to snatch a breath of air before my bruised and aching body was lifted from the icy water and, in one swift movement, tossed out of the bath. I landed with a sickening thud on the tiled floor of the bathroom, jarring every bone in my body. As I lay there panting for breath, Sister Magdelen threw a towel at me, and sneered, "Dry yourself boy, then get off to bed."

At the bathroom door she turned to look at me, and hissed, "Let that be a lesson to you, my lad. Hold your tongue in future and re-member, you're just an orphan, a nothing."

As she closed the door behind her, I heard her mutter to her part-ner, as they parted on their final rounds of the night, "That'll teach him to treat us with respect, Sister Anthony."

Drying myself with the damp towel, I crept upstairs and slipped between the sheets, to lie shivering. With tomorrow's outing all but forgotten, I lay weeping, nursing my bruised and aching body. I was a mere slip of a lad at the age of twelve and a half, and being small in stature was no match against the brute strength of a couple of enraged nuns, determined to make an example of me. Without a soul to tell my troubles to, or lodge a complaint, I lay there and cried myself to sleep.

A gentle touch on my shoulder next morning was enough to rouse me from a fitful sleep, and opening my eyes, I looked into the friendly face of my pal, Paddy.

"Wake up, Brandy," he urged. "We'll be going on our outing soon. You'll have to hurry and get yourself dressed."

Sunshine streamed through the open window of our dormitory on that bright summer morning of August 1931. But I could not, for the life of me, join in the laughter and merrymaking with other boys, who were getting ready for the day's outing. Throwing back the bed-clothes, I noticed a cluster of bright red welts on my arms and legs, that were turning black and blue. As I made ready to get out of bed, Paddy came over and whispered, "What's the matter, Brandy?"

Seeing the bruises on my arms and legs, he gasped, "Oh gosh, who on earth did that to you?"

He had been fast asleep when I was forcibly taken from my bed in the middle of the night, and had no idea what happened to me. I refused to talk about the treatment I received at the hands of Sisters Magdelen and Anthony. Just to mention the pain and suffering I endured would, I felt sure, cause my tears to fall like rain drops.

"Well, never mind, Brandy," said Paddy, doing his best to cheer me up. "You'll have a chance to get even with whoever did that to you today. Just wait and see," he said.

His words of encouragement seemed to help me forget my aches and pains as I quickly dressed in white shirt, grey shorts and socks, with white plimsoles. Then, having finished breakfast, we made ready to hop aboard two South Down coaches, waiting outside the convent gates.

"Don't forget to bring your football boots along with you, Brandy," Paddy reminded me. "We're playing the nuns at soccer today."

Prompt at eight o'clock that morning, two coachloads of excited girls and boys set off from the convent on their annual outing, for a day they would long remember. Seated at the rear of each coach, where they could keep their beady eyes on us, were two stern-faced nuns, who escorted us wherever we went. While driving through the town of Littlehampton, they demanded we be quiet.

Sitting well out of earshot of the nuns, I sat with Paddy Ryan, Haystack Jones, Dipper Dykes, Podgy Barnes, Lofty Towers, Cross-eyed Smith, and Bully Bromwhich who was to Captain our football team. Together we discussed our annual soccer match, against the hooded terrors, due to take place that very afternoon, determined to give them a taste of their own medicine.

Little more was said as we drove down country lanes in a northerly direction past quaint little hamlets tucked away amid rolling hills, in the beautiful County of Sussex. Skirting the green hills of Surrey, we sped on into the County of Hampshire and stopped at a small convent in Aldershot, close to an army barracks, where a group of nuns waited to greet us. We were now given permission to leave the coach to wander at will around the outer perimeter of the barracks, to stretch our legs.

Strolling around the grounds, we stopped to admire a life-sized statue of the first Duke of Wellington, Arthur Wellesley K.G. There he sat in life-like pose astride his charger and at the base of the statue was an inscription describing him as the most famous British general of the nineteenth century.

Lunch was taken at twelve o'clock and by one-thirty that afternoon, all was ready for the soccer match, due to take place on a football pitch inside the barrack grounds. Our team Captain, Bully Bromwhich, rubbed his hands together with a measure of satisfaction, when he read the names of the nun's team. "This is your chance to get even, Brandy," he grinned. "Sister Magdelen is goalkeeper for the nuns."

Sister Anthony, a dainty-looking fleet of foot nun, nicknamed the Peacock by the boys, had a violent temper when roused, and was down on the team sheet to play in the halfback position.

At one-forty-five that afternoon, the referee blew his whistle to start the game, and from the kick off we allowed the nun's centre forward to slip through our defence to shoot the ball past our goalkeeper, fat boy Podgy Barnes. Bully Bromwhich had given him instructions to let the nuns score the first goal, allowing them a little encouragement. From the restart, we took control of the game and slipped through their defence like a knife slicing through butter, intent on giving them a football lesson they would not forget in a hurry.

Trapping the ball with ease, our outside left, Lofty Towers, slipped it to Bully Bromwhich, who dribbled the ball towards Sister Anthony, waiting in a midfield position. As she challenged him for possession of the ball, Bully Bromwhich caught her in the midrift with a hefty shoulder charge, knocking the wind out of her. Grinning from ear to ear, he left her lying there on the field of play and passed the ball out to our right wing where it fell at the feet of Haystack Jones, who took the ball upfield toward the nun's goalmouth. Slipping through their defence with the greatest of ease, Haystack passed the ball across to me, waiting in centre field.

"It's all yours, Brandy," he hollered, "now shove it in the back of their net!"

Dodging Sister Magdelen's clumsy attempt to take the ball from me, I scored effortlessly. The score was now level one goal apiece until I managed to score a second and a third, to make it three goals to one in our favour. When, on my way upfield with the ball to score a fourth goal, Sister Magdelen, the goalkeeper, came charging toward me, in an attempt to grab the ball, I heard a shout of, "Sock it to her, Brandy," from Lofty Towers that seemed to spur me on.

I recalled how she had nearly drowned me during the night and, in that instant, I relived the pain and suffering all over again. Like an angry bull seeing red, I lunged at her, as she tried to pick the ball up, and, lifting my right foot back, aimed a terrific kick at the ball with all the strength I could muster, determined to score that vital goal.

As the toe of my boot clattered into her right ankle, the ball shot past her outstretched legs into the net. She gave an agonized squeal of pain, as her shiny red face turned the colour of chalk.

She collapsed in a heap in front of me, like a deflated balloon, to lay writhing in agony on the grass.

"Er, sorry, sister," I mumbled somewhat apologetically, trying hard to suppress a laugh. "Soccer's a tough game, you know."

Dashing back upfield, I took up my position at centre forward and waited for the referee to restart the game. There were the usual loud protests from our opponents saying one of there number was injured, that went unheeded, until the referee spotted the inert body of Sister Magdelen lying prostate in the nun's goalmouth.

A shrill blast on his whistle stopped everyone in their tracks and brought a protest from our Captain Bully Bromwich, who asked, "What's the matter, ref? Why have you stopped the game?"

"I think she's in need of help up there," the referee replied, point-ing to the goalkeeper, lying at the far end of the field, like a stranded porpoise.

"She's kidding you, ref," Bully Bromwich laughed. "I saw her eyelids flutter when she tried to get up. She's just having a rest."

As he spoke, two first aid men from St John's Ambulance, ap-peared on the field with a stretcher, and several nuns gathered around their injured goalkeeper. Placing her on the stretcher, they carried her off the field of play, to the ribald comments from several convent boys among the spectators.

"Don't forget the flowers!" shouted one boy, as another hollered, "Make sure they're dandelions!"

Shouts of, "Well played, Brandy" echoed around the ground, as I left the football field and entered our dressing room to change.

"She won't bother us for a while," grinned Haystack Jones. "You didn't half give her a wallop, Brandy."

"Serves her right," said Paddy. "She's had a taste of her own medicine, let's see how she likes it."

Throughout the rest of the day, little was seen or heard of either nun who accompanied us to Aldershot and appeared to be in no fit state to bother us, after Bully Bromwich and I flattened them on the soccer pitch. We were left to roam around the barracks at will, until it was time for us to return to the house of horrors at Littlehampton.

Sunset appeared to linger that day, as it slowly spiralled toward the western horizon, colouring the evening sky in hues of red and gold. For it was now mid-summer and the sun appeared reluctant to bid us adieu as it hovered above rooftops in a circle of fire, threatening to explode at any moment. Its sudden departure left us wandering about in semi-darkness as evening shadows quickly drifted in, prompting one and all to hasten to our respective coaches. In buoyant mood, we hurried aboard and sped away as darkness closed in accompanied by a canopy of stars twinkling in the night sky, while our voices raised in song echoed throughout the silent countryside.

Seated at the rear of the coach, our two escorting nuns, Sisters Anthony and Magdelen, listened in stony silence, to our rendition of Good Old Sussex By The Sea. Sister Magdelen sat nursing a badly swollen ankle with her hands hidden in the folds of her black habit, and looked straight ahead. Sister Anthony, on the other hand, lay moaning on the seat beside her companion, and massaged her bruised ribs. As a result of a heavy shoulder charge from Bully Bromwhich, it was pay back time, so she got no more than she deserved. Taking advantage of their inability to protest, Podgy Barnes and the rest of our team sang to our hearts content, as we sped through the silent Sussex countryside.

Our team Captain had given fair warning to Sisters Anthony and Magdelen before the game started, saying accidents do happen and people get hurt during a football match. This was simply pay back time for the pair of them who were nothing more than brutes, and got what they deserved for their cruel treatment of innocent children. Having finally settled an old score, we were in a joyous mood when arriving at the convent that night, and surprised to see a strangely subdued Sister Rose waiting to greet us in the refectory. For once in her life, she chose to treat us like human beings and offered each boy a cup of hot cocoa, instead of chasing us off to bed because the hour was late. Having to miss the day's outing, she no doubt had been informed of the accidents that befell Sisters Anthony and Magdelen from nuns arriving ahead of us. She must have thanked her lucky stars she wasn't on that coach trip, to receive the same treatment as her companions.

During the final week of our summer holidays, we were taken to Arundel Park, some four miles distance from the convent. And, although we were all dog tired after the long walk to get to our destination, we were more than happy to have the freedom to wander around the lake and wooded areas of the park. In this truly magnificent setting covering an area of twenty one square miles of parkland, one finds herds of deer, pheasants, peacock and rabbits, roaming their natural habitat.

Overlooking this scene of historic splendour from another period, stands Arundel's Norman castle, an ancient monument built in 1066 during the reign of William the Conqueror, attracting visitors from the four corners of the globe.

·   ·   ·

The following day, sudden change in the weather brought sullen skies of grey drifting across the landscape with the sun no more than a dull red glow, peeping above the far horizon. Abruptly the sky darkened and raindrops the size of penny pieces splashed across the dormitory windows, leaving criss-cross patterns on the dust-laden glass. It was a sure sign summer was almost over and the holidays were drawing to a close. It was also time to welcome back those of our friends fortunate enough to spend a few weeks at home.

Their return later that week coincided with Sisters Anthony and Magdelen leaving, amid loud cheers from all the boys, who were glad to see the back of them. Their departure made life a little easier for the boys at St Joseph's when Sisters Clare and Bernadette returned to duty and once again took charge of our dormitory. Unlike their predecessors, who were often brutal, this kind and caring couple treated us like human beings. Their very presence radiated a feeling of happiness, where none previously existed, because of their willingness to lend an ear to any child with a problem.

Back at St Catherine's for the start of a new school term in September of 1931, we saw many new faces among its pupils. As expected, the enormous figure of Molly Malone, our head mistress, was seen waiting at the school gates, welcoming parents of new arrivals. As large as life, she waited there bell in hand until several children strolled aimlessly into school, before raising the heavy object aloft. For a moment all was still, then her uplifted arm swung through the air in a huge arc. The clanging of the bell could be heard for miles around and pupils, fearing they'd be marked absent, panicked in their dash to school before the gates closed.

The month of September saw a continuation of the long hot summer with prolonged spells of dry weather, turning leaves red and gold rather early. Then, all too soon, our Indian summer weather tended to peter out as October crept in, with spells of intermittent rain and overcast skies. By the month's end, bitterly cold winds sweeping along the English Channel saw temperatures drop overnight with morning frost, turning the landscape into a blanket of white.

November, a dull and dreary month at the best of times, saw the annual lighting of bonfires, that took place on the fifth, a notable event in the British calendar celebrating the gunpowder plot of 1605, a period of much unrest in the country when a certain individual named

Guy Fawkes conspired with others, to blow up the Houses of Parliament. Fawkes himself was found hiding in a cellar below, and was subsequently hanged.

This also happened to be a time of year when children at the convent were normally privileged to enjoy watching the annual firework display, from dormitory windows. So it came as quite a shock to everyone when Sister Rose refused to allow us to watch the fireworks. She said it was the work of the devil and the possession of fireworks at St Joseph's Convent was strictly forbidden.

She was on duty that night and made every effort to prevent any child from watching the annual firework display. As a precautionary measure she covered all dormitory windows with seldom-used storm shutters, long before the celebrations began.

Determined not to miss the fireworks display, Bully Bromwhich told Podgy Barnes to wait until the Sister on duty put out the gas lamps and left on her nightly rounds, before opening the shutters. He then told Squeaker Smith to keep a lookout at the head of the stairs leading into our dormitory, to warn us in good time when Dewdrop, the night sister, returned.

As darkness fell, the night reverberated with the sound of exploding fireworks, followed by a brilliant display of colour. Peering through our dormitory windows, we watched with bated breath as a huge bonfire in Farmer Williams's field, directly opposite, was set alight, casting an orange glow in the night sky. Suddenly a fusillade of skyrockets, roman candles and fire crackers were seen to light up the sky in a breathtaking spectacle.

All too soon the celebration drew to a close with a series of loud explosions from dozens of thunder flashes and skyrockets, streaking across the night sky, ending in a riot of colour few boys at the convent. had ever been privileged to witness.

Long after the excitement of the firework display had simmered down, Lofty Towers suddenly remembered Squeaker Smith was still waiting outside the dormitory, keeping lookout. "Blimey, he'll be frozen stiff by now. Don't you think it's time we let him in?" he asked Bully.

"Yes, you can let the frozen turd in now," said Bully, who had a score to settle with the Squeaker.

"You can come in now," whispered Lofty, opening the door.

The Squeaker didn't need telling a second time. He shot past Lofty faster than a greyhound off the leash to tumble into bed, shivering like a leaf. Laughing like a jackass at Squeaker Smith's misfortune, Podgy hurriedly closed the storm shutters over the windows of the now silent dormitory, before the sister on night duty returned.

November's bitterly cold weather left many convent children suffering from chilblains and mumps as December swept in with darkening skies, cold easterly winds, and winter's first fall of snow. As it fell, gale force winds caused huge drifts four foot deep to pile up along country highways and byways, preventing children from outlying districts attending school. The landscape was hidden beneath a blanket of white, giving the countryside a touch of originality with the approach of Christmas.

Meanwhile, arrangements to celebrate this joyful event at St Joseph's Convent were well advanced. Dining-room walls festooned with decorations added a splash of much needed colour to brighten the drab surroundings. In one corner of the dining-room, fairy lights twinkled amid the branches of a Christmas tree, with a collection of parcels round the base.

Nobody was more surprised than I when the nun on duty called out my name and handed me one of the parcels. I stood for a moment staring at my name written on the package in bold black letters, wondering who could have sent this to me, until the nun on duty hollered, "The parcel is for you, Brandon, so sit down and open it."

A buzz of excitement filled the air as I opened the parcel, while my friends looked on. Inside was a model of a London bus full of mouth watering cream biscuits my pals and I managed to sample, before the nun on duty took them away.

We now looked forward to the New Year, and whatever surprises lay in store for us.

January, as usual, swept in with sullen grey skies and bitterly cold east winds, blowing in ever-increasing ferocity along the English

Channel. Down came the snow in non-stop flurries, obliterating the landscape for miles around. Our walk to school, on Monday morning, was rather hazardous after the heavy fall of snow over the weekend had frozen solid.

With the playground at St Catherine's inches deep in snow, it soon became a battleground when children arrived, hurling snowballs in all directions. The battle was at its height when Miss Press, deputising for our head teacher, Miss Malone, appeared on the playground, wrapped in heavy winter furs. She looked pale and sylph-like, standing on the snow-covered ground with a bell in her hand. Glancing nervously at her wrist watch, she slowly raised her right arm and shook the bell vigorously. Its urgent peals sent pupils running helter skelter to their respective classes.

Somewhat different in appearance, Miss Press was the prim and proper type. Slimly built and dainty with a mop of dark brown hair swept back off her forehead, the pale face and watery eyes looked out of place behind thick-lensed glasses. She was also hard of hearing, so pupils in her class nicknamed her 'Eggy.'

Toward the end of January 1932, I received the expected picture postcard and postal order for one shilling. As usual, it was unsigned, and simply said, "To wish you a happy birthday, Ronald."

Handing me the card, Sister Rose exclaimed, "I think its about time you gave a penny to the church, for a candle!"

To which I replied, "Oh! I don't think so, sister. The church has plenty of money. They've just bought Father Morrisey a new bicycle."

The words had hardly left my mouth, when her hand swung out in a huge arc and walloped me one on the ear, spinning me round like a top.

"How dare you speak to me like that, you nasty creature!" she fumed. "Go and face the wall, immediately."

Needless to say, I spent my birthday with my nose pressed up against the dining-room wall, counting the cost of a careless slip of the tongue.

After a bitterly cold winter, with more than our share of frost,

snow and freezing rain, the arrival of Spring came as a welcome relief. Stirred from a period of hibernation by the sun's warmth, prim-
roses, snowdrops and crocus appeared in hedgerows as if by magic, in
a vast array of colour. Gardens resounded with the song of the thrush,
and chatter of white vested magpie. Soon the chaffinch, skylark, reed
warbler and many other songbirds, back from their winter's retreat in
southern climes, joined with the trill of the blackbird.

Warm sunny spells, with an occasional shower, encouraged the
forsythia's yellow blossom to appear, as did sticky buds on horse
chestnut trees. Having laid dormant throughout the long winter
months, they slowly shed their protective coats for a mantle of green.
Then all too soon, this profusion of colour from May's blossom tended to fade with the approach of summer, by which time Bully had
simmered down. His threat to get even with his head teacher was long
abandoned. All was forgiven it seemed when Miss Malone permitted
him to join the rest of the boys on the playing field, at the start of the
cricket season.

Mid-way through the month of July, Miss Edison, our gym mistress, decided it was time the Morris Dancing team put in some practice. Having been idle during the winter months, it was necessary
we prepare for our annual school fete, due to take place at the end of
summer term of July 1932. As a member of the team, I welcomed the
opportunity to get out of a stuffy classroom, to enjoy a breath of fresh
air. In the midst of rehearsals, our head mistress, Miss Malone, who'd
been watching the country dancing team at practice, left her study and
was seen to approach me.

Taking a wooden baton from my hand, she gave one of her rare
smiles, and in a voice loud enough for everyone present to hear, announced, "You won't be needing this, Ronald. You're going home to
your mother."

Mouth agape, I simply stared at her and stammered, "But I don't
have a mother, miss. You must be mistaken, I'm an orphan."

She could see I was upset and placed an arm around my shoulder
to comfort me, saying, "The Mother Superior will see you when you
return to the convent, Ronald."

LUCK WAS MY COMPANION

A buzz of excitement spread among my friends, as word went round. "Hey," said Podgy, "did you hear what Molly Malone said to Brandy? She's just told him, he's going home to his mother."

As if in a dream, I heard the bell ring for the end of classes and, waiting at the school gates, our escorting nuns took us back to the convent. The moment I arrived, I was ushered into the Mother Superior's study.

Rising from her chair as I entered the room, she picked up an envelope from her desk, and beckoned me to her. Handing it to me, she said, "Here is your birth certificate and a photograph of your mother, who wishes to take you home. Your name is Rowland Charles Marshall, not Ronald Brandon."

"But, I don't have a mother," I protested. "Sister Rose has never tired of telling me I am an orphan, and have no parents. Now you tell me my mother wants to take me home?"

This left me wondering who I really was and, shaking my head in disbelief, I asked her, "Is my name Brandon or Marshall?"

Waving my protests aside, the Mother Superior rang a bell, and from an ante-room a nun, wearing the white veil of a novice, appeared. Taking me by the arm, she led me away from the study, and into the refectory beyond. Sitting with her arms tucked in the folds of her habit in her favourite chair, was Sister Rose – a person who'd shown neither love or kindness to myself or any of my orphan friends, in all my years at the convent.

Her pale granite face was wreathed in smiles as I approached, reminding me of a gargoyle. She appeared quite friendly, having forced herself to make an effort to speak to me. "You'll be leaving us soon, Ronald," she cackled in her squeaky voice. "We'll be sorry to lose you."

What a load of rubbish I said to myself and simply passed her by, as if she did not exist. What I really would have liked to say to her was, "And it will be jolly good riddance to the lot of you!"

Although I was happy enough to be leaving this horrible place, I was apprehensive at having to say goodbye to my convent friends, to meet a mother who was a complete stranger to me.

CHAPTER 3

HOME WITH MOTHER

Although I hated being shut away in the convent, I was a little frightened when the time for parting neared, wondering what the future held in store for me. I knew nothing about my mother or any family she might have.

Nevertheless, I looked forward to meeting my mother, if only to ask her why she had put me in such a horrible place to be ill-treated by these hooded terrors, when I needed her. And why she waited ten long years before taking me home and, in so doing, turned my life upside down. She did however send a copy of my birth certificate to the Mother Superior of the convent establishing my identity, and for that I was truly grateful. My birth certificate gave my name as Rowland Charles Marshall, not as Ronald Brandon, an orphan at St Joseph's convent.

On a bright summer's morning, at the end of July 1932, I bid goodbye to my friends at St Joseph's, the place I called home since childhood. Accompanied by a solemn-faced nun, I was taken to the railway station in Littlehampton, to catch my train to London. At the station, the nun eyed me up and down in a somewhat disapproving manner and, pointing to a bench, said, "Sit there, and don't move until your train for London arrives."

Pausing long enough to catch her breath, she looked me over once again, as if I were something the cat had dragged in, and added, "and don't you forget to say your prayers."

With that, she turned on her heel and was gone. As she disappeared from view, so did the last trace of the fear I lived with at the convent for ten long years, and a feeling of joy filled my boyish heart. No longer was I subjected to a rigorous code of rules and regulations, one obeyed without question. I was now free, to slip into the station bookstore like any other child in town to buy a comic, without having to ask permission. The reading of books, comics or magazines from the outside world was they said, the work of the devil. An evil influence on young children, and strictly prohibited within the convent walls. Now, undeterred by threats that the almighty would punish me for daring to read such blasphemy, I buried my nose in the colourful pages of my comic.

The rumble of an oncoming train caused me to look up and see a pennant of black smoke flying from the engine's squat chimney, with a cloud of steam escaping from the huge steel belly. As it entered Littlehampton's tiny station, smoke poured from the engine in a thick black cloud, blotting out the morning sun. I felt the railway station itself shudder as the train drew to a halt at platform two, where I waited to step aboard. Then a perspiring engine driver was seen to lean from his cab, and wipe his sweat-laden forehead with a red spotted handkerchief.

Suddenly, the peace and quiet of a lovely summer's morning was filled with the sound of carriage doors flying open and slamming shut, as passengers with excited young children, off to the seaside, tumbled out.

"Is this the train for London?" I asked a man in uniform, who I noticed was carrying a green flag.

"Why, yes, sonny," he replied, "but you've plenty of time. She won't be leaving for another ten minutes."

Strolling along the platform, I peered anxiously into every carriage, until an empty compartment caught my eye. Hurrying inside, I sat by a window and, peering out on the now silent railway station, suddenly realized I was on my own. It was at this point my thoughts turned to the many friends I'd left behind and, remembering the good times we'd shared over the years, a feeling of loneliness swept over me.

I wanted to run back to the convent to be with them, but the years of suffering I had to endure since childhood, at the hands of some of those brutes who called themselves Sisters of Mercy, would never be forgotten. There was no way on earth I would ever set foot inside that house of horrors again. It is a vow I have kept to this day.

A shout of 'all aboard,' followed by a shrill blast on the whistle, and we were off. From my seat beside the window, I watched the stationmaster resplendent in his railway uniform, wave a large green flag. Then, like a greyhound straining at its leash, the train gave a shudder and jerked forward, surprising late arrivals looking for seats. Caught off guard, several were thrown together in a heap and, as the train gathered speed, a cloud of steam escaped from its steel belly. In a flash, we slid past groups of people out on the station platform waving goodbye, to family and friends.

As my train left the station, a feeling of nostalgia rose within me as the Sussex countryside came into view. Would I perchance see such beauty again I wondered, as we sped on through the rolling downs. Then once again my thoughts were of the mother who waited for me, at London's Victoria station. Never having set eyes on me for the past ten years, would she recognize me or simply pass me by, I asked myself?

I did have a photograph of her in my pocket, given to me by the Mother Superior before leaving the convent, which I felt sure would help me to recognise her. Shrugging off lingering doubts running through my mind, I tried to convince myself all was well and I would find her waiting for me.

Mile after mile the train thundered along at breakneck speed with the wind tearing at my thin summer clothing as it whistled through the open window of the carriage, where I was sitting. Rising from my seat, I chanced to pull on a leather strap hanging below the window, slamming the window shut. The noise earned me a stern rebuke from my fellow passengers sitting opposite each other in the carriage, their noses buried in the financial section of *The Times* newspaper.

Dressed in pin-striped suits of similar colour, they could have passed for twins, heading for an office in the city. Apparently not on speaking terms, for neither uttered a syllable, it was simply their style of dress that caught the eye, enabling one to make comparisons. Meanwhile the elderly gent who appeared to be fast asleep in a corner of the carriage, opened his eyes and, mumbling to himself somewhat incoherently, dropped off to sleep again.

Slipping off my boots, I stretched out on the seat opposite the old man to get some shut-eye, and closing my eyes, listened to the click-erty clack of the wheels, as we sped along.

Wakened with a start by the squealing of brakes as the train slowed to a crawl, I rubbed the sleep from my eyes and watched the bowler-hatted gentlemen carefully fold their newspapers and sit there, looking to neither left or right. They appeared to show little interest in the tall grey buildings we passed when entering the City of London, whereas I, on the other hand, felt a surge of excitement grip me. Neither moved as the train inched her way forward beneath Victoria Station's glass covered roof, where it jerked to a halt.

This brought an immediate response from the two gents who smoothed down the jackets of their pin-striped suits, took time to adjust their bowler hats at a jaunty angle, and moved towards the carriage door. Only then did they decide to give the old chap, who had by this time woken up, no more than a cursory glance as they left, without saying a word. If, however, their discourteous behaviour annoyed the old man, he passed no remark and simply shrugged his shoulders, in a gesture of defiance, as if to say, 'who cares.'

A look of concern spread across the gentleman's face when I was about to leave the train, for he politely asked, "Is there anyone here to meet you, sonny?"

"Yes, thank you," I replied. "My mother will be waiting for me."

A smile creased the weatherbeaten face, as it wrinkled up like a sheet of brown paper, revealing a set of gleaming white teeth. With a nod of approval in my direction, he took his leave of me, and was soon lost in the crowd. Stepping off the train, I followed a group of travellers along the platform, hoping my mother would be waiting for me. At the station exit, I handed my ticket to a uniformed railway man and was caught up among a jostling crowd, ambling along behind a railway porter with his luggage laden trolley.

My mother,
Caroline Elizabeth Marshall.

Caught up in the middle of a crowd milling around outside the station exit, I was unsure of my bearings and on the verge of tears as I wandered blindly on, into the path of a young woman with her back to me. As she turned, I heard her startled cry of, "Rowland!"

Arms outstretched, she came to greet me. There was little doubt she was my mother. A perfect likeness of the lady on the photograph tucked away in my pocket. Of medium build with dark brown eyes that positively sparkled, she looked a picture of elegance in a smart black coat with soft fur collar. The matching hat, worn at a jaunty angle, failed to hide a cluster of soft brown curls peeping beneath its tiny brim.

Brushing aside a tear, she engulfed me in a warm embrace and as her lips brushed my cheek, I caught the fragrant odour of a heady perfume she wore. Holding me close to her bosom, she gave an involuntary shudder as a tear she tried so hard to suppress trickled down onto my cheek.

Looking into her tear-stained face, I whispered, "Please don't cry, Mother."

Holding me tight, she smiled through her tears and said, "It's been such a long time, Rowland, my dear, I thought I'd lost you."

. . .

Leaving Victoria Station, we walked arm-in-arm through a maze of narrow streets, past dark grey buildings towering above me. Their closeness worried me greatly for I feared they might topple over, and engulf us. I gave a sigh of relief as we boarded our bus for Wimbledon and sped off, across several steel bridges spanning the muddy waters of the River Thames.

Leaving the smoke-laden atmosphere of London, we entered the County of Surrey lying to the south of the River Thames, where old world cottages lay in close proximity to each other. Alighting from the bus in the picturesque village where Mother lived, we walked a short distance, before arriving at the place that was to be my new home.

Recently decorated, the house was built of red brick with a well-kept garden and neatly cut lawn, bordered by a display of brightly coloured flowers. Opening the front door, Mother took me by the hand, and said, "This is your new home, Rowland."

From the rear of the house, an elderly gentleman welcomed Mother home, giving me no more than a cursory glance, as I set foot inside his front door. Tall and pale of face, the man was slightly built with sandy coloured hair, thinning on top. A small tobacco-stained moustache, clipped in military style, adorned his upper lip. The deep set eyes looked me up and down without showing the slightest interest, and, by the look on his face, he was not pleased to see me.

Mother introduced the man as my stepfather, Mr Martin, who gave no more than a curt nod in my direction, and was gone. Following Mother into a neatly-kept kitchen, I saw a boy of two, named Colin, seated at table with Edward, a baby of no more than six months, in a high chair, playing with the remains of his breakfast. Too young to understand, they sat there staring at me, perhaps wondering who I was, when Mother told me they were my stepbrothers.

. . .

As the days and weeks passed, I became accustomed to my new way of life, although at times I felt lonely and wished I were with my old convent friends, Paddy Ryan, Haystack Jones and Podgy Barnes. Were it not for Mother encouraging me to join the local boy scouts where I made many new friends, I might have run off to God knows where.

Rising at my usual time of six o'clock next morning, an eerie silence pervaded my tiny bedroom. I missed the usual chorus of good humoured chatter among my convent chums, not forgetting the stern voice of the nun on duty, demanding we be quiet, or rebuking a child for making too much noise, under threat of punishment, for anyone who dared disobey.

·   ·   ·

Mother's call for breakfast saw me hurry down stairs to the kitchen, where a steaming bowl of hot porridge lay on the table. When the meal finished, I offered to help with the dishes, which she politely refused, saying, "You'll be starting work soon enough, Rowland, so go and enjoy yourself with your friends," adding, "I'll take you to see your grandmother in London as soon as it's convenient. She is anxious to see you."

"Oh, do I have a grandmother?" I said.

"You have aunts and uncles, too," Mother replied. "Some of whom you will meet later."

A change in the weather, during the first week of September, saw an angry red sky dotted with fragmented banks of black cloud drift in, followed by gale force winds and torrential rain. The downpour was enough to prevent my stepfather, who was employed in the building trade, from going to work that morning. Taking advantage of this opportunity, Mother decided to take a trip to London. Beckoning me into the kitchen where she was busy with the breakfast, she whispered, "I've arranged to take you to visit your grandmother today, Rowland. Your stepfather has agreed to look after the children until we return."

My polite good morning to Mr Martin, when he came down for breakfast that morning, was rewarded with no more than a grunt. He appeared quite upset and in a foul mood, simply because he was left to look after the children. Not wishing to remain in the house any longer than was necessary, I busied myself in the kitchen, helping Mother clear away the breakfast dishes. We had to catch an early bus to Wimbledon to avoid being caught in the traffic if possible. The morning drizzle turned to a downpour as we stepped from the bus on reaching our destination.

With the rush hour at its height, Wimbledon underground station was as busy as a hive of bees, people hurrying off to work in all directions. Fearing I'd get lost in the melee, Mother took me by the hand and led me toward a nearby lift, where we were packed in like sardines. As the lift gates closed behind me and the ground beneath my feet moved, a gasp of alarm escaped my lips. Were it not for Mother's protective arm round my shoulder, and her whispered, "We have to go below ground to our train," I would have panicked.

Deep down in the bowels of the earth, the lift jerked to a halt and as the gates slid opened, I heaved a sigh of relief as we hurried onto the station platform. From the mouth of a tunnel, I heard a rumble like that of thunder and, as if by magic, a row of lights appeared, rushing toward us at breakneck speed. With a swoosh, a train sped on past Mother and I waiting there, slowed down with a squeal of brakes and jerked to a halt. There was a loud hissing noise like escaping steam, as the carriage doors slid open. No sooner had the last passenger tumbled from the train, Mother hurried me into the nearest carriage, saying, "Come along, Rowland, we mustn't miss this train, or we'll be late getting to Grandmother's."

We barely had time to settle in our seats as carriage doors closed and we sped off through a maze of dark tunnels, heading for the city. The rocking motion of the train, as it rode the rails, soon had me nodding off to sleep, until Mother tapped me on the shoulder waking me with a start, and whispered, "This is our stop, dear." As the train screeched to a halt, the stationmaster shouted, "Peckham Rye, anyone for Peckham Rye?"

Alighting from the train, we found ourselves propelled along by a jostling crowd toward the lift and, in a trice, were whisked up to ground level. I was relieved to see the light of day once again where the heavens had opened up and rain lashed down by the bucketful, soaking us to the skin. So ended the first of many trips I was to make, back and forth, on London's underground railway system, during the short period of time I was to live with my mother. It was an experience I was not likely to forget in a hurry.

I was anxious to see my grandmother who lived in the town of Peckham, a suburb of London lying on the south bank of the Thames, boasting many beautiful old buildings in the neighbourhood ranging in style from early Victorian to Tudor and Gothic. Dotted here and there, houses with letter slots of burnished brass, brightly polished door knobs and white muslin curtains on the windows, looked out of place beside others, with holystoned steps leading to the front entrance.

Small in stature, Grandmother, in a black velvet dress with starched white apron, welcomed Mother and I with open arms. The dark hair, streaked with threads of silver and grey and brushed back off her forehead, was fastened at the nape of the neck with a black velvet bow. Her finely chiselled features and dark brown eyes simply oozed warmth. She appeared to be the type of grandmother any child would love.

Casting an approving eye over me, she smiled, and said, "Goodness, you have grown into a fine boy. Tell me, how were you treated at that convent?"

"Not very nice, Grandma," I replied hesitantly. "They used to beat me unmercifully. I lived in fear of them."

"Well, they can't touch you now, my dear," she replied and reproached Mother for leaving me at St Joseph's Convent. "I for one never trusted those so called holy people, professing to care for young children."

As she finished speaking, a young man accompanied by a pretty girl arrived and, taking me by the hand, Grandma said, "Come along dear, I want them to meet you."

Ushering me into a cosily furnished parlour, she introduced the couple to me. "This is your Uncle Ernest and his lady friend," she said with a smile.

A smartly dressed young man in his late twenties with dark brown hair parted down the middle, Ernest left his chair to shake me by the hand, and welcomed me into the family. Then, begging to be excused, Grandmother slipped into the kitchen to help Mother prepare lunch, leaving the door slightly ajar. From time to time snatches of conversation between the two women drifted into the parlour, and I heard Grandmother's voice, calm and precise, scolding Mother for not standing up to my stepfather.

"You should have taken the boy away from that dreadful place a long time ago, never mind Mr Martin's protests," she said.

For a moment all was silent, then I heard Grandma plead with Mother, "Why can't you bring Caroline home, dear, surely she would be of great help to you?"

Mother's reply was interrupted when Uncle Ernest rose from his chair and, knocking on the kitchen door, went in with his lady friend to say goodbye. Offering their apologies for having to leave so early, the young couple said goodbye and left.

As the front door closed behind them, I slipped into the kitchen and found Mother sitting there, staring into space. So I asked her, "Who is Caroline?"

My question seemed to upset her for she turned quite pale and angrily replied, "You have no business asking questions that do not concern you. It is also rude to listen to other people's conversation."

By the tone of her voice, I could see she was upset, so I decided not to question her further. Not another word passed between us until Grandma appeared as if from nowhere, to announce lunch was ready. She had, it seemed, stepped in to avoid what might have developed into an awkward situation between Mother and I, allowing her time to regain her composure. I could see Mother was most unhappy that I should want to know the identity of this girl named Caroline, for she refused to even mention her name.

It was Grandma who cleverly changed the course of our conversation during the meal, suggesting Mother should take me to visit an uncle living in Downham, Kent, the following week.

I was determined to find out who Caroline was and, waiting until Grandma cleared the dishes from the dinner table, I followed her into the kitchen. Seizing this opportunity to speak to her alone, I asked, "Would you like me to help with the washing-up, Grandma?" to which she replied "Why, of course, dear," and suggested Mother take a rest.

Closing the kitchen door, Grandma took me aside and said, "Your mother was most upset that you should question her about this young girl, Rowland. There are some things we grown-ups would not wish to discuss with our children."

"But, Grandma," I protested, "why shouldn't I know who this person named Caroline is? Can't you tell me?" I pleaded.

I had, it seemed, taken her by surprise by questioning her on such private matters. But instead of scolding me as Mother had done, she drew me to the far side of the kitchen and whispered, "Caroline is your sister. That is all I am prepared to tell you, dear."

Open-mouthed, I stood for a moment as if shell-shocked, then spluttered, "If Caroline is my sister, why won't Mother talk about her?"

I wanted to question her further, but she would have none of it. With a shake of her head, she stopped me in mid-sentence. Then placing a finger to her lips indicating I be silent, she motioned me to carry on with the chores. Her warning was given none too soon for, at that precise moment, Mother chose to pop into the kitchen, to ask, "Have you finished helping Grandma with the dishes, Rowland? It'll be dark soon, and I don't want your stepfather worrying."

Before leaving Grandma, we promised to visit her again in the near future, then made ready to go. Boarding a bus to Peckham underground, we passed huge wooden hoardings with coloured posters, advertising Andrew's Liver Salts, Craven 'A' Cigarettes, and Cadbury's Cocoa, the one bright spot in an otherwise dull and dreary area of a city, where life was seen to move at a fast and furious pace. What frightened me was the speed with which the trains hurtled through dark subterranean tunnels, a mode of travel completely foreign to me.

My journey into London during the rush hour that morning was far from comfortable. I found it rather frightening, so I asked Mother if we might stay on the bus until reaching Wimbledon, but she would not hear of it.

"There are no buses running from Peckham to Wimbledon," she replied, "so we'll have to take the train. It's getting late, and your stepfather will be angry if I am not home in time to cook his tea."

Our travelling companions on the journey home were a lively group of young men in uniform and, being curious, I asked Mother who they were.

"Oh! They're in the Navy," she replied, adding, "Your father served in the Royal Navy for many years."

She rambled on for quite some time about my father, which I found rather surprising, seeing she refused to tell me about my sister, Caroline. I wondered was she living with my father, so there and then, decided to ask her. Without thinking my question might hurt her feelings, I asked her point blank, "Where is my father?"

Mother sat there immobile, as if made of stone, looking neither to left or right. For a fleeting moment I watched the beautiful face change a whiter shade of pale and a tear she'd tried to hold back, lodged in the corner of her eye. Like a dewdrop at dawn it hung there, then slowly trickled down her cheek to nestle on the collar of her coat.

When next she spoke, her face wore a pained expression and with a sigh, she said, "Maybe I should have told you long ago, Rowland, that your father was badly wounded during the war and never recovered."

Placing a hand on her arm, I whispered, "I'm sorry if I've upset you, Mother."

"Oh, that's alright, dear, you're not to blame," she replied. "My loss has at times been very hard to bear," she ventured to say, before lapsing into a period of silence. No further words were exchanged between us during the rest of the journey home, both content to remain silent with thoughts of our own.

As the evening sun dipped below the rooftops, we arrived at Wimbledon's Underground Station and, in gathering dusk, Mother and I stepped from the train. Out in the street we stood beneath a street lamp's eerie glow to wait for a bus. Stepping aboard the vehicle as it drew to a halt, we sped off into the country, and in the blink of an eye the twinkling lights of the village loomed up to welcome us home.

Alighting from the bus, Mother hurried home because the hour was late, with me struggling to keep up with her. Not a chink of light could be seen as we approached the house, with Mother fearing the worst. No sooner had she put her key in the door, Mr Martin shouted from the kitchen. "Is that you, Carrie? Where on earth have you been all this time?"

"It's only once in a while I go out and leave you to look after the children, Percy," said Mother. "Surely that's not too much to ask of you, dear. It's been raining hard all day so you couldn't go to work now, could you?"

"Yes, I'm aware of that," was the curt reply, "but I couldn't put a foot outside the house, and I've got no damned tobacco."

"Very well, I'll send Rowland up the road to get some for you, dear," she replied, hoping this would pacify him.

I didn't hear his mumbled response as Mother appeared from the kitchen to put some money in my hand, and said, "Will you slip up to the corner shop and get your stepfather some Nut Brown tobacco, dear?"

The money for his tobacco was, as usual, given from what little Mother had left from her meagre housekeeping allowance, which often meant we had to go without food. This sort of thing happened during prolonged spells of wet weather, throughout the winter. During times like this, when he was laid off work, there was very little money in his wage packet at the end of the week.

Mother would solve the problem as she had done so often, by the only means available. Waiting until Mr Martin returned to work, she would wrap up his blue serge suit and brown boots in a neat parcel, and off she would go to the nearest pawn shop. The few shillings she was given by the pawnbroker in return for the clothing, would provide the family with groceries for the rest of the week. A practice whereby many a poor family was able to survive during the Depression of the twenties, and early thirties.

Often the butt of many a bar room joke, the old man's suit was nicknamed 'Indigo.' In it went to the pawnshop on Monday, and out it would come on a Saturday.

Constant rows over money in the Martin household erupted into a slanging match when Mother had nothing to give the old man for his weekly ounce of tobacco. Whereupon he would say to Mother, "That boy of yours is not my child. I'll not be held responsible for his welfare!"

He then suggested Mother should send me out to look for a job in the village, to help out with my keep.

"He's thirteen, Carrie," I heard him say. "There are boys much younger than him helping their families out doing odd jobs of work, such as delivering the morning papers."

This confirmed a suspicion I had from the outset, that my addition to his family was most unwelcome and as far as he was concerned, I was nothing more than a burden to him. Although I was considered rather small for a boy of thirteen, I had a voracious appetite, a legacy from my convent days when I was forced to eat all of whatever was put in front of me.

To keep the peace and avoid further unpleasant scenes between the two of them, I decided to look for a job myself, to help with the family budget. This, I hoped, would maybe stop my stepfather moaning at Mother over what he described as the extra expense I'd burdened him with. So, for the remainder of my summer holidays, I made every effort to find a job. There was none to be had and, come Monday of the following week, I was due to attend my new school for the start of term.

Shortly before I started, the headmaster and a member of the Education Board paid Mother a surprise visit. Mother seemed to know the gentleman rather well for they chatted away for some time before she decided to introduced me to him, saying, "This is Mr Turner, the head teacher from your new school, Rowland."

Tall in stature, sharp of eye and an elegant dresser, he had carefully groomed hair receding slightly at the temples and brushed back off the forehead, showed a pronounced tinge of grey. Smiling broadly, he came to meet me and, shaking me by the hand, said, "Hello, young man, how are you? Your mother has just been telling me all about you."

He then asked if I'd made any friends in the neighbourhood, and how things were in general. During the course of our conversation, he suddenly stopped to ask, "How do you like being home with your mother? It must be quite a change for you?"

"Oh! It's quite nice here, Mr Turner," I replied, not wishing to upset Mother by telling him I did not see eye to eye with my stepfather.

"Then, I'll look forward to seeing you at school," he replied.

He wished me well, and left. As he walked away, I had a feeling Mother must have spoken to him about the convent, having already asked me not to tell anyone where I had come from.

With the summer holidays drawing to a close and the new school term about to start, I spent each weekend in a never ending search for work. There was no money to spare for bus fares, so I was forced to walk the streets in all kinds of weather, without the benefit of an overcoat to keep me warm. Around midday, pangs of hunger gnawing at my stomach, saw me devour a jam sandwich Mother had given me. My breakfast each morning was nothing but a slice of bread and dripping, with a cup of water to wash it down.

Calling at village stores, I told shopkeepers I was willing to take on any job of work they cared to offer, but my luck was out. I continued to trudge the streets each weekend, come rain or shine. Footsore and weary, I would return home at the end of each day with the rubber plimsoles Mother bought rather cheap from Paddy's Market in London leaking like a sieve. As November's bitterly cold winds swept in, a chance meeting with Gordon Holmes, a pal of mine, gave me an opportunity to work for W. H. Smith & Sons, a well established newsagents. I happened to be the smallest of three applicants waiting for an interview and, entering the office, I got that sinking feeling in my stomach.

The manager, a solidly built giant of a man in his late fifties with a crop of greying hair, eyed me up and down as one would a lame donkey, and somewhat disapprovingly, remarked, "You're a bit small for the job, lad. Do you think you'll manage to cock your leg over the crossbar of one of our machines? The bicycles we use to deliver papers are quite big, sonny."

"Oh, I'll manage that easily, sir," I replied. "I must get a job because I'm starving, and my mum needs the money."

A wave of pity must have swept over the man when he saw the hungry look on my face, holes in my threadbare jacket, and the toes poking out of my black rubber plimsoles.

"Alright, lad, let's see what you can do," he said, escorting me out of his office.

I was taken inside a huge packing shed where he pointed to a row of red painted bicycles leaning against a wall and said, "Let's see you ride one of those, son."

Anxious to please, I gripped the huge handlebars and leaped over the crossbar as though my life depended on it, and landed with a sickening thud in the saddle. The pain started somewhere in the lower region of my crotch, then shot up to my throat, making me gasp for breath. An array of bright stars clouded my vision and, in that short space of time, I felt sure I'd done myself a mischief. With my pride somewhat dented, I gritted my teeth and hung on grimly to the handlebars of the huge red machine, circling the area twice, much to the satisfaction of the manager, who stood watching.

"Alright lad, we'll give you a month's trial and you can start on Monday morning," he said. Then he broke into a fit of laughter.

My day began with the muffled tones of an alarm clock waking me with a start, at five-thirty sharp. Groping around my bedroom in the dark, I managed to switch the thing off, before it disturbed the rest of the family. From the window in my bedroom, I could see the lights of town spreading across the horizon, for it was not quite break of day. With little time to waste, I slipped into the bathroom and washed my face in cold water, that chilled me to the bone. Slipping into my clothes, I crept soundlessly down the stairs into the kitchen where I ate a large slice of bread and dripping Mother had prepared for me the night before.

Removing my threadbare jacket from a peg on the back of the kitchen door, I slipped it on and, without making a sound lest I wake the sleeping household, hurried out into the cold morning air. With the wind whistling through a thin summer jacket I wore on that bitterly cold and frosty November morning of 1932, I set off for the nearby town of Wimbledon. Quickening my stride in an effort to keep warm, my plimsoles tended to slip on icy patches on the road's frozen surface, forcing me to slow down.

Long before I reached the newspaper office of W.H. Smith & Sons, a luminous glow in the dawn sky ahead warned me of its impending rise. Beneath the glare of floodlights inside the depot, I could see a number of people hurrying back and forth, loading bundles of newspapers into waiting delivery vans. The clamour of men's voices exchanging pleasantries or issuing orders could be heard above the throbbing engines of the waiting vans, ready to take to the open road. As I stood watching this feverish activity taking place at such an unearthly hour, I was confronted by a tall freckle-faced lad.

"Hey, is your name Marshall?" he asked, removing his cap to mop a perspiring brow.

"Yes, it is," I replied. "What do you want?"

"I've been looking all over the blooming place for you," he grumbled. "I have to help you with your paper deliveries this morning, so hurry up or we'll be late. Our customers are waiting for their daily paper."

"What's your name?" I asked, noticing his close cropped head of ginger hair.

"Stuart's the name, but just call me Ginger. The rest of the lads do, so one more won't make any difference," he remarked offhandedly and told me to follow him.

We entered the huge loading bay where a row of red painted bicycles were loaded with morning papers, ready to be delivered.

"That's your machine at the end of the row," Ginger grunted, pointing to a bicycle with an unusually large bundle of papers lodged in the front carrier.

I took one look at the red monster, and stammered, "Do I have to ride that one?"

"Why, what's the matter?" my freckled-faced companion asked. "I thought you could ride a bike," he said, with a sly grin.

"Of course I can," I replied, with an air of bravado, "but I haven't been on a bicycle for some time."

"That's okay then," said Ginger, "you'll soon get used to riding it, just watch me."

Grasping the handlebars and in one swift movement that would have done credit to a ballet dancer, he cocked his leg over the cross-bar of the bicycle with the greatest of ease and landed gently in the saddle. Admiring the boy's skilful manoeuvres, I stood glued to the spot in silent wonder as he proceeded to hop on and off the machine several times, with the ease of a bird leaving its perch.

"That's the way to do it," he laughed. Then offering the bicycle to me, said, "Here, you get on."

Standing alongside the huge red monster, I eyed it warily, wondering how a mere strip of a lad like me would manage to get the morning papers delivered. Why, the damned thing was enormous. The handlebars towered above my shoulders and fastened to the front of the bicycle was a wire basket holding a huge bundle of morning papers, which I felt sure would block my vision. Panniers fastened to either side of the rear wheel crammed with papers would certainly pose further problems if ever I managed to reach the road.

Ginger wheeled the bicycle, from the comparative warmth of the loading bay, into the cold morning air. Then turning to me, he said, "Here, you take hold of the handlebars while I hold the bike steady at the back, until you get on. So come on, let's hurry now," he said, "we're running late."

In the glare of a street lamp, I could see large patches of ice glistening on the road ahead and looked at the bundle of papers, balanced on the front of the bicycle, with some misgiving. I knew there was no way in Hell I'd be able to see where I was going, and this I felt sure spelt danger for me. But there was little I could do about it right now because my ginger-haired companion was getting impatient, and wanted to be on his way.

"C'mon, Marshall," he growled, "let's get moving. We're late."

Hoisting my leg over the crossbar, I felt at ease as my foot touched the pedal, and my rear end settled in the saddle. Then an unexpected shove from behind sent me hurtling down the road, with the sound of Ginger's laughter ringing in my ears.

Off I went at breakneck speed down the ice-covered road with a bundle of newspapers obscuring my view. With some difficulty, I managed to steer the machine on its downhill course, as it gathered momentum on the road's frosty surface. Suddenly, a large patch of ice appeared on the road ahead, in the beam of my bicycle lamp. A tremor of fear shot through my body when I realized there was nothing I could do to avert an accident, and disaster stared me in the face.

As the front wheel slid from beneath me, I hit the kerb with a sickening thud and lost my grip on the handlebars when a privet hedge surrounding a nearby garden loomed up ahead of me. The bicycle was torn from my grasp and, as we parted company, I found myself sailing over the hedge, to land with a dull thud on a well-kept lawn. Stunned and immobile, I lay there with the morning papers fluttering around me like confetti after a wedding ceremony, and a cluster of brightly coloured stars exploded inside my head as I passed out.

A babble of voices woke me from my stupor and I heard one wag say to his pal, "Blimey, I've never seen a flying bicycle before." Another laughed, and said, "I don't think he's had much practice, his three point landing was lousy." To which his companion remarked, "Oh! I think he'd make a jolly good trapeze artist."

The morning papers I should have delivered to my customers, lay scattered around me when Ginger Stuart arrived on the scene and, seeing the state I was in, broke into a fit of laughter. "What happened to you?" he said.

"You know darn well, Ginger," I shouted. "It was you who sent me careering down the icy road and caused this accident, didn't you?"

"Where's your bike then?" he grinned.

"There's the blasted thing!" I snapped back, pointing to my bicycle lodged in the privet hedge. It was hanging at a crazy angle among the branches, its lamp winking at me. It looked like something out of space squatting there, daring me to move.

From a nearby dwelling house, an elderly gentleman appeared on the scene and, seeing me lying there, asked, "Are you alright, sonny?"

Rising unsteadily to my feet, I brushed off a few sprigs from the privet hedge lodged in my jacket and, feeling the lump on my head, replied, "I've a few bumps and bruises, otherwise I'm alright, thank you."

"Are you sure there's nothing broken, son?" he asked.

"No, I don't think so," I said, "I can still move my arms," and brushed off the remnants of the privet hedge stuck to my coat.

"Let's give a hand to pick your papers up," he suggested, calling on everyone to help gather the morning newspapers, lying around the gentleman's garden. Meantime, my companion was occupied trying to straighten the front wheel of my bicycle.

When the last of the newspapers had been gathered, I thanked everyone for their help and, retrieving my bicycle, began delivering the morning papers to my customers. When I'd finished, my ginger-haired companion gave no more than a grunt of satisfaction and, on parting company, shouted, "You can take your bicycle back to the depot now," and waved me goodbye.

None the worse for wear, I arrived home a rather tired but wiser boy. With the passing of time, I managed to ride the red bicycle just as skilfully as Ginger Stuart, my freckle-faced companion.

.   .   .

It was now mid-December, a time of the year when the building trade experienced the usual slump, and as expected, my stepfather was put on short time, leaving Mother struggling to make ends meet, with the meagre housekeeping allowance he gave her. Not wishing to stir up a hornet's nest between myself and my stepfather, I took on an extra job of work at the United Dairies, helping the roundsman with his Saturday and Sunday milk deliveries. This, as expected, turned out to be no easy job.

Starting at six a.m. prompt, I might be lucky to finish around three in the afternoon. My day was spent running around with a dozen bottles of milk in a wire basket, delivering to his customers. No mean feat for one so small as yours truly, little more than knee high to a grasshopper. At the end of a hard day's work, for which I was paid the handsome sum of two shillings and six pence, I would crawl back home exhausted, to have the money snatched from my hand by my stepfather.

On occasion, inspectors from the company would take over the books of a roundsman on his day off, to check they were in order. Many young boys like myself, eager to earn an extra shilling or two to help with the family budget, refused to work with one particular inspector, seeking to avoid him like the plague. Don't trust him, the lads warned me when I first arrived at the dairy in search of a job, he takes a delight in playing nasty tricks on his hired help.

I needed the money, to help my mother, and rather stupidly accepted a day's work with this character because my mother had no food in the house. Sad to say, I became his next victim.

Seeing me waiting at the depot gates, he shouted, "C'mon, if you want a job, son, but make it snappy!"

In desperate need of a few shillings, I never gave it so much as a second thought and, throwing caution to the wind, jumped at the chance of a job. As I hopped aboard his milk float, the inspector yelled, "Let's go," and gave the poor old horse such a sharp crack with his whip, the frightened animal took off like a bat out of Hell. Before I had a chance to sit down, he galloped away from the company's milk depot like a Roman charioteer, with me hanging on grimly to the seat I was supposed to be sitting on. As we shot past the depot a group of boys waiting outside, shouted, "Watch him, Marshall!"

Shaking his fist at one young fellow making insulting remarks to him, the inspector perched high up on his milk float as we drove on. Sublimely indifferent to their taunts and cat-calls, his eyes were glued on the road ahead as he sat there immobile, like an overstuffed statue of Buddha. A person of enormous proportions, he was anything but athletic, with his movements slow and cumbersome. He seemed quite content to allow the horse to trot at a steady pace and, looking neither to the left or right of him, said not a word, choosing instead to keep tight hold of the reins, in the sausage-sized fingers of his podgy white hands. Red-cheeked and weather-beaten, he would whistle out of tune, while the ginger moustache on his upper lip bristled like the back of a hedgehog.

Little was said as we galloped on and I wondered if he was cooking up something to catch me out, knowing he had a habit of playing tricks on new recruits. But as time went by and nothing untoward happened, I had my doubts whether a well-intentioned warning cry of 'Watch him, Marshall' from an irate boy at the depot, was indeed necessary. The man seemed quite amiable and, as the morning wore on, became rather talkative, even to cracking jokes. Was he by chance lulling me into a sense of false security, I wondered.

It was late afternoon when we chanced to stop outside a large brownstone house and, checking his book, he said, "This is our last call, son. We can go home after this."

Placing several bottles of milk in my wire basket, I was about to deposit them on the lady's front doorstep, when he shouted, "Don't leave the milk there, son, take it round the back. That old dear's rather fussy."

His friendly attitude gave no warning when he politely said to me, "Now you won't forget to pick up all the empties, will you, son?"

At the rear of the house, I found a dozen or more empty milk bottles on the old lady's doorstep, waiting to be collected. Quickly loading them into two wire baskets I carried with me, I hurried back to where the inspector waited for me, a short distance away. With the reins gripped in one podgy hand and his whip in the other, he sat atop his milk float. He waited until he saw me hurrying back with my baskets full of empty bottles and burst out laughing.

"You'll have to run much faster than that to catch me, son!" he shouted, "Come on, it's getting late!"

I was within striking distance of his milk float when I heard the crack of his whip, as he shouted, "Giddy-up, Lass!"

Like a winged messenger he took off at an amazing speed and left me to struggle back to the dairy with two baskets of empty milk bottles, as best I could, his mocking laughter ringing in my ears, as he disappeared from view.

Footsore and exhausted, I arrived back at the dairy where Spotty Wilson who'd fallen foul of him the previous week, waited to greet me.

"I warned you about that old devil," he grinned.

I threw the empty bottles down in disgust, and went into the dairy looking for the fat slob. Seeing me, he started to grin like a Cheshire Cat who'd just stolen someone's milk and, holding out a fat grubby hand, offered me the money I'd worked so hard for.

"Never mind, son, you'll sleep without rocking tonight," he laughed.

Snatching the money from his sweaty paws, I screamed at him, "You big, fat pig, I'll never work for you again!" and limped off home, while he rubbed his podgy hands together with glee.

With the approach of Christmas, a cold easterly wind brought winter's heaviest snowfall to-date and, with it, a lack of money in the Martin household. As usual, my stepfather was laid off work so I was forced to trudge back through the snow to the United Dairies depot, in search of work. Conditions underfoot were not exactly favourable for one to be standing around in bitterly cold weather, but times were hard and, like many boys around the neighbourhood, I was eager to earn a few extra shillings to help my hard-pressed family.

Arriving at the depot, I joined a group huddled together for warmth against a bitterly cold wind, hoping to be offered a few hour's work. There were eight of us waiting there and as each milk float left the depot, our numbers slowly dwindled, until there were three of us left. Then Spotty Wilson caught sight of the ginger-haired inspector about to leave on his round, and shouted a warning, "Watch out, lads, here comes Fatty!"

At the depot gates, the inspector pulled up alongside us and asked each boy if he would help him with his milk delivery. When his offer of work was refused, he turned nasty, and made insulting gestures. As he galloped away he gave us a two-fingered salute, certainly not the kind a cub would greet his scoutmaster with.

This upset Spotty Wilson, who returned the compliment in the shape of a large snowball that hit the inspector in the neck, and before he'd a chance to see who'd thrown the missile, we were out of sight.

However, he knew who was responsible and lost no time in reporting the incident to the bosses who informed us we would receive no further offer of employment at the United Dairies. Although the extra money did help to buy badly-needed food for the family, the situation was not desperate, because I still had my job at W.H. Smiths delivering early morning papers. My family could at least enjoy a decent Christmas dinner, then we'd see what the New Year had in store for us.

CHAPTER 4

THE CALL OF THE SEA

An urge to sail the seven seas when just a boy was inherited from my father, whose career with the Royal Navy began at the tender age of sixteen. With school boy enthusiasm, I was eager to learn all I could about the great oceans of the world, and ships that sailed their turbulent waters. Anxious to continue my studies as we entered the New Year of 1933, I looked forward to going back to school, as the festive season drew to a close. Bored with having nothing to do during the holidays, school would come as a welcome relief.

Browsing through the school library's collection of well thumbed books, a seamanship manual caught my eye. Inside, I found a wealth of information about ships of the Royal Navy and Merchant Service, to which I had a strong leaning. Whenever possible, much of my time was given to studying books describing the day-to-day life of seamen aboard cargo vessels and ocean liners, their trade routes and various ports of call. There were pictures of knots and splices, the ship's compass, and a complete A to Z table on the Morse code, a subject of great interest to me.

Every available minute of my free time at school was spent in the library pouring over this old seamanship manual, while other boys were out in the school playground. Long before reaching my fourteenth birthday, my mind was set on a career at sea and, with my nose to the grindstone, I learnt all I could about life aboard ocean going ships. In fact, I hardly noticed the early months of the year slip by.

Reaching the ripe old age of fourteen, it was time for me to put the seamanship manual aside, and prepare for the end of term exams. On a humid day at the end of July, I sat at my desk in the elementary school I attended, pouring over an exam paper set before me. As the town hall clock struck the hour of ten, the examiner's voice boomed out, "You have one hour to complete the paper in front of you, so knuckle down to it, and good luck."

A momentary silence was broken by the sound of pens scratching paper, as the school's fourteen-year-olds worked against the clock, in an effort to complete the exam paper within the allotted time.

The summer holidays were well under way when I received the letter I eagerly awaited to say I had passed my exams, much to the delight of Mother.

Having passed the entrance exam for higher education, I left elementary school, to attend St Joseph's College in Blackheath, London. Strictly a non-coed establishment, our teachers were Catholic Brothers, who insisted pupils adhered to the rules and regulations laid out. Suitably attired in a school uniform of grey flannel trousers, green jacket with badge emblasoned on the breast pocket and a cap encircled with two yellow rings, I was admitted to this seat of learning.

The school itself was a large greystone building situated in one of the more secluded suburbs of town, away from the hustle and bustle of daily life. Because of ongoing family problems at home with my stepfather, it was arranged that I be boarded out, close to the school. So before the start of the new term, Mr Turner, the school headmaster, took me to see a Mrs Beresford who ran a small boarding house nearby, where I was entrusted into her care.

Mrs Beresford, having lost her husband shortly after their marriage during the early part of the First World War, was left childless, and devoted her life to caring for young boys such as myself, in her well-run establishment. A kindly silver-haired motherly type of lady, in the habit of wearing heavy tweed suits, she appeared to enjoy her role as foster mother to five or six young pupils, who affectionately called her Ma Beresford.

Discipline practised over many years, like everything else at the school, was strictly adhered to, with mechanical precision. In their teachings, pride of place was given to the study of religion. It was a stark reminder of my childhood days at the convent, where one's daily life revolved around learning the catechism by heart. Here at St Joseph's College things were much different, for I was never subjected to the kind of punishment I received from nuns at the convent in Littlehampton, whose treatment of orphans was nothing short of brutal.

Games, such as cricket and rugby, were played here at various times of the year on the school playing fields, under the paternal eye of a games master. Although the game of football was looked upon as of secondary importance, it was never discouraged. Being as I was small in stature, my classmates, who towered above me on the rugby field, christened me 'Tich.' My position as scrum-half often saw me tossed around like a rag doll, leaving me covered in bruises. While accepting rough play as part and parcel of a game where I invariably managed to come off second best, my time at this school was as far as I can recall, a very happy one.

Prior to my leaving St Joseph's College in 1935 at the age of sixteen, I received a visit from Mr Turner who acted as my guardian, in the absence of Mother. When asked what sort of career I would like to follow, my immediate reply was, "I'd like to go to sea."

"Why on earth do you want to go to sea?" he exclaimed.

Shrugging my shoulders, I replied, "Oh, maybe I've inherited it from my father, who went to sea as a young boy."

Responding with a kindly smile, he said, "Well, if that is what you really want, I'll see what can be done for you."

Leaving St Joseph's College, I arrived home to be greeted by Mother, who told me my stepfather had arranged for me to take a job as an errand boy with J.H. Sainsbury, the village grocer.

"I'm not wasting my time pedalling a bicycle around the village,"

I protested. "There are no long term prospects for me in that sort of work."

I was most upset my stepfather would do this behind my back, so I wrote a letter to Mr Turner seeking his help. In reply, he told Mother arrangements were already in hand for me to attend a Sea Training College.

As expected, my stepfather accused me of deserting the family, when hard pressed to make ends meet. Mother, in her wisdom, decided it would be best to let me do what I had set my heart on, a career at sea. It was a subject that caused much ill-feeling between my stepfather and myself until the day I left home.

After a cold and bitter winter with wind, rain, and a heavier than expected fall of snow, we welcomed a change to spring-like weather around the time I was destined to leave home, to learn about life in the seafaring fraternity. Venturing inside the portals of a sea training college accompanied by Mr Turner, I was introduced to the officer in charge. With the college situated close to London's dock system with the River Thames a short distance away, it was possible to watch, from classroom windows, ocean-going ships and barges sailing up and down the river.

Built of red brick, the college had at some time in the past been used as government offices. The building itself was sectioned off into separate classrooms where pupils were taught subjects such as navigation, wireless telegraphy, and courses on seamanship.

Before leaving college, pupils were expected to possess a lifeboat efficiency certificate and have familiarized themselves with the workings of a ship's lifeboat. It was also important one acquired a reasonable knowledge of the equipment in them, in case of emergency. As a country boy, I found it very exciting to sit and watch large ocean liners and cargo vessels, sailing up and down the Thames at any time of day.

Ships operating around Britain's coastal waters or out at sea would, according to the rules of the road as written in seamanship manuals, give way to sail. The River Thames, for instance, was a good example. Deep sea vessels trading up and down its reaches were often seen giving way to wooden barges under full sail, running before a strong westerly wind. It was also interesting to note each merchant ship carried distinctive markings or colours painted on their funnels, giving one an indication of the company to which the vessels belonged and their trade route.

Filled with boyish enthusiasm and a spirit of adventure, I prepared for my first voyage to sea in March of 1936. I was a mere seventeen years of age when Mr Appleton, a school instructor they nicknamed Seedy, took me to the King George V Dock to join the *S.S. Ardmere*. Arriving at dockside, I was taken on board a rusting hulk ready for the breaker's yard, no bigger than a cross channel ferry running from Dover to Calais.

The vessel's name painted on her bow was hardly legible beneath a coat of dirt and rust, a sure sign she'd never had a lick of paint on her rusting steel plates in many a long year.

Eyeing the rusting vessel somewhat suspiciously, I turned to my instructor, and asked, "Have I to sail on that, sir?"

"Oh, she's not that bad, son," he said, looking her up and down. "She looks a good solid tramp steamer to me. You could be sailing on a lot worse than her, believe me."

I had no idea there were ships sailing the seven seas called tramp steamers, so I asked the instructor, "Why do you call the ship a tramp steamer? There aren't any tramps on board, are there, sir?"

Suppressing a laugh, he went on to say, "Ships having no regular trade route of their own, are often chartered or hired from small companies, for the purpose of carrying general cargoes to ports all over the world. That is why they are classed as tramp steamers. Maybe you ought to take a look around the ship before you sign on. I think you'll find it quite interesting," he advised.

Leaving me to roam the ship's deck at will, I chanced to wander through a steel door leading to the ship's galley, where the crew's meals are cooked. Measuring twenty feet by eight and spotlessly clean, the galley's steel cooking range ran along its entire length. I stood for a while admiring rows of gleaming saucepans neatly arranged on a steel grating, just above the stove.

A noise from behind caused me to turn sharply as the huge galley door slid open and I found myself facing a coloured man, as black as the ace of spades.

"What you look for, white boy?" he asked. His melon-sized grin, showing two rows of huge white teeth, put me in mind of a crocodile about to swallow its prey.

Never having seen the likes of him before, I was frightened to death, and said, "I don't want anything, mister, I'm just looking round the ship," and took to my heels. Like a greyhound let out of its trap, I made a hurried exit for the ship's dining saloon, hoping to find Mr Appleton. He was nowhere to be seen so I guess I just panicked and ran headlong into a weather-beaten old man, wearing a dark blue seaman's jersey, strolling along the ship's deck.

"What's the matter, sonny, have you lost something?" he asked, squinting at me through watery eyes.

"No," I gasped, "but I've just seen a great big black fellow in the galley. He fair put the wind up me."

"Ah, that's Smokey, the ship's cook," he laughed. "Comes from Africa. Oh, you're alright now, son," he assured me. "They don't eat the white man any more, they'll steal from you instead."

"Are you a member of the ship's crew then, mister?" I asked, somewhat hesitantly.

His sun-tanned face cracked wide open in a shark-sized grin, revealing a row of tobacco-stained teeth. "Parker's the name, sonny," he announced, holding out a calloused hand. "My friends call me Nosey," he chuckled.

As we chatted away, Mr Appleton, who'd been searching the ship for me, hurried towards us.

"Come on, son, they're waiting for you to sign on," he said, "so make it snappy."

Inside the ship's dining saloon, he pointed to one of several chairs placed around an oblong table covered in a green baize cloth, and motioned I be seated opposite the Shipping Master. He said, "You're next to sign articles, son."

Smoke from a cigar, gripped firmly between the Shipping Master's teeth, drifted lazily up to the ship's deckhead and hung there, above his bald head. He appeared to be one of those solemn faced individuals who took his time before choosing to look up from some documents in front of him, to study my face. As I sat before him in the smoke-filled atmosphere, he looked me up and down, studied me for a while not saying a word, content to chew on the butt of his cigar. The gold-rimmed spectacles hanging perilously on the end of a large red nose, reminded me of an over-ripe tomato. Leaning across the table, he asked, "Are you the young radio operator joining this ship?"

My polite response of "Yes, sir," was answered with no more than a grunt, as he withdrew a sheaf of papers from a black briefcase and, placing them in front of him, asked, "Your name, young man?"

"Rowland Charles Marshall, sir," I replied timidly.

Then without raising his eyes from the paper he was signing, he droned on, "Your age, next of kin and home address, please."

Above the dull throbbing of the ship's dynamo housed in the nearby centre castle, the Shipping Master's pen scratched out the information I had just given him. Moving easily across the paper the noise reminded one of a mouse trying to escape its would-be captors.

Suddenly he stopped writing and chanced to look up at me, to ask, "Do you wish to leave an allotment, sonny?" The only allotment I was familiar with was a vegetable patch rented from the local council, by my stepfather.

"He wants to know if you wish to leave part of your wages to your mother each month," said Mr Appleton.

"Yes, I'd like to do that," I replied.

"Then sign right here on the dotted line," said the Shipping Master, pushing the document in front of me.

As we left the ship, Mr Appleton said, "Well, son, what do you think of her?"

"I didn't expect to sign aboard an old wreck like that. Why she doesn't look seaworthy and she's quite rusty, sir. "

"Ah, that's because she's been laid up, son. Once she gets a fresh coat of paint on her she'll be as good as new," he enthused.

The *S.S. Ardmere*, a vessel of some six thousand tons built during the First World War, had a flush deck and coffin stern, with little to offer in the way of comfort to those who sailed in her.

Having had an opportunity to see for myself the pathetic state of the vessel, my instructor's attempt to present a glowing picture of a ship that looked to me a heap of old junk, did nothing to boost my confidence. Her razor thin deck plates bent to the touch, and were it not for a multitude of cockroaches holding hands below deck, I felt sure she'd fall apart.

The ship's crew, hailing from different parts of the globe, turned out to be a motley crowd, to say the least. The seamen and officers came from places scattered far and wide around the British Isles, while the stokers came from West Africa. Her engineers were mainly inhabitants of Scotland who complained bitterly about the state of her clapped out engine. Just to mention her speed brought a painful grimace from the Chief Engineer who, when asked about her performance, would angrily declare, "Why, she couldn't pull you out of bed!"

Of one thing I could be certain, she was going to be my constant companion for the next two years, whether I liked it or not. Moreover, I was ordered to report back on board the vessel at eight the following morning, ready to sail on the midday tide. With this in mind, I hurried home where Mother awaited my return, unaware it would be many a long day before she would see me again.

Recalling the events of my day on arriving home, I told her all had gone well, and I'd signed on for a period of two years.

"Two years, Rowland!" she gasped. "My goodness that's an awful long time, dear. What will you be doing?"

"We might come home before the two years expires," I said, to allay her fears.

As soon as the evening meal ended, I decided this was perhaps an opportune moment to ask her, once again, for my sister Caroline's address. So I offered to help her with the dishes and waited until my stepfather was out of earshot, before attempting to broach the subject.

As soon as we were alone, I put the question quite bluntly to her, saying, "As you are well aware, Mother, my one desire is to see my sister. It would be a nice gesture, on your part, if you could give me her address, so I can correspond with her while I'm away at sea."

She recoiled, as though stung, and a look akin to fear clouded the beautiful face, to quickly disappear as she regained her composure. In total silence, we stood facing each other and, save for the ticking of the kitchen clock growing louder with each passing second, no sound disturbed the quiet of evening. Then, as on previous occasions when my request fell on deaf ears, it left me wondering, was the past haunting her? Were there skeletons in the family cupboard she dare not speak of for her own peace of mind, I asked myself.

Bitterly disappointed when she refused to divulge my sister's whereabouts, I turned on my heel, intending to leave her standing there in the kitchen. I heard her anguished cry of, "Rowland!"

It sounded like a plea for help, forcing me to turn about and face her. I could see she was distraught, and near to tears. Her quietly subdued voice faltered slightly when next she spoke, for she said, "You must understand, dear, there are some questions I find impossible to answer, such as the present whereabouts of your sister." Pausing to catch her breath, she said, "At the moment she is being well looked after, that is all I am prepared to say."

Reaching out she took my hand, and squeezed it gently. Her voice little more than a whisper, she pleaded, "Please don't press me further, dear." Tears, she fought so hard to hold back, suddenly cascaded down her cheeks, prompting me to place an arm round her shoulder.

"Please don't cry, Mother," I begged. "I didn't mean to upset you."

Through her tears she murmured, "I understand your one aim is to be in touch with your sister and who can blame you, dear, but there are some things I simply cannot discuss with you."

It was then I realized nothing would be gained by pursuing the matter further and, deciding it was time for me to say goodnight, edged toward the foot of the stairs.

"I'll have to hurry up and pack now, Mother," I said, changing the subject. "I'm due to report on board the ship at eight o'clock sharp in the morning."

"I expect you'll need an early breakfast then, dear. I'll give you a call at six, if that's alright with you," she replied.

Bidding her goodnight, I retired to my room and finished packing my bags. Slipping into bed some hours later, I tossed and turned into the small hours, before dropping off into a fitful sleep.

In response to Mother's early call, I awoke to face a cold grey dawn, with a March wind whistling through the trees. Slipping into the bathroom, I hurried through my ablutions, not wishing to be around when my stepfather woke. Making as little noise as possible, I quickly dressed and, gathering up my bags, tip-toed quietly downstairs to the kitchen, where Mother waited for me. She seemed rather reticent and withdrawn at the breakfast table that morning, certainly not her usual chirpy self, so quite casually I asked her, "Is there anything troubling you, Mother?"

Pausing to look me in the eye for a moment, she answered, "No, everything's fine, but why do you ask?"

It was at that precise moment, she dropped her guard and I detected the first sign of panic, a deep-seated fear she was about to lose me again. And with a sigh, she said, "You're going to be away an awful long time, dear, however the decision is yours and I respect that."

"Is my stepfather upset?" I asked, in an effort to change the course of our conversation.

Her response put me at ease, when she said, "Your wish to go to sea has nothing to do with him, the choice is yours. No doubt an urge to sail the sea lies deep within you and no one can alter that, and I for one would never try to stop you from going."

Then as an afterthought she said, "Two years is such a long time, dear, but you will write as often as possible, won't you?"

Promising to keep in touch I reminded her it would be some time before we reached our first port where I could post a letter to her, which according to reliable sources, would most certainly be on the West Coast of Africa. Glancing at the clock, I noted it was time for me to be moving and, as I prepared to say goodbye, a feeling of sadness welled up inside me.

"I must be off now, Mother," I said, somewhat reluctantly. Her arms reached out to hold me in a farewell embrace and as my lips brushed her cheek, I could see she was about to cry.

"I'm going to miss you, dear," she whispered and, as she held me close to her, I felt the warmth of her tears trickle down my face. "Go with my blessing," she murmured, "and may the good Lord keep you safe."

Slipping from her warm embrace, I picked up my sea kit and stepped out into the cold morning air. Bracing myself against a blustery March wind driving dark clouds scudding across a grey overcast sky, I strode toward the bus stop. Looking back, I saw her waving from the doorway and was tempted to run back, to that lonely figure standing there. But I daren't and with a final wave I walked right on, until I was out of sight.

I was not to know this would be the last time I would ever see my mother.

Alighting from the bus at Wimbledon Underground Station, I sought what little warmth there was to be had, hanging on to a mug of hot tea from the station buffet. When my train arrived, I hopped aboard and journeyed on through London until reaching the King George V Dock, on the north bank of the Thames. Through a thin veil of morning mist hanging over the dockside area, I caught sight of what I believed was the *S.S. Ardmere*.

A closer inspection revealed the vessel's name was cut into her bow, the white paint having long since obliterated. Stepping on board just before eight a.m., I was directed to my quarters on the after end of the bridge by a young African steward. Inside the tiny cabin that was to be my quarters for the next two years, I realized how Alice must have felt, entering Wonderland. Everything was so small and compact, it must have been designed for a midget.

The cabin measured six by ten, with a bunk bed squashed up against the ship's side. A tiny porthole, above my bunk, allowed a minimum of daylight to filter in and, during stormy weather, steel deadlights attached to the porthole were screwed down to stop the sea from rushing in. Morning ablutions were carried out over a washbasin which was in danger of parting company from its fixture on the ship's bulkhead.

Everything in the cabin was lumped together and, as I took stock of my surroundings, it suddenly dawned on me that unless anything unforeseen happened, I had to live with this for the next two years. Not a comforting thought I must say, to spend this period of my life aboard a rusting hulk the rats had long since abandoned. How much easier life might have been, had I chosen to pedal a bicycle around the village for the local grocer, is open to question. It was too late for regrets. I had to honour my contract and knuckle down to it, so I set to and unpacked my bags.

Wardrobe space, on this museum piece, was limited to a small cupboard, the size of a sentry box. Not that I expected anything palatial, mind, just comfortable. Why a mouse would have difficulty finding a place to hide in my cabin, it was so small. Beneath my bunk a large drawer with two brass handles looked an ideal place to pack my small garments in but, when I tried to open it, the front section fell off. I reported the matter to the Chief Steward who just grinned, and remarked, "Oh, I wouldn't worry too much about that, sonny. The damned ship's ready for the scrap yard. How she stays afloat is a mystery, so for God's sake, don't cough too loud or she'll fall apart."

In the midst of all the confusion, the senior radio operator named Perkins, knocked on my cabin door to say, "Hello there. Are you the new Sparks? I'm your number one," he said, and shook my hand.

This, I might add, is a nickname given to all radio operators aboard ships, in the seafaring fraternity.

"Yes, my name is Rowland Charles Marshall," I replied.

"There's no great hurry," he said, "so, when you've settled in, can you slip up to the radio room?"

"Is there someone on board who can repair this broken drawer?" I asked. "The darn thing fell apart when I pulled it from under my bunk."

"Don't worry about that, son, Chippy will fix it for you," he assured me.

"Who's Chippy?" I asked, thinking it was some kind of joke they played on new recruits.

"Oh, he's the ship's carpenter," said Perkins as he left my cabin. "You'll find him in his workshop under the fo'c'sle head."

Packing the last of my clothes away, I stepped out on deck and, climbing a companionway onto the boat deck, knocked on a door marked radio room and went inside.

Seated at a small table, Perkins looked up from some papers he was studying, to welcome me in. Tall and angular in appearance, he looked every inch a sailor. From the suntanned face that creased up when he smiled, one could not fail to notice he'd spent much time in the tropics.

Moving to one side, Perkins allowed me to squeeze into a radio cabin much smaller than anticipated. It was barely eight foot square. On one wall a mass of dials, switches, clocks and radio equipment covered an area of the cabin, leaving scarce enough room for a small table and rickety chair.

"It's a good job we're both skinny," said Perkins cheerfully, "or we'd never get in."

My introduction to the radio room aboard the *S.S. Ardmere* was most interesting, with Perkins explaining the use of each piece of equipment. There were coloured wires, switches and dials fixed to the wall of the radio cabin, flashing on and off at various intervals. As I took my leave, Perkins asked, "Did you get the drawer in your cabin fixed?"

"I'm afraid not," I replied, "I haven't had time."

"You had better see the carpenter before we sail," he warned. "He'll be too busy later."

Clawing my way through a tangled mass of ropes and wires cluttering up the foredeck, I managed to get to the carpenter's workshop, underneath the fo'c'sle head. The place was in darkness, so I called out, "Are you there, Chippy?"

A shaft of light pierced the gloom as the door of his workshop slid open an inch or two and somebody wearing thick-lensed glasses squinted at me from inside the room for a minute or two before opening the door.

A wizened old man, in torn overalls and open necked shirt, stood in the doorway, and asked, "What can I do for you, son?"

Bronzed by the sun, the carpenter's face, etched with deep lines, reminded me of a shrivelled up prune, a legacy one might say of many years sailing up and down the West African coast. Examining the broken drawer, he gave a toothless grin and said, "There's not much I can do with that, my old son, the things knackered."

"It's the drawer from under my bunk and I've nowhere to put my clothes," I told him.

"What you need is a coat hanger," the bald one said in mock surprise, acting as though shocked.

"No, I'm afraid I don't have any," I replied. "Is there some place where I could buy them?"

"Don't worry," he said, much to my surprise, "I'll soon find you something to hang your clothes on." From his workshop, he fetched a handful of rusting nails and a heavy claw hammer, and offered them to me.

"What on earth are these for?" I asked, rather puzzled.

"Didn't you want some coat hangers, sonny?" he declared.

"Why, yes," I replied, "but these aren't coat hangers."

"Are they not?" he laughed. "And where the Hell d'you think you are, matey, in the bloody Ritz Hotel?"

Refusing his offer of a hammer and nails, I left the workshop and returned to my cabin, as a derisive ripple of laughter from the old chap followed me. Retracing my steps along the foredeck, an uncanny silence filled the air. The cursing of longshoremen entangled in masses of wire strewn around the foredeck, was heard no more, all was as quiet as a cemetery.

The loading of the vessel having been completed, and dock workers were battening down the hatches, before leaving the ship. With the S.S. Ardmere due to sail on the midday tide, lunch was taken earlier than usual that day and, as I entered the dining saloon to take my seat at the table, Perkins shouted, "Come on in, son, while there's food on the table, we've a right crowd of gannets here."

A chorus of laughter in the dining saloon appeared to upset Prendergast, the First Mate. The tall wiry chap had steely blue eyes, goatee beard, and a deep-seated scar down the right side of his face, the result of a bar room brawl in New York. He turned out to be another of those miserable devils one has the misfortune to sail with, from time to time.

A blast on the ship's whistle, warning all personnel the vessel was ready to leave port, sent crewmen in the midst of eating lunch hurrying from the dining saloon to standby stations. From my position on the wing of the bridge, I watched the pilot enter the wheel-house and give an order for the engine room to stand by. Then moving over to the engine telegraph, he pushed the lever forward to slow ahead and, as he did so, the engineer on duty down in the engine room set the ship in motion.

The clatter of the ship's windlass on the fo'c'sle head suddenly ceased as the last of the vessel's mooring ropes were heaved inboard, and tugs secured to the ship fore and aft took her in tow. Easing the S.S. Ardmere gently away from her berth, they towed her into the murky waters of the River Thames.

On a bitterly cold morning in March of 1936, under skies of grey and drizzling rain, I watched my final link with Mother fade in the distance. She was far beyond my reach, and maybe sitting by a comfortable warm fire at home. Gazing at a fast disappearing coastline, I took stock of the vast expanse of water between myself and the shore before deciding it was more than the few lengths of my local swimming baths, which was all I could manage. Realizing the distance between myself and the shore was too great, I decided to knuckle down to my job aboard this latter-day Noah's Ark, and make the best of it.

Approaching the Thames estuary, the S.S. Ardmere slowed down, allowing the Pilot to descend a jacob's ladder into a motor launch alongside the ship, waiting to take him ashore. With a gale force easterly wind blowing in from the North Sea tossing the tiny boat about like a cork, the pilot found leaving the vessel a difficult task to undertake. Meanwhile, numb with cold waiting for his launch to come alongside the ship, the man was left swinging to and fro on the end of a jacob's ladder.

Risking life and limb, he stood on the lower rung of the ladder swaying in the wind as the launch managed to come alongside the vessel at the third attempt, allowing the pilot to hop aboard the tiny craft. With a shout of 'Bon Voyage' and a wave of his hand, he was swallowed up in gathering mist.

Leaving the Thames estuary, we entered the North Sea, where the wind had by this time increased to gale force eight easterly. As night closed in, mountainous waves buffeted the old tub about, shaking her from stem to stern, each time her propeller left the water.

It was on this gale-swept night in March of 1936 that I entered the radio cabin aboard the *S.S. Ardmere* for my first spell of duty, where I was to spend the next four hours listening to a chorus of dots and dashes, bouncing over the air waves.

"There's nothing to report at the moment," said Perkins, slipping off the headphones and handing them to me as I entered the radio room. "If you have any problems, give me a call," he said, and bid me goodnight.

With the door of the radio room ajar, I sat gazing out to sea watching vessels of every description pass to and fro along England's southern shores, heading for their various destinations. Sitting there, I recalled seeing the towering White Cliffs of Dover rising majestically above the windswept waters of the English Channel and, in passing, realized it would be two long years before I would see them, or Mother, again.

Altering course as Dover's cliffs appeared on our starboard hand, we sailed in a south-westerly direction along the English Channel. Altering course abeam of Lands End, a following wind on our port quarter caused the ship to pitch and roll her way toward Ushant, on France's West Coast.

Dawn had yet to break when Perkins arrived to take over in the radio cabin and remarked, somewhat casually, "I suppose you know we're heading for West Africa, Rowland?"

"Seeing we'll be away for the next two years, I don't suppose it matters where we go," I replied.

"No, I guess not," laughed Perkins.

"Well," I said at length, "there's nothing to report, so I'll nip below for a bite to eat as I'm feeling a bit peckish."

The wind had increased from force eight to nine by this time, causing me to run for cover as I left the warmth of the radio cabin. Gazing toward England's southern coast, I stood for a moment, watching the lights ashore appearing to dance in the darkened skies. From St Catherine's Point further along the shoreline, fingers of light swept the storm-tossed waters of the English Channel. As ever, the Eddystone lighthouse carried out its never-ending task, protecting men who sailed the seven seas.

It was now late afternoon and as the weather deteriorated, I began to feel sickly. Much against an inner voice that bade me no, I decided to take a chance and eat my evening meal. Seated at the dinner table, I was about to swallow a spoonful of soup when a jovial devil-may-care sort of chap sat down beside me. A little on the tubby side, with a mop of fair hair and blue eyes that twinkled mischievously, he smiled, and said, "Hello there, my name's Gilchrist, Second Mate on this old bucket of rust," and offered his hand.

Seeing this was my first voyage to sea and I looked decidedly green about the gills, he was quite concerned and asked, "Are you alright, son?"

"I'm feeling a little under the weather right now," I told him.

With the ship pitching and rolling in seas lashed by gale force winds, I got that sinking feeling every time she nose-dived into a trough. As she struggled to break surface, I felt as if my stomach was trying to catch up with me.

"You'll have to be careful what you eat," said Gilchrist. "The worst is yet to come."

"What do you mean?" I groaned, as my stomach cartwheeled.

"I don't want to alarm you, Sparky, but I guess you might as well know what's in store for us," he said. "I've just had the weather report and there's some real nasty stuff waiting for us, in the Bay of Biscay."

I detected a note of warning in his voice, and questioned him, "What do you mean by nasty stuff?" I asked.

"Rotten lousy weather," said Gilchrist, a worried look on his face. "Nothing like the wind and pitter-patter of raindrops you get at home. Oh, no, Sparky lad, there's a ruddy force nine gale brewing out there."

Whether it was intended to shock me, his remark managed to do just that, as with arms akimbo in a gesture of hopelessness, he said, "I wouldn't mind that so much, but the arse is falling out of the bloody barometer."

Preferring to ignore his seafaring jargon the like of which had never before sullied my ears, I remained silent. How was I to explain to this worldly wise character that yours truly was raised in a convent, shielded from the evil outside world, with all its devilish practices. I was about to vacate my seat in the dining saloon when I felt the vessel give a sudden lurch forward and decided to hang on, when her bow appeared to dig ever deeper into the storm tossed seas.

A roar of laughter went up from personnel at the meal table, when the ship took another nose dive and the contents of a jar of pickles shot across the table, to land in my lap. It was at this point I rose, unsteadily to my feet. Scooping up the pickles, I took them out on to the open deck and flung them overboard.

While the ship continued pitching and rolling head on into mountainous storm-swept seas, I sought refuge in my cabin.

On leaving the dining saloon, I was given a timely word of warning from Barker the Second Steward, a real old salt who'd travelled far and wide. "Batten yourself down tonight, young fellow," he advised, "and make sure your porthole cover is screwed down tight, or you'll get washed out of your cabin."

Tottering around my cabin on unsteady legs, I worked to securely fasten a deadlight, covering the porthole. Meanwhile the ship continued to bounce around in the teeth of a gale like an Egyptian belly dancer with a dose of the trots, as I hung on desperately to whatever I could, until the task in hand was accomplished. Feeling the need for some shut eye, I lay down and listened to the storm, praying the ship's bulkhead alongside my bunk would not cave in every time a huge wave sought to crash up against it.

With clockwork precision, she buried her bow in the raging seas, causing her propeller to leave the water and thrash the air, shaking the vessel from stem to stern like a rag doll. In the teeth of the force nine south-westerly gale, the ship made little headway against mountain-ous seas sweeping over her rusting deck, as she nose-dived her way across the Bay of Biscay. Counting each giant wave and fearing it would be my last, as it crashed against the bulkhead in my cabin, I finally managed to drop off into a fitful sleep until rudely awakened by a seaman sent to waken me, for my next spell of duty.

"Come on now, Sparks, show a leg there," came the raucous voice of the old seaman.

"It's almost midnight, son, and time you were on duty," he added.

It was then I felt the ice cold water from the seaman's sou'wester splash over my face.

Waking with a start I leapt from my bunk like a scalded cat, al-lowing my bloodshot eyes to focus on the old seaman who'd roused me. Wrapped in heavy oilskins and thick rubber seaboots, his craggy face took on a ruddy glow, in the dim light of my cabin. Water con-tinued to drip from his oilskin clothing, forming a large puddle in my cabin, as he stood there watching me get dressed.

"What's the weather like out there?" I asked the old chap.

"It's not fit for a dog to be out, young sir," he replied, "and what's more there's a howling bloody gale raging out there. So take my ad-vice and put a warm coat on," he said, blowing on his fingers.

"Why, is it that cold?" I replied.

The old seaman was about to leave my cabin when he laughed, and turned to ask, "Cold, did I hear you say, Sparky?"

He put his shoulder up against my cabin door and giving it a hefty shove held it open, allowing a blast of cold air to fill the cabin. Then stepping out on deck, he hollered, "It's cold enough to freeze the balls off a brass monkey out here," and, slamming the cabin door shut, he left.

Heeding the old seaman's advice, I donned a warm duffle coat and woollen hat, prepared to face the elements, as I stepped out on the open deck. Driving rain and gale force winds hit me head on, knocking the very breath out of me. Its sheer intensity flattened me up against the steel bulkhead outside my cabin, delaying my dash for cover. Ahead of me lay a companionway I somehow had to climb, before reaching the warmth and comfort of the radio room.

Gripping a small safety rail on the bulkhead, I planned my next move, at the same time watching each huge wave as it crashed on the ship's rusting deck, to scare the Hell out of me. Never before in my life had I experienced such awful weather and, having second thoughts about my choice of a career at sea, I asked myself, "What on earth am I doing out here in the middle of nowhere?" as another great lump of water thudded against the ship's side, causing her to shudder violently. I guess it was too late for regrets, I'd made my choice and had to jolly well get on with it.

Releasing my grip on the safety rail, I made a dash for the companionway, climbing the steps two at a time. I was halfway up the ladder when this heap of scrap-iron gave a funny sort of twist and roll, leaving me hanging on by my fingertips. Then a huge green sea swept over her lower deck covering me in a shower of salt spray as I hung there helpless, too frightened to move.

There and then, I decided a career in the radio room was not for me. I got claustrophobia every time the door closed to shut me in. I wanted to be out on deck so I could see what was going on, not penned up in this rabbit hutch of a radio room. Unless, by some miracle, we returned to the U.K. beforehand, I had to remain on board this scrap heap until I'd finished my two-year agreement.

It took me a few minutes to gather my senses before I was able to claw my way to safety, and reach my objective on the upper deck. Soaked to the skin, I staggered into the radio cabin, whose inner warmth was a relief from the bitterly cold hurricane force winds bat-tering the old tub. Surely this was the worst possible sort of weather to encounter, and on my first trip to sea.

"Hello, young fellow, you've made it," laughed Perkins. "Why don't you take a seat while I give you all the gen."

"We had a distress signal from a small coasting vessel with engine trouble off Cape Finisterre asking for assistance," said Perkins. "She's lying off the North-West Coast of Spain, wallowing in heavy seas."

I noticed Perkins had marked the distressed vessel's position on a chart, lying on the table in front of him.

"I'm afraid there's nothing we can do to help her," said Perkins. "We're miles out of reach."

Checking a map of Europe hanging on the wall, he pointed to Ushant on the French coast, and said, "This is our present position, Rowland."

"I suppose they'll have problems of their own up on the bridge, steering clear of French fishing trawlers with their nets spread-eagled all over the place. Never mind, that's his pigeon," grinned Perkins, pointing to the navigation officer on duty, who at the time was pouring over some maps in the chart room.

It was just after midnight when Perkins left the radio room and bid me goodnight. As I stood in the open doorway my attention was drawn to a collection of tiny white lights dotted around us, as the *S.S. Ardmere* staggered on through the Bay of Biscay.

I closed the door of the radio room and slumped down in a battered old armchair, the only means there was to snatch a rest in such a confined space. Through the open porthole of the radio cabin, I watched mountainous seas crash down on the ship's paper-thin deck, and winced each time it caused her to roll on her beam ends.

Without warning her bow would suddenly disappear into an ever deep trough of foaming green ocean from which she seemed unable to resurface, as her propeller thrashed the air and shook the very guts out of her. My God, I gasped, as another gigantic wave smashed against the ship's side, standing the old tub on her beam ends. Why on earth, I asked myself, did I decide to take up a sea going career?

Leaving the radio cabin, I staggered out on the open deck and managed to reach the bridge where Gilchrist, the Second Mate, was busy pouring over his charts.

"Hello, young Sparks, what can I do for you at this ungodly hour of the morning?" he asked, as I toppled head first through the doorway of the chartroom.

"God, I feel awful," I said, collapsing into an empty chair near his desk.

"I know what you're going through, my old son," he said, with a sympathetic smile. "We've all had our share of it at one time or another. Stay on dry tack," he advised. "And mind you leave the greasy food alone."

The very mention of the word grease sent a sickly feeling round my stomach, causing it to cartwheel around like a mad thing, completely out of control.

"You'd better stay out in the fresh air," Gilchrist suggested. "The stuffy atmosphere of the radio cabin will make you feel worse."

Back in the radio room, I sat by the open door, allowing the wind and salt spray to do its worst. It was either kill or cure, anything to stave off an attack of sea-sickness that I felt sure was inevitable. If my memory serves me right, the next three days were a nightmare. Like a fish out of water, I lay motionless on the ship's cold steel deck as huge green seas washed over me, every time she nose-dived into a trough, giving my stomach a chance to empty out a little more. Although by nature I was inclined to be skinny, my stomach appeared to swell up like a poisoned pup's. In short, I looked like a pregnant broom handle.

It was lunchtime when Barker, the Second Steward, a kindly soul with my best interests at heart, came looking for me, and found me stretched out on the foredeck. Peering into my deathly white face, his soothing voice, begged, "Ain't yer gonna eat something, Sparky, lad?"

I felt sick inside and wincing involuntarily, groaned, "Oh God, no."

But there was no stopping him, he insisted I should have something to eat and tried to coax me into the dining-room, saying, "We've got some nice juicy pork chops on the menu, son, now we don't want to waste them, do we, lad?"

The very mention of pork chops spelt disaster, its effect was to urge me to be violently sick. My stomach spun round and round like a ferris wheel and everything I'd eaten in the last two days, was quickly regurgitated. In a state of total collapse, I was lifted bodily from my watery surroundings, into the warmth and comfort of my cabin, where I dropped off into a much-needed sleep, helped in some small way with a sedative, administered by the Chief Steward, who issued all medicines on board in the absence of a doctor.

Forty-eight hours after collapsing on my bunk, suffering from the ravages of sea-sickness, I woke to the sound of the ocean lapping gently against the vessel's rusting steel plates. During that time, the weather had abated somewhat, causing me no further bouts of sickness, although my innards felt they didn't belong to me. It did, however, take a while before my dose of sea-sickness over the past few days eased off and I regained my sea legs. Then life aboard this rusting heap of junk they called the *S.S. Ardmere* became tolerable once more, as she entered calmer waters of the South Atlantic.

Off the northwest tip of Spain, a change in the weather saw the sun pierce an early morning mist, drying our clothes with its warmth. Deck chairs, stowed away since the previous voyage, were set out, allowing off duty personnel to enjoy a well-earned spell of sunbathing. It was at this point in the voyage, I first set eyes on Frederick Collie, the ship's Captain, who hailed from the Isle of Man, and had seen service with the Royal Navy.

Small in stature, he had a large hooked nose covered in a mass of black hair, that took pride of place on his weather-beaten face. In keeping with naval tradition, he carried out an inspection of his ship every Monday morning, weather permitting, as regular as clockwork. The routine led one to believe he really imagined he was still in command of a naval vessel instead of a rusty old tramp steamer fit for the scrap heap.

The inspection team stood to attention on the boat deck, dressed in their Sunday best, waiting for the Captain to appear. As he stepped onto the open deck, the First Mate, Chief Engineer and Chief Steward saluted *Herr Capitain* and followed him around the ship, the morning sun glinting on their gold-braided uniforms. Old timers among the ship's crew looked at his carry-on as taking things a bit too far for a rusty old tramp steamer. I happened to be an innocent bystander, drinking a mug of tea in the ship's galley as the inspection team passed by, and chanced to overhear one of the seaman criticizing his Captain.

"'Ere," said old Nosey Parker to Jimmy Boyle, "what d'yer make of the Skipper with his blooming inspections? He thinks he's still in the Royal Navy, the pompous little sod."

"Couldn't agree with you more, Nosey," said Jimmy, "'e's nothing but a big 'ead."

CHAPTER 5

NEW HORIZONS

Beneath a cloudless sky of blue, the morning sun sparkled like diamonds on the waters of the South Atlantic, as the *S.S. Ardmere* approached the Island of Madeira, our first port of call. Like a jewel in the crown, this island, the largest of an archipelago lying off the NorthWest Coast of Africa, enjoys a mild climate, amid lush tropical and semi-tropical plant life. A wonderland of charm and beauty, Madeira's economy is centred on agriculture, and an internationally famous wine.

This sparsely-inhabited island was discovered in 1418 by the Portuguese explorer Joao Goncalves Zarcothe, and colonized by his country some years later. Not until the latter half of the past century were tourist hotels built in and around the island capital of Funchal, a world-renown winter holiday resort and playground for the rich and famous.

Sailing into the harbour at Funchal, the mere beauty of this sub-tropical island renewed an urge within me to follow my chosen career at sea which had diminished somewhat, due to a nightmare passage across the Bay of Biscay. My first encounter with the cruel sea and its changing moods was an experience I was not likely to forget in a hurry. As we neared our berth, mooring ropes were passed ashore and the ship's steam winches groaning under the strain, heaved her alongside the wharf. Fenders placed over the ship's side to protect the vessel's paper-thin steel plates, were of little use. The merest bump was enough to send a shower of rust, clouding the island's clear blue waters.

No sooner had the ship berthed, local traders swarmed aboard the old tub, hoping to sell their wares. There were brightly coloured scarves, caged birds and small souvenir barrels filled with Madeira wine. In broken English, one of their number cried, "Hey, amigo, you wanna da nice a canary, him plenty sing?"

The crafty fellow, knowing the bird was unable to whistle a note, gave his prospective customer a smile that would hypnotize a crocodile and, holding the cage in front of his face, imitated the bird's whistle.

Such was the cunning of the islanders and many seamen were duped into buying these so-called songbirds, only to discover when the ship was miles away, all the damn thing could do was to chirrup seed! There were, of course, many seamen who liked nothing more than to indulge in a drink of the island's renowned Madeira wine and in disposing of the potent brew like there was no tomorrow, would wake hours later with a very sore head.

Having discharged a small assignment of cargo from the vessel's hold onto the wharf for transport up island, it was time for us to leave. So, saying farewell to the Island of Madeira, we headed south toward Dakar on the coast of North West Africa, our course taking us within hailing distance of two islands of the Canaries group, Las Palmas and Tenerife.

Before reaching Dakar, sun helmets were issued to European members of the crew, with instructions to wear them each day, from sunrise until sunset, a precautionary measure against sunstroke due to extremely high temperatures reaching one hundred and twenty degrees in the shade.

Described as an economic centre for market gardening, Dakar has an expanding industry producing food products, fertilizers, cement and textiles. Designated as the capital of French West Africa in 1902, the town itself is linked by rail to outlying regions of Mali and Mauritania. Occupied by U.S. forces during World War II, Dakar is today an educational and cultural centre.

As soon as the vessel berthed, native workers arrived to discharge a cargo of coal briquettes from the ship's holds. Working throughout the day, with temperatures in excess of one hundred degrees, they toiled on, their sweat-soaked bodies glistening in the midday sun were as black as the coal. As night fell and the last slings of cargo were landed ashore, native workers battened down the hatches and hurried ashore, leaving the crew of *S.S. Ardmere* to wash layers of coal dust off her deck as she headed out to sea, for a breath of fresh air.

Arriving off Bathurst at daylight, the Captain requested the engineer on duty to stop the ship's engine and, following a short pause, gave the order of slow astern. Suddenly a thunderous roar shattered the morning silence as her anchor cable rattled down the hausepipe to a depth of five fathoms, as the ship drifted astern. Fore and aft mooring ropes were carried ashore in small boats, the bow rope fastened to a steel post buried in the sand, her stern rope secured to coconut trees on the beach.

Within easy reach of the Atlantic's cooling waters, a group of white painted bungalows were nestled in the shade of tall coconut palms. Nearby, children at play frolicked in the surf as it rolled back and forth, in a flurry of white foam. The golden sands and tall green palm trees of this native settlement looked inviting to a perfect stranger like myself, visiting the continent of Africa for the first time.

On my one and only trip ashore next day, I passed a collection of corrugated tin shacks and mud huts sheltering local inhabitants, hidden away amid a background of jungle greenery. Plumes of smoke from wood fires were my only guide to their whereabouts as I ventured into dense undergrowth hidden from the beach.

Facing an off shore breeze it was merely by chance I caught a whiff of human excreta rising from a row of shallow ditches, a makeshift toilet for natives living in the area. Hurrying back aboard the ship, I decided there and then, this would be the last time I set foot ashore in Bathurst. Thankfully, our stay here was limited to a few short hours before it was time for the *S.S. Ardmere* to haul in her fore and aft mooring ropes, heave up the anchor and head out to sea once again.

Steaming south, our vessel arrived off Freetown some twenty-four hours later and, anchoring in the bay as night closed in, we waited for the arrival of two hundred native cargo workers at daybreak. Shipping companies trading around Africa were held responsible for the welfare of all native cargo workers aboard their ships, for whatever length of time it took to discharge and load the vessel. Food provided for native workers by the company on a daily basis was cooked on board by one of their number.

There were, however, no toilet facilities provided for the natives who had to make do with a structure put together by the ship's carpenter the day before our arrival. This makeshift toilet was simply a canvas-covered wooden box with platform attached, placed over the stern of the ship and fastened to the rails with stout ropes.

A moderate breeze blowing in off the ocean that evening was a welcome relief from the day's searing heat but, as night fell, I along with the rest of the ship's crew were forced to seek refuge in our cabins, from swarms of marauding insects. Mosquitoes and flies of varying size from the minute midge to the huge cocoa beetle, chose to descend on the ship in their thousands, forcing one and all to stay in their cabins, which were as hot as a baker's oven.

Wet with perspiration I lay beneath a mosquito net in my cabin that night, listening to swarms of unwelcome visitors buzzing around my ears, before dropping off to sleep. Waking at intervals throughout the night, I was sorely tempted to step out on deck for a breath of fresh air, but this infernal buzzing of winged monsters seeking entry into my mosquito net was enough to discourage even the bravest from committing such a foolish act. I felt certain I'd be eaten alive, with lumps as big as duck eggs all over my body.

Daylight afforded little respite from the night's humid atmosphere and, as the tropical sun raised its head high above dense jungle greenery to focus on the ship, the heat was so intense you could fry an egg on her steel deck. Riding at anchor, the vessel rolled from side to side in a large sheltered bay opposite the sprawling native township of Freetown. Smoke, from wood and charcoal fires on the shore, rose lazily into the clear morning air forming a thin blue curtain above a cluster of nearby palm trees, amid a collection of mud huts on the waterfront. In the foreground, taking pride of place, the town's only licensed establishment provided food and shelter for one brave enough to step inside that cockroach-infested domain. Dominating the skyline, the white-fronted City Hotel (an imposing sight against such a squalid background of tin shacks and mudhuts) acted as a landmark for ships looking for a safe anchorage.

From the town's market place at first light, one heard the babble of native voices echoing across sunlit tropical waters, disturbing the morning stillness. Congregated around a wooden jetty jutting out from the shore, a collection of small boats were busy loading various tropical fruit, such as bananas, coconuts, mangoes and limes. Their ultimate goal, to grab whatever rich pickings were to be had aboard.

A shout of 'here they come' gave ample warning to seamen aboard the ship, as a barge carrying two hundred native cargo workers and their belongings was seen to bear down on the *S.S. Ardmere* lying peacefully at anchor. A feeling of unease came over Slim Prendergast, the ship's First Mate, as he watched them approach the vessel. A hurried glance at his much-prized accommodation ladder hanging over the ship's side and the damage the barge might do to it as it came alongside, was enough to give him a dose of the trots.

It was unthinkable he would allow this unruly mob to damage his prized possession as they charged aboard the ship, and he shuddered at the thought. The situation facing him was nothing short of desperate, for he knew there was no way on earth he could stop this boisterous crowd of natives about to descend on his ship that was be their home for the next three months.

Hearing the shrill blast of the tug's steam whistle, Prendergast

turned to a seaman standing nearby and gestured toward the barge
loaded with native workers.

"Here comes trouble," he moaned. "Get those fenders over the
ship's side as quick as you can, before they cause any damage."

As the tug with its bargeload of human cargo in tow, neared the
vessel's side, Prendergast's nerves were on edge. He simply stood
there as if frozen to the spot, and tried to visualize the awful mess he'd
have to clean up after them, if he didn't act quickly. Unable to stand
the suspense any longer, he seized hold of a megaphone and screamed
at the native who captained the tug, "Ahoy there, slow down," he hollered. "You're coming ahead too damned fast!"

Receiving no reply from the Captain of the tug, Prendergast
started to wave his arms up and down signalling to the tug with its
barge in tow, to slow down. From the wheel-house aboard his tiny
craft, the native tug Captain mistook this as a greeting and waving back in reply, propelled his barge toward the ship at full speed.
Prendergast seized the megaphone once again and shouted angrily at
the tug's Captain, "Never mind all the crap, Sambo. Just watch you
don't smash my bloody accommodation ladder with that heap of junk
you've got there!"

The poor fellow was helpless to avert a collision, which now
seemed imminent and, fearing the worst, Prendergast ordered two
of his seamen to lift the accommodation ladder clear of the water.
Uproarious bursts of laughter and cheering were heard down on the
barge as it thudded into the vessel's stern end with an almighty wallop, buckling the ship's paper thin plates. The impact was more like
a miniature earthquake that sent a sudden tremor through the barge,
scattering its human cargo in all directions. It then slid halfway along
the vessel's starboard side before coming to rest, underneath the up-
raised accommodation ladder.

For a moment there was a stillness in the air, until one heard a
cry of welcome from native stokers among the ship's crew to their
countrymen down on the barge. This encouraged several natives to
scramble up the vessel's accommodation ladder as it was lowered to
the water's edge, causing this surging mass of humanity to fight each

other for the privilege of being first to step aboard the ship. Looking on helpless to do anything, Prendergast wrung his hands in despair as the barge with its human cargo thudded repeatedly against the accommodation ladder, splintering the woodwork.

Fearing his prized possession would be smashed to bits, Prendergast appealed to the tug Captain, "For God's sake, stop them before they destroy it altogether!"

Receiving no reply, he lost his temper and, leaning over the ship's side, hollered, "What in Hell's name is going on down there?"

A momentary silence settled on the barge as all two hundred startled natives looked up toward the ship's deck, the whites of their eyes popping out like organ stops. For a moment, nobody dared move until one of their number blew his bugle, in an effort to break the deadlock. Then all Hell let loose and, once again, two hundred excited natives en masse clawed their way up the ladder. Racing wildly around the ship with what little possessions they carried with them, some individuals who knew the ropes found a place to hide their precious belongings.

Down on the after deck a group of seamen, deep in conversation, watched the performance as native workers scrambled aboard. Nosey Parker, one of their number, was the old salt I met when signing on the ship, and got to know quite well during the voyage. He also appeared to be the eldest among this motley crowd, who answered to nicknames such as 'Snowy' White, 'Shifty' Sullivan, Jim 'The Book' Doyle and Taffy Davis 'The Welsh Nightingale.' Last, but not least among them, were the terrible twosome of Ted 'The Plonker' Bigmore and Paddy 'The Spud Basher' O'Rourke. Doyle, the youngest and craftiest among them, seeing me on the upper deck, sidled up to say, "Watch out, Sparky lad, we're being invaded. These natives are taking over the ship."

Even as he spoke, several were seen heading toward the after end of the ship intent on being first to christen their new toilet, hanging over the vessel's stern. Since it was expected to fly a flag, or ensign, at the stern, naturally it was a bar room joke among seamen up and down the coast to nickname the natives' toilet the West African

Ensign. Uproar and confusion followed, as the workers fought each other for the privilege of being first to use it.

A fresh water pump underneath the fo'c'sle head, supplying the entire crew of the *S.S. Ardmere*, was a precious commodity, one could never afford to waste on the coast of West Africa. A need to conserve the ship's fresh water was vital, since ports along the coast where fresh supplies were to be had, were few and far between. Many natives aboard the ship, never having set eyes on a water pump, looked upon this modern invention of the white man as if it were a toy to play with, until Captain Collie gave orders for the pump to be locked up and the key given to the native head man, allowing the use of it only at certain times of the day.

A concession from the company allowed seamen on vessels, trading down the West Coast of Africa, to hire a native mess boy, when arriving at the port of Freetown. His duties were to clean out the quarters, and fetch food from the galley. With this in mind, they chose a native they'd hired on a previous trip, named Joe Beef. Many Africans, in agreement with their employers, used names of English origin. For example, the native in charge of the Captain's launch called himself, Half Past Five, a name he was quite proud of.

.   .   .

Splashes of red and gold slowly melted away as the evening sun slipped beneath the far horizon, shedding an iridescent glow across the now silent bay, as the *S.S. Ardmere* prepared to leave Freetown. Above the chatter of native voices preparing to bed down for the night, one heard the anchor chain groaning and squealing on its way down to the chain locker, as it was hauled in-board. For a brief moment, an eerie silence followed whilst the anchor cable was stilled in the gathering dusk and a pencil of light from the fo'c'sle head stabbed the darkness, lighting up the water, beneath the ship's bow.

Swinging idly to and fro, her starboard anchor, covered in mud, was hosed down and heaved into place. Suddenly, the stillness of this tropical night was interrupted as the plaintive voice of Prendergast rang out. "Anchor's a'weigh, sir!" he informed the Captain.

"Aye, aye, mister mate," came the Captain's response, as he paced up and down the bridge deck. "Secure anchor and go below."

Turning to Dawson, making his first voyage as Third Mate, the Captain gave the order, "Engine slow ahead." This brought an immediate response from the ship's engine room. Moving sluggishly at first, the old tub began to shiver and shake as her propeller thrashed the water, in an effort to set her in motion. With some reluctance, she slowly inched her way out to sea, until a command from the Captain for full speed ahead caused the vessel to shudder uncontrollably.

When it seemed she would shake the guts out of herself, she slowly gained momentum, and headed out into the wild blue yonder. In that instance, I felt sure I heard the cockroaches, down in the ship's holds, breathe a sigh of relief. The twinkling lights of Freetown, seen as no more than a reddish glow in the night sky, disappeared below the horizon. Caressed by cool evening breezes, our living quarters eventually cooled down, allowing the ship's crew a measure of comfort throughout the long night, with the exception of yours truly.

Sitting on the boatdeck, beneath a star-studded tropical sky, I waited for the sound of the dinner gong, as the old tub rolled from side to side, on a lazy ocean swell. Fascinated, I sat watching a reflection of the moon on the Atlantic's velvety waters dancing up and down with each movement of the ship. As often happened, during my initiation into the seafaring community, a moment of peace and tranquillity was rudely interrupted. Out of the darkened night, 'Shifty' Sullivan sidled up to whisper, "You'd better make sure your cabin is locked while you're on duty, Sparky. The bloody pirates are on board now."

"Pirates?" I replied. "I haven't seen any. When did they arrive?"

"Oh! Come on now, Sparky," he scoffed. "Didn't you see that crowd of tea leaves board the ship in Freetown?"

"Tea leaves, Shifty. What are they?" I was wondering what on earth he was talking about.

He gave a grunt, and said, "Those natives running wild all over the ship. They're bloody thieves, Sparky mate, that's what they are."

His remark surprised me, for I replied, "Oh! Surely they're not that bad, are they?"

"Listen to me, Sparky," he warned. "They'll pinch the laces out of yer boots an 'ave the cheek to come back fer the eyelets. So watch 'em, d'yer 'ear me, son? Take heed of an old salt, cos I know these buggers. If it moves, they'll lift it."

Thanking him for his advice, I slipped into my cabin to wash and brush up as the gong for dinner sounded and, locking the door, hurried down to the dining saloon. Our conversation, during the meal that evening, centred around our next port of call, where we hoped to get shore leave.

. . .

Arriving off the port of Takoradi, as the morning sun raised its head above the horizon, we caught sight of Sekondi, a once-thriving surf-port, now commercially obsolete with the opening of the harbour at Takoradi. Sekondi, a mixture of old and new buildings on a hill side adjacent to a stretch of sandy beach, was once said to have one of the finest harbours along the coast of Africa. Takoradi, a modern sea-port town constructed in the late nineteen-twenties, lies in the Gulf of Guinea a few miles north of the equator and is now the main trading centre for the entire area of the Gold Coast, exporting commodities such as cocoa beans, palm oil, rubber, bauxite, gold and manganese.

Night was closing in as the *S.S. Ardmere* approached Takoradi to take a pilot on board the vessel, to guide us into harbour. Moored alongside her berth, the ship's crew could settle down to a comfort-able night's sleep at this seaport town with its modern facilities. Since leaving the port of Dakar several weeks ago, the *S.S. Ardmere*'s crew had little sleep. Anchored off ports with a lack of berthing facilities, rolling around on ocean swells, the ship simply bobbed up and down like a cork.

Our stay at Takoradi allowed the ship's crew time to visit the shopping area in the nearby town of Sekondi or enjoy a swim on the beautiful beach, before leaving that evening. By sun-up we arrived off Accra, capital of the Gold Coast, another of several ports where harbour facilities were non-existent. All ocean-going ships, calling at the port, were obliged to anchor half a mile from the shore. Cargo arriving for the port of Accra was then transferred from ship to shore in surf boats, manned by a dozen natives paddling the craft out to the ship through waves of rolling surf.

Lying at anchor off the port of Accra, Gilchrist, the *Ardmere*'s Second Mate, came to my cabin advising me to close the porthole at night, adding, "and make sure your ventilator is facing the wind, or else you'll suffocate."

Having previously been warned by seamen Shifty Sullivan, I asked Gilchrist, "Why are you telling me this, and what do you mean?" Thinking it was some sort of joke, I waited for the inevitable punch-line.

"Oh, I'm not joking, young Sparks," he said. "After you've closed your porthole and locked the cabin door, you'll find the heat unbearable. You'll be glad of what little fresh air comes down the ventilator. If you fail to lock your cabin, while we're lying at anchor at Accra, it will be picked clean should natives from the surf boats manage to get on board, and some of them will, I can assure you," he warned.

Then wagging his finger as if to caution me, he added, "Now you won't forget what I've told you, will you, son?" And with a grin he left, allowing me to turn in for the night.

A shortage of fresh vegetables was reason enough for Morrison, the Chief Steward, to send a message ashore to the company's agent in Accra, requesting a fresh supply. Seeing a number of surf boats filled with his provisions arrive alongside the ship next morning, he had good reason to be pleased and began rubbing his hands together, with a feeling of satisfaction. A consignment of beer he'd ordered from the Accra brewery had arrived with his fresh produce, and was about to be hoisted aboard. Several heavily laden surfboats made the gruelling journey through boiling surf, much to the delight of watching seamen.

With shore leave out of the question and little else to occupy their time while off duty, it was not unusual for seamen to spend the long evening hours in idle gossip and drink, which no doubt pleased the Chief Steward, who'd sell nuts to a monkey, and went out of his way to encourage seamen to spend their hard earned money on his beer.

Drink was also a means of solace for seaman Nosey Parker, a man content to spend the night boozing, when possible. His close associates, alas, were few in number because of his heavy drinking and, at times, his drunken behaviour. In an inebriated condition, he would wander aimlessly around the afterdeck muttering to himself, giving his shipmates the impression he was losing his marbles, so to speak.

Suffering one of his periodic bouts of constipation, as many of his ilk were prone to do, Parker turned to medicine, by way of change from alcohol, hoping this would help cure his affliction. He tried mixing the medicine and beer with disastrous results for an unsuspecting young native, the seaman's mess man, answering to the name of Joe Beef.

Now Parker was in the habit of drinking copious amounts of a medicinal black draught he'd obtained from the ship's medicine chest, and kept the concoction in an empty beer bottle. Having purchased his quota of beer for the night, he decided to mix the black draught with a little of the beer he'd just bought. Taking a couple of bottles of beer and his bottle of black draught with him, he slipped away to his usual spot on the after deck and sat in his favourite chair, allowing the golden elixir to quench his thirst.

Late that evening, Joe Beef went looking round the ship for his friend 'Massa' Parker, well aware he had purchased a few bottles of beer earlier that day. Like a shark seeking its prey, Joe was determined not to miss out on a free drink, unaware his voracious appetite for a beer would lead to his own downfall.

Seeing his old friend, Nosey, stretched out in his chair on the after deck, stoned to the eyeballs, with an array of bottles around him, Joe took the opportunity to bum a drink. Waking the drunken Parker, he pleaded with the old man in his pigeon English, "Please, Massa Parker, I beg you, give me small beer."

Parker's bloodshot eyes struggled to focus on the young native, and recognizing his mess boy standing by his side, he said, "Hello, Joe, d'yer wanna drink?" Picking up the bottle nearest to hand, Parker offered it.

"'Ere yer are, Joe, finish it off," he croaked.

A grateful Joe Beef readily accepting Parker's offer, put the bottle to his lips and took a huge gulp, then spluttered, "Oh, Massa, that no good beer, me no likee."

"Aw co'mon, Joe, drink it up," Parker urged. "Go on 'ave another, it'll do you good, son."

The mess boy swallowed it down, then looked at the old seaman, an agonized frown on his face. Moments later he said, "Massa, I go now."

Without as much as a backward glance, Joe Beef was up and running as fast as his legs would carry him, to the after end of the ship, in an almighty hurry to get to the West African Ensign, hanging over the stern.

"Now where the hell yer going, Joe?" Parker shouted.

But there was no reply. All he could hear was Joe Beef's feet pounding along the after deck in a desperate bid to reach the ensign on time.

"Why, the ungrateful bugger," old Parker grunted.

Slumping down in his comfortable chair, he dozed off once more, unaware of the commotion he'd caused among native workers. Milling around the ship's stern, they looked on helplessly and listened in silence to the anguished cries of distress from one of their number. Turning a deaf ear to his mess boy's cry for help, old Parker lay there snoring his head off until a native began to shake him, in an effort to waken the old seaman out of his drunken stupor.

"Massa Parker, come quick," pleaded the native. "You come quick, Massa," he begged. "Joe Beef gonna die!"

Reluctant to move from his comfortable chair, the old sea dog cursed the native who dared to disturb his slumbers and, peering through bloodshot eyes, muttered, "Wa'sa matter, Sambo, can't you bloody sleep?"

"Massa, come now," begged the hapless native.

Parker rose unsteadily to his feet and, like a ship without a rudder, weaved his way toward the after end of the vessel. Padding along behind him, the bare foot native, who by all accounts was calling on his witch doctor for help, chattered away in his native lingo. Pushing his way through a sea of black faces, Parker caught sight of Joe Beef, squatting on his haunches in the native's toilet. He appeared to be in great pain as he gazed to the heavens, as if in meditation. His eyes rolled around his head, as he pleaded, "Oh Lord, ha' mussy. Ooh! Lord, ha' mussy!"

Seeing the unfortunate Joe Beef writhing in agony and hanging on grimly to the stern rails, Parker turned to face his native companions who looked on helplessly and, laughing aloud, said, "Now yer don't wanna worry bout 'im, mates," and, jerking a thumb toward his mess boy, said, "Why, he's just having a good crap, me hearties."

Then holding his nose between thumb and finger, Parker said to his mess boy, "Gaw'd, you don't 'arf stink, Joe. Yer must've dropped yer guts."

With a grunt of disgust, he made as though to walk away, then turned to admonish the poor fellow once again, saying, "Now, ah've told yer before about drinking too much beer, matey, serves yer right. I don't think yer'll need any more beer this trip, Joe. You'd better stay on the water wagon."

.   .   .

Morning appeared out of a cloudless sky of blue with the tropical sun spreading an orange glow across a wide expanse of still water, as it rose slowly above the horizon. Since break of dawn, native cargo handlers carried on discharging the last few tons of goods we had for the port of Accra, loading them into surf boats waiting alongside. The ship's steam winches, having worked flat out since early morning taking cargo from the vessel's holds, ceased their clattering shortly after midday, when the job was finished.

Making ready to leave port, Captain Collie gave orders to heave up the anchor and, as the ship got under way, a loud blast on the steam whistle warned small craft in the vicinity to keep clear.

Gathering speed, the old tub began to pitch and roll in a heavy sea swell and time after time sought to bury her nose in the ocean, as she headed out to sea. With little cargo in her holds to give her stability, she was cumbersome, and slow to respond to the helm. Veering about in all directions, we sailed on down Africa's West Coast day after day in a southerly direction, on this heap of rusting junk. Every mile drew the vessel nearer the equator, where temperatures as high as one hundred and twenty degrees in the shade were the norm.

There was little respite from the stifling heat off the African desert other than a slight breeze through a tiny porthole in my cabin, caused by the movement of the vessel. Luxuries such as electric fans were for the privileged few, like Captain Collie, Prendergast, Morrison and McIntosh, our Chief Engineer. However, an insufficient supply of electricity to operate a fan gave little comfort to the occupants in the cabin's steamy atmosphere, for as one character quipped, there ain't enough power in the blasted fans to blow a fly off the wall.

Because the heat was so intense, many Europeans among the ship's company took to sleeping out on the open deck beneath mosquito nets, which proved to be a blessing in disguise. Life without the nets on deck would have left us at the mercy of swarms of mosquitoes invading the ship each night in search of their meal.

Since parting company with England's green and pleasant land, my time at sea appeared to move on rather quickly for I'd had more than my share of surprises in these last three months. It was not without some misgiving, I found myself enjoying life at sea and was now accepted, one might say, as part and parcel of a motley crew aboard the *S.S. Ardmere.*

A vessel well past its date with the breaker's yard, she was as many an old sea dog would say, 'a pig of a ship in half a gale.' Dancing lightly over the waves, like some burlesque queen, her mood would suddenly turn violent, at the mere mention of gale force winds. She did everything but capsize and at the same time, the old tub did her level best to shake the guts out of you.

It was in times such as this, I found out who my friends were. A kindly chap with my best interests at heart, like the Second Steward, who in the teeth of a gale in the Bay of Biscay found me lying in the scuppers spewing my heart up, and whispered in my ear, " 'Ow'd yer like a couple of nice pork chops fer dinner, Sparky lad?"

To all intents and purposes, I was still a greenhorn, or as many an old salt would say, 'wet behind the ears.' I had much to learn about life at sea at the tender age of seventeen, so until I'd spent the necessary length of time in my chosen career, I would not, so to speak, have gained my sea legs. As an innocent abroad, raised in a convent is entitled to be, I was in all honesty, totally ignorant of the ways of a seafarer. Never before had I heard language as used by these men. It came as something of a shock to hear them cursing, but I soon learnt to live with it.

Not that I would apportion blame on any particular individual, or point the finger, that it was simply by chance I came face to face with the seamier side of life at sea when my ship berthed at the West African port of Lagos.

Arriving at the mouth of the Niger River, we picked up a pilot and continued on our way up river to Lagos, capital of Nigeria. Our journey thus far was slow and laborious. Even with the *Ardmere*'s clapped out engine working overtime, we made little headway against the current and a fast flowing tide. On our starboard side, we viewed the colonial splendour of the Governor's Residence, a sprawling white painted building with neatly tended gardens, lying close to the waterfront. Across the river lay the town of Appapa, a hive of activity with its up-to-date berthing facilities, where ships of all nationalities discharged machinery and general cargo. Homeward bound vessels would load whatever exports of raw material the country had to offer, such as palm kernels, cocoa beans, ground nuts and hides.

Berthing alongside the wharf at Appapa, I received a letter from Mother with the usual news from home, such as my stepfather had been laid off work, or someone had let the canary out of its cage and the cat had eaten it. Thanking me for leaving her a monthly allowance from my wages, Mother would add, "Even so, my day-to-day life is a struggle to make ends meet." This was her way of telling me she'd had to give my stepfather money for tobacco.

Sadly, there was never a mention of my sister Caroline or her whereabouts in Mother's correspondence, which I found most disappointing. It now seemed futile to ask, leaving me no option other than to wait until I returned home to look for her, whenever that might be.

CHAPTER 6

THE SEAMIER SIDE OF LIFE AT SEA

Shortly after our arrival at Lagos, Perkins the senior operator informed me one of the insulators on the ship's radio aerial was damaged, and should be replaced immediately.

"You'll have to ask the Bo'sun for a couple of his men," said Perkins. "He's an obliging chap so there should be no bother. Ask him if he'll get his men to haul the aerial down from aloft."

Standing six foot tall in his stockinged feet, the Bo'sun looked every inch an old sea dog, if ever I saw one. Slimly built, with not an ounce of fat on his wiry frame, he looked as though he could do with a good meal. "Why, I've seen more meat on a butcher's knife," a seaman was heard to remark.

Bronzed beneath a tropical sun, the weather-beaten face was partly hidden by a huge handlebar moustache. I watched him amble along the foredeck toward me, like a seal in the mating season, hollowed cheeks puffing in and out. It was then I realized why they'd nicknamed him 'The Walrus.'

The wizened face broke into a smile, as he came to greet me, revealing several discoloured front teeth, the result of chewing plug tobacco.

"What can I do for you, young Sparks?" he asked as we met. "If it's money you're after, you're out of luck, son," he said, with a grin.

"No, it's your help I need, Bo'sun," I replied.

"Don't they all, Sparks," he said. Then giving a chuckle, he asked, "So what can I do for you, lad?"

"We have a damaged insulator that needs replacing on our radio aerial. Could you have it lowered down on deck, so that I can see to it?" I asked.

"Oh Hell," groaned the wily old devil. "I'll have to stop my men before they nip ashore for a bit of black velvet."

I gave him a puzzled look, and said, "What do they need black velvet for, they should have bought some in England?"

With a nudge and a knowing wink, he quipped, "I guess they're after a bit of the *other*, son."

"A bit of what other?" I countered, hoping he didn't think I was stupid.

Stroking his handlebar moustache, he gave me a funny sort of look, and asked, "How old are you, son?"

Uncertain as to his reason for wanting to know my age, I proudly answered, "I'm seventeen, Bo'sun, but why do you want to know?"

"Then tell me, sonny," he said, "where the Hell have you come from, a blooming monastery?"

With that, he burst out laughing, and said good-humouredly, "Alright, son, wait there until I detail a couple of my men to lower the aerial for you."

Taking me to one side while the work was in progress, he did his best not to shock me, while trying to explain the seamier side of life at sea. Being brought up in a religious background one might describe as sheltered, I found his many nautical expressions hard to comprehend, knowing very well they would never be found in the good book. Yet I quickly came to realize that life at sea was a world apart from one educated in a convent.

Meanwhile, two seamen busily engaged up aloft trying to release the triatic stay, gave a warning shout, "Lookout, below!"

From a height of about fifty feet, a steel spike hurtled down on the deck below, barely missing the Bo'sun and myself, standing directly underneath. Like a pair of scalded cats, we managed to leap clear and, shaking his fist menacingly at the men aloft, the old fellow screamed, "You stupid sods! What the Hell are you trying to do, kill us?"

Ashen faced, he turned to me and gasped, "Christ Almighty, we were damned lucky there, Sparks. We could've both been killed."

Gazing aloft, he ranted and raved at the seamen, pouring out a tirade of abuse. "I know you're after my job," he hollered. "You'll not get rid of me that bloody easy."

Snowy White, the younger of the two seamen, made an effort to apologize. "Sorry, boss, it was an accident!" he shouted, trying to placate the infuriated old devil.

"Accident, my arse!" hollered the Walrus, and with an air of disgust he walked aways off.

Standing to one side, I waited until the triatic stay was lowered on deck. Quickly replacing the damaged insulator, I moved out of harm's way as it was being hauled aloft once more and placed in its original position. Thanking the Bo'sun for his help, I left the scene as a further stream of curses directed at the men aloft escaped the old man's lips.

"Just look at them, Sparks!" he bellowed, pointing aloft. "They're sitting there like a couple of vultures waiting to pounce," he sneered.

Back inside the radio cabin, I assured Perkins all was well and the radio aerial having been repaired, should now be in working order.

"By the way," he said with a grin, "how did you get on with the Bo'sun? He's a funny old cuss, don't you think?"

"Oh, I guess you could say that," I replied. "But I'm afraid his language was rather choice."

Perkins gave me a sidelong glance. "What do you mean, Rowland?" he asked.

Grinning sheepishly I replied, "He said his men wanted to nip ashore for a bit of black velvet, while he made reference to the local native girls."

"Oh! Take no notice of the old reprobate," said Perkins. "He'd lead an angel astray if she cared to listen to him. You have to look out for yourself while you're away at sea, Rowland, so be sure you stay on the straight and narrow," he advised.

He went on to lecture me on the do's and don't's of how one should behave while aboard ship, pointing out pitfalls and serious consequences that no doubt would follow, should I stray off the straight and narrow. And, with a friendly wag of the finger, he warned, "Take heed of what I'm telling you, Rowland, and leave the dusky maidens alone, otherwise you'll come to grief. You're far too young to understand the ways of the world, right now."

It was his final comment that worried me, when he said, "Just imagine what your dear old mother would say if you ran into any serious trouble."

Watching a number of seamen return aboard drunk that night, I was more than grateful for the advice Perkins gave me, and thanked my lucky stars I took the time to listen to him. It brought to mind that well-known phrase I'd heard so many times, "But for the grace of God, there go I."

With the sun slow to rise above a bank of low cloud out on the eastern horizon next morning, it tended to get hot and sticky around midday. Having risen since dawn's early light, native workers stripped to the waist working below deck were discharging the last few slings of cargo for the port of Lagos. Now the task of cleaning out the ship's holds was to be undertaken, before a new consignment of cargo was hauled on board, for our return journey up the coast of West Africa.

Leaving Lagos, we set course for Port Harcourt, lying up one of many tributaries of the River Niger, some thirty miles inland from the sea. Navigating many twists, turns and sharp bends in the fast flowing river, was at times hazardous, and our journey slow and cumbersome. Reaching a sharp bend in the river, the vessel ran into difficulties when the old tub's clapped out engine refused to answer the helm, and failed to stem a fast-running tide. In order to avoid unnecessary damage to his ship, Captain Collie ordered the First Mate, standing by on the fo'c'sle head, to let go the starboard anchor.

A cloud of red dust shot in the air as the anchor and five fathoms of rusty cable left the ship's chain locker, to rattle down the hausepipe. Hitting the water with a splash, the anchor disappeared below the river's muddy surface as the *Ardmere* surged ahead. There was no stopping her now, she had too much way on her and failing to slow down, she dragged her anchor.

Suddenly her stern swung to starboard and, as she drifted inshore, all manner of vegetation in her path was swept aside, including the native's toilet on the after end of the ship. Oblivious to the danger he faced when using the toilet at such a critical moment, the native occupant sitting on the throne ended up clinging to the branches of a nearby tree, his cry for help echoing throughout the jungle.

Watching this performance from the ship's after deck, a group of seamen roared with laughter. "Ask him if there's any coconuts up there!" shouted Snowy White.

Arriving on the scene, much too late to see what had happened, the ship's carpenter stood there, surveying the wreckage. Seeing the West African Ensign he'd spent many hours putting together hanging in dense undergrowth ashore, shattered beyond repair, he blew his top. "Good grief!" he shouted, shaking his head in disbelief. "What the Hell's happened here? There's all my bloody work wasted," he moaned.

The native cargo worker, waving frantically from the tree-top, caught his eye, so Chippy asked seaman Doyle, standing nearby, "How did that stupid bugger get up there?"

"I suppose he felt homesick," laughed the seaman, "and slipped ashore for some oranges."

"He didn't have to take the West African Ensign with him," said the carpenter. "I've no timber left to make another."

As the vessel pulled away from the river bank, the native's cries for help were heard by Captain Collie, directing operations from the bridge.

Turning to his First Mate, he said, "What the Hell's he doing up there, Mister Prendergast?"

"They forgot to bring that damned West African Ensign inboard again, and he appears to have been using the toilet at the time, " replied the Mate.

"We'll leave the stupid sod up there," Captain Collie replied. "I'm not stopping my ship to pick him up. He can find himself a bloody canoe to take him up to Port Harcourt."

Against a backcloth of stars twinkling in the night sky, tiny fingers of light punctured the far horizon as Port Harcourt, our next port of call, loomed ahead of us. Night had long since spread its mantle of darkness over this tiny township carved out of the African bush, where a bite from the mosquito was likened to that of a kick from a mule. No sooner had the vessel berthed, than a row erupted among native workers, when one of their number found their toilet was missing. The situation got out of hand altogether when the carpenter refused to put a makeshift toilet together for them, when requested to do so by Prendergast.

"I've no damn timber left," said the carpenter. "They'll have to hang over the ship's side to empty out, until you order more."

Leaving the pair arguing the toss on the after deck, I retired to my cabin for the night, which was hotter than the ship's stoke hold. With the sound of native voices squabbling no more than a distant murmur against a background of crickets chirruping in the nearby jungle, I slipped beneath my mosquito net. Feeling relatively safe I soon dropped off to sleep, knowing there was little chance the winged monsters buzzing around my cabin would be feasting on me that night.

A shaft of morning sunlight filtering through the porthole pierced the semi-darkness in my cabin's oven-like temperature. It was shortly after six a.m. and the sun, already high above the horizon in this tropical outpost, quickly dried up what little moisture remained of the morning dew. Out on the open deck, native workers, having toiled through the night, were busy covering numbers one and two hatches with tarpaulins. The clatter of the ship's steam winches having ceased, the last slings of cargo were discharged ashore.

Even at this early hour of the morning, the temperature in my cabin had reached the lower eighties, causing me to perspire profusely. Stripping off my pyjamas, which by this time were soaking wet, I enjoyed the luxury of a cold shower. Taking time to finish dressing,

I locked the door of my cabin and set off for a brisk walk around the ship's deck, before my day's work began.

Passing by the ship's accommodation ladder, a native cargo worker I recognized as the fellow we'd left stranded in the bush the previous day, approached me. Pointing to the bridge, he shouted in a mixture of pidgin English, "Him, Captain, no bloody good, leave me in jungle."

Waving his arms about like some wild thing, he said, "Look me, Massa, I plenty scratch. Tear all cloth," he said, showing me his torn shirt and trousers.

"Me see Captain now, Massa!" he demanded.

His bloodshot eyes swept round the deck and, belching loudly, he staggered a little closer to me. It was then I caught a whiff of the native firewater he'd been drinking, so I tried to pacify him, saying, "Captain sleep now, better you come back later time."

Refusing to move away, he muttered, "I wait, Massa, I wait. Me make plenty trouble for Captain, him very bad man."

Standing my ground, I barred his way up to the boat-deck and informed him there was no point in disturbing the Captain, at such an unearthly hour. Shielding his eyes from the glare of the sun, he gazed toward the heavens for a moment, as if seeking advice from his witch doctor. Receiving none, he belched louder and shuffled away, muttering threats to the Captain's person. It was well past midday when, in a more sober frame of mind, the native was taken before the Captain, who reprimanded him for failing to do his duty, and fined him for being absent without leave.

Toiling throughout the heat of the day beneath a tropical sun can be thirsty work and reason enough for seaman to hit the bottle, when their day was done. With an ample supply of beer available on board at a reasonable price, some seamen preferred to drown their sorrows in a locally brewed liquor from the sugar cane, nicknamed 'jungle juice,' a native brew with a one hundred percent alcohol content, powerful enough to drive a car.

Legend had it, the golden nectar acted as an insect repellent, against the deadly bite of the mosquito. This no doubt was another old seafarer's yarn, simply to encourage seamen to drink the stuff. Many, like moths attracted to the flame of a candle, ventured ashore at night, thirsting for a sip of the potent brew, and purchased a bottle of firewater to drown their sorrows. Having drunk their fill, they would somehow manage to crawl back aboard the ship in the early morning hours, collapsing in a drunken stupor on their bunks.

The morning sun appeared as no more than an orange ball of fire as it rose high above the eastern horizon as the Bo'sun set off along the after deck, to rouse his men from their quarters. Like a mother hen caring for her brood of chicks, he shepherded his men over the ship's side into a small boat moored alongside the vessel, ready to start the day's work. His orders from Prendergast were to get some rusty patches on the ship's starboard side painted before leaving Port Harcourt, so he urged his men on.

But as usual, the terrible twosome of Paddy O'Rouke and Ted Bigmore were still feeling the effects of their previous night's binge, and complained of having sore heads.

"Serves yer right," laughed the Bo'sun. "Drinking that bloody jungle juice would rot the soles of yer boots, never mind yer guts."

Leaving the two men commiserating with each other as they painted the ship's side, he slipped away to his cabin, hoping there would be no further interruptions from the rest of his men. Settling down in his chair to enjoy a pipe of tobacco, he heard the melodious voice of Taffy Davis, our Welsh nightingale, who enjoyed nothing more than to exercise his vocal chords. He decided to entertain his shipmates with a rendition of *Men of Harlech* and burst into song.

As he toiled away at the rusty patches on the ship's starboard side, Taffy spotted a large mango fly that had settled on his new paintwork and, in attempting to flatten it with his brush, he missed the winged monster. It must have been attracted to the colour of the red paint for it returned to the scene some minutes later and chose to settle on Taffy's backside, sinking its poisoned barb in his rear end.

An agonized howl of pain rent the air with Taffy dancing around the boat, as if he'd been injected with a dose of the screaming Abdabs. Scrambling up a jacob's ladder as fast as his legs would carry him, he hopped around the deck like a scalded cat, rubbing his backside and howling like a banshee. The noise disturbed the old Bo'sun in the midst of his daydreams.

Leaving the comfort of his cabin, where he'd been enjoying a quiet pipe of tobacco, the old man ambled along the after deck, wondering what all the commotion was about. Seeing one of his men gingerly massaging his rear end he shook his head in despair, as he could tell there was trouble brewing.

"Now, what the Hell's going on here?" he moaned. "Can't I get five minutes peace!"

"Whose bright idea was it to send us down in that damn boat?" shouted Taffy Davis.

"Why, what's the matter, Taffy?" the Bo'sun asked.

"I'll tell you what the matter is," snarled Davis. "I've just been stung on the arse by a bloody great mango fly."

To a burst of applause from his shipmates, who in the meantime left the boat and arrived back on deck, Taffy poured out his tale of woe. But the old Bo'sun saw no reason to feel sorry for him, and quipped, "Now you should be so lucky, my son. I've been up and down this here African coast for nigh on twenty years, and never had the honour."

Twenty-four hours later, Taffy received some sort of treatment from the Chief Steward, for a huge swelling on his backside. The bite from the mango fly was to keep him out of trouble, for the remainder of our time in port.

Our departure from Port Harcourt, some two days later, came as a welcome relief from the humid jungle atmosphere where swarms of mosquitoes and nocturnal creatures pestered one throughout the hours of darkness. Back out at sea, I stood on the open deck for some minutes enjoying a breath of fresh air as the *S.S. Ardmere* moving lazily down the coast, nosed her way south across the equator to Matadi, our next port of call. First discovered by the Portuguese explorer Diego Cao in 1487 and colonized in 1908, Matadi lay on the left bank of the Congo River in Equatorial Africa. The site was chosen as the main seaport for the Belgian Congo, because of its favourable position to the Atlantic Ocean.

Slowing down on our approach to the river estuary, a native pilot, familiar with the hazardous twists and bends along the river, took command of the vessel, until arriving at Matadi. As night closed in, mosquitoes, cockroaches, cocoa beetles, praying mantis and all manner of nocturnal insects arrived in their thousands, to make life intolerable for the ship's company. Attracted by the powerful arc lights, they covered the ship's deck throughout the long hot night.

In 1936, the Belgian Congo, in many respects, was not as far advanced as other parts of the African continent colonized by Europeans, where the quality of life for the native population was seen to be greatly improved. Out in this sparsely-inhabited jungle wilderness of the Congo, street lighting was virtually non-existent. Therefore strict rules and regulations were in force during the hours of darkness in the native township of Matadi. If, for instance, you chose to venture ashore at night, you were obliged by law to carry a light of some description. Failure to do so was punishable with a fine or worse still, one might even find themselves incarcerated in one of their foul smelling native jails.

From the boat-deck aboard the *S.S. Ardmere* next morning, I was able to get a bird's eye view of the town's many beautiful white walled bungalows, situated along the river bank. These, no doubt, would be occupied by families of the local European community, while hidden from view in a clearing way back in undergrowth amid a background of jungle green, a collection of mud huts housed the natives. A short distance away stood the town's one and only hotel, the Metropole, a fine example of Gothic architecture in all its splendour, set among brightly coloured magnolias and lawns of green velvet. It was a welcome sight for any thirsty seafarer wishing to indulge in a quiet drink to while away the daylight hours, sheltering from the infernal African sun.

Providing you were skilful enough to navigate a course from the ship to within reach of the hotel precincts, drink was readily available to those in need, at any time of the day or night. But one also had to be wary of thieves lurking around the darkened streets of town at night seeking to waylay any individual from the ship, foolish enough to venture out alone. This of course proved to be no stumbling block for some seamen aboard the *S.S. Ardmere* who worked each day from eight a.m. until five p.m. Monday to Friday. Weekends being days of rest allowed the crew ample time for shore leave.

To this end, one or two seamen among the crew managed to slip ashore during the day to sample a native alcoholic drink, produced from the sugar cane. An urge to drink his fill of this local jungle juice prompted a particular character among the *Ardmere*'s crew to set foot ashore during the hours of darkness. This so-called golden elixir, one purchased from the local inhabitants, was a means of satisfying a craving for seaman Paddy O'Rouke, well known for patronizing native townships up and down Africa's West Coast. Unable to satisfy his craving for a mere glass of ale, which he called 'the staff of life,' he became more accustomed to supping the native jungle juice.

As soon as the ship's gangway touched the quayside, he was off ashore. Like a bloodhound searching for its quarry, he'd wend his way along a well trodden path, to the nearest native village. There he would sup the native brew, until the tap ran dry. Then around midday, when the sun was at its highest and even the natives themselves sought relief from the heat of the day, Paddy was seen to stagger into the town's Metropole Hotel, seeking to further satisfy his thirst.

Supping more than his share of the local booze, he was seized with a sudden urge to relieve himself, and found the only available toilet in the hotel bar occupied. It was then he remembered seeing a couple of decorative pots filled with tropical flowers, on his way into the establishment. Faced with such a dilemma, he decide to take what he considered to be the easiest way out of an awkward situation.

What have we here, he said to himself, as he left the hotel in a drunken stupor and came upon the flower pots. This looks a likely place. Noting the soil was parched and dry Paddy decided the plants were in need of water and promptly obliged, by discharging a considerable quantity of diluted jungle juice into each flower pot.

An irate native gardener looking on, asked, "Why you do that, massa?"

"S'matter, Sambo," said Paddy. "Ain't yer ever seen anyone 'avin' a squirt before? I'm saving you the job of watering them, sunshine."

The gardener's response was to report the matter to the manager of the hotel. Within minutes, the local police were on the scene to witness Paddy's drunken performance, and promptly locked him up in the local jail. His bosom pal and boozing partner, Ted Bigmore, decided to venture ashore later that day in search of his friend and, calling at the native village, was told "Big man Paddy drink plenty fire water, him go hotel now."

Arriving at the Metropole Hotel, the manager informed Bigmore his friend had been thrown into the local jail and was likely to remain locked up there, unless he paid for the damage he had caused to the hotel's property. Bigmore was off like a shot from a gun.

"Where is he now?" Bigmore asked the native policeman on duty. When told Paddy was in jail, he demanded to see him, to which they duly obliged, then locked him up to keep Paddy company.

Early next morning, an agent from the company's office ashore boarded the ship to inform the Captain two of his men were locked up in the local calaboose. Waiting until after lunch, Captain Collie called Slim Prendergast to his cabin, and requested he go ashore to secure the release of the two men in jail.

"Can't trust that damned Irishman O'Rourke, or that useless idiot he goes ashore with, out of your sight for a minute," the First Mate complained to the Captain. "I'd leave the pair of them to rot in jail if I had my way," he moaned.

"That's not possible, Mister Prendergast," the Captain replied. "We have to leave this place while there's daylight. I don't want to be steaming down river after dark, it's too dangerous. You'd better ask the Bo'sun to detail one of his men to accompany you ashore."

When the Bo'son told seaman Snowy White to accompany Prendergast ashore, he replied, "Why do I have to go with that miserable sod? It's him we should leave in jail."

Down in his quarters on the after deck, Snowy made ready to go ashore and was asked by his shipmates, "Where are you going?"

To which he replied, "Paddy's in trouble again and I've got to go with that jerk Prendergast to the jailhouse, to bail him out."

"What the Hell's he been up to now?" asked Taffy Davis.

"Drunk as usual," laughed Snowy. "He's probably had too much jungle juice, I'll bet."

"That's nothing unusual for him," said Nosey Parker. "A sniff of the barman's apron, and he's sozzled."

Sullivan, a grizzled old sea dog, lay stretched out on number four hatch, like a corpse waiting for the undertaker's wooden box to arrive. Wakened from his midday nap by the noise going on around him, he suddenly sprang to life and, rubbing the sleep from red-rimmed eyes, hollered, "What the Hell's going on now?"

"Paddy and his side-kick, Bigmore, are in jail," said Snowy, "and I've to go ashore with Prendergast to get them out."

"They're damned lucky they have money to spend on drink," Sullivan moaned. "I've a wife and four kids to support, how the Hell can I afford to go boozing?"

"You should have tied a knot in it when you got hitched up," laughed Jimmy Boyle, who they'd nicknamed 'The Philadelphia Lawyer.' His verbal wit and offensive criticism of the old man being quite sarcastic at times, enraged old Sullivan.

"What do you know about marriage, sonny?" the old man shouted angrily. "You're too young to understand what it's all about. Why, you are still wet behind the ears. You think kids come from under gooseberry bushes, and I bet you're still a virgin," he sneered.

It was old Sullivan's final remark that took the wind out of young Boyle's sails and left him speechless, when the old fellow quipped, "I don't suppose you've dipped yer wick yet, have yer, sonny?"

A heated argument between the two threatened to get out of hand until the Bo'sun's call to resume work left the cocky young Boyle with his pride somewhat dented.

Meanwhile, seamen O'Rourke and Bigmore were released from a darkened cell where they'd spent the night, and staggered out into the light of day. Shielding his eyes from the glare of the sun, O'Rourke squinted at Snowy White and Slim Prendergast, waiting to escort him and Bigmore back to the ship.

"Any chance of a drink, Mister Prendergast?" Paddy asked the mate. "Me throat feels like bloody sandpaper and, what's more, I'm as dry as a bone."

"You want a drink, do you," sneered the Mate. "It's milk you need, not alcohol, you can't get drunk on that."

Paddy nudged his pal, "D'yer hear that, Ted, the miserable sod won't let us have a drink."

"Aw, c'mon back to the ship, Pat," whispered Bigmore. "I've got some jungle juice stowed away on board."

Bigmore and O'Rourke accompanied by the First Mate and Snowy White, trudged slowly back aboard the ship.

It was not until late that afternoon they faced Captain Collie, a fearsome looking character reminding one of Bligh of the *Bounty*. Like many an old sea dog he was rugged in appearance, broad shouldered and muscular, the sun-tanned face marred by a scar down the left side of a large hooked nose. An ex-naval officer and strict disciplinarian, he would never tolerate ratings from the lower deck misbehaving during the voyage. As a shareholder in the company, he cared little for the comfort of his crew, and made sure the food aboard his ship was never wasted. In condescending to look up from some papers he was studying on his desk, he asked Prendergast to show the offenders in.

"Well?" he asked the two seamen standing before him, "And what sort of excuse have you to give for your behaviour?"

Shifting nervously from one foot to the other, O'Rourke broke the silence. "Well, 'twas like this, sir," he explained. "I thought I'd wet me whistle so I nipped ashore fer a quick one."

"So how did you land in jail?" the Captain inquired.

Paddy thought for a moment, and said, "Ah! I remember now, sir, me tank wanted emptying and I couldn't find a loo."

"So you decided to water the flowers, O'Rourke," Captain Collie retorted sarcastically.

"Yes, and damned near killed them with the rot-gut he was drink-ing, sir," Prendergast chipped in. "It's strong enough to kill an el-ephant, never mind flowers."

"And what happened to you, Bigmore?" the Captain asked, a sar-donic smile on his face.

Bigmore remained tight lipped, as he watched the Captain scrib-ble a report in his log book.

"What's the matter, haven't you a tongue in that thick head of yours?" Captain Collie asked him, rather irritably. "I suppose you just went there to hold O'Rourke's tiny hand, did you?"

Bigmore chose to remain silent, much to the annoyance of the Captain, who with a wave of his hand, said to Prendergast, "Take this useless pair out of my sight. They'll be logged a day's pay for being absent without leave, and charged for any expenses they've incurred while ashore. See that it's deducted from their wages, Mister Prender-gast," he instructed.

Dismissing the drunken pair, he said, "You'll remain on board until further notice."

In the seamen's quarters down on the after deck, Jimmy Boyle waited to hear what Snowy White had to say, as he entered the foc'scle, grinning like a Cheshire cat.

"So what happened to the pair of them?" Jimmy asked.

"Oh! Paddy's been serenading the natives with a rendition of *It Ain't Gonna Rain No More*, outside the Metropole hotel."

"And what the Hell's wrong with that?" old Sullivan wanted to know.

"There was nothing the matter with the song," laughed Snowy. "He decided to water the flowers with his hosepipe at the same time. Said they needed livening up."

"You mean he pissed on 'em," said old Parker.

"Good for him, boyo," quipped Taffy Davis. "They must have needed a drink in this awful heat."

Young Boyle, choosing to quote a passage from his gardener's manual, said, "Like most humans, flowers like music."

"But they don't fancy jungle juice or Irish liquor," grinned old

Sullivan, who motioned for silence from the rest of his shipmates as O'Rouke and Bigmore set foot inside the fo'c'sle.

"Where's the booze, Ted?" the Irishman asked his pal. "I'm as dry as a bone."

It was long after the nightly chirruping of crickets had ceased that seamen Bigmore and O'Rouke, having consumed their fill of jungle juice, dropped off to sleep, each caressing an empty bottle.

Peeping above the eastern horizon, the morning sun quickly spread its warmth across a wide expanse of the Congo's silent waters, embracing the row of white walled bungalows lying along the river bank. Greeting a new day, anguished cries from gulls on the wing woke the old Bo'sun from his slumbers. Seeing the hour was late, he dressed rather hurriedly and stepped smartly out on deck, determined to make ready for an early start to the day's work. Hurrying along the after deck as fast as his bandy legs would allow him, he entered the seamen's quarters, to rouse his men from their bunks.

"Come on now, me lads!" he hollered. "Show a leg there."

Receiving no reply from Bigmore and O'Rourke, he warned them, "You'd better get out of yer ruddy louse traps right now, cos we're sailing on the early morning tide."

The pair woke with a start.

"Hell," said Paddy, "it feels like someone's been standing on me blooming head."

"Serves you right fer drinking that rot-gut," said the Bo'sun.

"Is our tea made?" quipped Taffy, rubbing the sleep from his eyes.

"You want me to bring you tea?" said the Bo'sun in mock surprise. "Where the Hell d'you think you are, son, at the bloody Ritz Hotel?"

Sullivan and Parker were the first to leave their bunks and hurried along to the galley in search of the native mess boy they'd sent to make the tea, and found him sitting on a bench in the galley arguing the toss with his countryman, the African cook.

"Where's our tea, Joe Beef?" Parker asked the boy, who sat gazing at the kettle.

"Him water no boil long before dis time," he told the seaman. "I come quick now, Massa," said Joe.

Then seeing the ship's African cook was busy over his hot stove, old Sullivan shouted, "Morning, Snowball, what have we got for our breakfast?"

Beads of perspiration running down his face, the cook turned and grinned at the two seaman. Showing a set of gleaming white pearlies a crocodile would have been proud of, he quipped, "Okay, Chalky. Today I give you curry rice."

"Cor blimey, not again," moaned Sullivan, who turned to Parker and said, "D'yer hear that, Nosey, it's another dollop of duck shit and hailstones he's giving us. That Chief Steward must think we're bloody coolies."

A complaint to the Chief Steward, who like the ship's Captain happened to be a shareholder of the company, fell on deaf ears.

"You can take it or leave it," he told them bluntly. "I couldn't care less."

Upset by the Steward's off-hand attitude, the men decided to send a deputation, headed by Jimmy Boyle, to the Captain. But once again, an eloquent speech by the professed sea lawyer outlining the men's troubles, fell on deaf ears. Captain Collie's prompt reply was the same as the Chief Steward's. "You can eat it or damn well starve."

.   .   .

Leaving the humid atmosphere and primitive conditions of this Belgian outpost on the Congo River, the *S.S. Ardmere* set sail from Matadi on her return journey up the coast of West Africa. Calling at several ports we visited on our journey south, small amounts of cargo were taken aboard the vessel as we ventured further north. By the time we reached our final destination of Freetown, Sierra Leone, the ship was loaded down to her plimsoll marks. It was now time for the two hundred natives from the area, who were hired to work aboard the vessel during her voyage up and down the African coast, to return to their homes ashore.

As the last boatload of native cargo workers left the ship, everyone breathed a sigh of relief, realizing this rusty old tub we called home would be ours until we returned, once again, to the coast of West Africa. Clearing up the mess the native workers left behind was cause for loud cursing by the crew who had the unenviable task of spending hours washing down the ship's deck, with a strong solution of disinfectant.

Evening came upon us suddenly and, with the setting sun no more than a splash of red and gold, I watched as it turned into a ribbon of fire before slipping ever so gently beneath the western horizon. Lulled by the gentle motion of an Atlantic swell, I sat gazing toward the shore, but my thoughts were not of the palm fringed coast of Sierra Leone we'd left behind. I now looked forward to my first visit to America as we set sail for New York.

CHAPTER 7

A GLORIOUS SIGHT

Beneath a star-studded tropical night sky, a full moon bathed the *S.S. Ardmere* in radiant light, as she rode a gentle ocean swell. The old tub creaked and groaned beneath the weight of a cargo of cocoa beans in her holds and a consignment of mahogany logs, lashed down on the open deck. It was shortly before midnight that I left my cabin and climbed a companionway leading to the radio room, where I was due to begin my four hour stint of duty. Perkins answered my knock and opened the door of the tiny radio cabin, inviting me in. Motioning for me to take a seat, he handed over the headphones, saying, "There's nothing to report, so you should be okay for a while."

From a small locker next to the transmitter, he picked up a book he'd been reading and sighed wearily, "I guess I'll hit the sack."

With a cheery goodnight, he closed the door behind him, leaving me with my thoughts. For the next four hours, I had to sit there listening to an incessant chorus of dots and dashes bouncing over the air waves, with the headphones clamped to my ears. Alone in the dead of night, I sat cramped up in the tiny cabin, swaying from side to side in rhythm with the ship, as she swung first to port and then starboard. Riding a moderate ocean swell, she pitched and rolled over the Atlantic's glassy waters heading in a nor'westerly direction for the U.S.A., our next port.

I had brought a book with me to while away the lonely hours between midnight and four a.m., referred to by men who sailed the seven seas, as the death watch. The reason given was, any crew member suffering with a tropical disease such as Malaria, Blackwater Fever, etc., tended to kick the bucket so to speak, during these unearthly hours. Being miles away from land they would be sewn up in a canvas bag, with a couple of steel firebars for company, and dispatched to a watery grave.

Checking the calendar, it surprised me to note we were nearing the end of June and that I'd spent the entire last four months on the mosquito-infested West African Coast, having left England in early March. During that period I'd suffered much discomfort, from bouts of prickly heat and fevers, from which there seemed no escape. There was, it seemed, little one could do to avoid conditions such as these which are prevalent in many tropical countries, where each and every day was alike.

We were now well on our way across the South Atlantic bound for the U.S. and, as I sat in the tiny radio cabin with a symphony of dots and dashes pounding my ears, my thoughts turned to Mother and home. Why, I asked myself over and over again, did she never mention my sister Caroline in any of her letters, choosing instead to talk about other members of the family? I had to carry on with the same old routine of bed and work day in and day out until reaching New York where, I hoped, a letter from Mother would be waiting for me.

An uneventful passage, it took the *S.S. Ardmere* almost three weeks, by which time the weevils that joined us in Africa had settled down, when we duly arrived at the mouth of New York's Hudson River. An early mist caused many an anxious moment on the bridge as the morning wore on, then slowly dispersing to allow a pilot to board the ship. With the clouds lifting to give way to bright sunny weather, the *Ardmere* was allowed to continue her passage up river to anchor opposite the Quarantine Station, where we were ordered to await clearance from the Port Health Authorities.

It was then we noticed a hive of activity taking place in the immediate vicinity with ocean-going liners and small coastwise freighters, appearing to line up along the river. This unusual performance prompted Captain Collie to exclaim, "There must be something going on here. I've never seen such a huge collection of ships."

Lined up along the Hudson River, passenger liners and small coastal craft were decked out fore and aft, with flags of every conceivable colour. Then, as if by some prearranged signal, all Hell broke loose when every ship in the vicinity opened up with a series of loud blasts on their sirens. The noise was simply deafening.

Suddenly a cry of "There she is!" from the duty officer caused a flurry of excitement, with every member of the ship's crew rushing over to the starboard side of the vessel. Looming up on the horizon one saw the silhouette of a huge liner, drawing ever closer.

"Why, it's the *Queen Mary!*" Perkins shouted, with a burst of boyish enthusiasm.

The latest addition to the Cunard Company's passenger fleet had arrived in New York on her maiden voyage, and the city was agog with excitement. From out of the morning mist she came upon us, decorated from stem to stern with a multitude of flags, made up of every colour of the rainbow. One could only stand and gaze in wonder at her three huge red and black funnels and gleaming white painted superstructure, that sparkled in the early morning sun, giving an added dimension to her enormous size.

Majestic in her every move, she certainly looked a wonderful sight as she sailed gracefully up river, with all the aplomb of a Queen. This surely was one of the proudest moments in the history of the British Merchant Service and the men who built her at John Brown's shipyard, on the River Clyde in Scotland. As she passed the Statue of Liberty, her sirens boomed out a vibrant salute to attendant ships, stationed along the river.

In reply, she received a deafening chorus of welcome. It was a privilege indeed to have witnessed her maiden voyage.

Meanwhile, the *S.S. Ardmere* was ordered to wait at the Quarantine Station for a doctor from the Port Health Authority, who failed to arrive until the great ship had passed us by. Only then was it possible for the doctor to carry out his long awaited medical inspection of African members, among the ship's crew, a customary procedure vessels entering the port from tropical countries had to undergo. Native firemen and Stewards were told to line up on deck for a short arm inspection, before the vessel was allowed to proceed up river to her berth. This was said to be merely a precautionary measure against the risk of contagious diseases carried into the U.S. by nationals from countries ravaged by Malaria, Yellow Fever and Small Pox.

As the doctor passed down the line inspecting them, each man was asked to take out his ding-a-ling, and squeeze it. At the far end of the line, a young native stoker struggled to release the zip on his trousers when, suddenly, his ding-a-ling flopped out and hung there, like a length of black rubber hose. Seeing its enormous size, the doctor remarked good-humouredly, "I guess you weren't behind the door when they were dished out?"

A melon-sized grin spread across the stoker's face and proud as a peacock, he replied, "Oh no, sah, ah's born wid dat."

To which an onlooker among the seamen shouted, "Somebody must have trod on it as he walked away, Doc."

The remark saw the doctor double up in a fit of laughter, and exclaim, "Wait until they hear this one at the hospital. They'll be in stitches."

Given clearance by the Port Authorities to continue our journey up river to her berth, I stood in silent awe as the *S.S. Ardmere* sailed past Manhattan Island, and marvelled at the size of its skyscrapers. The Empire State Building, being the tallest, stood in isolated splendour, head and shoulders above them all. It was, by any stretch of the imagination, a wonderful sight to behold. The dingy appearance of many large buildings I'd seen in the great City of London, were small in comparison and no match against these lofty giants.

Struggling to stem the Hudson River's fast-flowing tide, the *S.S. Ardmere* moved sluggishly upstream on her approach to Brooklyn Bridge, connecting the shore with Manhattan. Nearing her berth, she was taken in tow by two escorting tugs, who shepherded her alongside. Thus ended a long and tedious voyage which was much longer than anticipated owing to engine failure in mid-Atlantic. As expected there was no booze left on board when the vessel arrived in New York and several members of the ship's crew, eager to satisfy their craving for a glass of lager, couldn't wait to slip ashore.

Like lemmings, who for some unknown reason habitually threw themselves off cliff tops into the sea, many seamen could not resist the temptation. Ever ready to quench their thirst, they charged toward the ship's gangway en masse and when just about to set foot on American soil, their path was blocked by none other than Prendergast. Standing at the ship's gangway he held up his hand, like a London Bobby stopping the traffic in Picadilly Circus, and said, "Sorry, lads, there's no shore leave until Customs have cleared the ship."

"Wha'dya mean, chief," said Snowy White. "Can't we nip ashore for a glass of lager?"

"Not until they know what you have to declare," sneered Prendergast.

"Yes, and we all declare you're a bloody nuisance, mister," jeered old Sullivan. "That's all we've got to say."

As they drifted back toward their quarters, the First Mate shouted after them, "Maybe we ought to keep you all on board. How will that suit you, my lads?"

Howls of derision, curses and threats to his person were hurled across the deck, as the seamen trooped back to the fo'c'sle.

"We can't let him get away with that," said Paddy O'Rourke, as together they discussed ways and means of getting even with the First Mate.

"Leave it to me," said Paddy as the debate finished and the men returned to their quarters. Answering a knock on the door of a cabin he shared with his pal Ted Bigmore, Paddy came face to face with an American Customs Officer.

"Good morning, sir," said Paddy, doing his best to create a good impression. "Won't you come in?"

"Good morning, boys," echoed the officer. "Now don't mind me, just carry on as usual."

The Customs Officer then took a folding stick and flashlight from his bag and tapping the ship's bulkhead, shone his flashlight behind a row of steam pipes into small crevices. Using a tiny mirror attached to the end of his stick, it was now possible for him to see if there was any contraband hidden away there. When the officer had finished searching, the seamen were asked to open their suitcases, so that the customs official might check its contents. O'Rouke was the first to open a small holdall he carried with him and, detecting a hint of Irish brogue in the officer's voice, winked at his pal Bigmore.

"So, it's from Africa you are now?" said the Customs Officer.

"Yes, and a stinking hole it is to be sure, sir," says Paddy, putting on the blarney.

"Well, let's forget the formalities, shall we," said the Customs Officer. "Murphy's the name, boys."

With his brain working overtime, O'Rouke quick as a flash held out a grimy and somewhat calloused hand, and offering it to the official, "Patrick O'Rouke at your service, Mr Murphy," he said with a grin.

Touching his forelock in some form of salute, he shook the officer's proffered hand, saying, "Well now, Mr Murphy, it's grand to meet someone like yourself from the old country."

The officer studied him intently for a moment and in his broad Irish accent cagily asked, "And what about you now, Patrick, have you anything more you'd like to declare?"

From beneath his bunk, O'Rouke dragged out an old canvas kit-bag that had seen better days and tipping it up, emptied the contents on his bunk.

"There ye'are, Mr Murphy, sir, that's me lot," said Paddy.

Glancing at the untidy heap of clothes spilling out of the bag, the officer soon lost interest in its contents. There was nothing more than a pair of seaboots the worse for wear, a cracked shaving bowl, cut-throat razor, and a faded photograph of some distant relative. Never having to undergo such a thorough search before, Paddy was inquisitive and asked the officer, "And what would you be looking for now, Mr Murphy, sir?" he said.

"Well, I guess you boys don't have any," said the office. "The place is clean."

"And what in the Lord's name would I be wanting to hide from you?" said O'Rouke, acting the innocent.

"Surely you've heard of Irish Sweepstake tickets now, boys?" grinned the official. Paddy's eyes lit up in mock surprise, when he realized this was a golden opportunity for him to get even with Prendergast. Turning to his pal Bigmore, he winked, "Did you hear that now, Ted? This here gentleman's looking for Sweepstake tickets, of all things. Now what was it you were telling me about them?"

"Oh, it was nothing much," said Bigmore, "just a few snatches of conversation I heard before we arrived here," he confessed.

"About what?" asked the officer, who now seemed very interested in what he had to say.

"Why don't you tell the gentleman about it, Pat?" said Bigmore, "You can explain it much better than me."

Facing the Customs Officer, O'Rouke rambled on, "Well 'twas like this, Mr Murphy, sir," said Paddy, trying hard to make it sound none too serious, yet holding the man's attention.

"Me mate here was coming off the bridge a few nights ago, having done his spell at the wheel, and as he walked along the deck, he heard these voices. Now he couldn't see too much through the cabin porthole, Mr Murphy, sir, because the curtains was partly drawn. But he remembered hearing someone mention Irish Sweepstake tickets, for this month's Derby."

Hesitating long enough for the officer to say, "Well go on, and what did you see through the porthole?"

O'Rouke continued to lay it on thick and heavy. "Now you'll never believe who it was me pal saw, Mr Murphy. I tell you it fair shook 'im up it did when he saw it was Prendergast, the First Mate."

"There you are, officer," said O'Rouke and, rambling on with a touch of the blarney, said, "You can't trust any of them, sir. Fancy all these foreigners taking tickets out of the country and robbing the poor Irish folk of a livelihood, what do you think of that, Mr Murphy?" said Paddy.

"Hmmm," said the officer. "This fellow you speak of, Patrick. Was that him I passed as I came up the gangway?"

"Ah, for sure, officer, he was the very one. Him with the three gold stripes on his coat sleeve. The very man, Mr Murphy," echoed Paddy's mate, Ted Bigmore. "And more than likely, he's waiting for his contact on the shore to come and collect the tickets, sir."

"Thanks for the information, boys," said Customs Officer Murphy, as he left the cabin. "I'll not mention your names."

As soon as the officer was out of sight, Bigmore turned to O'Rouke, and grinning like a Cheshire cat that's stolen someone's milk, said to him, "You're a sweet talking sod, Paddy. I've never heard such a load of bull-shit, in my life."

"Ah, but it'll sort that bloody Prendergast out, Ted," quipped the crafty O'Rouke. "Then we can scarper ashore."

Meanwhile, Customs Officer Murphy joined his companion who'd been rummaging through the African stoker's quarters and the pair of them walked along the after deck, toward the ship's gangway. About to step ashore himself, Prendergast was busy talking to a longshoreman.

Exchanging the usual "good morning" courtesies when seeing the Customs Officers, Prendergast asked, "Is there anything I can do for you gentlemen?"

"Well now," said Customs Officer Murphy, "come to think of it there is. We've searched the crew's quarters and if you'd oblige us, we'd like to make a start on the officer's cabins."

"Search the officers?" said Slim Prendergast, who obviously was taken by surprise and stammered, "What for, they don't usually bother with us?"

"Oh, it happens now and again that we get these special instructions," said the Customs Officer, following Slim up onto the boat deck.

"What are you searching for?" Prendergast asked the officer.

As it so happened, it was at this particular moment O'Rouke and Bigmore decided it was time for them to hit the road and, as the pair of them strolled nonchalantly toward the gangway, they spotted their arch enemy Prendergast, with the Customs Officers.

Standing outside his cabin on the boat deck, the First Mate was arguing with the officers, and as Paddy passed by he heard him say, "But I haven't got any damned Irish Sweepstake tickets," and angrily protesting his innocence, retorted, "Why do you keep on asking me what I've bloody well done with them? I can hardly afford a tram ticket on the wages I'm being paid here."

Suppressing an urge to burst out laughing, they hurried off ashore. Then, in the seclusion of the customs shed, roars of Cockney and Irish laughter rent the air, as the pair rolled around in hysterics. "That's stopped his gallop!" said Bigmore. "Who the hell does he think he is, trying to stop our shore leave?"

"Aw' c'mon, Ted," said Paddy, "let's go and have a drink before I die laughing."

Following a cursory examination of Prendergast's cabin, the tumult and shouting was allowed to simmer down, with the First Mate still protesting his innocence. Although professing to know nothing about the Sweepstake tickets they assumed he was smuggling into the country, the customs officials insisted he must remain on board until further inquiries were made. It appeared as if O'Rouke had managed to convince the customs authorities that the First Mate was indeed a regular carrier of contraband, and put the skids under his arch enemy.

At lunch that day, the First Mate felt distinctly uncomfortable, when receiving sidelong glances from several of his fellow officers. Things got completely out of hand when Morgan, the Chief Engineer, jokingly asked Prendergast, "D'you have any of those Sweepstake tickets to spare, Mr Mate?"

This was too much for the enraged Prendergast who, rising from the table, pointed a finger at Morgan and leered, "Why don't you stuff an oily wad in that big mouth of yours, Chief? You're too damn nosey."

A brief exchange of sarcastic wit between the two antagonists was enough to put a seldom seen smile on the face of Captain Collie, nicknamed 'The Manx Tiger.'

Not wishing to get involved in a heated argument, I left the warring couple to sort things out for themselves and hurried along to the gangway, with the intention of slipping ashore unnoticed. Assuming the coast was clear, I was about to set foot on the ship's gangway when my path ashore was blocked, by none other than the Bo'sun.

"Ullo there, young Sparks," he said. "Off ashore, are you?"

"Just taking a quick look around town, Wally," I said, with a grin.

"Well, don't hang around the dock area, Sparky boy," he warned, "They'll cut yer blooming throat for five cents."

"Oh, I think I'll just slip up town then, maybe it's safer there."

But there was no stopping the old sea dog who seemed determined to lecture me, saying, "A smart young lad like you will 'ave to watch the ladies, son. You're only seventeen so you don't want to catch a dose of the pox now, do you?" he added, with a sly grin.

"The pox, Wally?" I replied, somewhat alarmed. "Do you mean chicken pox? I've had measles and mumps when I was young, but I've never had that. Is it dangerous?" I said, rather timidly.

His face took on a purple hue and I thought the old fellow was going to explode as he searched for suitable words to explain what he meant. Eyeing me in a paternal manner, he said, "Dangerous, did I hear you say, boy? Why it could ruin you fer life. This place is rotten with it so, take my advice, son, and give the pretty girls a miss, 'cos if you go with them your thingy could drop off. Why, you could even go blind, lad. Now you wouldn't like to go back home to yer dear old mum without a thingy and carrying a white stick, would you now?"

The very thought of walking about without a thingy and having to use a white stick, tap-tapping my way along the pavement because of blindness, sent a feeling of abject horror coursing through my body. The old chap was so convincing he had alarm bells ringing in my head, as I stammered, "I'll keep clear of them, Bo'sun, I promise. I'll just have a quick look around the shops, and come right back."

Taking a taxi, I high-tailed it up town to visit the large depart-

ment stores and paid a hurried call to Gimble's and Macy's, on Fifth
Avenue. When heading in the direction of Times Square, I was about
to hail a taxi back to my ship, having decided I'd had enough for one
day, when the plaintive cry of a familiar voice assailed my ears.

"Oi there, Sparks, where yer dashing off to? Come over 'ere an
'ave a drink with us?"

"Good grief," I muttered to myself when seeing who it was. "How
unlucky can I get?"

Sitting on the sidewalk, as large as life, were Paddy O'Rourke
and Ted Bigmore, each hugging a large jug of cider, or some other
concoction. No doubt the pair of them had set out to paint the town
red but how on earth they managed to reach an uptown New York
shopping area, seeing the state they were in, was beyond comprehen-
sion. Their usual hunting grounds were the nearest pub outside the
dock gates.

Making an excuse that I needed to get to a washroom, I shot away
like a bat out of Hell. As expected, the pair of them did not return
aboard ship until late that night, and were again in trouble with the
law. No sooner had they crawled up the ship's gangway, than they
slipped into the galley, and helped themselves to the remains of a
leg of lamb. Then having quickly disposed of the meat, they offered
the bone to a Customs and Excise guard dog, in an effort to coax the
animal on board the vessel.

Although our stay in New York was somewhat limited, I did manage to squeeze in another visit to many of the big stores, on my last
day ashore. Bearing in mind to keep an eye out for Paddy and Bigmore, I made sure they were nowhere in the vicinity, and hurried
along Fifth Avenue. Passing Times Square, I stopped to post a letter
home to my mother, in reply to one I received from her when arriving
here. Heeding the old Bo'sun's warning about catching galloping dry
rot or some other contagious disease, I called in at the nearest drug
store.

Along with some toiletries such as face soap and razor blades, I
purchased a small bottle of disinfectant as a safety measure against
infection, before returning aboard the ship. Unfamiliar as I was at

the time with the behaviour of seafarers, that old devil chose to put the frighteners on me, with his seaman's jargon. I was, to all intents, still inexperienced in their way of life or, to put it mildly, an innocent abroad.

CHAPTER 8

BACK TO DARKEST AFRICA

An unexpected change of orders cut short our stay in the U.S.A. That's not unusual for tramp steamers like the *S.S. Ardmere*, who had no regular trade route and were liable to be sent all over the globe to pick up cargo. It came as no surprise when the vessel was ordered to leave New York harbour, on a morning cloaked in heavy mist. Loaded down to her plimsoll line with a full general cargo, the old tub met the choppy waters of the North Atlantic head on, her thin deck plates groaning beneath the weight. Like most of her crew, she seemed reluctant to make the long arduous trip across the South Atlantic, back to West Africa.

Steering a south-bound route, our return journey across the Atlantic was smooth and uneventful, with never a ship in sight. It was also rather boring unless one was privileged to catch sight of a flying fish skimming the unruffled waters by dawn's early light, which would give rise to a bout of excitement. Leaping up from the ocean, many of these fish were caught in the fresh southeast trade winds and landed on the ship's deck, where Rusty, the ship's cat, forever on the lookout for a tasty meal, lay out of sight waiting for them to arrive so he'd enjoy fresh fish for his breakfast.

Battered by strong head winds whistling through the rigging, the old tub, with perfect timing, dipped her bows into every deep trough with a resounding thud, rattling her thin hull. We were now off Africa's West Coast and, with the rainy season in full swing, the *S.S. Ardmere* faced gale force winds and sudden heavy rain squalls before limping into Freetown, Sierra Leone, our first port of call. Waiting to meet us were the same old invading hordes of native cargo workers, waiting to pick us clean.

Amongst the first to step aboard was the ever faithful Joe Beef, who once again offered his services as the seamen's mess boy.

"Hello, Massa Parker," said Joe, saluting the old sea dog. "I wait you dis long time, sah. Me your mess boy, one more time."

Remembering old Parker as the person responsible for giving him a dose of the trots on the previous trip, Joe said, "You give no more bad beer, please, sah."

"Alright, Joe, take your gear aft before the rest of the bandits take over," said Parker, rising from his huge teakwood chair, as though he were a tribal chief. Then strolling along to his quarters on the after deck, he informed the rest of the seamen Joe Beef was once again their mess boy.

"He hasn't come for another dose of the shits, has he?" laughed Snowy White. "He might put some of the witch doctor's jollop in your tea this trip, Nosey, so you'd better watch out."

Within the hour, two hundred native workers swarmed aboard and like an army of ants ran in all directions, over the entire ship's deck. Some went looking for a place to hide their belongings, while others were seen to make a bee line for the fresh water pump underneath the fo'c'sle head, only to find it padlocked. As a safety measure, once again, the key had been given to the natives' head man to limit the amount of fresh water used.

As night fell, some semblance of order was restored among the natives who, by this time, had settled down as the *Ardmere* heaved up anchor, and slipped quietly out to sea. Standing on the open deck I watched the lights of Freetown fade in the distance. Sporadic spurts of flame from bush fires further along the coast lit up the night sky until seen as no more than a flicker in the inky blackness, to suddenly disappear from view. Then, all one could hear was the faint swish of water slapping against the ship's side, as she carved her way south, through the Atlantic's silken waters.

Morning saw a build-up of black cloud scudding across the far horizon to blot out the sun, an ominous sign we were in for a heavy downpour with the rainy season about to commence. A period of violent thunder with flashes of lightning that lit up the darkened sky, warned us rain would surely follow in its wake. Suddenly, the wind increased and down it came, falling in huge droplets the size of penny pieces, that bounced around as if on springs as it hit the ship's steel deck. As the heavy showers lashed the vessel, Gilchrist, the navigation officer, slipped into the chartroom to don his oilskins, then once again stepped out onto the open bridge to face the elements.

Nervous as a kitten and on edge, he strode up and down the bridge keeping a weather eye open for other vessels operating in the area, until a burst of heavy downpour accompanied by flashes of lightning drove him back in the wheel-house for cover. Once inside, he found it impossible to see little more than a few hundred yards ahead. This time the tension had proved too much for him, forcing him out on the starboard wing of the bridge to face the elements.

It was late that afternoon when the S.S. Ardmere entered Takoradi harbour, one of the more modern seaports along Africa's West Coast, with a cargo of 200 tons of kerosene. Work on discharging the vessel began immediately, allowing off duty crewmen little more than an couple of hours to nip ashore for a quick drink. The privilege was denied seamen O'Rouke and Bigmore, whose shore leave had been cancelled until further orders by Captain Collie. Surprisingly, this did not seem to bother the pair of them, as they watched their shipmates trooping off ashore.

Not to be denied a sup of the local brew, O'Rouke sent Joe Beef ashore to purchase some of the Palm Wine from a nearby native village. The pair were, at this moment in time, quietly congratulating each other with having made such a crafty move, and chose to wait for the mess boy to return aboard.

Night had fallen by the time I finished my evening stroll around the ship's deck when, beneath the glare of the vessel's arc lights, I caught sight of Joe Beef. The lad was bent double as he staggered up the ship's gangway, with a heavy load on his back. He was about to set foot on board the ship when a dark clad figure, hidden from view on the lower deck, stepped out of the shadows and stopped him in his tracks.

Prendergast took the startled Joe Beef by surprise, saying, "What you got there, boy?"

Dropping his heavy load on deck, Joe Beef shook with fright as he opened up the sack for the First Mate, enabling him to examine its contents. Bending low, Prendergast put his head inside the sack, and reeled back as though stung. "What the hell is this you've got here?" he yelled. "It stinks to high heaven!"

"Him tombo, sah," said Joe Beef, a puzzled look on his face. "Dis very good Africa palm wine, sah," he proudly announced.

Screwing up his face in disgust, Prendergast snorted, "Where d'you get this stinking concoction from, the bloody sewer? It's enough to poison a donkey."

Fearing he was in trouble, Joe Beef muttered, "Dis not for me, sah," and pointing to the sack holding two large calabashs of the horrible brew, he pleaded, "Him for big Massa Paddy, sah. He speak him no go shore-side, get plenty headache. Him tell me, Joe Beef, go bring plenty Tombo."

"Ah, so that's his bloody game," sneered Prendergast, giving the two jars of palm wine a hefty kick, to send the contents spewing out over the ship's deck.

Rousing the seamen from their quarters, Prendergast ordered O'Rouke and Bigmore to get buckets and brooms, to clean up the stinking mess. Under the watchful eye of the First Mate, they toiled long into the hours of darkness, scrubbing the deck clean. Only then were they allowed to slink off to their quarters, without so much as a sip of the jungle juice they craved.

·   ·   ·

Our departure from the port of Takoradi next morning was delayed by a violent thunder storm and gale force winds sweeping along the coast, bending tall palm trees in its path like an archer's bow. It was almost midday by the time we left the harbour to head in a southerly direction towards Lagos, our next port of call. Following an overnight stop at Lagos to replenish our dwindling fresh water supplies, we were expecting to move on south to Port Harcourt, where the remainder of our cargo of kerosene was to be discharged ashore. But, as so often happens with tramp steamers, our trip was cancelled at the last minute, and the kerosene quickly transferred onto a small coastwise vessel.

Leaving her berth alongside the wharf at Appapa, the *S.S. Ardmere* was ordered to anchor up one of several mosquito-infested creeks in the vicinity, to await further orders. So here we were stuck up a swampy creek surrounded by dense jungle, as far as the eye could see, where suffocating night temperatures defied description and a goodnight kiss from one of several million mosquitoes in this breeding ground, guaranteed you a dose of the screaming Abdabs. Why, I kept asking myself, was I stupid enough to think life at sea among this green jungle horror was my forte? I could so easily have been swanning around on a bicycle at home, earning an easy living at Sainsbury's, the family grocers.

After wallowing in that stinking green Hell, for what appeared to be a lifetime, we were finally allowed to leave our jungle hideaway, and ordered to proceed south. Running short of coal, the vessel was forced to call at Durban in South Africa to replenish her depleted stocks, and told to wait there for further instructions. Arriving in the port after an uneventful four-day passage down the African coast, we at least had the benefit of cool ocean breezes, a breath of clean air, and a stroll along the dockside to stretch our legs. Other than that, there was little for many of us to do except watch a group of native convicts arrive each morning, to start work on Durban's new breakwater.

Closely guarded by native warders armed with assegais, the pris-

oners, in leg irons, were chained to each other as they toiled throughout the day, beneath a blazing tropical sun. Short periods of rest were
taken for drinks, but any unofficial break in between by a prisoner
was rewarded with the tip of a warder's spear in his backside.

Wishing to go ashore, I approached a Dutch overseer who had
just boarded the ship, and asked, "How does one get into town from
here?"

"You could hire a taxi that will probably get you halfway to town
and then break down, so why not take a rickshaw?" he said, pointing
to a half-naked Zulu, wearing nothing more than a feathered head-
dress and a leopard skin jock strap covering his loins.

"How much do I pay the chap with the rickshaw?" I asked.

"Chap," he replied, giving me a rather puzzled look. I knew he did
not understand what I meant, so I said, "My friend and I want to go up
town, so how much do I pay him?" I said, pointing to the Zulu.

"Oh, the kaffir," he laughed aloud. "Never pay them what they
ask for, give 'em half."

"But he's a big fellow," I said, "supposing he argues with me?"

"Kick his arse," was the man's response.

Well, I said to myself, this is not the sort of situation a skinny seventeen-year-old greenhorn like me would ever wish to get mixed up
in. A second glance at the Zulu's rippling muscles on his huge torso,
caused me to hurriedly change my mind. Why the fellow might take
me to some lonely spot and eat me, I feared. So I decided, after all, I
could quite easily see everything I wanted to of the port of Durban,
from the safety of the ship's deck. As luck would have it, our stay here
was limited to the time it took the ship to bunker.

Before leaving Durban, Captain Collie decided to fill the vessel's
ballast tanks to give the old tub some stability, as we headed for God
knows where. Nobody on board seemed to have a clue as to which
direction the vessel was heading except the Captain and, being a se-
cretive sort of individual, he would never inform any of his crew until
we were off the port.

Leaving harbour as night was falling, the *S.S. Ardmere* ran into
fierce south-easterly winds and a huge sea swell that tossed the old

tub about like a piece of cork, as she pitched and rolled her way up Africa's East Coast. With a following sea underneath her stern, the old girl would lurch forward, burying her nose deep in the ocean. Then without warning, her after end would rise clear of the water to shake the vessel from stem to stern, her propeller thrashing the air like some wild thing. Fearing this might cause serious damage to his ship, Captain Collie requested the Chief Engineer report to him, in his cabin, on the top deck.

"Can't you ease the engine revs down, Chief?" the Captain asked him, when he appeared on the bridge. "You're shaking the very guts out of her."

"I've already told that idiot on watch down in the engine room to ease the throttle when she takes a nose-dive, I can't do more than that, Captain."

"She'll fall apart if we don't watch out," the Captain moaned. "There's only a layer of rust and the rats holding hands down below that's keeping the bloody ship afloat," he went on.

The situation went from bad to worse when the ship's carpenter checked the fresh water tanks and, finding our drinking water perilously low, reported the matter to the Captain. The *S.S. Ardmere* was halfway up the East African coast and about to head across the Indian Ocean when Captain Collie decided to call in at Mombassa, our nearest port to hand.

Lying close to the equator, Mombassa, Kenya's main port, has a natural harbour and ships arriving there have an opportunity to replenish their supply of fresh water and if necessary fruit and vegetables. An overnight stay here was more than sufficient for any human being in the oppressive heat of this tropical cauldron where the temperature reached one hundred and twenty degrees, in the shade.

At night, once again, life was made intolerable for all concerned, by the swarms of mosquitoes and nocturnal creatures from the outlying swamps. The point was emphasized by a chance remark from an irate seaman who, when asked if these insects bothered him, remarked, "Why, they've got hobnail boots on, and the kick of a mule."

Leaving Mombassa at daybreak, the *S.S. Ardmere* set off on her long journey across the Indian Ocean, bound for Colombo, capital of Ceylon. It was late afternoon, some six days later, when the ship dropped anchor in one of the many beautiful bays surrounding the island, where our stay was no more than a few hours. Here again, we replenished our depleted supply of fresh water before setting off for our next port of call, wherever that might be.

From the deck of the *S.S. Ardmere* I surveyed the town's inviting palm-fringed beaches with stretches of sun-kissed golden sand, caressed by clear blue waters of the Indian Ocean.

How I envied the young native children frolicking about in the rolling surf and longed to be with them, instead of pacing the deck of this rusting hulk, with scant relief from the stifling heat.

As evening approached, the setting sun's orange glow lit the far horizon, where it remained for a few fleeting seconds. Then, surrendering to the fast approaching hours of darkness, it slipped gently out of sight, plunging us all into darkness.

CHAPTER 9

INDIA'S PERFUMES AND PALACES

In the inky blackness of a moonless night, the *S.S. Ardmere* hoisted her anchor, and headed back out to sea. Keeping within sight of land, the old tub wallowed in an off-shore sea swell on her journey up India's West Coast to Calcutta, capital of Bengal. With no berths available, the ship's anchor cable was used to secure her to buoys in midstream on a fast-flowing Hoogli River. Within a short space of time, a flotilla of barges laden with sacks arrived alongside the ship, whereupon all Hell broke loose.

There was so much arguing and fighting among the Indian barge crews as to whose barge was to be discharged first, Prendergast threatened to cut them all adrift. Order was finally restored and work on loading the ship with a cargo of rice and gunny bags went on ceaselessly during the weeks that followed.

On this my first visit to India, I was appalled to see large families of the poorer class Indian, known as untouchables, living in squalid conditions on board these barges. The water they drank and washed in was from the polluted Hoogli River, where vultures were seen to feed off dead bodies drifting down its length.

With class distinction much in evidence in India as a whole, the only means of earning a living for many of the poorer classes like the untouchables, is by begging on the streets. Is it any wonder when strangers visit this country they are often surprised and saddened as I was, when accosted in the street by infants in ragged clothes pleading for money. Arms outstretched, they approach the stranger, with cries of "Baksheesh, Sahib."

Much as I would have liked to further explore this historic city of Calcutta, which started as a trading post for the then British India Company way back in 1690, for me the place had lost its appeal following my one and only venture ashore. This far flung land of fragrant perfumes, silks, spices and beautiful white marble palaces written about in children's storybooks, as far as I was concerned ceased to exist. The bubble burst, so to speak, when I first set foot ashore. The aroma of eastern promise replaced by a pong of stale curry and a foul smelling odour of cow-dung, lying in sun-baked village streets. It was with a feeling of relief and sadness I left the port of Calcutta some weeks later, with the cry of hungry children ringing in my ears, mindful never to return.

Our journey, via the Cape of Good Hope to the West Coast of Africa, was anything but hopeful for those of us aboard when the weather turned nasty as we neared Capetown. Lying gunnel deep in the ocean, *Ardmere* fell victim to a strong south-easterly gale that lashed the ship, spewing heavy seas over her rusting deck. Rounding the Cape, a huge sea swell caused her to dance about like a marionette or bury her nose into bottomless troughs. At times I feared she would turn turtle never to resurface. But the old tub did her best to maintain a top speed of five knots and, at the same time, shake the guts out of us.

Approaching the Gulf of Guinea, a short distance from the equator, the *Ardmere*'s crew seized every opportunity to shelter from the intense heat, beneath an array of canvas awnings, erected around the bridge and crew's quarters. It was with a feeling of great relief we reached the more temperate climate of Duala, a seaport in the Cameroons on Africa's West Coast, administered by the French. More especially, since members of the ship's crew were forced to work in sweltering heat from dawn to dusk, they now had sufficient cover from a tropical sun that burnt you to a cinder.

It was here, in Duala, the bulk of the *Ardmere*'s cargo of rice was discharged. With number two and three hatches empty, exports of the country's minerals, hides, timber and other raw materials for the U.S.A. were loaded on board the vessel. Of strategic importance to the country, Yauonde, the capital, relies on a railway link with Duala for imports of foreign goods. In keeping with many ports along Africa's West Coast lying up jungle-infested rivers, Duala had its nightly patrol of winged monsters to contend with, forcing the ship's crew to sweat it out each night beneath mosquito nets, hot and miserable. I found sleeping throughout the hours of darkness an impossible task, more like asking for manna from Heaven. Asking to have an electric fan installed in your cabin was liable to cause the Captain to have an apoplectic fit.

The loading of cargo aboard having been finally completed, a consignment of mahogany logs bound for the U.S.A. were securely fastened down to her deck fore and aft. It was with unbounded joy that I felt the old ship's engine tremble beneath my feet, as we steamed north for Takoradi. Having spent the last three weeks seeking relief from a tropical sun so fierce it could have dried up the sea, I felt relief. Although Takoradi, our next port of call in the equatorial Gulf of Guinea, boasted much the same tropical atmosphere as that of Duala, we were able to enjoy the benefit of cool sea breezes, instead of the unbearable jungle heat we left behind.

Daybreak saw the morning sun peep above the horizon, sending an orange glow across the ocean's stillness as we slipped into Takoradi harbour, where a handful of natives waited to take the ship's mooring ropes. By mid-morning, dock workers arrived to discharge what little remained of our cargo of gunny bags from India and to clean out number one and four holds, leaving them empty. Following a short break for lunch, consignments of cocoa beans lying on the quayside were hurriedly stripped of their waterproof coverings, and work on loading the *Ardmere* began again in earnest. From early morning until long after dusk, natives worked throughout the choking heat of each day, with a short break for their midday meal. By the end of our second week in Takoradi, the loading of the ship had been completed and all that remained was to batten down the hatches, and the old tub was ready for sea.

It was time for the *S.S. Ardmere* to set course for Freetown, our final port of call. Sailing due north under skies of blue, we were blessed with just a hint of a breeze off the Atlantic Ocean.

Our journey, however, was to take longer than anticipated due to engine failure, leaving the old tub to limp into Freetown, Sierra Leone, for much-needed repairs. Our orders were to move up a narrow creek on nearby Sherbro Island, where we dropped anchor close to an old wooden jetty, hemmed in by swamp and jungle.

From his vantage point on the boat deck, Captain Collie watched a small tug towing a string of barges loaded with chrome ore, toward his ship. Sensing they were approaching much too fast and appearing to be out of control, he shouted a warning to the Captain of the tug, instructing him to slow the vessel down. Wringing his hands in despair, when his order was not carried out, he winced as though in pain, when the barges thudded against the ship's side. The impact shook the vessel from stem to stern denting her thin plates. A cloud of rust from the ship's side was seen to shoot high in the air, colouring the river in a reddish brown dust.

"Is there no one looking after my ship, mister?" he asked Prendergast, who at the time seemed at a loss for something to do.

"Get Bo'sun to put a couple of his men on the port side to watch these stupid natives," the Captain moaned. "They'll sink my damn ship if you let them. Just look at this idiot," he growled, as another barge slammed against the ship's side.

Seamen Parker and Sullivan waited for the next load of barges to come alongside, with strict instructions to stand by with fenders ready to cushion the impact, thus avoiding further damage to the ship. Fearing he would miss his target by a mile, the tug Captain in charge of operations made a valiant effort to avoid a head-on collision with the ship, as it rattled her plates, then bounced off the vessel in another shower of rust.

Watching this performance from the boat deck, Captain Collie vented his anger on the two seamen, who stood there laughing.

"They've damaged my blasted ship," Captain Collie shouted, "and you damned fools stand there grinning like a pair of Cheshire cats!"

Sullivan, a crafty old sea dog who knew the ropes, spread his hands out in an apologetic gesture, and replied, "It's only the rust that's fallen off, Capt'n."

"Rust, be damned. We could have sprung a blasted leak," Captain Collie retorted.

"Well, that's saved us the bloody job of chipping the rust off," Sullivan said to his mate, Nosey Parker.

"Yes, it'll give the weevils down in the holds a chance to get a breath of fresh air," grinned Nosey. "They've been dying to escape."

Fearing they had buckled the plates on his ship, Captain Collie himself ordered a boat to be lowered over the side of the vessel, while he inspected her. Seeing there was no serious damage, he ordered the Bo'sun to see that his men were set to work with paint and brush, to cover the rusty patches.

Loading of chrome ore continued as night was falling in this God-forsaken, swamp-infested, green Hell out in the middle of no-where. In a moment of madness, I threw caution to the wind and took a moonlight stroll around the boat deck and receiving a goodnight kiss from one of many thousands of tiny winged monsters. I was soon to learn the little devil had the kick of a mule. Having neglected to use a mosquito repellent I kept in my cabin, I would fall victim to the dreaded Malaria.

CHAPTER 10

THE DREADED MALARIA
CATCHES UP WITH ME

Some twenty-four hours later I felt a little dizzy, and my head started to spin round like a top. An uncontrollable bout of shivering gripped my body, cartwheeling me into space. Buckling at the knees, there was nothing I could do to save myself from falling. As the steel deck came up to meet me, I simply drifted aimlessly, into oblivion. I found myself entombed in a place of darkness, from which there seemed no escape.

Suddenly, a pinpoint of light appeared to lead me out of that long black tunnel into the light of day, where soft white clouds brushed my face in passing. Regaining consciousness, I was vaguely aware of a dark-skinned man, standing at my bedside, in conversation with a person nearby, whom I recognized as Perkins, our senior radio operator. The coloured man said, "I'll have to give him an injection."

Bending over me, Perkins whispered, "You are going to be alright now, Rowland."

A whiff of surgical spirits assailed my nostrils as the native doctor attending me wiped my arm with a piece of cottonwool, and muttered, "Just a little jab, Mr Marshall."

I tried to remain calm as the needle bit into my flesh, but could do nothing to stop myself from plunging into a bottomless pit. I became one of the many thousands who have fallen victim to the dreaded Malaria, a disease from which it is said, few survived. A bout of fever can attack people suffering from Malaria or any one of several diseases out in tropical climates without warning, favouring neither young or old. Diseases such as Malaria, Blackwater Fever, Yellow Fever and Dysentry are said to be a curse among the European community out here in darkest Africa, where in many instances the victims indulge in bouts of drinking, brought about by sheer boredom.

Then again it could well be caused by an accumulation of all three but, in any event, death can come swiftly. So for many there is no time to linger, while relatives and nurses tip-toe around the patient's bed, making comforting noises. Just how I managed to survive to tell the tale, when many young men before me simply perished, I will never know. Suffice to say I did not get away scot-free, for during the next six years, I was to suffer periodic bouts of the dreaded disease.

It was now late December of 1938, when the *S.S. Ardmere* once again sailed into New York, where bitterly cold easterly winds iced up our snow-covered decks, looking more like some skating rink. The ship's Captain reported to the Port Health Authority that I was suffering with a tropical disease, whereupon they insisted I be sent to hospital immediately. From our berth in Brooklyn, I was quickly transferred to the Long Island College Hospital and left in a small ante-room, to await a visit from the doctor.

"Hello, can I help you?" asked the young man in white hospital garb, who happened to pop his head around the door. "Where have you come from?" he asked, looking me up and down.

"I've just arrived on a ship from Sierra Leone, West Africa," I informed him.

"My goodness, you look ill," he said. "Are you suffering from some malady?"

The very mention of the word Malaria saw his face light up in surprise. "Malaria, did you say, sir?" he repeated. "Would you care to come this way, please."

I was shown into a small laboratory, where a group of young men, dressed in similar attire, were busy conducting some sort of experiment among a collection of test tubes and bunsen burners.

"We have a visitor from Africa with a tropical disease," my guide announced to his fellow workers. "Malaria no less, I believe. Is that correct, sir?" he asked.

My reply was lost in a tinkle of glass being swept aside as a dozen medical students gathered around and, like werewolves baying for a victim's blood, took samples from my fingers. I was fast becoming a human pin cushion and, were it not for a kindly nurse who happened to be passing by and released me from the clutches of these young students, I might have been bled dry. I was most grateful to the young lady who then escorted me to a ward in the hospital where I was placed under observation, until my ship was ready to leave New York. Meanwhile, I was visited by some sympathetic old ladies who brought me presents of cookies, candy and magazines, making life pleasantly tolerable.

"So you're from Africa," my visitor would say. "Why it must be awful for you out there what with the heat, and all those wild animals roaming about."

Comfortable in my new surroundings, I soon adjusted to the luxury afforded me in hospital, and wished my ship would sail off without me. Sadly this was not to be, for all too soon Captain Collie and his bosom pal Prendergast, like a couple of black clouds on the horizon, put in an appearance at the far end of the ward. Peeping from beneath the blankets, I watched as their beady eyes scanned the room, looking for me. It was just a matter of time before they arrived at the foot of my bed, where they stood exchanging glances. Prendergast's face quickly underwent a change from white to crimson, seeing the huge assortment of goodies I'd been tucking into.

"I hope the company isn't paying for this lot?" he grumbled. "Just look at all the chocolates he's been eating, Captain."

Several glossy magazines and papers lay on a table at my beside with a half empty box of chocolates and packets of cookies donated by kindly old dowagers, on their weekly visits. It was Prendergast who removed the blankets covering my head, and grunted, "Come on, son, you've been here long enough. You'd better get dressed and hurry back on board. We're leaving on the morning tide."

"Yes, you've cost the company enough already," Captain Collie whined. "We can't allow you to stay here in the lap of luxury, any longer."

Back on board the ship that night, I dreamt the Captain and First Mate were shipwrecked, many miles away. The pair were adrift in an open boat that leaked like a sieve as they held hands and sang *Let's Be Buddies*, while it slowly sank beneath the waves.

Next morning, I was wakened by the noise of the ship's steam winches, heaving our mooring ropes inboard, and chose to stay in my bunk, thinking of what might have been. Cursing my luck and Captain Collie for dragging me back aboard this heap of junk, I gazed through the porthole in my cabin as skyscrapers on Manhattan's skyline came into view, and quickly faded in the distance. With New York and the Hudson River far astern, we dropped our pilot off at the estuary before reaching the open sea. I then realize that life could have been so much easier for me if those two jerks had left me in hospital, to be spoilt by those dear old ladies who visited me.

Out in the Atlantic heading south, a cold north-east wind and following sea caused the vessel to pitch and toss about like some wild thing, dipping her bow into every trough. Off Cape Cod, a blinding snow storm delayed our arrival at Boston until the following day, when our deck cargo of mahogany logs was hurriedly discharged ashore. Leaving on the morning tide, we then sailed on to Philadelphia, where a small cargo of kerosene was taken on board. At the end of January, amid snow showers and a good deal of fog, we left Philadelphia for Norfolk, Virginia, to replenish our dwindling supply of coal.

Arriving at Norfolk the following morning, bunkering the ship with some two hundred tons of coal took no more than a couple of hours. So it was late afternoon that same day, when the *S.S. Ardmere* with a full complement of cargo made ready to leave port. Creaking and groaning under the weight of all that cargo, she forged ahead, to enter the cold unfriendly waters of the Atlantic. In deciding to take a southerly route, we hoped to avoid running into bad weather that lay in our path. We were now en route for the West Coast of Africa, which at the earliest would take the *S.S. Ardmere* with her top speed of six knots, the best part of three weeks. This of course was providing her weary engine behaved herself, and did not throw in the towel.

With my ship due to make landfall within the next few days, I wondered if Mother had taken the time to write, her letters having been few and far between, over the past six months. This tended to worry me, for I had no way of knowing if all was well at home. In a matter of weeks my two-year contract with the company was due to expire, bringing to a close the most exciting chapter of my life, so far. I would at times pause to look back and remember my upbringing as a young child, in the cloistered atmosphere of a convent. I had, during my two years at sea, come to learn about life as it really was, seeing for myself much that amused or shocked me. I would now, doubtless, return home a wiser young man.

As expected there was no letter from Mother when I arrived at the African Port of Freetown, Sierra Leone, a disappointment I sought to overlook knowing I was soon to be on my way home to England. I started packing my personal belongings and prepared to board a waiting launch, with several other members of the ship's crew who were also leaving the rusty old tub that had been my home for two years. Memories of my time aboard the *S.S. Ardmere* both good and bad flashed through my mind in a trice. I had to confess, there were no regrets.

On landing ashore at Freetown, all members of the ship's crew due to be relieved were accommodated at the City Hotel, a large white-fronted building on the edge of town, equal in status to that of a second-class boarding house back home. A swashbuckling Greek, who imagined he was Errol Flynn, ran this flea-bitten hotel and treated his native staff like a bunch of pirates, which of course many of them were. The place was comfortable to a degree, if you didn't mind the flies doing the breast stroke in your soup. In the lounge, a radio purchased from some hard-up seaman provided music from a bygone era, and was by all accounts the only source of entertainment the hotel had to offer its guests.

As an alternative, if one could call it that, you could spend the evening listening to the rumble of jungle drums somewhere out in the bush, or a rendition of *O Sole Mio* from Paddy O'Rourke, in a drunken stupor. Otherwise, you might as well plug your ears with cotton wool and try to get some sleep, remembering, first and foremost, to use the mosquito net provided for your benefit, or suffer the consequences.

Having experienced several bouts of Malaria during the course of my time in Africa, I was most anxious not to jeopardize my chances of a passage home, and made a point of using my mosquito net every night. There was no way on earth I would want to end up in a native hospital. Paddy O'Rourke, however, seemed immune to the mosquitoes' deadly bite, which led me to believe there might be a grain of truth in his conviction that the native jungle juice acted as a deterrent in warding them off. Along with his buddy Ted Bigmore, the pair would dance the night away with native girls in the nearby village, to the non-stop rhythm of the tom-toms.

From my window at the hotel next day, I watched the *S.S. Ardmere* as it sailed away. As an inexperienced slip of a lad of seventeen, with no idea what life at sea was all about, I was thrown in at the deep end, as one would say, and quickly gained my sea legs. Having to witness many amusing incidents among drunken seamen after a night on the tiles, so to speak, reminded me of a quotation from one of many books I'd read, 'If only we could see ourselves as others see us.'

With little first-hand knowledge of life at sea, I was, to all intents and purposes, an innocent abroad when joining the *S.S. Ardmere*, an old tramp steamer. Much of the coarse language used by seamen in their everyday lives aboard ship was hard for me to understand at first but, like many a young lad making his first trip to sea, I soon learned to live with their nautical jargon, often said in a humorous manner. Now that my contract with the company had expired, I waited for a passage home on the *M.V. Accra*, a passenger ship due to arrive at Freetown that day.

Standing out on the waterfront with some of my shipmates, we watched as the silhouette of a ship on the horizon grew larger with each passing minute. She was within hailing distance when one of the seamen exclaimed, "That's the *Accra*, so we'll soon be on our way home, lads."

Back at the City Hotel, where I'd spent two weeks of complete boredom, lunch was being served amid a hubbub of excitement, the main topic of conversation centred on the burning question, how soon would we be on our way home?

M.V. Accra carried passengers between England and the west coast of Africa.

It was late afternoon when we received word, from the company's agent, we were to take passage aboard the *M.V. Accra*, now lying at anchor in the bay. To whoops of delight, everyone hurriedly packed their bags and were taken down to a small jetty, where we spent a couple of hours waiting for a launch to take us out to the ship.

With dusk closing in, I stood on the boat deck and felt her powerful engines begin to throb beneath my feet, as they suddenly burst into life. Soon the twinkling lights of Freetown were no more, as they slowly disappeared in the gathering gloom. The vessel picked up speed, and headed out to the open sea.

Early next morning, I wakened to the cry of gulls on the wing waiting for the usual bucket of garbage thrown overboard from the ship's galley. For a while, I lay on my bunk listening to the gentle lapping of the waves against the ship's side, and from the upper deck above my cabin, there came the clumping of crewmen's seaboots. Deck scubbers, scraping back and forth as they went about their morning chores, hosing down the ship. Rising slowly, I washed and dressed and left my cabin for a morning stroll around the upper deck, before venturing into the dining-room for breakfast.

We were now three days out from Freetown and approaching Cape Finisterre, the southernmost point in the Bay of Biscay, when the weather quickly deteriorated. With the vessel struggling to maintain a steady speed of fifteen knots against gale force winds, a previously calm sea whipped up into waves of mountainous proportions, which threatened to swamp us, the storm's ferocity easing in intensity as we approached the English Channel's calmer waters.

It was now March 6 of 1939, and I was about to catch my first glimpse of England's southern coast since leaving some three years earlier. Entering Plymouth Sound, the *M.V. Accra* was taken in tow by attendant tugs, shepherding the vessel alongside her berth. Shortly after the ship had received clearance from the Customs and Port Health Authorities I was given a railway ticket to London, and allowed to disembark. The *M.V. Accra* had already slipped quietly away from Plymouth, destined for her home port of Liverpool.

Hailing a taxi, I asked to be taken to Plymouth railway station and, waiting to reach my destination, my thoughts turned to Mother and home.

CHAPTER 11

A SAD HOMECOMING

"Here you are, sir, Plymouth Station," said the taxi driver, helping me out with my luggage. Paying him in excess of the fare he'd asked for, I took stock of my surroundings. Like most seaside towns in England during winter, Plymouth Station was deserted except for a handful of sailors from the nearby naval base, who appeared to be going on leave. At the ticket office, a pale-faced individual in a crumpled railway uniform scrutinized the travel voucher I'd given him and, pushing his black peaked cap to the back of his head, took a good look at me. For a minute or two his watery eyes studied my suntanned face, as if to satisfy himself I was not on the wanted list, before he chose to ask, "And what can I do for you?"

"I'd like a ticket to Victoria Station, please. That's if you're not too busy," I replied, tongue in cheek.

Closely inspecting the green railway voucher I'd handed him, he produced a ticket from a drawer in his desk, and once again eyed me with suspicion. In parting, he said, "Go to platform four, over the bridge." Then as if reluctant to part with further information, he added, "Your train is due in half an hour."

Hesitating a moment, I asked, "Is there somewhere warm where I could wait until my train arrives?"

"There's a waiting room on platform four," he replied, and carried on reading his morning paper.

The waiting room, a relic of past grandeur when railways were a joy to behold, had been stripped bare of seating, and was nothing more than an empty shell. On a graffiti-covered wall, in this cold and derelict place, a once ornate mirror hung from its rusting chain at a grotesque angle, the glass shattered beyond repair. Travellers seeking to rest awhile would find little comfort here except an overpowering smell of urine, the result of a drunken visitor's calling card. Out on the railway platform a machine that once held penny bars of Nestle's chocolate stood empty, red paint peeling from its rusting iron frame. With no place to shelter from biting March winds, I huddled up in my dufflecoat and paced up and down the station platform.

The sound of an approaching train destined for London was music to my ears. Standing there braving bitterly cold east winds, I looked on anxiously as it pulled in, a pennant of white steam gushing from its squat funnel. As it ground to a halt, carriage doors swung open and tired passengers tumbled out and trudged wearily on to the station exit, glad of an opportunity to stretch their cramped and aching limbs. Stepping into an empty compartment, I stowed my luggage in the rack provided above the seats and, brushing some muddy footprints off the red upholstery, sat down to rest. Having just arrived home from Africa, I was chilled to the bone.

No sooner had I sat down when a shrill blast on the station master's whistle spurred a uniformed railway guard into action and, as the train jerked forward, he hurried along the platform, slamming carriage doors shut as he went. The noise echoed through my compartment like a clap of thunder and, as he waved his green flag to indicate all was clear, he disappeared in a cloud of smoke.

Patches of morning fog hid much of southern England as we travelled north, slowly dispersing by the time my train arrived at Victoria Station in London. As it squealed to a halt, a pall of black smoke from the engine drifted up under the station's glass-covered roof, black with layers of dust and grime accumulated over the years. The light of day was failing to penetrate many areas.

Carrying two holdalls with all my worldly goods, I pushed my way past bustling crowds toward the station exit. Stepping into a waiting taxi, I asked to be taken to the nearest Underground station where I would catch my train for Wimbledon, then a local bus home. With Mother having failed to answer my letters during the last six months, I approached the house I called home with some misgiving. Maybe she was upset with me because I had written to say I was determined to find my sister. Or was it because of some dark secret she felt she must hide from me?

Now that I was back home, she might at least explain why she had not written to me.

Knocking gently, I stood back from the door and waited to see the look of surprise on her face, when seeing me on her doorstep unannounced. An infant's cry from within gave no indication that anything was amiss for I remembered she had two small children to look after when I left. As the front door swung open, I was surprised to see a young woman standing there, with an infant in her arms.

"Is Mrs Martin in?" I asked.

The young lady looked perplexed and shook her head. "I'm sorry, sir," she said, "I think you've come to the wrong house. There is no one living here by that name."

"But this is 32 Merton Road, isn't it?" I questioned. "My mother lived here when I left to go to sea."

"I'm afraid I can't help you," she said, apologetically. "Why don't you ask the lady next door? She must have known Mrs Martin, as she's been living here for some time."

Somewhat bewildered I turned away and called on Mother's next door neighbour, Mrs Barnes, who wasn't exactly a wealth of information either. She simply said that Mother had left the area some months earlier and, whilst on friendly terms with her, had no idea where she'd gone. The situation I now found myself in was nothing short of desperate, there was no one to whom I could turn. My inquiries at the local council offices having also proved fruitless, a feeling akin to panic seized me. Not only had Mother deserted me, she'd left me homeless. This was something I hadn't bargained for.

Saddened and bitterly disappointed by Mother's disregard for my welfare, I retraced my steps to London, and sought help from the local police. The only information I could give them was the last known address of my Grandmother, a Mrs Ashby, whose address, as far as I could remember, was Rye Lane, Peckham. Promising they'd try to find her, my final glimmer of hope faded later that day when police informed me she no longer lived there, and advised me to seek refuge at the sailors' home, where I could obtain temporary shelter. With limited means of support and little chance of finding my mother, I had no choice other than accept the advice of the local police, and set off to look for the sailors' home.

The Sailors Home at the East India Docks, with a view inside its prison-like interior. Sleeping was impossible here.

I soon found out this grim-forbidding greystone building they called the sailors' home was no hotel. If anything it was a replica of London's Newgate Prison, as seen in the days of Charles Dickens. It couldn't have been any worse. Pressing a rust-encrusted button on the front door of the building brought an immediate response from an old man, reeking of stale tobacco, who stared at me through pink-rimmed eyes.

Welcoming me in with a toothless grin, he rubbed his pale white hands together in an effort to keep warm. Then, poking around a dimly-lit office, he produced a tattered ledger and handing it to me, said, "Sign here for your room, son, it's five shillings a week."

Giving me the key to my room, he proceeded to lecture me on the pitfalls one encountered in such places, saying, "Make sure yer put one of yer boots under each leg of yer bed. That way they can't pinch them, son."

From the ground floor, I climbed up a flight of wrought iron stairs leading to a narrow corridor where occupants lived in tiny cubicles. At the far end was a small communal washroom and lavatory. Carrying a horse blanket the old man had given me, I unlocked the door to my room and looked around. It came as something of a shock when I saw a window in the room protected by steel bars. I had no way of knowing whether this was to prevent intruders from breaking into the sailors' home, or stop drunken inmates suffering from a bout of the D.T.'s from throwing themselves out.

Accommodation at the sailor's home offered the stranded seafarer little comfort and, seeing I had no alternative, I was obliged to stay there for the time being. It was either that or sleep on the street. The room was sparsely furnished with an old iron bedstead and a tattered straw mattress, referred to by members of the seafaring community as the donkey's breakfast. In a far corner of the room was an old fashioned washstand holding a cracked and discoloured basin and water jug that had seen better days. On the floor, shattered beyond repair lay a mirror, its rusting chain hanging on the wall. Suffice to say no sane person stayed too long in this establishment where one was assured of a quick passage to the nut house, if they dared to linger.

A cold March wind whistling through gaping great holes in the window of my room turned it into an ice box. Eyeing the thin straw mattress on the bed with suspicion, I had no doubt an army of bugs nestled inside, waiting to attack me as I slept. Bearing in mind the damage these blood sucking creatures could cause to one's person, I chose to leave my clothes on and wrapped a blanket around the mattress, to stop the red devils' escape. Using my jacket for a pillow, I covered myself with my dufflecoat and laid down, exhausted, to sleep.

In the dead of night, I was rudely awakened by a series of unearthly screams from some demented drunkard down on the lower landing, chasing pink elephants. The noise was enough to rouse the entire fraternity of this glorified doss house, many of whom staggered around on drunken legs. The tumult and shouting eventually subsided, so I returned to my room and, finding sleep impossible, lay in a semi-conscious state until break of dawn.

The light of day brought scant relief to my pain-racked body, after a night of torture lying on a bed of iron. A glance around the room filled me with an urgent desire to remove myself from this damp and depressing establishment as fast as my legs would carry me. The night's performance served to speed my departure, without so much as a bite to eat.

Leaving my luggage at the nearest railway station, I took the tram to Leadenhall Street in the City of London, where I hoped to find employment with one of several shipping companies in the area. Like a lost sheep, I wandered past tall office buildings keeping a weather eye open for a likely doorway I might squeeze into, if only to get warm. Stopping in front of a greystone building, the brass plate attached to the frontage caught my eye and, like a magnet, I was drawn toward it. A closer inspection revealed the name of a shipping company, one of which I'd heard glowing reports. With nothing to lose, I decided to take a chance and mounted the office steps.

It was nothing more than good luck that prevented me from being trapped in the revolving doors as they spun around. Approaching a young clerk at her desk in the foyer, I told her I was destitute and in desperate need of work. Taking pity on me after I explained the situation I was in, she directed me toward a room crowded with people whom I recognized as seamen by the clothes they wore, and was told to wait there.

"What's happening?" I asked a fellow standing next to me.

"We're hoping to sign on a ship," he replied. "There's very little work to be had around here, at the moment."

My practised eye knew in an instant to which department various members of this diverse gathering belonged, by their mode of dress. Stewards and cooks, in the catering department, were seen wearing collar and tie whereas seamen were more easily recognized, wearing dark blue jerseys. Among many seeking employment as deckhands were a mixture of Liverpool or Cockney characters. One often found a sprinkling among them of those quietly-spoken men from Scotland's far flung islands, the Outer Hebrides and Orkneys.

Questioned as to my presence in the office by a young clerk at the inquiry desk, I was ushered into a well-lit ante-room where my feet sank into luxurious carpets, warm to the touch. An elderly gentleman seated behind a large oak desk introduced himself as Captain Asquith retired and, pointing to a chair, he requested I be seated. He was rather tall and well-proportioned, his welcoming smile put me at ease immediately.

"Are you in the company's employ, young man?" he asked.

"I'm afraid not, sir," I replied, and told him I had just returned from a long engagement abroad.

"Well now," he asked, almost apologetically, "what can I do for you?"

Explaining the unfortunate position I now found myself in through no fault of my own, I set about convincing the gentleman I was homeless and in need of help. Showing him the discharge papers from my previous ship, I told him I suffered with claustrophobia every time I closed the door of the radio room and would like to join my next ship as Quartermaster. He left me for a moment to consult with a colleague in an adjoining room and quickly returned to ask, "Are you familiar with the compass and have you ever had occasion to steer a ship at sea?"

I assured him I had taken over steering my last ship on a regular basis, and had completed a course while attending sea school prior to joining my last ship. Dispensing with the usual formalities he said, "We have a vessel due to sail shortly and can accommodate you as Quartermaster. How soon can you be ready?"

Delighted to accept his offer, I signed aboard the *M.V. Seafox,* an intermediate class motor vessel of five thousand tons gross weight, capable of accommodating a dozen passengers, under the command of a Captain D. Saunders. Freshly painted and fully loaded with a general cargo bound for West Africa, she lay at her berth in London's K.G. five dock, waiting for her crew to join her.

CHAPTER 12

BACK ON THE HIGH SEA

Within forty-eight hours I would, once again, be back on the high seas, a sadder but wiser man. And I promised myself, come what may, the search for my sister Caroline would continue on my return to England. Time they say is a great healer but, sadly, the hurt my mother had caused me through her sudden disappearance left bitter memories that would never be erased. She had for some unknown reason chosen to cast me aside as she had done before.

The early morning sunshine glistened on the vessel's white painted superstructure as I stepped aboard the *M.V. Seafox* where seamen were busy clearing her decks of rubbish left behind by longshoremen, prior to leaving the Port of London. Nearby, two attendant tugs secured to the vessel fore and aft waited to tow her out into the River Thames. At a signal from the pilot directing operations, the tugs heaved the ship away from her berth and, as the lock gates swung open, she entered the river.

Out in mid-stream, our escorting tugs held us against a fast flowing tide until the ship's engines took over, then slipping their tow wires, headed back into dock. With reasonable weather ahead, we made good time in reaching the English Channel where a fresh south-westerly breeze caused the vessel to pitch and roll.

Our passage through the Bay of Biscay being moderately calm, the *M.V. Seafox* reached Madeira on schedule, where we stayed for a few hours. Moving on, we visited the islands of Tenerife and Las Palmas, where passengers were allowed to go ashore for a short period of sightseeing. Having no cargo to discharge in the port, our stay was limited to the time it took the ship to refuel before she headed south on her way to the West African port of Freetown, Sierra Leone.

Arriving at Freetown, we prepared for the usual invasion of native cargo workers about to descend on us. Strategically placed in position on the ship's stern was the West African Ensign. Fastened to the rails with stout ropes this rough toilet hung there, waiting for its first customer.

Leaving Freetown, the *Seafox* called at many ports I'd become familiar with along the coast during my first voyage of two years. There is no doubt that it helped broaden my outlook on life, seeing how the other half lived. Nothing surprised me any more, not even the men I sailed with. The everyday routine of life at sea soon became habitual.

Among the ship's crew, one found a joker or studious type of fellow, who'd spend his off duty hours with a book. Having a reasonable knowledge of Board of Trade rules and regulations, he was the one man chosen to speak up for his shipmates if things went awry. As far as the Captain of the ship was concerned, he was seen as no more than an agitator, out to make trouble.

Seizing every opportunity to nip ashore for a drink, many seaman somehow managed to crawl back on board the ship, hours later, in a drunken stupor. Jungle juice could be bought for one shilling a bottle. On one occasion, a number of seamen were seen to slip ashore and make their way to the nearest native village. Having supped more than their fill, Sniffy Wilkinson, the ringleader of this motley group, suggested they should go for a swim. How they ever managed to find their way to the beach in such a drunken state is a mystery and, arriving there, they invaded the private enclosure of the local European

Yacht Club. Stripping down to their birthday suits, they danced along the water's edge with a performance that might have earned an encore at the Follies Bergère.

Shouts of encouragement from the native populace attracted the attention of European residents, who threatened to call the police and have them thrown in jail. Not wishing to sample the inside of a smelly native prison, the seamen quickly donned their clothes to disappear into the dark of night.

The morning sun beat down on the ship's deck as only it can in the tropics where not a breath of wind stirred the Red Ensign, hanging from its flagstaff on the after deck. It was long after daybreak when a group of red-eyed seamen left their quarters and staggered into the light of day. As a result of their escapade the previous night, the ship's Captain demanded they report to him immediately.

Leaving his cabin, Captain Saunders stood on the boat-deck waiting for the men to appear, then asked who among them visited the local European Yacht Club last night. Receiving no response from the seamen, he conferred with a native policeman who had arrived on board his ship at sun-up, a burly character dressed in blue tunic and shorts.

With mannerisms similar to that of a witch doctor, he eyed each man suspiciously then, slipping a hand into his trouser's pocket, pulled out a dirty old grey sock. Holding it at arm's length he swung it to and fro muttering to himself, as if casting a spell. Then in pidgin English, he asked the seamen, "Who belong him?"

There followed a roar of laughter as seaman Sniffy Wilkinson stepped forward to examine the sock and, shaking his head in disgust said, "Him no belong here, him give much bad smell, like Arab's underpants."

With a sweep of his arm, Sniffy tossed the sweaty sock over the ship's side and addressing the policeman said, "White man on shoreside not like sailor man. Him no good, make plenty palava for seaman."

"So where were you and the rest of your men last night?" Captain Saunders asked Sniffy.

In one voice, Sniffy and the rest of the seamen insisted they'd never set foot ashore, having spent the night on board the ship playing cards. Snifty said this was the first he'd heard of the incident, then both he and the rest of his pals demanded an apology from the owners of the Yacht Club. This forced a smile from Captain Saunders who turned to the policeman and said, "I'm afraid there is little I can do to help, my ship is set to leave port later this afternoon." Warning his seamen as to their future behaviour when setting foot ashore, he dismissed them.

The day was hot and uneasy with banks of dark cloud drifting up over the far horizon as the *M.V. Seafox* prepared to leave her berth in Takoradi, into the face of a tropical storm. Banks of ominous black cloud drawing ever closer by the minute, engulfed the ship in a torrential downpour, a stark reminder the rainy season was upon us. Within an hour there were two violent rain storms, with bouts of thunder and lightning for good measure. Squalls of heavy rain beat down on native workers trying to cover numbers three and four hatches with tarpaulins, as the last slings of cargo were dispatched ashore. With flashes of lightning and peals of thunder reverberating across a darkening sky, *Seafox* slipped out of harbour, into the storm-tossed waters of the South Atlantic.

Daybreak saw the ship berthing at the town of Appapa, lying across the Niger River, opposite the Nigerian capital of Lagos. Here, at Appapa, vessels from around the globe are familiar with its modern wharf and railway terminus, adjacent to nearby swamp and jungle. The Seaman's Mission, equipped with a small bar, library and billiards table, lies in a clearing some distance from the wharf and serves as a meeting place for seamen who, at one time or another, had been shipmates. In the confines of this secluded outpost in the African bush, they would perchance meet once again to share a drink or two, and talk of old times.

Night was falling as we prepared to leave Appapa and head south toward the equator, having replenished our fresh water supplies. It was a commodity in short supply in many areas on the West Coast of

Africa, where a ship carrying maybe two hundred native cargo workers was obliged to economize on its use.

At dawn, the vessel dropped anchor off the island of Fernando
Po, a dense mountainous region covering one thousand square miles
of this former Spanish Protectorate, lying in the Bight of Biafra. Exports of coffee, cocoa beans and large quantities of timber cut from
the forests provided the island with its main source of revenue. As the
first ray's of sunlight coloured the landscape, a small tug with some
two hundred mahogany logs in tow approached the ship. A sudden
gasp of alarm escaped the officer on duty when the tug towing the
logs toward his ship appeared out of control.

It seemed that every boat and every Captain had the same problem. With the Skipper of the tug helpless to do anything to stop the
logs smashing against the ship's side, the impact shook her from stem
to stern, the noise effectively rousing the entire ship's company awake.
Native cargo workers, having managed to secure the logs alongside
the vessel, proceeded to heave them on board the ship throughout the
day, stowing them down in number three and four holds.

Then, as the tropical sun disappeared below a cluster of palm
trees on the far side of the island, I watched, fascinated, as a colony
of fruit bats left their nesting place where they had spent the night and
flew to the mainland to feed.

With two thousand tons of timber safely stowed in the ship's
holds, we left Fernando Po for Duala, the main seaport in the French
Cameroons. Here a railway linking the port to Yaounde, its capital,
carried the country's vital exports to vessels lying in the harbour.
Waiting for the *M.V. Seafox* to arrive, a shipment of cocoa beans was
hurriedly loaded on board, allowing her to leave at short notice to
return north to Lagos.

It was shortly after our departure from Duala that we listened
to an overseas broadcast from the B.B.C. in England and heard the
talk of war. Political unrest caused by Hitler's claims to territory on
Germany's borders had finally come to a head. Having laid claim to
Bohemia and Moravia from Czechoslovakia in the early part of 1939,
he now insisted the Polish port of Danzig belonged to Germany. It

was quite obvious Prime Minister Neville Chamberlain's efforts to appease Hitler when signing the Munich Agreement in September of 1938 had proved useless. With Europe once again in turmoil, the threat of war loomed ever closer.

Out here in darkest Africa, where the mere mention of war was for the moment of no concern to the populace, work on loading the ship carried on regardless. It was now late August and the rainy season having run its course, we once again experienced day temperatures well above one hundred degrees, with humid nights. When the last of our cargo was taken on board *Seafox* left Lagos and sailed north en route for Freetown, arriving at the port on the morning of September 1 of 1939. Our broadcast from the overseas service of the B.B.C. on that morning was suddenly interrupted by a solemn-voiced announcer saying, "Hitler's forces have invaded Poland." Great Britain now had no alternative but declare war against Germany.

Almost immediately, orders were relayed to all merchant vessels, in foreign waters, instructing them to cover the ship's white paintwork a dark grey and to darken brasswork. This caused a near panic when pots of grey paint and brushes were hurriedly issued to all and sundry on board the *M.V. Seafox*, in an effort to cover the vessel's white superstructure. Even the ship's name painted on her bow and stern were quickly obliterated.

News that Britain was now at war with Germany spread like wild fire among native cargo workers on board, who became restless in their hurry to leave the ship, as we approached their home base of Freetown. Within sight of Freetown the *M.V. Seafox* was stopped by Royal Naval vessels patrolling up and down outside the port's submarine defence system and escorted to a safe anchorage. Preparations for an emergency such as this had been in operation by the port authorities for quite some time, fully aware Hitler's U-boats were already prowling the oceans.

No sooner had the ship's anchor rested on the ocean floor, boats of every description came alongside the *M.V. Seafox*, allowing panic-stricken native cargo workers to pick up their belongings and hurry off ashore. Had they known German U-boats were already lurking in the vicinity of Sierra Leone, waiting to torpedo unsuspecting merchant ships, many would have risked swimming ashore, they were so frightened.

In any event, all British merchant ships were now under the jurisdiction of the government and therefore obliged to wait for instructions from the naval authorities before leaving port. Dusk had fallen by the time a naval officer arrived on board the *M.V. Seafox* with orders to sail, as she lay at a safe anchorage. Having received orders to observe a total blackout, Captain Saunders was told to wait until night had closed in before weighing anchor. Then, following astern of a naval escort, the *M.V. Seafox* slipped past the port's submarine defence system, and headed out to sea.

A mile or so out from the shore, an aldis lamp flickered on the darkened bridge of our escorting destroyer, sending a coded message that read, "You may now proceed with all possible speed to your final destination, and good luck."

With a final warning from our escort to make sure all lights were extinguished including those used for navigational purposes, the *M.V. Seafox* gathered speed and sailed off into the dark of night. Lookouts placed in strategic positions around the ship were instructed to keep an eye open for enemy U-boats as we zig-zagged our way home alone, prepared to face the unknown. It was now late September of 1939 and, with the war in progress, we had orders to steer a course to the west of the Bay of Biscay, keeping well clear of Ushant on the French coast.

Having encountered little sign of enemy activity indicating a war was in progress, when arriving in the English Channel my thoughts once again turned to Mother and home. Would I be able to find her, I asked myself and, in doing so, meet my sister Caroline?

As so often happens, the most carefully laid plans will go awry, as I was to learn, when *Seafox* was abeam of Lands End. A patrol vessel from Plymouth's naval base approached the ship with a change of orders and, much to my dismay, of our original destination, which should have been the Port of London. The *Seafox* altered course for

Liverpool. A change of orders due to the outbreak of war saw me put aside my plan to find Mother, for the time being.

Sailing in a northerly direction, the *M.V. Seafox* altered course rounding Lands End and, passing through St George's Channel, entered the Irish Sea. As night fell, coastwise vessels criss-crossing back and forth on trade routes between Ireland and Great Britain tended to keep our lookout men on edge. Without warning, several were seen to cross our bow in the inky black of night, showing not a glimmer of light, whereupon *Seafox* was forced to hurriedly alter course in order to avoid a collision.

Daybreak saw us steaming up the River Mersey, to the port of Liverpool, the busiest port in the northwest of England. Along the river silver-coloured barrage balloons suspended on long wire cables were placed in strategic positions around the dock area. Like guardian angels, they hovered above important installations, protecting them from the threat of low-flying enemy aircraft. Sailing along the City of Liverpool's busy waterfront, many historic structures catch the visitor's eye. Prominent among them are the twin towers of the Liver Building, exhibiting statues of the legendary Liver Birds perched atop green-encrusted domes, from whence the city derived its name.

Along a seven mile stretch of river, Liverpool's docks are serviced by an overhead railway system, with stations at various intervals, providing dock workers, seamen and those connected with shipping, access to vessels berthed therein. In time of peace, visitors to the port would see Cunard White Star or Pacific & Orient passenger liners, berthed at Princes Landing Stage, centrepiece of Liverpool's waterfront.

Abeam of Harrington Dock, the *M.V. Seafox* reduced speed, allowing attendant tugs to take the vessel in tow and shepherd her into her allotted berth. Only then were we informed the passenger liner *Athenia,* evacuating women and children to safety overseas, had been torpedoed by a German U-boat at the outbreak of war. Hearing of this terrible tragedy brought home to many of us the horror of war.

Berthing formalities having been completed, a clean bill of health from the Port Health Authorities allowed members of the ship's crew to pack their bags and slip ashore. Leaving my personal belongings locked away in my cabin, I took a taxi into town and called at the local police station. Informing them I was a stranger in town, I asked where I might find suitable lodgings during my stay in the area. They duly obliged and directed me to an address on the outskirts of town, in the Sefton Park district.

Outside a large brownstone house, I spoke to a Mrs Linden, the landlady, who agreed to give me board and lodgings. Thanking her, I cleared up some business that needed attending to on board the ship, before returning to the good lady's house with my bags the following day. The house was in a fairly quiet neighbourhood, on the outskirts of Liverpool's bustling city. Public transport in the area was available at regular intervals, allowing one reasonable access to the city centre. I soon settled down to enjoy a short period of leave with Mrs Linden's two teenage boys who, like many of their age group conscripted into the army, were home on leave.

Like thousands of young men before them, they would soon be shipped abroad, knowing they might never return. Although I myself was not subject to the usual rules and regulations like the armed forces, I was unable to move about as freely as I had done in time of peace.

I had planned a trip to the south of England but was liable to be recalled for duty before my leave expired. With the enemy dropping magnetic mines in shipping lanes around Britain's coastal waters, the war at sea became extremely hazardous.

Out on the high seas, German U-boats, operating in wolf packs, were causing havoc with our depleted merchant fleet, sinking every ship in sight. So many ships, bringing vital war supplies across the North Atlantic from America, had been sunk. These had to be replaced somehow. It was, therefore, necessary to reclaim a number of ships rotting away in breaker's yards around Britain's coast, ships that had lain idle during the Depression of the thirties, and press them back into service, in an effort to boost our merchant fleet.

CHAPTER 13

A TASTE OF WAR

To all intents and purposes, England was now a country at war, yet life continued apace largely in the same old easy-going manner. Were it not for the fact an exceptionally large proportion of young people were in uniform, one would never imagine a war was in progress. Men employed in shipyards and aircraft factories deemed necessary to help in the war effort were not, as a rule, drafted into the armed forces, although they were forbidden to leave their place of employment without permission, under the terms of the Essential Works Act.

Having recently arrived home following a four-month voyage up and down Africa's West Coast, I realized only too well that I could be called back for duty at a moment's notice. It, therefore, came as no surprise to receive notice, before my leave expired, to report to the Mercantile Marine Office in Liverpool immediately.

Along with many seamen home on leave, I was ordered to join one of several vessels rescued from the breaker's yard. No sooner had I set foot in the office, a pen was thrust in my hand and I signed on aboard the *S.S. Benbury,* a vessel of five thousand tons dead weight, built in the early nineteen hundreds, and reclaimed from the scrap heap. The moment I clapped eyes on her, she reminded me of another heap of scrap iron I had sailed round the world on, at the outset of my sea career, way back in 1936.

Several coats of paint covered her rusting hull, in an effort to disguise the paper-thin plates. Like many ships of her era, she had steel chains running along either side of the deck stretching from the bridge to her rudder astern, a system referred to as chain steering.

I was none too happy when it was rumoured the vessel was bound for New York, a journey one could best describe as perilous for a seaworthy ship in mid-winter. Surely this was tempting Providence, akin to committing suicide. At best *Benbury's* top speed of six knots would leave her at the mercy of the elements should we happen to run into stormy weather. Sailing its stormy waters, without a scrap of cargo in her holds to steady her, would be no picnic. At best, she'd be lucky to stay upright, whereas a fit of coughing might loosen the rivets in her rusting plates. Having said that, she'd more than likely capsize in a force eight gale.

.   .   .

In the early light of an October dawn, a watery sun chanced to peep from behind a formation of angry black cloud, giving rise to strong north-easterly winds and driving rain. Buffeted about as she entered the River Mersey's cold choppy waters, the *S.S. Benbury* struggled to keep in line astern with other merchant ships heading out into the Irish Sea, where naval destroyers waited to escort us across the Atlantic.

Arriving safely at Liverpool Bay, all vessels were ordered to form up into columns of three by our naval escorts, who then shepherded the convoy away from the main shipping lanes in the Irish Sea, where enemy U-boats waited to strike. Increasing speed in an effort to keep up with the rest of the convoy was too much to ask of the *S. S. Benbury's* worn-out engine, and as a result, a pall of black smoke issued from her funnel. This brought a reprimand from the convoy's C.O., who warned our Captain this was giving away our position to enemy submarines lurking in the vicinity.

With nothing but a few tons of ballast in the ship's holds to steady her, the *S.S. Benbury* had difficulty keeping up with the rest of the convoy. As a result of faster vessels complaining to the officer in command that the *Benbury* was a danger to them, he ordered us to take up station at the rear of the group. Late on the evening of our third day at sea, the weather turned real nasty and, with a force eight gale blowing, our naval escorts instructed all ships in convoy to disperse. Bidding all vessels farewell and safe passage, our escorting destroyers wheeled about to return to base.

Breaking away in orderly fashion some forty ships set course for their own particular destination and were soon out of sight, leaving the *Benbury* to zig-zag her way across the North Atlantic alone. Within the hour ships that accompanied us for the past three days were seen as no more than a smudge on the distant horizon. Without naval protection, we prepared to face the elements and enemy U-boats in our path and, as a precaution, placed extra lookouts at vantage points around the vessel. Mindful of these unfriendly waters, we were told to keep a weather eye open for any sighting of a submarine. We had quite a few anxious moments during an uneventful and uncomfortable crossing, but managed to make American shores.

On a bitterly cold morning in early November 1940, we arrived at the mouth of the Hudson River to be greeted with skies of grey and a curtain of thick fog hanging over the river estuary. We had difficulty in locating the pilot who took the *S.S. Benbury* to an anchorage off Ellis Island, where Immigration and Port Health officials boarded the ship. Checking our papers were in order, they carried out an inspection of the ship's crew before allowing the vessel to proceed up river to her berth. Moving at a snail's pace, the *S.S. Benbury* sailed passed the Manhattan and Williamsburgh suspension bridge amid the fog laden atmosphere to our berth at Brooklyn's Erie Basin. Within half an hour of the ship making fast, longshoremen, working in shifts, toiled night and day loading war supplies on board the vessel, a task they completed within a period of ten days.

Taking advantage of an unlimited supply of goods, either rationed or unavailable back in England, I decided to slip ashore on a shopping expedition. Visiting Macy's department store, it was my misfortune to bump into one particular member of our crew, seaman Paddy Mc-Grath. Passing the time of day, he told me he was newly-married and asked for my help in purchasing some articles of underwear for his young wife. As a single man of twenty-one, I was certainly less learned than he as to the type of lingerie women wore, although he somehow imagined I was. Having seen the frilly garments advertised in glossy magazines, I had a faint idea, so agreed to assist him.

Somewhat apprehensive, I approached the lingerie counter with Paddy in tow, where a charming young salesgirl smiled and dutifully asked, "Can I help you, sir?"

I told the young lady my companion had recently been married and wished to purchase some lingerie for his wife, but had no idea what the garments looked like. She smiled demurely and replied rather shyly, "Oh, that's alright, sir, I understand."

Placing several pieces of female apparel in a variety of colours and sizes on the counter, she chose a delicate pink slip and panties, and asked, "What size is your wife, sir?"

Turning to Paddy, a big raw-boned Irish lad, I said, "Do you know what size your wife takes?"

His face paled for an instant and, looking around the store, he pointed to an enormous lady standing nearby, saying, "Oi tink she's loike her over dere." Things really got out of hand when the young lady asked Paddy, "What size brassiere would you like for your wife, sir?"

The salesgirls at the lingerie counter were already giggling among themselves over Paddy's lack of finesse. His next remark brought roars of good-humoured laughter when he placed his two big maulers on his chest and said, "Is that them tings dey wear here?"

I asked him, "What size do you think your wife wears, Paddy?"

Slightly embarrassed, he again cupped two enormous hands to his chest and with a sickly grin said, "About dis big."

The two girls were in hysterics as they took their time to search, allowing them to regain their composure. I was anxious to get back aboard the ship but dare not leave Paddy loose in the store on his own. So I waited until the salesgirl had wrapped the articles and handed them to him. Without so much as thank you to the salesgirl, he panicked to get away from the fifth floor and with giant strides he leaped onto an escalator on its way down to the ground floor, clawing his way through the crowd to the front and disappeared. I gave a huge sigh of relief.

When details of my shopping trip with Paddy leaked out in the seaman's mess during lunch hour that day, it was greeted with howls of laughter. It was Johnson, the Bo'sun's Mate, who remarked, "You'd get a write up in the *New York Times* if you were to send them a report like that, Rowland."

"We've no time for that sort of tom-foolery," said Creswell, the Bo'sun, a grizzled old timer. "We sail on the morning tide."

.   .   .

On a cold winter's morning in mid-November of 1940, the *S.S. Benbury*, loaded down to her gunnels with war material, left New York's bright lights astern of her and sailed north. As darkness closed in, an order was given to douse all lights, as we were heading into a war zone and liable to be torpedoed by enemy U-boats said to be in the vicinity. Facing a head wind with heavy seas pounding her rusting deck, the old *Benbury* was forced to struggle every inch of the way on her journey north. Hugging Canada's eastern seaboard, the old tub creaked and groaned as she rode huge Atlantic rollers all the way up to Halifax. On arrival we were told to anchor close to a group of merchant ships, mustered in the outer harbour, waiting for a naval escort.

A message was sent to all vessels lying at anchor to maintain a strict blackout, a precautionary measure against pre-emptive attacks by enemy U-boats known to be operating in the area. The warning did nothing to boost the confidence of the crew of the *S.S. Benbury*, scupper-deep with a cargo of ammunition and war material in her holds.

"I doubt if the old tub would reach England's shores if we were spotted by U-boats," moaned seaman Royce, a real Joab's comforter at a time like this. "Why, a shot across her bow would see her disintegrate, never mind a bloody torpedo."

On our sixth day in the outer harbour at Halifax, a naval escort of four destroyers were seen to arrive and, in the fading light of day, an order was sent out to all vessels, prepare to leave. At a given signal, each ship hoisted her anchor and headed out of harbour, to form up into five columns of eight. Our convoy comprising a total of forty ships loaded with war supplies sailed off into the choppy waters of the North Atlantic.

Screened by our escort of naval destroyers, we left Halifax under cover of darkness, prepared for any emergency that might arise during the voyage home. We were some two days out at sea, when a fresh northerly wind suddenly increased in strength to gale force, making it extremely difficult to enable ships like the *S.S. Benbury*, with a top speed of no more than six knots, to keep up with faster vessels. By the end of our fourth day at sea, manoeuvres of any kind were impossible for many ships to carry out in the teeth of a gale, with mountainous seas running, and a forecast of worse to come. It was at this point the convoy's Commanding Officer ordered all ships to disperse, requesting each vessel make all possible speed to their respective destinations.

A warning from the naval authorities that the German battleship *Admiral Graf Spee* was operating in the South Atlantic had been issued to all ships prior to our leaving the port of Halifax. Our orders were to avoid contact with the armed raider at all costs, so our Captain decided to take a northerly route across the Atlantic to the U.K. Choosing to face the fury of elements in the North Atlantic in midwinter was, the Captain said, a risk worth taking, as an alternative to being sunk by the enemy.

We were now without the protection of our naval escorts, who by this time were long out of sight. Of the thirty-nine merchant ships who sailed with us four days ago, there was no sign. We were now on our own battling against a force nine gale in a desperate bid to keep the ship's head up to windward, fearing any deviation either way would see her capsize. Every ounce of speed was being squeezed out of her clapped-out engine and, in doing so, volumes of black smoke were seen to pour from her funnel. With our normal top speed of six knots reduced by half, we were a sitting duck for any one of a dozen or so U-boats known to be lurking in the area.

Faced with raging seas and near-hurricane force winds, that tossed the old tub about like a rag doll, we strained every nerve to ride out the storm. At the time, I was on duty in the wheelhouse, hanging on to the steering wheel for dear life, or anything that would help to keep me upright. There were moments when her stern-end would cork-screw out of the water like some wild thing ready to plunge the ocean depths, never to return. At times, I feared the ship might capsize and, going on bended knee, offered a silent prayer to my Maker for a safe passage home. Making little headway against mountainous seas for days on end and having to exist on sandwiches, hurriedly snatched from the galley, was nothing short of soul-destroying.

It was at this point in time that my thoughts swung back to those earlier days of our voyage. With nothing better to do to pass the time of day I sat chatting with a group of seamen, when the subject of religion cropped up. For many seafarers, this subject is a delicate matter to discuss on board any ship and was quickly pooh-poohed by old Creswell, the Bo'sun, as a load of hogwash. Professing to being an atheist, he insisted religion was for certain people who allowed themselves to be brainwashed. But in moments of peril at sea such as this, men whatever their creed were seen to go down on bended knee and offer a prayer to their particular maker for salvation.

It so happened I was going off duty one night during the height of the storm and found this avowed disbeliever on bended knee, so I stopped to ask him, "What are you doing down there, Bo'sun?"

Hesitating a moment, he replied, "Oh, I'm just looking for something I've dropped on deck."

I quipped, "It wasn't your Bible by any chance, was it?"

Mumbling to himself he hurried away, no doubt realizing he'd been caught out.

The raging storm that had tossed the old tub about like a puppet on a string suddenly abated, and all at once, turbulent seas, with waves that had reached forty feet in height, were as flat as a mill pond. Leaving no more than a ripple on the ocean's surface, a one hundred mile an hour gale had, in a manner of speaking, been reduced to a mere whisper, and a strange silence pervaded the ship. All one could hear was the gentle lapping of the sea against her thin plates. Thanking our lucky stars we had survived the worst of it was a relief to many of us, until a warning from Johnson, the navigation officer, renewed fears for our safety.

"Oh, we're not out of it yet," he announced solemnly, when I chanced to mention the weather while on duty that night.

"There's a hell of a lot more to come," he said. Then in a more sombre mood, he went on, "Why, we are only in the eye of the storm right now."

Even so, this break in the weather gave all on board a little breathing space, allowing the Bo'sun to rig safety wires along the ship's deck fore and aft, with all movable objects being securely fastened down.

Some twenty-four hours later, having passed through the eye of the storm, we once again faced the fury of wind and sea. Dusk was falling when, without warning, the ocean's stillness suddenly changed from the calm of a child's paddling pool to a raging storm. Mountainous seas once again lashed the ship, almost standing her on her beam ends. The old tub did her best to forge ahead during the height of the storm and appeared to be waltzing with death as she buried her nose 'neath the ocean's foam-laced green waters, pitching headlong into bottomless troughs.

Gyrating from one side to the other in an effort to rid herself of water lodged in her well-deck, the old *S.S. Benbury* was unable to escape the next gigantic wave that hit us. With a thunderous roar, it hurtled down on the hapless ship's boat deck, sweeping away the lifeboats on our starboard side like so much driftwood. Solid steel davits from which the lifeboats were suspended lay twisted and bent, like the stem of a flower. Terrified out of my wits as I gazed in awe at the ocean's fury from a position of safety on the boat deck, its devastating power filled me with foreboding. Once again, I thanked my lucky stars I was no longer a ship's radio operator with little chance to escape, if she were to suddenly capsize. The very thought scared me to death as I had suffered with claustrophobia, penned up in the radio cabin on previous ships. Now, being a Quartermaster, I could at least see what was going on, and should anything unforeseen happen to the vessel, I had a better chance of survival.

Witnessing a catastrophe such as this instilled in me the real meaning of fear and an ever-present reminder one must never take the sea for granted, its moods are unpredictable. The freedom of the sea lures seamen to her like a magnet, until the forces of nature take a hand and a storm like this crosses your path. There is nowhere for the sailor to run or hide, no freedom from nature at her ugliest, he must simply face reality and see the storm out.

Having used the greater part of our coal during the height of the storm, it was agreed we should either burn the wooden hatchboards to keep the ship moving or, heave-to, and leave the old tub to the mercy of the elements. Thankfully, neither was ever necessary for, by some miracle, the wild tempestuous weather of the past weeks slowly abated, allowing the *Benbury* to limp up the River Mersey into the port of Liverpool. In retrospect, a journey that should have taken ten days in the normal course of events, lasted a nightmare twenty-eight, leaving me in a state of shock.

When I recall the endless hours spent at the helm of the *S.S. Benbury* during that never-to-be-forgotten voyage, I wondered why on earth I ever decided to choose a career at sea. Without a backward glance at the rusting hulk that had miraculously survived hurricane force winds to bring me safely home, I stepped ashore on that morning in early January of 1940, with a song in my heart and a prayer of thanks to my Creator.

As my taxi headed home through Liverpool's darkened streets during the blackout, I saw little of my surroundings, a reminder, if indeed one were necessary, I was now back in a war zone. It did, however, effectively outline the futility of a war that added stress and mental strain to one during a voyage that, at best, could only be described as disastrous. There is no doubt it left its mark on me and, in like manner, the rest of the crew of the *S.S. Benbury*, for in truth, I was mentally and physically exhausted.

Answering my knock on her door that evening, Mrs Linden, my landlady, was taken by surprise, when seeing me standing on her doorstep and welcomed me back home.

"My goodness, Rowland, where have you been?" she exclaimed. "I expected you home long ago."

Not wishing to sully the good lady's ears with coarse or vulgar expletives one hears and learns to accept while at sea, I could not begin to describe to her the frustration, fear and panic I felt in the teeth of that storm. So I decided to satisfy her curiosity by simply saying the ship's crew were fed up when the vessel pitched and rolled around in a frenzy, somewhere out in mid-Atlantic. How could I adequately explain that we feared for our very lives when mountainous green seas forty feet in height thudded against the vessel's side, almost capsizing her? The dear old lady most certainly would not have understood had I tried to explain why life lines were strung along a ship's deck from fore to aft for one's own safety during violent and stormy weather. Or, the fear that rose within me when the old tub corkscrewed about in a frenzy like a drunken belly dancer, threatening to capsize and take me with her.

It would also be hard for me to describe the days and nights we spent soaked to the skin having to make do living on hard tack, until the storm abated. Then a strange silence that appeared to spread throughout the ship when the storm's fury was spent and one heard nought but the faintest sound of the ocean, brushing ever so gently against her steel plates. Only then did that rusty old tub, the *S.S. Benbury*, manage to crawl back from whence she came, the port of Liverpool. So, I reasoned with myself, landlubbers did not fully understand the ways of a sailor's life at sea, and that it was therefore easier for me to tell the dear soul, we were unavoidably delayed.

It was near the end of May 1940 and British forces were being evacuated from the beaches of Dunkirk, following the capitulation of France. Germany now turned her attention to Belgium who, against such overwhelming odds, were helpless to stop invading enemy forces sweeping around the Maginot Line. Hitler now proclaimed a war of total annihilation against his enemies and, on June 10, turned on Great Britain, unleashing heavy bombers in raids on the City of London, the heaviest since the outbreak of war. In one raid, the city centre was set afire by incendiary bombs resulting in the Guildhall and many old churches being destroyed.

My return to sea, during this period, saw me once again sailing back and forth across the Atlantic to the U.S. in a bid to bolster our flagging war supplies. By the time I returned to Liverpool in January of 1941, aerial warfare had intensified, with widespread bombing of many of our major cities, throughout the length and breadth of Great Britain. I therefore deemed it necessary to delay a planned visit south, in search of my mother and sister during this all-too-short period of leave, not wishing to travel through London during a blitz on the capital.

Putting this venture on hold, I found little to occupy my time until my leave expired, and chose to wander at will around the department stores in the nearby City of Liverpool, to do some shopping. It was here by chance I was befriended by a young lady working in one of the large stores in the area, and during a conversation, she told me her name was Marjorie Hulbert. From the outset we enjoyed each other's company and before long, romance began to blossom. But, all too soon came the time for parting. Once again, the call to duty saw me back on the high seas on a voyage to God knows where, with me promising to write to her, as soon as possible.

Since the end of June 1940, Britain stood alone against the might of Germany and its allies and, were it not for a Lease Lend Bill signed by President Roosevelt in early March of that year, our beleaguered country would have been in even more dire straits. However, an agreement was reached with America whereby they would send us unlimited supplies of war materials, plus fifty U.S. World War One naval destroyers and several merchant ships, to help make up the heavy losses suffered by our decimated fleet. It was now of the utmost importance to send several hundred merchant seamen to various ports in America to man these vessels, referred to as Liberty Ships, and bring them back to the U.K. laden with war supplies.

CHAPTER 14

THE DREADED MALARIA STRIKES AGAIN

R eporting for duty as soon as my leave expired, I hoped to be chosen to join one of many merchant crews sent to America, to man
the lease lend ships waiting there. I was less than enthusiastic when
told to join the *M.V. Kinersley,* an intermediate cargo and passenger
ship, under the command of Captain J.J. Smyth, a nervous shoot-on-
sight individual, nicknamed 'Two Gun Pete.'

The *Kinersley,* bound for West Africa, left the port of Liverpool
at the end of January 1941, with a small convoy of merchant ships
and an escort of four naval frigates, who remained with us for three
days. Once clear of home waters, the convoy, as usual, was ordered
to disperse, each vessel instructed to make all possible speed to their
final destinations. Ships using the normal South Atlantic trade routes
no longer feared an attack from the German battleship *Admiral Graf
Spee,* scuttled outside the harbour of Montivedeo by her Captain on
Hitler's orders.

When *Spee* had been free to plunder ships at will, no merchant
ship was safe, and to challenge this powerful raider was akin to suicide, bearing in mind the heavy armament she carried. Her supply
ship, the *Altmark,* engaged in the transfer of captured British seamen

to German Prisoner of War camps, had also been sunk by the Royal Navy and was now confined to a watery grave, at the bottom of a Norwegian fiord near Narvik.

Nevertheless, our indomitable Captain Two Gun Pete was determined to be ready when coming to grips with the enemy, and insisted his guns crew received regular spells of practice. Fully aware the gun mounted on the stern of the *M. V. Kinersley* was of little use as a deterrent against a surface raider such as the *Graf Spee*, her guns crew realized a single shot fired in anger against a powerful adversary would be suicidal. Even so, our swashbuckling Captain carried on regardless, never stopping to consider he was risking the lives of his men or his ship being sunk in the bargain.

In spite of these shortcomings, he chose to tempt Providence whenever a man on lookout up in the crow's nest reported seeing a ship appear on the far horizon, or anything that looked in any way suspicious, floating nearby. This was reason enough, for our gallant J.J. Smyth, to order his guns crew to stand by, ready for action. Times without number, this order was carried out against the advice of the officer in charge of the ship's guns crew, even though he informed the Captain his meagre supply of ammunition was being wasted unnecessarily. When the guns crew officer informed the Captain a need for caution was most imperative in dangerous situations, the defiant J.J. Smyth simply told his gunnery officer, "you are here to obey orders."

·   ·   ·

It was now early February of 1941, and as the morning sun chanced to peep above the far horizon, its shimmering light sparkled like diamonds on these calm waters. In the distance, we viewed the Spanish Island of Tenerife and, in the foreground, a long since extinct volcano towering upward beneath a sub-tropical sky. Like some prehistoric giant from bygone days, it hovered over the troubled waters of the South Atlantic, its inky blackness outlined against a sky of azure blue. By-passing the Island of Tenerife because of its friendly overtures

with Germany, one chose to recall happier times when visiting this
tropical island paradise during years of peaceful co-existence with
nations the world over.

Arriving off the French-administrated African colony of Senegal,
a hoarse cry of ship-ahoy was heard from the man on lookout up in
the crow's nest. The silhouette of a large naval vessel drawing ever
closer caused a flurry of excitement on the bridge. As if by magic,
telescopes and binoculars appeared, and half a dozen pairs of eyes
scanned the far horizon. Without stopping to consider the danger to
his ship or the men who sailed in her, our courageous Captain, Two
Gun Pete, adopted a death or glory stance. Throwing caution to the
wind, he ordered the guns crew to stand by for action.

As the distance between the two ships diminished, the heavy armament of the vessel bearing down on us was plainly visible, and one
could not fail to see she was a battleship. Tension increased by the
minute out on the gun platform, where a nervous guns crew waited,
realizing one false move on their part would be fatal. We were within
range of the naval vessel's guns, when a signal from her bridge requested we heave-to, and be recognized.

The gunnery officer suggested the Captain should allow his guns
crew to stand down. Adopting a threatening stance against such a
powerful adversary was tantamount to committing suicide, the gunnery officer declared.

The battleship continued to head in our direction at full speed
then suddenly altered course, swinging away down our starboard
hand. As she passed us by, we caught sight of a large French tricolor
flying from her stern and identified her as the *Richelieu*, one of two
Allied battleships on patrol in the area. Seeing her disappear, a sigh
of relief escaped the lips of Captain Smyth who ordered the helmsman to resume our original course for the port of Dakar, West Africa.
Many among the ship's crew feared she might have been one of several German surface raiders known to be roaming the high seas, so
lady luck was on our side.

It was now high noon and, with the midday temperature a blistering 120 degrees in the shade, the *M.V. Kinersley* entered the sun-

drenched port of Dakar. Late that afternoon, our guardian of yesterday, the French battleship *Cardinal Richelieu* entered the naval dockyard across the bay to replenished her fuel supplies. Our stay in Dakar enabled the *Kinersley* to top up her fresh water supplies before leaving that night under cover of darkness to set course for Freetown.

The morning sun had yet to rise as we dropped anchor in the harbour at Freetown and, as usual, two hundred native cargo workers, hired to load and discharge the ship's cargo up and down the West African Coast, swarmed aboard. Within the hour the *M.V. Kinersley* heaved up her anchor, and slipped quietly back out to sea. Steaming south along Africa's West Coast, we arrived off Takoradi at daybreak some two days later. It was here I fell victim to one of my frequent attacks of Malaria that continued to plague me since I first set foot in Africa, some five years previous.

During an early morning stroll around the ship, a feeling of nausea gripped me, followed by a bout of shivering. A violent headache forced me to hurry back to my cabin where I collapsed on my bunk and passed out. In my delirious state, I experienced moments of terror when falling into a darkened pit and, catching hold of some imaginary object to stop my descent, I grasped at thin air. Round in circles I spun, chased by monsters of varying shapes, sizes and colour. Standing before me, they would scream and taunt me, pointing to a black abyss below, where I was set to fall.

It was at this point the sickly smell of ether hit my nostrils, and a needle bit into my flesh. A loud popping noise, like that of a gun being fired, hurt my ears then all was quiet, as I floated away on a sea of comfort.

"You'll feel much better, now," said a young nurse at my bedside, when I awoke.

"Where am I?" I asked, looking around the brightly-lit room where I lay. Even before she chanced to reply, I realised I was in hospital and had, once again, fallen victim to the white man's bogey, Malaria.

After many weeks of careful treatment by nurses and staff at the hospital in Takoradi, I was pronounced fit enough to leave, which made the time for parting difficult. I felt as if I were losing old friends, one had grown to know and love. No praise of mine is too high to describe the care lavished on patients, by nurses and staff at this hospital. When leaving, I was given a medical card stating I suffered from Malaria. Handing it to me, the young nurse warned, "You will be prone to suffer further attacks of Malaria in the future. Make sure to carry this card with you."

Anyone who suffers from a tropical disease such as Malaria, Black Water Fever or Dysentery, will know the road to recovery is painfully slow. I'd lost a considerable amount of weight and was not fit enough to travel.

The responsibility for my welfare now rested with the shipping company, whose usual practise when a seamen fell ill abroad was to ship them home on the first available boat. They did, however, agree to me having a period of convalescence recommended by the hospital, and made arrangements to put me up at the Hotel Metropole, in the nearby town of Sekondi, for a period of peace and comfort.

Alexis, the hotel proprietor, a swarthy looking Greek with a black beard covering most of his handsome features, welcomed me on arrival, and instructed a native servant to take my bags to my room. Exchanging a few pleasantries, we sat drinking orange juice until it was time for lunch. From my bedroom window a panoramic view of the ocean lay before me. Gazing out, I watched giant Atlantic rollers gather speed, only to crash on the beach with a thunderous roar in a flurry of white foam.

Adapting to my new surroundings, I soon settled in and, rising early each morning, would slip down to the beach for a swim, before the heat of the day sent temperatures soaring. Lying there, I'd allow the cooling waters of the Atlantic to tumble over my feet, as the sun caressed my weakened body. I would then amble back to my hotel for breakfast. With little to occupy my time, I'd while away the hours until lunch reading a book from a well-stocked hotel library. Scanning local papers for news of the war in Europe was a waste of time and why I bothered is beyond me, for there was never a mention of hostilities to read in it.

Time being of little importance, I enjoyed each day as it came, without a care in the world. Mention of war among the European community out here on Africa's Gold Coast was a subject hardly ever discussed, for they were more concerned with their own daily lives. Nightly entertainment at the hotel was usually a movie show sponsored by the proprietor, who in turn was dependent on ships arriving from the U.K. with the latest films. Local European residents were then invited to the initial screening of world affairs. In doing so, it helped in some small way to keep the hotel on a profitable basis.

Newsreels covering various theatres of war, borrowed from passenger vessels arriving at the port, were of little interest to the European Community who preferred to ignore them.

From time to time, seamen arriving from the four corners of the globe would frequent the Metropole, the town's only decent hotel, to spend off-duty hours drinking ice-cold beer in a shady courtyard. Nobody gave a second glance to the scruffy old grey parrot languishing in its cage high above them, as they sat chatting away. Even tidbits from the crew of an American freighter visiting the port failed to get so much as a squawk out of him. But as often happens, seamen tend to drink more than their share of the local beer and as a result, sit there arguing and cursing each other.

If Alexis heard their unsavoury language, he would see them off the premises, fearing they would drive his local clientele away. But as often happens he was elsewhere at the time. As usual, Scruffy, the African grey parrot sitting in his cage high above with its head tucked under his wing, chose to remain silent.

It was some two days later when the American vessel having finished discharging her cargo left the port of Takoradi, much to the delight of the hotel's proprietor. With its departure, we witnessed the arrival of the *M.V. Abosso,* one of several passenger ships trading down Africa's West Coast, with the latest newsreel covering the war in Europe and the Far East. It was now late February of 1942 and, with Singapore having surrendered to superior Japanese forces earlier in the month, the European community gathered in the hotel courtyard next evening to watch the latest war film. As darkness fell a hushed audience sat with bated breath as the white-washed wall of the courtyard serving as a cinema screen, burst into life.

While pictures of the Japanese fleet leaving the scene after the bombing of Pearl Harbour were being shown, an eerie silence settled on the watching audience. Then suddenly, from the back of the courtyard there came the sound of laughter. Scruffy then let out a blood-curdling squawk, "You God-damned son of a bitch!" it screeched, as Admiral Tojo was shown inspecting his fleet on their return to Japan.

Amid scenes of hysterical laughter, parrot and cage were hurriedly removed from the courtyard, and deposited in the darkened doorway of the lounge by the hotel proprietor. Calling on the native responsible for looking after the bird, he demanded to know why the parrot had not been taken indoors earlier.

"Oh, I forget, sah," pleaded his native servant.

"Well, you can forget your damn wages this week," shouted the infuriated proprietor. "You've spoilt the film show for my customers."

There was only one option open to him if he valued his customers: he had to get rid of the bird. There and then, he decided he would sell it to any passing seamen who happened to drop in for a drink. It upset him to think the parrot had been in his possession for the past eighteen months, and had never uttered a word until now. Alexis cursed the American seamen who were responsible for the parrot's blasphemous behaviour.

As usual my day began with an early morning walk along the beach and light exercise to give much needed strength to my weakened body. The frequent spells of dizziness I tended to experience after leaving hospital slowly subsided with the passing of time. During the weeks that followed, there was a marked improvement in my health. As the weeks rolled slowly by with never a word from the shipping company responsible for my welfare, I imagined they'd forgotten all about me. In all honesty, I was in no hurry to leave my African paradise and having sampled the good life for the past couple of months, it came as something of a shock when I returned to the hotel for lunch one day, and found a letter from the company awaiting me.

Brief and to the point, the message read, "A passage home has been arranged for you on the *M.V. Accra* due within the next day or so, please report to this office as soon as possible."

Somewhat reluctant to relinquish the good life, I had an idea it was some pimply-faced pen pusher in the company's office back home who discovered my file, hidden among the archives. In deciding I was indeed a burden to the company, he'd probably arranged for me to be brought back into the field of play, so to speak. I was less than eager to report at the company's office.

"Ah, there you are, Mr Marshall," said the manager, grinning good humouredly, when I duly appeared at his office, "I'd almost forgotten about you. Come with me and I'll get you a boarding pass," he said, shepherding me into an adjoining room.

Seated in one of several cane chairs in his office, he went on to say, "The *M.V. Accra* arrives the day after tomorrow, so we would like you to get on board as soon as you can," and handed me a boarding pass. Then uttering the usual words of wisdom office managers are apt to give their employees when about to depart, he wished me bon voyage and was gone.

The morning sun, shining through the open curtains of my hotel room, woke me with a start and, heavy-eyed, I gazed at the remains of a farewell party the previous night. Seeing the hour was late and knowing I had to get on board the ship as early as possible, gave me little time to take a hurried breakfast. While down in the hotel foyer, Alexis had come to bid me goodbye.

"I'm sorry to see you go, my friend," he announced sadly. "You've become part of the fixtures. I must say I've enjoyed your company."

Thanking him for his hospitality, I replied, "Nothing is forever, my friend."

A spontaneous wave of the hand was all I could manage, as my taxi left, distancing me from that remarkable character. Soon the tropical paradise I was so reluctant to leave faded from view as the harbour of Takoradi came in sight. A feeling of depression hit me when seeing the ship that was to once again take me back to England. She looked a grim forbidding sight now in her wartime coat of battleship grey and appeared top heavy – a sure sign she'd roll the guts out of you in bad weather. I was stopped by the purser's assistant as I reached the top of the ship's gangway, who asked, "Your name, please?"

"Mr Marshall," I replied, hoping he might say there was no berth for me. But it was not my day. Glancing at the list of names in his hand, he turned to a native steward standing nearby, and spoke to him in pidgin English, saying, "You take him cabin number 41 on B deck, Moses."

"Yes, sah, I unerstan," said Moses, giving him a melon-sized grin.

Motioning me to follow him down a companionway, Moses directed me to my quarters. They were small and reasonably comfortable but there was a large notice pinned in a prominent position over the wash basin that caught my eye. It read as follows,

'No lights must be seen on the open deck,
after the hours of darkness.
All cabin port-holes and dead-lights must be closed
each night at dusk,
failure to do so will entail heavy penalties.'

As evening approached, the tropical sun's parting rays, sprawled across an ocean streaked with red and orange, slowly sank beneath the western horizon. Checking the vessel's lights were extinguished, the *M.V. Accra* slipped silently out of Takoradi harbour as dusk fell, steering a northerly course for Freetown. Beneath a star-studded tropical night sky, I stood on the boat-deck and watched pinpoints of light on the shore flicker in and out like fireflies in the jungle, to suddenly disappear. Sailing close to the coast of West Africa we were obliged to alter course within hailing distance of Sherbro Island, and arrived at Freetown as dawn was breaking. Patrolling up and down outside the port, naval vessels escorted us through the boom defence system to an anchorage in the bay, where native cargo workers were quickly dispatched ashore. A small amount of cargo was then taken on board the vessel, while we awaited orders and, with the approach of evening, prepared to leave port.

Dusk was upon us as the anchor was heaved in-board and with the ship in total darkness, we were ordered to follow astern of our naval escort. As soon as the *Accra* had passed Freetown's boom defence system, our escort bade us bon voyage, and we set course for England and home.

It was early March of 1942 when I arrived back in Liverpool to overcast skies of grey and bitterly cold winds gusting along the choppy waters of the River Mersey. Spring had yet to arrive in this part of the northern hemisphere still languishing in winter's grip. Facing such dreadful weather, I longed to be back under the blue skies and warm tropical beaches I'd left behind.

Standing out on the open deck of the *M.V. Accra,* I waited for the berthing of the ship to be completed when a sudden bout of shivering gripped me, forcing me to seek the warmth of my cabin. Having just recovered from an attack of Malaria, the damp atmosphere of England's northern climate had an adverse effect on me. As soon as we were given clearance by the Port Health Authorities, I hurried off the ship and without a backward glance, headed home, sure of a warm welcome when arriving.

"My goodness, what a lovely surprise!" said my landlady, answering my knock on her door. "You're looking nice and sunburnt. Did you have a good trip, Rowland?"

Comfortably seated in front of a blazing fire, I told the good lady I'd been plagued by another bout of Malaria while on the coast of Africa. It was due to the many weeks I had to spend in convalescence that prompted her to remark, "But you look so well, Rowland."

As soon as I had time to settle in, I had every intention of taking a trip to the south of England, in another effort to find my mother. Without her, any chance I might have of meeting my sister Caroline were slim indeed. Meanwhile, I had to go in search of warmer clothing which I promised myself I would do when visiting the City of Liverpool on the morrow. A bitterly cold March wind with intermittent showers of rain greeted me, as I stepped off the train at Liverpool's

Central Station. Like the rolling of a drum, the rain beat a tattoo on my protective umbrella, as I hurried toward the town centre.

Approaching Lord Street, the main shopping area in the city, I was forced to seek shelter from a bitterly cold east wind that cut through the tropical clothes I wore, like a knife cuts through butter. Within reach of warmth and shelter inside a brightly lit department store, I felt my knees buckle, and realized there was no way I'd make it. Gripped by a feeling of nausea, I staggered on, and in reaching for an imaginary door handle, grasped at nothing but thin air.

The pavement came up to meet me with a sickening thud, and a million stars exploded inside my head. Then mercifully, darkness enveloped me, bringing a measure of welcome relief to my fever-ridden body. But, as anyone who has experienced the ravages of Malaria will tell you, the nightmare scenes one experiences are never far away.

Sadly, many seamen were never lucky enough to survive to tell the tale, as I did.

CHAPTER 15

OUT OF THE FRYING PAN AND INTO THE FIRE

Pursued by demons and grotesquely shaped animals of varying shades and hues, I ran blindly on. As they closed in on me, I fled into a darkened forest, only to fall headlong into a yawning chasm, from which there seemed no escape. Down I plunged into a bottomless pit, their screams of demonic laughter taunting me as I fell. Then a cool hand, brushing my fevered brow, served to wake me from this awful Malaria-induced nightmare.

Bathed in a pool of my own perspiration, I lay perfectly still knowing the slightest move on my part would cause the bedclothes to squelch.

"Where am I?" I asked the young nurse standing at my bedside, for I remembered little if anything that had befallen me.

"You are suffering from a relapse of Malaria," she replied, "and are being cared for in the tropical ward of Liverpool's Royal Infirmary."

"I remember walking through the city's shopping centre," I remarked, "and must have passed out." Fortunately, I happened to be carrying the medical card with me that stated I was suffering with Malaria.

Wincing with pain when I touched my bandaged head, the young nurse attending me smiled, and said, "You've had a bad fall, Mr Marshall, so try to get some sleep now, the doctor will see you in the morning."

The sound of curtains being drawn across the window of the ward next morning served to wake me from my fitful slumber and, once again, all the old aches and pains of yesterday coursed through my fever-ravaged body. The effects of my last morphine injection were slowly wearing off and, although in a semi-stupor, I could hear the moans and groans of other patients in the ward. Like myself, they suffered from one of many diseases one is prone to when in tropical countries world wide. A number of patients in the ward suffered with Dysentery, an infectious diseases, rampant in many backward countries where drinking water and sanitation leave much to be desired. Lying in a horizontal position with the foot of the bed slightly raised, sufferers are administered periodic enemas to flush out the bowels.

It was shortly after midday when the ward sister, resplendent in her neat blue uniform, arrived at my bedside, with two white-coated gentlemen.

"Ah, you're awake," said the elder of the two. "How do you feel now, Mr Marshall?"

"Not well at all," I replied. "I've suffered the most horrible nightmares."

"Malaria will cause you to hallucinate while the fever rages," the elderly gentleman remarked, somewhat sympathetically. He then went on to introduce himself, and the young man with him. In a voice with a pronounced Scottish accent, he said, "My name is Professor Yorke and my partner here is Dr Adams. We specialise in tropical diseases. Tell me, young man, how long have you suffered with this malady?" he asked, a note of anxiety in his voice.

"About six years," I replied, recalling my first attack in 1936. I also told him I suffered periodic bouts of Malaria throughout those years.

Conferring with his partner, he said at length, "Well, young man, we have a new treatment for Malaria, which has proved very successful. This, I feel confident, will rid you of the disease from which you are suffering and, in the fullness of time, you should make a complete recovery," he replied. And with a kindly smile, he left.

The course of treatment prescribed by Professor York was then administered night and day with monotonous regularity for a period of six weeks. Although I was feeling weak due to losing so much weight, I was allowed to leave hospital with a clean bill of health when my treatment finished. Discharging me from the hospital, the good doctor Adams said, "You are now free of the disease."

Hopefully, I could now look forward to a life free from the ravages of Malaria. Before leaving hospital, I paid Professor Yorke a visit to thank him personally for the care and attention he gave to so many like myself, suffering from tropical diseases.

Rising from his chair as I entered his office, he shook me warmly by the hand and, with a smile, said, "You are now well on the way to a full and complete recovery. Maybe looking a little pale, but that is only to be expected after what you have been through." He then studied me closely for a minute and asked, "How do you feel in yourself, Mr Marshall?"

"Rather weak, but otherwise, quite well," I replied.

A look of concern clouded his face for he went on to say, in a most friendly manner, "I'm afraid I must warn you, any future visit to the tropics on your part should be avoided at all costs."

"But, why doctor?" I asked, unaware of the danger I faced.

Without mincing his words, he warned, "Although you are now free of the Malaria virus, to risk further infection could be fatal. Therefore, I strongly advise you to stay clear of tropical areas if humanly possible."

He seemed most concerned for my future wellbeing, insisting I heed the warning he'd given. Thanking him, I left the hospital deep in thought and returned to my lodgings, on the outskirts of Sefton Park, to consider my options. Although I'd fully recovered from Malaria, I had lost a considerable amount of weight, and looked as thin as a rake. Clothes that once fit me snugly, hung in folds on my emaciated body. I looked like a scarecrow in some farmer's field.

Seeing me in such a poor state of health gave rise to a look of concern from the landlady, when I arrived at my lodgings. Her kindly voice asked, "Whatever's happened to you, Rowland? Come on in and I'll get you a nice cup of tea." Then, looking me over, she remarked in her broad Lancashire accent, "Aye, lad, ya looks awfully thin. Why, I've seen more meat on a pigeon."

Sinking into a comfortable armchair, my thoughts turned to Professor Yorke's warning, especially his concern for my health. What was I to do, I wondered?

The letter he gave to me on leaving hospital clearly stated I was unfit for further sea service. With the war in progress, merchant ships and the men who sailed in them were now under the jurisdiction of the British Government. No longer could a seaman pick and choose ships he wished to sailed on, as one did in time of peace. So, if perchance I was ordered to sign aboard a vessel destined to end up in the tropics, I might not be lucky to survive. So there and then, I decided this was a golden opportunity to give up my sea career.

Without seeking permission from my company or the shipping office, neither of whom thought to get in touch with me when I entered hospital some five weeks earlier, I decided to spend a little time recuperating, then find myself a job ashore. This would also allow me time to visit my girlfriend each weekend, in the nearby town of Birkenhead. We could visit the beautiful City of Chester with its old Roman walls and Tudor style timbered houses, lying at the head of the River Dee estuary.

With my health improving each day, I also decided to venture south and try once more to look for my mother. She had, for some unknown reason, decided to leave the Morden, Surrey area at the time I was due home after an absence of two years. It was now early May of 1942, some six years having past since I last saw her. This was the first opportunity available to me since the outbreak of World War II to head south in search of her.

Packing a small bag, I took an early morning train from Liverpool's Lime Street Station and arrived at Euston Station in London around midday, where a late spring sun failed to penetrate a heavy curtain of smog hanging over the bomb-scarred city. Most noticeable were the many fine buildings burnt to the ground during an endless succession of day and night bombing raids on the city, leaving the country's capital in a deplorable state. Smoke blackened and bomb scarred buildings dotted the landscape. Its many streets lay empty with nothing but the remnants of derelict houses still standing, its occupants having long since moved elsewhere.

Taking the train from Kings Cross Underground, I journeyed on via Victoria to Wimbledon, a happy hunting ground of mine as a young boy. Booking into a boarding house in the area, I planned to spend a week or two making inquiries, in the off chance someone might know of Mother's whereabouts. Should I be fortunate enough to find her, after all this time, I felt sure she would have a change of heart, and agree to put me in touch with my sister Caroline. With this in mind, I travelled around for miles each day on numerous trains and buses to out of the way places, to no avail. What little information I was given led me up a blind alley.

Footsore and weary, I would return to the boarding house each night, thinking maybe tomorrow my luck would change, but that tomorrow never came. As the second week of my search drew to a close, I realized it was futile going on and nothing would be gained by hanging around my old stomping-ground, knowing, once again, I'd drawn a blank. With a heavy heart, I returned to the boarding house in Wimbledon and, packing my few belongings, took the train back north, arriving at my lodgings feeling the fates had cheated me.

Arriving home, I was left with little money to pay for my lodgings. The journey had depleted my funds, so I set to looking for a job. As a seafarer, I was familiar with the working of ships and figured my best chance would be in the local shipyards, which were busy since the outbreak of war, repairing naval and merchant ships damaged in action.

Wasting little time, I boarded the local ferry to take me across the River Mersey into the town of Birkenhead, where I entered the ship repair yard of Rollo Grayson & Clover. A few discreet inquiries gained me access to the company's main office and an interview with

Mr Mercer, the stores manager. Like many north countrymen, he was tall and heavily built with a mop of unruly ginger hair, and ruddy complexion from working long hours outdoors. He seemed an understanding sort of chap, whose easy going manner made it possible for me to talk with him, as he lent a sympathetic ear to my plight.

When I explained how I'd been left in such an unfortunate state of affairs, he readily agreed to offer me a job, instead of turning me away as others had done. Thanking him for his kindness, I returned home to sort out some clothes from among my seafarer's kit that I imagined would be suitable to wear while working at the shipyard. At seven o'clock the following morning, I waited in line outside the shipyard gates with several hundred men and women, in the process of clocking on.

Within minutes of the shipyard gates closing, one heard the pounding of the blacksmith's steam hammer echoing throughout the yard and clatter of pneumatic drills hard at work, replacing steel plates on ships under repair. I myself was rather fortunate to be employed in the stores department, away from the deafening noise reverberating throughout the yard. Working alongside a young lady named Margaret, one of several employed at the shipyard, my day was occupied with handing out nuts and bolts of various sizes, copper piping, packets of steel and brass screws, and other material necessary for carrying out repairs.

Margaret – one might refer to her as a buxom lass built like a battleship – was more than capable of holding her own against any man, and moreover quite nimble in spite of carrying much excess weight. Wearing blue overalls and industrial gloves to protect her carefully manicured hands, she would serve her customers with speed and precision.

Pale of face with deep blue eyes and heavily rouged lips that would pout provocatively when upset, she would not put up with backchat from fellow workers who tried to take advantage of her, and often they got more than they bargained for. Such occurred, for instance, when a young lad was sent to the stores for a roll of felt by the shipwright for whom he worked. Unaware he was treading on thin ice, the young fellow approached Margaret, who at the time happened to be at the counter serving, and in his broad Yorkshire accent quite innocently asked, "Aye, lass, is this where ah gets felt?"

Taken by surprise, she glared in astonishment at the big farmer's lad standing in front of her, and lifting a huge forearm the size of a pit prop, she replied, "Come round here, sonny, and you'll feel the weight of this."

Amid roars of laughter from a nearby group of workers waiting to be served, the young lad hurried away, returning some minutes later with the shipwright who'd sent him to the stores. Hearing of the lad's stupid remark, he apologized to the young lady and, collecting his order, left the stores, cursing the hapless fellow for his hapless remark. Instances such as this gave a much-needed touch of humour to one's life, at a time of nerve-jarring tension when the City of Liverpool suffered day and night attacks of indiscriminate enemy bombing.

Working from dawn to dusk, seven days a week, left little time for the simple pleasures of life, such as going to the movies. It was dangerous to venture out after dark due to nightly bombing raids on the town of Birkenhead where I lived, and the nearby City of Liverpool. So for the time being, my girl friend and I decided we would spend our evenings together at her home, where we listened to the radio.

Reports of heavy losses among merchant vessels at sea, due to the submarine menace, did nothing to bolster one's confidence, at a time when Great Britain stood alone against the enemy. Also mentioned was the plight of people on the Island of Malta, who were under constant siege, having to face an enemy determined to starve them into submission. It therefore came as no surprise that I should receive a letter marked urgent, when arriving home from work one evening.

Inside was a neatly typed message from the Ministry of Shipping in Liverpool, requesting I report to their office immediately.

CHAPTER 16

AN UNFORGETTABLE JOURNEY

Arriving at the shipping office, around nine a.m. the following morning, I was told to see a Mr Repp, the senior shipping clerk. His office was normally busier than a hive of bees with endless queues of seamen hanging about looking for jobs, but on this particular morning it was as quiet as a graveyard. The place was deserted except for an old man sitting at his desk arguing the toss with an irate seaman, and instinctively I had a gut feeling something was amiss. Why should men suddenly avoid the place as though it were infected with the plague?

Seated behind a roll-top desk, Mr Repp, a pasty-faced individual whom I felt sure had never ventured further out to sea than an occasional trip across the Mersey on the local ferryboat, refused to listen to the pleas of an elderly seaman.

"I'm not fit for sea, Mr Repp," the old man said. "I'm blind in one eye."

"Oh, that's alright," said Repp, somewhat sarcastically. "Don't let that worry you. The doctor's always half-pissed so you could have a leg missing and he wouldn't notice it."

Scribbling a note on a scrap of paper he handed it to the seaman saying, "Take this to Dr Reeves for your medical, and make sure he signs it."

My God, I thought to myself as I handed this Mr Repp a letter I received from my family doctor to say I was unfit for sea. I haven't a snowball's chance in Hell of staying ashore with this nut.

A sardonic smile split old Repp's face in half as he read the letter and, in a taunting voice charged with malice, pointed to a door and sneered, "The Manager's Office is over there, sonny."

Taking the letter from his claw-like hand, I knocked on the door of the manager's office, as instructed. A rustle of papers from within suddenly ceased, and an authoritative voice shouted, "Come in."

The genial smile on the face of the smartly-dressed gentleman sitting behind a large oak desk, was that of Commander E.R. Nicholson, an ex-naval officer in charge of Merchant Shipping for the Liverpool area Western Approaches. Looking up from the manuscript he was studying, he asked, "And what can I do for you, young man?"

"I was instructed to report here," I replied, and handed him the letter I'd received from the Ministry of Shipping.

Examining the document he smiled, and said, "Hmm, you've been adrift for quite some time, young fellow. What happened to you?"

"I've been receiving treatment for Malaria at the Liverpool Royal Infirmary," I replied.

"Oh dear," the gentleman exclaimed. "But you're quite alright now, I take it?"

"I'm afraid not," I answered. "I have here a letter given to me by Professor Yorke, the specialist who attended me at the hospital, advising me to give up my sea career."

"Yes, I see," he exclaimed. "You arrived home in March and it's now early July. What have you been doing since you left hospital?"

"I've been working in the local shipyard," I replied.

"You've been working ashore," he spluttered, "and who gave you permission to leave the Merchant Service?" he wanted to know.

I simply shrugged my shoulders and replied, "I had no idea I needed permission to leave the service."

"You could be in serious trouble, young man. Don't you realize there is a war on? The *Essential Works Act* came into force to stop people like you from leaving their place of employment without permission. You're a candidate for the army if you don't get back to sea pretty soon and you could also run into trouble when you have to leave your job at the shipyard, and go back to sea."

I then told him I was a radio operator on my first voyage to sea and suffered with claustrophobia shut up in a poky radio cabin, so I changed my job. Since then I have signed on each vessel as a Quartermaster.

I was hoping he would say we have no vacancies for your position at the moment, so we will call on you when one is available, but it was not my day.

His next remark floored me, when he said, "There's a ship over in Victoria Dock, Birkenhead, in need of a Quartermaster, so you can sign on aboard her or join the army, the choice is yours."

Depositing the specialist's letter in his waste paper basket, he gave an impatient grunt and, handing me a note, said, "Give this to Mr Repp next door, he'll sort things out for you."

I handed the note to old Repp sitting behind his roll-top desk ordering men to join ships, even though they had certificates from their doctors saying they were unfit for sea. He looked, for all the world, like a judge handing out death sentences to these seamen, deriving some form of sadistic pleasure in doing so.

In an attempt to antagonize the old devil, I went up to his desk, and asked, "Are you Mr Ripp?" and waited for his response.

The watery eyes glared at me over the top of horn-rimmed spectacles and, white-faced, he snarled at me, "The name's Repp if you don't mind, Mr Marshall." Specks of white foam oozed from the corners of the thin bloodless lips and, leering at me across his desk, he mocked, "And what may I ask did the manager have to say to you?"

"He asked me to give you this," I replied, placing the letter on his desk.

A scrawny hand reached out to snatch at the document and, reading it, he cast suspicious glances in my direction, perhaps thinking I'd written the letter myself. With an impatient grunt, he put the letter in his desk and allowed a sickly grin to spread across his hawk-like face.

"Didn't you know there's a war on?" he leered. "If you think you can stay ashore, you're sadly mistaken, sonny. You'll have to go back to sea or get drafted into the army, take your pick."

Remembering discretion as the better part of valour, I decided it best not to goad him into having a fit by telling him where he could shove it, and kept a still tongue in my head. Seeing I was unresponsive to his snide remarks, he took a notepad from inside his desk and wrote down the name of a ship berthed over in Birkenhead Docks, due to sail on the evening tide.

"The doctor will be there to examine you before you sign on, so get there as fast as you can, and take your luggage with you," he growled. "Make sure you are there on time, or else."

He never bothered to finish the sentence, but I knew, only too well, he meant that I'd be shanghied into the army. So in reply, I asked, "What part of the globe is the vessel bound for?"

"You're not supposed to know," he scowled. "Didn't I tell you there was a war on?" he added sarcastically. "She's sailing on the evening tide, that's all you need to know."

Back at my lodgings, I realized I had no other option but to sign on the ship. Old Repp's veiled threat left me no alternative. There was no way I was going to allow him to shanghai me into the army.

When I told my dear old landlady I had to go back to sea, she was so upset, bless her heart, for she remarked, "You shouldn't have to go back after the terrible illness you've suffered, Rowland. It's most unfair."

"There's a desperate shortage of seamen to man the ships," I replied, realizing the dear old soul had no idea what life at sea was like.

Hurrying up to my bedroom, I packed my bags and gathered a few odds and ends I might need, including some photographs. One was a faded picture of Mother I always took with me wherever I went, the only one I possessed and treasured. After a hurried meal, I prepared myself for the task ahead. I left the house that summer of July

1942 with little time to reach my destination, hurrying off down the road to board a tram that took me to Liverpool's Pier Head, where I boarded a ferry across the Mersey, to join my ship.

Arriving at Birkenhead, I hopped into a taxi and asked to be taken to Victoria Dock where the *M.V. Waimarama* was berthed. As we passed through the dock system, my taxi driver pointed to a large vessel berthed on the far side of Victoria Dock and shouted, "That's her lying over there!"

The *M.V. Waimarama,* a vessel of around eleven thousand tons dead weight and painted a battleship grey, loomed up ahead of me. Her superstructure

The ill-fated M.V. Waimarama.

towering skyward like some avenging angel was to haunt me for years to come.

A hurried glance around the deck as I stepped aboard the vessel brought a gasp of alarm. "Why, she's a damned armed cruiser," I said to myself, noting her heavy armament. There were half a dozen freshly painted gun platforms welded to her deck fore and aft, with surface and anti-aircraft guns of every description. Not until I set foot inside the saloon to sign on and took stock of its emptiness, did I suspect something was amiss. Then I spotted old Repp sitting there as large as life in vulture-like pose, waiting for me to arrive. Otherwise the place was as quiet as a graveyard, so quiet, I swear I could hear the moths fluttering about inside the pocket of the old devil's blue faded serge suit.

Seeing me, he rubbed his thin bony hands together gleefully and, like the proverbial fly caught in the spider's web, I saw myself as another victim caught in his trap. The bloodless lips parted and an insipid smile creased the pallid face, revealing rows of yellow tobacco-stained teeth. Pointing to a cabin door marked doctor, he sneered, "He's waiting for you in there, sonny."

Inside the room, I came face to face with Doctor Reeves, a tall balding man, well past his prime. Somewhat scruffy in his mode of dress, he could have been mistaken for a horse doctor as the cabin reeked of horse liniment, and a none-too-pleasant smell of stale liquor.

Looking me up and down, he belched loudly, and asked, "D'you wear glasses?"

"No, I can see perfectly well, thank you," I replied.

With little more than a cursory glance in my direction, he squinted at me through bloodshot eyes and announced, "All right, you'll do." In between a series of muted grunts and groans, his pen scratched out a note which he handed to me saying, "Give that to the clerk."

Glancing at his report, which I found hard to understand, I took it back to the wily old Repp, who snatched the paper from me.

Scanning the note he grinned sardonically and said, "You're fit enough, sonny, so sit yourself down over there. The Shipping Master will arrive shortly."

Dressed in a navy blue suit, the Shipping Master, a man in his late fifties, finally arrived and took his seat at a baize-covered table in the ship's dining saloon. Spreading a document in front of him in a hollow voice, he proceeded to read out a list of Board of Trade rules and regulations. Stopping now and again in mid-sentence, he would emphasize the penalties stated therein, then pushing the paper in front of me said, "Sign here, son."

With the usual formalities of signing on completed, he informed me, "All personnel are on board the vessel, ready to leave on the evening tide."

"Good grief, it doesn't give me much time to get myself ready," I complained.

My remark was rewarded with a stern rebuke from the Shipping Master, who rounded on me, saying, "There's no time to waste, my lad, time and tide wait for no man," and eyeing me coldly, said, "I suppose you realize there is a war on?"

Given little time to worry about the predicament I now found myself in, I hurried to my allotted cabin to unpack my bags, mulling over the events of the past twenty-four hours.

Scurrying around the ship, like an army of ants, dock workers were busy loading the last of the ship's cargo into her holds, in an effort to enable her to catch the tide. It was at this point I noted the vessel carried an additional complement of army and navy personnel on board, among the ship's crew. Seeing this, there was no doubt in my mind the *M.V. Waimarama* was bound for some secret destination only the Captain of the ship was aware of.

It was also unusual to note that every man jack of her previous crew from Stornaway in the Outer Hebrides or some other far flung island in Scotland, would leave the ship, without so much as a backward glance, after her last voyage. Having heard on the grapevine the ship was bound for some hostile battle front, they left in an almighty hurry and didn't wait to see if it were true.

Now it was rumoured the vessel was bound for Australia so an air of mystery hung over her, more especially since the heavy armament the ship carried was likened to that of an armed cruiser. I somehow had a gut feeling we were heading into trouble and the voyage we were about to embark on would prove to be like no other before, with the possibility many of her crew would not return.

As darkness enveloped us, a pale moon began its final ascent toward the heavens and the longshoremen having completed the task of loading, the vessel slipped quietly off shore. It was only then one heard the murmur of voices from small groups of seamen standing around the deck, lost in animated conversation.

Beneath the light of the moon, the *M.V. Waimarama* left her berth and move to the river entrance, to await further instructions. Being a heavily-laden ship, her draft of twenty-eight feet would not allow her to leave the dock until near the top of high water. When it seemed the incoming tide was taking forever to rise to the necessary height, the lock gates holding us fast in the dock basin slowly parted.

With our passage out to sea now clear, the pilot gave an order to let go of the vessel's mooring ropes, fore and aft, as attendant tugs took the ship in tow. With a feeling of unease, I stood on the deck of the *Waimarama* as it slid through the lock gates into the fast-flowing River Mersey. My last link with England's shores was about to fade from view. Suddenly, the deck beneath my feet trembled as her powerful twin engines burst into life. As the vessel swung to starboard to face the incoming tide, she gained momentum and headed out to sea. With her engines increasing speed, the pilot ordered his tugs to let go of their tow-ropes, allowing the vessel to be on her way. Little did anyone realize, except maybe her Captain, that this was merely the beginning of a nightmare voyage that none but a handful of her crew would live to remember for the rest of their lives.

Abeam of Holyhead, the order slow ahead was given, as a motor launch came alongside the ship and took our pilot away. Bidding us *bon voyage*, he gave a wave of his hand and was swallowed up in the dark of night, allowing the *Waimarama* to make all possible speed to her destination, wherever that might be. Were the truth but known, we were about to embark on one of the bitterest convoy battles of the Second World War, destined to send the *Waimarama* and most of her crew to a watery grave.

· · ·

Awakened for my spell of duty around midnight, I quickly dressed and, reaching the bridge, entered the wheel-house, to relieve the man at the helm. Checking our course on the gyro compass, I could see we were heading in a northerly direction. Where in God's name is this ship going, I asked myself, since we most certainly were not bound for Australia. Rumour spread like wildfire throughout the ship that the vessel was to rendezvous with a convoy bound for Russia, as we headed further north. Heavy armament recently installed on the vessel, plus the inclusion of extra personnel drafted on board from the army who manned the guns, and naval personnel taking over signals, gave weight to this supposition.

Our arrival at the port of Gourock in Scotland the following evening was cause enough for concern to every member of the ship's crew. Lying at anchor, no more than a few cable lengths ahead of us, lay a group of merchant vessels of similar design, accompanied by a large oil tanker. All were heavily armed, with surface-to-air missiles and, apparently, waiting for orders from the Naval Authorities as to their final destination. Patrolling nearby, in a mist-shrouded background, lurked the ghostly grey shapes of several naval escort vessels, forming a protective screen around this gathering of ships.

In the fading light of evening, a morse lamp from the naval base ashore sent a message instructing the *Waimarama* take up an anchorage near vessels waiting there. With darkness closing in, we dropped anchor. The clanking of the ship's anchor cable as it slid down the hausepipe, echoed across the silent waters. With a loud splash, the anchor came to rest at a depth of six fathoms and from the darkened bridge, the ship's Captain barked out an instruction, "Secure anchor and go below, Mr Mate."

The reply echoed back and forth across the bay, "Aye, aye, sir."

On the morning of August 2, 1942, a curtain of mist hung over the Firth of Clyde. With the aid of a pair of binoculars, it was just possible to get a clear view of a number of vessels anchored close by. Weighing up the situation at hand, one could not fail to notice this concentration of fire power among this gathering of heavily-armed merchant ships, and realize there was trouble brewing.

The crew of the *M.V. Waimarama* were still unaware of her destination until the Captain ordered the ship's company to muster on deck after breakfast that morning. This was a most unusual occurrence for a merchant ship, enough to set alarm bells ringing. The seamen, gathered on the ship's foredeck, could only hazard a guess as to what this meeting was about. A rumour, via the galley wireless, that we were steering a course for Murmansk, spread throughout the ship like wildfire until the Captain appeared on deck, requesting everyone pay attention to what he had to say.

He then told the ship's company he had just received word from Naval headquarters in Gourock concerning the ship's final destination, and asked for complete silence while he read out the following message, "The *M.V. Waimarama* has been detailed to join a convoy, codenamed Pedestal, bound for the relief of Malta."

Before he could utter another word, there were loud protests from several members of the deck crew, who complained bitterly, "We've been bloody shanghied," one seamen shouted angrily.

"Why didn't they ask for volunteers?"

Calling for calm, the Captain continued to read the message, saying, "The people of Malta are at this very moment facing an enemy determined to starve them into submission, it is therefore of the utmost importance this convoy gets through at all costs."

Having listened at length to the Captain describing the people of Malta's plight, an undercurrent of discontent, predominant among the seamen, quickly subsided, when again he pleaded with them, and said, "Surely, there is no man among you who would have these unfortunate people starve to death?"

In the deathly silence that followed, nought was heard other than the mournful cry of gulls, wheeling above. With a brief word of thanks to all concerned, the Captain dismissed the ship's company, allowing them to continue with their normal duties and their thoughts. An air of uncertainty hung over the vessel, as this bright summer's day ended with the setting sun. Seen in the distance as a ball of fire tinged with flashes of orange, it sought to linger a while, like some warning angel, before slipping beneath the far horizon.

As night closed in, an aldis lamp from the naval base ashore, flashed out a coded message to each vessel, requesting they heave up anchor and move out to sea. In response, a ghostly grey collection of heavily-laden merchant vessels slipped stealthily away in the dark of night from Gourock, Scotland, to rendezvous with their naval escorts out at sea. In all a total of eleven ships, comprising the cream of the British merchant fleet accompanied by three American merchant vessels, the *Almeria Lykes*, *Santa Elisa* and the oil tanker *Ohio*, set sail for Malta, on the night of the third of August, 1942.

Commander A.G. Venables, R.N, in charge of the convoy, took passage aboard the merchant ship *Port Chalmers,* while the main body of our naval escort under the command of Admiral Syfret met the convoy off the Clyde later that night. Steaming at a speed of fifteen knots, our journey being uneventful thus far, we arrived off Gibraltar, during the early hours of August 10. Unseen by the enemy, convoy and escorts slipped through the Gibraltar Straits in dense fog. Not until late afternoon of that same day, was our position made known to the enemy. At the time, our convoy was well into the Mediterranean.

At this point, the convoy codenamed Pedestal was joined by a naval task force from Gibraltar, comprising of two battleships, three aircraft carriers, six cruisers, and twenty-four destroyers. It was a powerful force to be reckoned with, outnumbering the convoy of merchantmen they were escorting, by three to one.

It was at daybreak on the morning of August 11 when enemy aircraft spotted the convoy and thereafter shadowed us continuously, in spite of special attention paid to them by our carrier-borne fighters. Around midday, when our convoy was approximately 550 miles from its destination, Spitfires from the aircraft carrier *H.M.S. Furious* flew off to their new base on the Island of Malta, to replace losses to the island's defence force.

At approximately 1:15 that afternoon, German U-boat *U.73* successfully penetrated our defensive screen and fired four torpedoes at the *H.M.S. Eagle*. A series of violent explosions were heard, as the missiles struck home, setting the vessel afire in her midship area, putting her out of action. Listing sharply to starboard, she drifted astern as aircraft waiting to take off on her flight deck slid into the water, followed by members of her crew.

Burning fiercely, she began to sink, slowly at first, then reluctantly she slipped beneath the clear blue waters of the Mediterranean. A column of water from the crippled vessel's engine room shot into the air, as she slowly disappeared from view.

Within a matter of eight minutes she was no more. Escorting destroyers managed to rescue 900 out of her compliment of 1160 men including her Captain L. D. Mackintosh and, as dusk fell on the evening of the eleventh, the convoy experienced its first air attack. A large formation of German high level and torpedo bombers, swooping in from the west, managed to escape the attention of our fighters in the failing light. Luckily, all salvos missed their intended targets. A concentrated barrage of anti-aircraft fire from the guns of every ship in the convoy managed to repulse this attack and, at the same time, accounted for several of the enemy being destroyed.

Dawn was colouring the eastern horizon on the morning of August 12 when renewed enemy air attacks were intercepted by carrier-borne fighters, some distance from our convoy. Few, if any, enemy aircraft managed to slip past to attack the merchantmen. This however proved to be just a preliminary skirmish by the Luftwaffe and its allies, their most ferocious effort so far until the convoy was abreast of the Sardinian airfields, around noon on that day. Then out of a clear blue sky they came, a combined force of some eighty torpedo bombers, dive bombers and fighter bombers. In a perfectly-timed raid, they swooped down on the convoy. The attack, which lasted for over an hour, did little damage. Our only casualty was the merchant vessel *Deucalion*, forced to leave the convoy, and later destroyed by the enemy off the Tunisian coast.

Further attacks by large forces of German dive bombers quickly followed, only to peter out before any serious damage was inflicted. Not to be denied the chance of another kill, a lone enemy dive bomber sneaked in out of the morning sun, as I strolled along the boat deck. Sweeping in low among the convoy, it raked the *Waimarama* with a volley of cannon fire. Taken by surprise, I dived headlong beneath a nearby lifeboat, unable to move, and watched with bated breath as her wooden deck was ripped to shreds.

The Captain's Steward caught unaware by this sneak attack had just left the wheel house with his tea tray in hand and was halfway down a companion ladder, when he stumbled and fell. Landing with a sickening thud on the boat deck, he lay perfectly still.

Leaving his place of shelter when the attack had subsided, one of the ship's engineers shouted, "Are you okay?" and rushed to assist him. Stunned and badly shaken, the Captain's Steward slowly raised his head. In shocked silence, I watched a jagged gash above his right ear pump out blood that spilled onto his chest, turning his white shirt front crimson.

"Where the Hell did that sneaky sod come from?" he groaned. "I thought the square-headed bastard had done for me, that time."

Late that afternoon, we passed through an area where the main concentration of enemy U-boats made numerous attacks on the convoy and, were it not for the vigilance of our escorts or precise timing of emergency turns made by the merchantmen, serious losses could have occurred. Throughout the long daylight hours, repeated attacks by enemy aircraft were driven off as a result of concentrated fire power from every ship in convoy, momentarily turning the sky black.

While a fusillade of exploding anti-aircraft shells tended to blot out a brilliant August sun, a coded message was sent to all ships in convoy warning of an apparent enemy attack by U-boats. Several torpedoes were fired in our direction. But, once again, precise timing of several emergency turns made by the convoy avoided serious losses. There was no let up by the enemy, as the fight raged on, forcing battle weary guns crews to remain at action stations until late into the evening of the twelfth. As darkness closed in, sporadic bursts of tracer were seen to zoom across the night sky during a brief exchange of fire between our escorts and Italian E-boats, based at Sardinia.

Nerves on edge, after a night of continuous attack by submarine and E-boats, guns crews made ready at first light of day to meet an expected onslaught from superior enemy forces. Shoulders strapped firmly into the harness of anti-aircraft guns, grim-faced crews stood by to repel further enemy attacks that were to last for the remainder of the day. There was no respite for the merchantmen when, out of a setting sun, huge formations of enemy bombers swooped down on the convoy.

With a thunderous roar on they came like a plague of locust, intent on devouring everything in sight. Squadrons of high level and dive bombers, unwavering in their determination to obliterate every merchant ship in convoy, made desperate efforts to stop our life saving cargoes of much needed food, hospital supplies and oil, destined for the starving population on the Island of Malta.

As night fell on the night of August 12, repeated attacks by enemy submarine and E-boats continued unabated, as the convoy altered formation from four to two columns. Passing through the narrow Skerki Channel at eight p.m., a torpedo struck the oil tanker *Ohio* and, although badly damaged, she managed to remain with the convoy. Even so, repeated submarine and E-boat attacks by the enemy afforded the convoy little respite when two further merchant ships, the *Clan Ferguson* and *Empire Hope* were lost. Also hit was the *Brisbane Star*, a torpedo striking her bow, forcing the vessel to leave the convoy. She eventually managed to limp into Malta, a day or so later.

Rounding Cape Bonn at midnight, it became apparent that several enemy E-boats were operating in the area when, at one a.m., on the morning of August 13, a violent explosion was heard some way ahead of the convoy. The cruiser *H.M.S. Manchester,* torpedoed from close range and out of action, was slowly sinking stern first when the *Waimarama* passed her by, some minutes later. We also learned it was marauding E-boats slipping in and out of the convoy during the hours of darkness that unleashed a series of torpedoes that had damaged the *Manchester*'s propeller shafts, bringing her to a standstill.

Between the hours of 3:20 and 4:30 a.m., further crippling attacks by enemy torpedo boats accounted for the loss of another five merchantmen. Following some distance astern of the main body, four of the convoy, the *Wairangi, Almeria Lykes* and *Santa Elishia,* and most probably the *Glenorchy*, were all sunk. This was a cruel blow indeed, after the convoy had ventured thus far with great success.

The battle continued throughout the dark of night, with special attention being given to the oil tanker *Ohio*. It seemed the enemy were determined to destroy her valuable cargo of much-needed oil at all costs before she reached Malta. They attacked her ceaselessly. In her wake the remnants of once proud ships and their gallant crews, who joined battle with the enemy, were left ablaze, as the depleted convoy continued to fight every inch of the way to its final destination.

·   ·   ·

Throughout the hours of darkness, red balls of fire strung out along the horizon as far as the eye could see, were all that remained of merchant vessels sunk in battle. Amid a sea littered with wreckage lighting up the night sky, survivors from sunken ships, many badly injured, waited to be picked up. From the deck of the *M.V. Waimarama*, I surveyed this horrific scene of death and destruction, unaware that I too would be in much the same predicament, come the morning.

CHAPTER 17

NO PLACE TO HIDE

In circumstances favourable to the enemy, continuous attacks by Italian E-boats based at Pantellaria dominated the hours of darkness. An exchange of gunfire during these skirmishes saw tracers criss-crossing the night sky with naval vessels firing parachute flares aloft, in an effort to protect the convoy. This enabled our escorts to destroy several enemy torpedo boats before they had a chance to press home an attack.

Daybreak on the morning of August 13 brought little relief for battle weary crews aboard the few remaining merchant ships left in convoy. Within striking distance of enemy airfields in Sicily, we now faced a much bigger threat of attack from dive bombers. Rising at seven a.m. that morning, I managed to snatch a hurried breakfast before my turn of duty in the wheel-house at eight o'clock.

Surveying the battered remnants of our convoy, I noticed the hours of darkness had claimed at least six merchant ships sunk, and two damaged, with an unknown number of escort vessels. I was, however, surprised to see how many merchant ships and their gallant crews had managed to survive during a night of mayhem, when the odds were so stacked against us.

Taking advantage of a lull in the ongoing battle for supremacy of the Mediterranean, I took the opportunity to think. Everything seemed peaceful and quiet after a night of carnage. It was hard to imagine how anyone, engaged in this do or die battle for survival, had come through unscathed. Which brought to mind a phrase from that man of letters, Samuel Johnson, who said, and I quote, "Being on a ship at sea is like being in prison, with every chance of being drowned."

It was now imperative we remained forever on the lookout against surprise attacks by the enemy, at any given time. Whilst our over-worked guns crews snatched a welcomed breather, they stood ready and waiting for the next enemy onslaught, one that arrived all too soon. Climbing up a companionway to the bridge, I entered the wheel-house at 7:55 a.m. to relieve the helmsman on duty. At that precise moment warning flags hoisted from the foremast of every ship in convoy signalled an enemy air raid was imminent. It was at this point a strangled cry of alarm from the duty officer, out on the starboard wing of the bridge, was cut short as a formation of JU 88 dive bombers swept in for the kill.

With a plane passing at mast height over the *Waimarama,* a stick of bombs landed on the vessel's foredeck, igniting her deck cargo of high octane and setting off a series of violent explosions that rocked the vessel, turning her into a raging inferno.

The force of the blast was enough to lift me off my feet, throwing me up against the rear wall of the chartroom. There I lay stunned and momentarily helpless, as flames quickly engulfed the surrounding area. Badly shaken, I rose unsteadily to my feet, and found breathing difficult in the intense heat. Acrid fumes from burning oil and timber choked me.

Fighting for breath, I looked on helplessly as flames swept through the vessel's tinder dry superstructure with lightning speed to encircle me. Glass in the chartroom windows, caught in the blaze, crackled viciously, to melt away instantly. I was trapped in that cauldron of fire, flames creeping ever closer. Where to run? Nowhere to hide.

Gasping for breath in the intense heat, escape from the raging inferno seemed virtually impossible, and terror clutched at my heart.

Fearing my life would come to a dramatic and painful end, on bended knee I beseeched the Lord to help me in my hour of need. Truly believing I was about to die, I offered this silent prayer to my Maker, and begged of Him, "Lord, if my time has come, please let it be quick."

·   ·   ·

Scenes from childhood moved swiftly through my mind as I stood rooted to the spot, waiting for the flames to devour me. I pictured Mother waiting to meet me at Victoria Station in London for the very first time, as a thirteen-year-old and, as she faded from view, Grandma appeared. Bending low she whispered, "Caroline is your sister, my dear boy."

Never having set eyes on my sister, I begged the Lord to spare me this one time, that I may, with His blessing, fulfil a boyhood dream. As vital seconds ticked away, I found myself caught up in a combination of fear and deep emotion. My lungs screamed out for air, as the blistering heat and dense smoke from the burning oil all but choked me. Suddenly, a series of violent explosions below deck rocked the ship and, in the blink of an eye, fire swept through the vessel's holds, tearing the heart out of the *Waimarama* and igniting her cargo of hospital supplies, food and ammunition.

Then a strange rumbling sound, from the port side of the bridge, attracted my attention. As I gazed in that direction, the scene that caught my eye caused my heart to skip a beat. It was as if my prayers had been answered, and the hand of Providence was reaching out to guide me. For one fleeting second, the curtain of fire between me and salvation parted and, in that vital moment, I had a clear view of that area of the ship.

A section of the port wing of the bridge was as yet untouched by the raging inferno and there, before me, lay a miraculous avenue of escape, some thirty-five to forty feet away. Hope anew welled up within me. If only I could make it, I said to myself, realizing I must first run through a dense wall of fire. I was also aware in desperate situations such as this when every second counts, one has little time to lose. It was now a matter of life and death, so I had to act quickly. Of one thing I was certain, I could not rely on others to save me. I had to save myself.

Picking up a steel helmet from among debris littering the chart-room floor, I placed it firmly on my head. Then raising my eyes heavenward, I offered a prayer to a merciful Lord, who had, so far, seen fit to spare me. With precious seconds ticking away, I placed my hands over my face for protection and inhaled what little air there was to be had. Holding my breath, I dashed headlong through a rapidly lengthening curtain of fire. Nothing more than sheer terror urged me on, as I dashed blindly on through that wall of searing fire, licking hungrily at my bare flesh, forcing me to fight every inch of the way.

On and on I ran, with the sickly smell of death in my nostrils. I felt as if I had entered the gates of Hell itself as I ran through a solid sheet of fire, with smoke and burning oil squeezing the breath out of me. Choking back a need to scream with pain, I stumbled blindly on in a desperate bid to reach the port wing of the bridge and safety, before it was too late.

Suddenly, a rush of cool air brushing my hands told me I had, by the grace of God, managed to escape from a cauldron of fire. I was blind in one eye, my hands were badly burnt and swollen twice their normal size, but I was alive. It was nothing short of a miracle I escaped certain death and I thanked the Lord for saving my life. While every move I made sent excruciating pain shooting up my arms, I realised there was little time to waste. If I did not hurry off the ship, now in danger of blowing up and sinking, she would take me with her.

In between several loud explosions within the vessel's holds, I heard the frantic cries for help from some of my shipmates, trapped below deck. Their pleas were cut short by agonized screams of pain, as fire engulfed them. It made my blood run cold, but I was helpless to do anything to relieve their suffering. I knew the vessel was loaded with ammunition and would blow up at any moment. With this in mind, I realized my only avenue of escape was to take to the water.

A hurried glance over the ship's side renewed fears for my safety.

My only avenue of escape appeared to be cut off. The *Waimarama*'s deck cargo of high octane, having set the ship afire, spread to the ocean and ignited fuel oil spewing from her tanks, setting the sea ablaze. The situation was desperate indeed, as fire raging around me crept closer by the second, and more violent explosions from ammunition in the vessel's holds, shook her from stem to stern. Fearing the next blast would be my last, I rid myself of the steel helmet and some outer clothing, arranged my life jacket as best I could, said a hurried prayer, and dived headlong over the side of the ship, into a sea of fire. In a desperate bid to survive, I plunged deep into the ocean and, holding my breath, swam beneath the surface.

I remained submerged for as long as humanly possible, constantly aware of agonizing pain shooting up my arms with every stroke I made, as I swam away from the ship as fast as I could. If I failed to put enough distance between myself and the blazing oil surrounding the vessel, all my efforts would have been in vain. With this in mind, I held my breath until I felt as if I were about to burst. Then slowly expelling air from my lungs, I surfaced in the middle of a large patch of fuel oil that had somehow separated from the rest of the debris, covering me in a black gooey mess.

Although the fire was quite some distance away, heat from the blazing oil all but scorched the back of my neck. Watching the stricken vessel burn fiercely from stem to stern, I realized how lucky I was to have made such a miraculous escape. Then all at once a series of violent explosions, from ammunition stowed down in the *Waimarama*'s holds, shook her as one would a rag doll. Fearing I'd be sucked down with her, I swam away from the stricken ship as fast as I could.

I soon found swimming extremely difficult because my hands were badly burnt, so I turned on my back and propelled myself away from the ship, kicking out strongly with both legs, until I could go no further. Thoroughly exhausted and suffering intense pain, I felt unable to swim another stroke and simply lay there, watching the crippled vessel in its final death throes. Then an enormous explosion below deck rent her apart. With a gigantic shudder, the huge steel masts that had survived many a storm at sea snapped like a couple of carrots and

My ship, the M.V. Waimarama, *is torn apart by exploding ammunition and fuel. Within moments, it would sink, leaving only debris and burning oil to mark the watery grave of so many sailors.*

caved in, toppling like nine-pins onto the deck below. Feeling I was in no immediate danger now, I watched her, as she spewed out a dense cloud of black smoke and burst into a ball of fire, to slowly sink.

Drifting past mounds of fire foam and chunks of flotsam bobbing about in the water, the *Waimarama* disappeared from view, and I shuddered to think what might have been. All that remained of the doomed vessel was a sea littered with debris as far as the eye could see. Lying there, I felt reasonably safe, floating amid the wreckage with nought but a pall of black smoke towering skyward, marking the spot where my ship met an untimely end. Having fought bravely throughout, she'd taken most of her gallant crew with her and, but for the grace of God, I too might have perished with them.

Still the battle raged on, the sound of gunfire and a distant rumble of exploding bombs could be heard above intermittent chatter of anti-aircraft fire. As the day wore on, an eerie silence descended over these troubled Mediterranean waters where not too long ago peace and tranquillity were totally absent.

Having made strenuous efforts to put distance between myself and the sinking ship left me so exhausted, I lay immobile. Body tensed and nerves on edge, I listened for the slightest sound, believing there was every possibility I'd be rescued. Due to a lack of sleep since passing through the Straits of Gibraltar into the Mediterranean Sea, I dropped off into some much needed shut-eye. Wakened by a noise like that of a stiff breeze rustling through the trees, I was startled out of my wits. Afraid to make the slightest move, fearing it might be the enemy looking for survivors, I lay perfectly still, as though dead.

In the stillness of time, I chanced to peep through my good right eye and gazed in awe at the amazing sight that lay before me. No more than a stone's throw away, the ghostly figure of a young woman appeared to hover just above the water in front of me. Emanating from her being, an iridescent light surrounded this sylph-like figure, clad in gossamer white robes, with a girdle of brilliant azure blue. With arms outstretched, she appeared to beckon me to her.

My reaction was one of fear. "Is this real or is it nothing more than a figment of my imagination?" I asked myself, closing my eyes.

Suppressing a need to shout for help, I tried to assure myself whatever it was I had seen would vanish just as suddenly as it appeared. Waiting several minutes to allow this strange being or what ever it was to disappear, I chanced to peep once again. But there, as before, this beautiful vision was positioned just above the water, beckoning me with greater urgency.

"My God, I'm hallucinating," I said to myself. "The heat of the sun must be driving me crazy."

Suffering intense pain and dizziness, I could not bring my eyes to focus on this heavenly being and, strange as it seemed, the pain I suffered slowly receded. An overpowering feeling of calm surged through my body in her presence, enabling me to move with greater freedom. I needed to get closer, if I were to find out what it really was, and instinctively began to swim with greater urgency.

Putting extra effort into every stroke, I swam, with consummate ease, toward my objective to narrow the distance between myself and this angel of God. The faster I swam the further away she drifted from me, all the while still beckoning me on. I was soon exhausted by my efforts to get near her and, feeling I had expended every scrap of energy and could swim no further, lay gasping for breath. I had, it seemed, stretched myself to the limit and, closing my eyes, lay motionless.

Still alert, the sound of voices breaking the afternoon stillness startled me. When I looked for guidance from this angel-like being, she appeared to have vanished. Slowly the excruciating pain that left me a short while ago, returned to torture my body once again. Meanwhile, the mumbled conversation I'd heard from a distance appeared to grow louder, so I kept perfectly quiet. It might be the enemy searching for survivors, I said to myself, remembering I was close to the Italian island of Pantellaria. The thought of being picked up by the enemy did not appeal to me – I'd no wish to spend my days rotting in a prisoner of war camp.

Suddenly, a peal of laughter echoed across the now silent waters of the Mediterranean, disturbing the morning's stillness. "You daft bugger, they'll shoot us if they see you wearing your hat!" the voice went on.

Recognizing that the voice belonged to one of my countrymen was music to my ears. I hardly noticed the rush of pain to my hands when, with some difficulty, I managed to take a whistle from the pocket in my life jacket. Carefully placing it between swollen lips, I blew as loud as I could, and waited for some response. There followed a lengthy silence of probably five minutes, then a voice shouted, "Where the Hell are you?"

Careful not to alarm them, I responded by blowing on my whistle again, to which the voice replied, "Keep blowing, we'll make our way over to you."

Surrounded by mounds of fire-foam floating on the water, I appeared to be hidden from view at the time, making it difficult for them to locate my position. Suddenly two startled men, guided by the sound of my whistle appeared, as if by magic, from behind a collection of floating debris.

The men appeared to be hanging on to a cabin door they salvaged from the wreckage of the sunken ship and, seeing me, propelled themselves through the water to get closer. Keeping an eye on me as if I were from another planet, they allowed me to share the floating debris they'd salvaged. The elder of the two could see I was covered in fuel oil and stammered, "Where the Hell have you come from to be in such a mess?" His partner butting in, added, "What colour are you, black or white?"

"I was a member of the crew of the *M.V. Waimarama*," I mumbled through swollen lips. "Fortunately I managed to get off the ship before she sank, following an attack by a formation of Ju 88 dive bombers. Like yourselves I'm white, and my nationality is British," I replied.

"My God, you were damned lucky to get off the ship alive," they said, and told me they were naval gunners seconded to the *Waimarama* for the voyage to Malta. It was at five minutes past eight on the morning of August 13 when they opened fire on a formation of JU 88s coming out of the sun, who appeared Hell-bent on sinking the ship.

Arthur, a reporter for his local paper in time of peace, and the elder of the two naval ratings witnessing the attack on the *Waimarama* by enemy dive bombers, later described her sinking as follows, "The merchantman *M.V. Waimarama,* steaming toward Malta at a speed of thirteen knots, appeared to be singled out for this attack. A near miss by the leading aircraft was followed by a direct hit from a salvo of bombs from the second. No merchant ship on earth could withstand that sort of punishment, and survive. Missiles landing fore and aft of the bridge caused a tremendous explosion, setting her deck cargo of octane afire. It was at this point my shipmate and I, manning an Oerlikon anti-aircraft position on the port wing of the vessel, saw fit to leap into the sea and swim for our lives.

"From a safe distance, we watched as the vessel burst into a huge ball of fire, and a column of black smoke from the stricken vessel rose slowly skyward. A second explosion saw her huge steel masts telescope inwards and fall into the heart of a roaring furnace below. Her cargo of ammunition below deck ignited in a sheet of fire which swept the vessel from stem to stern, and resulted in a series of violent explosions down in her holds.

"Listing to starboard, the *Waimarama* suddenly righted herself then disappeared without trace, in a matter of seconds. A later report on the sinking said a third Junkers dive bomber, coming in for the kill, was itself caught up in a mighty explosion from the stricken vessel, to disintegrate in mid-air."

He went on to report, "It seemed unimaginable that anyone could survive such mass destruction. Sadly, many of her crew perished as a result of a shattering explosion that tore the vessel apart. Few, if any, were expected to come out alive. There is no doubt the *Waimarama* was the bombers' main target on that fateful morning of August 13, 1942. Enveloped in a blazing inferno, with little chance to escape, the crew of this ill-fated ship faced certain death, a mere handful surviving, as she vanished without trace."

Because my hands were badly injured, my companions decided to place me between them on the cabin door salvaged from the wreckage.

Hemmed in on all sides by the enemy, we had no idea in which direction we were heading. With the sun at its full height around midday, my comrades divested the upper part of their naval uniforms. To keep the sun from burning them to a cinder, they would every now and again take to the water, to cool off. While they were busy bobbing up and down in the water, I watched a dark smudge on the far horizon, grow bigger with each passing second.

"I think there's a ship over there," I mumbled excitedly, when my companions came up for air.

Watching the distant object for a moment, Arthur, with a look of elation on his sunburnt face, turned to me and cried, "By jove, I think you're right, son," and started waving his arms about, as if we'd just won an important victory.

"Look, she's coming this way," his partner Nobby Clarke shouted. "I hope they've seen us."

Her outline, now clearly visible as she drew closer, sent Nobby into raptures. "It's one of our L-Class frigates. I can tell by her superstructure," he exclaimed.

"She must be looking for survivors," said Arthur. "Let's try to attract their attention once more."

While the pair of them waved frantically, I placed my whistle between swollen lips and blew as hard as I could. Our moment of

On the attack: Junkers Ju 87 Stuka

ecstasy at the thought of being rescued suddenly evaporated, however, with the sound of distant gunfire. We were helpless to do anything and watched in dismay as the vessel we imagined was about to come to our aid decided to alter course.

Junkers dive bomber as shown in this newspaper photo. This was the type of plane that sank the Waimarama *and killed so many brave men.*

Her propellers thrashed the water wildly, as she wheeled to starboard and our would-be rescuer took off in the opposite direction. The deathly silence that followed was shattered by the all-too-familiar sound of an approaching aircraft. With bated breath we watched as it skimmed low over the water, heading directly toward us.

The plane's markings now clearly visible, Arthur yelled out a warning, "Duck for God's sake," he shouted. "It's a bloody Jerry!"

The warning came none too soon, for I quickly released my grip on the cabin door I'd been clinging to, and disappeared beneath the Mediterranean's oily waters. Suddenly a short burst of cannon fire from the enemy aircraft raked the wooden plank above us, the noise sending shock waves echoing below in a deafening crescendo. Like my comrades, I remained submerged until I felt my lungs would burst, when a desperate need to take in some fresh air forced me to surface. Gasping for breath, I swam toward the cabin door floating nearby and hung on to it for dear life as my two companions, white-faced and badly shaken, surfaced simultaneously.

Shaking his fist at the now-distant enemy aircraft, Nobby Clarke screamed, "You murdering bastards, trying to kill us when we're helpless!"

Turning to Arthur, he gasped, "That son of a bitch was using us for target practice."

"Hell, that was a bloody close call. I thought our number was up," said Arthur. "We'll have to keep a sharp look out in case he decides to come back, and have another go at us."

The sun, having almost burnt the three of us to a cinder during the heat of the day, began to cool down somewhat as it slipped toward the western horizon. Not even a bird on the wing was seen in the vast emptiness of these troubled waters.

Night was fast approaching and we were alone, our one chance of rescue long out of sight. Fearing I might have to spend the night in these waters sent shivers through me. My injuries hurt so much I was in desperate need of something to relieve the awful pain, and prayed rescue might be near at hand.

"I wonder what the time is?" Nobby remarked rather casually. "We seem to have been in the water forever."

It was then I chanced to look at the watch on my wrist. Why I'll never know, for it was burnt beyond recognition and useless. The steel strap left a red weal on my forearm and, in like manner, the watches belonging to my two companions were waterlogged and useless. We had no way of knowing the time of day but did, however, notice the sun took on a reddish hue as the light slowly faded.

In gathering gloom, a tiny white light, out on the far horizon, caught our attention. It appeared to be bearing down on us at a considerable speed and, within minutes, the outline of a small ship came in sight. Although we were unaware of her identity as she drew nearer, silhouettes of her crew moving around the foredeck were clearly distinguishable.

"I think it's one of our escorts," exclaimed Arthur excitedly. "We're going to be alright now, lads!"

Without warning, her propellers thrashed the water and she slowly moved astern, to stop a little to our right. Caught in the vessel's backwash, we drifted toward her starboard side where the officer in charge, seeing us in the water, ordered his men to lower a scrambling net over the ship's side. Leaning over the rails, he addressed us like long lost friends, saying, "Nice to see you safe, boys. Hop aboard."

Surprised to hear such a jocular remark from the young officer, Arthur quipped, "What the Hell do you think we are, matey, bloody monkeys?"

A chorus of muffled laughter from members of the crew standing nearby was quickly stifled when a senior officer appeared.

"You'd better send a line down for our friend here," said Arthur. "His hands are badly injured."

Darkness having closed in by the time my two companions were helped aboard, I lay motionless in the water, until assisted by a member of the ship's crew. Entering the water, he fastened a canvas belt under my arms. I was then hoisted aboard the vessel in a state of collapse, and placed on a stretcher. In the beam of a flashlight held by one of the crew, I caught a glimpse of two red and gold bands on the uniform of the officer attending me. From past experience, I knew he was the ship's doctor. Turning to a seaman in attendance, the officer remarked, "I'll need to give him a shot of morphine. You had better cut his trouser leg open, while I give him a jab."

The destroyer HMS Ledbury *picked my burnt body up out of the water.*

Drawing a wicked-looking knife from its sheaf, the seaman with a deft stroke sliced through the oil-soaked fabric of my trousers. A shiver ran through my body as a swab touched my bare thigh and an odour of medical spirits assailed my nostrils. I felt the needle bite into my flesh, and a numbness pervaded my body, relieving me of the awful pain I suffered, soon to render me unconscious.

At the crack of dawn, our rescue ship, the destroyer *Ledbury*, came under a concentrated attack by enemy aircraft. The noise from her guns woke me with a start. In an exchange of gunfire, the escort vessel opened up with every available weapon in her armoury, and for a while the noise was deafening. Then all was quiet, save for the moans and groans of row upon row of rescued seamen, lying around me, filling every available inch of space on the vessel's mess deck.

Night brought scant relief to the battle-weary guns crew, as *Ledbury* continued to be harassed by raiding E-boats, slipping in and out of the convoy with sporadic exchanges of gunfire throughout the hours of darkness. Racing to the aid of the crippled tanker *Ohio*, still afloat after receiving a terrific pounding from the enemy, our destroy-

er *Ledbury* was joined by destroyer *Penn*, and the minesweeper *Rye*. Together they towed the stricken vessel in the direction of Malta, in spite of constant enemy air attacks. During the next two days, anti-aircraft crews on *Ledbury*, *Penn* and *Rye* worked overtime to keep the enemy

The tanker Ohio *takes a hit and is seriously damaged while making her way to Malta.*

at bay. We survivors, sleeping on the ship's mess deck tables, were given little time to rest during these incessant sharp exchanges of gunfire.

Lying in semi-darkness aboard the rescue ship, I recoiled in fright when seeing ghostly figures moving around the mess deck, until I was informed it was the guns crew, who wore white flash hoods when in action. During this time, the escort vessels, aided by guns on the stricken *Ohio* joining in the fray, kept up a continuous barrage of anti-aircraft fire, fending off desperate attempts by the enemy to destroy *Ohio*'s precious cargo of fuel oil.

By dawn's early light on the morning of August 15, I wakened to a tremendous burst of cheering. The beleaguered tanker *Ohio* had just entered the Island of Malta's Grand Harbour, in a sinking condition, supported on either side by her naval escorts. Having fought off

Arrival of the first ships into Malta. The broken tanker Ohio *is guided into Malta harbour by the* HMS Ledbury *and* HMS Penn.

continuous air attacks since daybreak of the thirteenth, she was welcomed by thousands lining the harbour. As soon as she berthed, little time was wasted salvaging the 10,000 tons of fuel she carried. It was a welcome relief in helping the besieged island hold out against the enemy's attempt to starve them into submission.

Of the fourteen merchant ships that set sail from the port of Gourock in Scotland, a total of five, the *Port Chalmers, Rochester Castle, Melbourne Star, Brisbane Star* and the severely damaged tanker *Ohio,* reached their destination. Ships set afire through enemy action, many carrying dangerous cargoes of aviation spirit and high explosives, lost most of their gallant crews.

As the cheering and shouting subsided, badly-wounded survivors from the ill-fated Pedestal convoy, aboard the escort vessel *H.M.S. Ledbury,* waited to be taken to hospital. Alone with my thoughts in the aftermath of that bitter battle, I lay on a mess room table and gazed in horror at the carnage created by man's inhumanity to his fellow man. Bodies packed together like sardines lay around me swathed in bloodstained bandages, hiding horrific wounds. Nothing disturbed the quiet of this peaceful morning, save for an anguished cry of pain from some wounded soul, who like myself, waited for a sedative to relieve his suffering.

A squeal of brakes on the quayside announced the arrival of an ambulance with a team of medical staff, who boarded the vessel to attend the injured survivors. One by one, the wounded were stretchered ashore to the waiting vehicles and hurriedly whisked away from the harbour area, before the start of another enemy bombing raid on the island. Bumping and bouncing along narrow mountain roads, no better than cart tracks, the ambulance took off with all possible speed, shaking the living daylights out of me.

Interrupted on its journey by sporadic enemy air raids, the ambulance eventually arrived at an Army Hospital, near the tiny village of Mtarfa. Skidding to a halt on the gravel driveway, our noisy arrival alerted members of staff, who placed all badly wounded survivors on stretchers, transferring them to a ward set aside for Naval and Merchant seamen. Inside a brightly-lit operating room, the smell of ether

Survivors from merchant ships are taken off escort vessel Ledbury *in Malta.*

stung my nostrils, as I waited to be attended to. I recall feeling no pain when a needle was jabbed into my arm, just the sound of voices trailing off into a distant murmur.

Weakened by the loss of blood and hunger, a morphine injection left me powerless to stop myself falling into a black abyss, as it took hold. Gyrating around in ever-decreasing circles, I plummeted into space, as my tormented body danced crazily before me. With the smell of death pervading the air around me, icy fingers reached out to touch my cheek. I recoiled in terror and, once again, searing flames ravaged my pain-wracked body. As the fire spread, my frantic cries for help went unanswered. There followed an eerie silence, and all was stilled.

Night had fallen by the time I regained consciousness, aided by a damp sponge brushing my fevered brow and the gentle voice of a young nurse, whispering, "You are in safe hands now."

I tried to touch my face and found my hands held fast by a cumbersome dressing, pinning them to the bed. Looking up at the young nurse standing at my bedside, I asked, "What have they done to me?"

"You are very ill," she said, "so try to get some rest, sir."

Through sleep-laden eyes, I watched her disappear down the ward, as darkness claimed me once again.

Wakened next morning by the rattle of medicine trolleys trundling past my bed, I found myself in a brightly-lit hospital ward painted in shades of white and pastel green. On either side of the room, nurses were busy attending survivors. As comrades in arms, we fought the good fight in a never-ending struggle for supremacy of this island. It was nothing short of a miracle I or any of my comrades aboard the *Waimarama* escaped from that blazing inferno of a ship, with death staring us in the face.

I now found myself with badly burnt hands encased in oilskin gloves. It came as something of a shock, finding I was unable to carry out the everyday things we take for granted in life. Like a child cared for by its mother, I was dependant on nursing staff at the hospital to wash, dress and feed me. I felt helpless and just wanted to shut the world away.

Closing my eyes, I allowed my mind to wander at will, recalling how recent events might have turned out different had I been allowed to say I was unfit for sea. Alone with my thoughts, a female voice cut short my daydream to ask, "Would you care for a drink?"

Suffering blurred vision, I found it hard to focus on the young nurse standing at my bedside holding a large cup. Bending over me she placed a tube from the receptacle against my lips, allowing me to siphon up the liquid in my own good time.

"Is the pain too much for you?" she asked, watching me grimace each time I moved.

"Yes, it's getting worse," I replied. "But I'll be alright," I assured her.

Smoothing down the bed clothes, she drew a mosquito net over me and whispered, "I'll be back in a moment." Then she hurried off down the ward.

Minutes later, the ward sister arrived at my bedside and, lifting the bedclothes, rubbed my leg with a cotton swab. "Just a little jab, Mr Marshall," she said, producing a hypodermic.

An involuntary shudder ran through my body as the needle bit into my flesh, then the sea of pain on which I floated slowly subsided.

"You'll be alright now," she announced abruptly, covering me with the bedsheets.

Bleary-eyed, I watched her walk away, leaving the young nurse to tidy my bedclothes and replace the mosquito net over my bed, before I passed out.

Roused from a fitful sleep by the tinkling of glass on a passing medicine trolley, I watched the dawn breaking. Even at this early hour, hospital staff were administering medicine to survivors and dressing their wounds. The young Maltese nurse attending me arrived at my bedside with a bowl of warm water, soap and towel, and placed them on my bedside locker. With a smile, she said, "Good morning, did you sleep well?"

"Yes, thank you, I slept like a top," I replied.

Dipping the flannel in warm water, she moistened my face, taking care not to wet the dressing covering my left eye. Then, taking a bottle of liquid from a pocket in her uniform, she poured a little on my head and massaged it in, to soften a mass of black fuel oil stuck to my hair. With deft strokes she ran a small comb through the tangled mess to complete my morning ablutions as the ward sister arrived, with another medicine trolley.

"We'll give you a morphine injection to help ease the pain after we've dressed your hands, Mr Marshall," she said.

I felt a searing pain, as warm saline water trickled through the oilskin gloves covering my hands, to slowly subside as the morphine coursing through my veins rendered me, once again, unconscious.

As the first light of dawn spread its silver lining across the eastern horizon each morning, I lay awake listening for the rattle of the trolley as it trundled down the ward. It was now six a.m. and the ward sister in her white starched uniform stopped at my bedside to administer the morphine injection, before attending to my hands. It was a duty performed with clockwork regularity by these angels of mercy, for many weeks to come.

CHAPTER 18

TOO MUCH RED TAPE

Throughout their long history, British military hospitals have sought to maintain a rigid code of discipline, in times of peace and war. Here on the beleaguered Island of Malta, where hunger and death walked hand in hand, army rules and regulations reigned supreme. Red tape, aptly described as bull shit by the majority of young servicemen stationed here, was strictly adhered to by all rank and file, no matter who. Members of staff in the upper echelons of the medical service were not slow in pulling rank on junior ratings, and often took it upon themselves to adopt this mightier-than-thou attitude.

The Matron in charge at this army hospital, for instance, was a fine example of this long standing tradition, demanding all and sundry jump smartly to attention, at her command. Soon after my arrival at the hospital, she entered the ward where I lay abed, determined to make her presence felt.

A large number of patients in my ward were badly-injured survivors from the convoy. The last thing they needed was for a dominating personality, wearing a dark blue uniform with a white lace bonnet distinguishing her from her nursing staff, to let it be known she was the boss. Standing six-feet-tall and heavily built, she would rumble up the ward like a Sherman tank at her usual time of ten o'clock each morning, giving orders to her subordinates, like a postman delivering mail.

On this particular morning, she called her hospital orderlies to attention and addressed them in a manner befitting the time-honoured tradition of a sergeant on parade. "We have an important visitor arriving here shortly to inspect this hospital so I expect the place be neat and tidy," or words to that effect. "Now I hope I have made myself clearly understood!" she barked, with emphasis on the word "clearly." Then turning on her heel, Matron marched off, leaving hospital orderlies to carry out her instructions to the letter.

"That, I presume, is the matron in charge," I remarked, smiling at the young Maltese nurse dressing my wounds.

For an instant, her bright young face clouded over, then just as quickly the radiant smile reappeared. A shrug of her tiny shoulders was enough to express her feelings, as if to say, I have no choice but to obey Matron's orders. Then bending low she whispered, "Noblesse oblige," a well-known phrase, I felt suited the occasion, referring to people in high office who should behave more generously or nobly towards others in the lower ranks.

Then, skilfully changing the subject before I could reply, she asked, "Have your family been notified you are in hospital?"

Hesitating, I replied, "I have no family. I lost touch with my mother, some years ago," adding, "my grandmother told me I have a sister but never having met her, I've no idea where she is."

The young nurses brow wrinkled, as if in deep concentration and a look of concern crossed the elfin face. "You've no idea where she is?" she said, in shocked surprise. In a sympathetic gesture, her hand reached out to brush my cheek, with the tenderness of a mother comforting her child. "Oh, I'm sure you'll find her, one day," she whispered.

Tidying the bedclothes, she made ready to leave and, with a cheerful smile, said, "I'll have to go now, sleep well."

Around ten-thirty next morning, the rasping voice of the Regimental Sergeant Major, calling his orderlies to attention, woke me with a start. All service personnel in the ward, able to stand on their feet or on crutches will do so, he ordered. Then with the usual salutations, our long-awaited important visitor set foot in the ward to carry out his inspection. Accompanied by the Matron in charge and a retinue of hangers on, they strolled down the ward, stopping now and then to talk to patients as they went. Reaching the foot of my bed, the visitor, an elderly man dressed in khaki uniform, stopped to gaze down at me.

Standing head and shoulders above the rest, he was red of face with large bushy eyebrows protruding from beneath a peaked cap. Standing at my bedside, he studied my bandaged face for a minute and bending low, hollered in my ear, "And how are you today, my lad?"

Temporarily deafened, I recoiled as if shot, and replied in a none too pleasant manner, "I'm feeling damned awful, how are you?" and moaned, as another spasm of pain shot through my arms.

Turning to one of his uniformed cohorts, dripping with gold braid, he asked, "Who is this young fellow and why hasn't he shaved this morning?"

Examining the chart hanging at the foot of my bed, the gold braided individual turned to his superior and announced, rather brusquely, "His name is Rowland Charles Marshall, a merchant seaman from the recent convoy, sir."

"Hmm," grunted Red Face, and turned away.

He moved to the bed next to mine occupied by a Naval Marine, name of White, whom they nicknamed 'Knocker.' The poor fellow lay prostrate, with a couple of days' growth covering his face. Seeing Red Face as someone of importance, he gave a nervous cough as the man drew near, and struggled into a sitting position. It was at this point, a gold-braided member in the party, whom I later learned was this person's adjutant, picked up the seaman's medical chart from the foot of his bed, and read out the following, "Name, White, in service with the Royal Marines. Admitted to hospital August 14, shrapnel wounds to right arm and leg."

"Why haven't you shaved today?" Red Face asked a pale-face
Knocker White.

Receiving no reponse he turned to the young naval officer in attendance and announced, rather abruptly, "Put him on a charge. We
can't put up with this sort of thing in the services."

This again was nothing more than a typical example of the army's
inhuman behaviour to a serviceman wounded in battle. Why the poor
fellow couldn't raise his hand, never mind shave himself. I, too, was
soon in hot water, having incurred the wrath of none other than the
Matron in charge.

It was late that evening when she came charging up the ward like
an enraged bull intent on goring the matador, and stood at the foot
of my bed. Glaring at me she thundered, "Your behaviour today was
absolutely disgraceful!"

Taken by surprise, I asked, "So what have I done, to warrant such
attention?"

"You were extremely rude to a very important visitor this afternoon!" she rapped out.

"Then what would you have me do, dear lady, after he'd almost
deafened me," I replied indignantly, "kiss him?"

For a moment, I thought she was going to throw a fit when the
ashen grey face turned the colour of beetroot, as she fought to catch
her breath. Drawing in great gulps of air, her huge bosom rose and fell
like the heaving waves on a storm-tossed sea. Then having regained
her composure, she rounded on me once again, screaming, "Didn't
you know who that gentleman was?"

"Oh, was I supposed to?" I asked, feigning a look of hurt
surprise.

"That was Lord Gort, G.O.C. Malta," she crowed indignantly.
"And you had the nerve to make insulting remarks to him."

"So what would you have liked me to do, madam, the sailor's
hornpipe?" I taunted.

"You don't have to be so vulgar!" she snapped back at me and,
stamping her foot on the floor in rage, she rambled on, "You merchant
seamen are nothing but trouble. I'll be glad to see the back of you."

Infuriated by her sarcastic remark, I rounded on her and said, "Many of my comrades perished trying to save the likes of you from starving. Maybe you should thank your lucky stars that you're still alive. You are so indoctrinated with rules, regulations and red tape, you go raving mad when your authority is challenged."

My final comment all but knocked the skids out from under her when I added fuel to the fire, saying, "Didn't anyone ever tell you an army marches on its stomach? These men are hungry and are in need of food," I retorted, "not an extra dose of discipline!"

Mouth agape, she studied me for a moment with a look of distaste. "You," she said at length, "have to be the nastiest person I've met in a long time."

Seeing this as an opportunity to further annoy her, I remarked, "Thank you for your kind words, madam," adding, "I need them like a hole in the head."

With a toss of her broad shoulders, she turned away and marched down the ward in silence. As the door slammed shut behind her, the sound of cheering erupted round the ward. Out on the verandah, a cockney voice piped up, "Good on yer mate, it's about time someone took her down a peg."

But for an occasional air raid disrupting the peace and tranquillity of our everyday lives, things had now returned to normal. Especially after my verbal exchanges with Matron, who was most conspicuous by her absence. Maybe finding herself outnumbered by a large contingent of merchant seamen, she probably feared a backlash from men who'd risked their lives to relieve Malta's hungry population, and decided to give our ward a wide berth. Although the amount of food salvaged from our decimated convoy was proportionately small, in comparison to what we hoped to get through, it did at least for the time being ease the threat of starvation.

As with the island's population, hospital patients also suffered through a lack of nutrition. Our only means of supplementing a meagre allowance of food, was to eat the local grown fruit, such as grapes and tomatoes. There was of course a penalty attached to the unwary

who, in failing to wash the fruit, risked severe abdominal pain followed by a dose of the trotters, commonly known as Malta Gut.

At first light each morning, I listened for the sound of the medicine trolley, an unwelcome reminder that it was once again time for
my hands to be dressed, before I'd a bite to eat. I had now been confined to my hospital bed for many months, in the care of a wonderful
young nurse. So it came as a pleasant surprise, one morning, to hear
the sister in charge of my ward, say, "You can get up, as soon as I've
finished dressing your hands, Mr Marshall."

Carefully removing the oilskin gloves protecting my hands, the
ward sister proceeded to cover them in a thin layer of vaseline gauze,
before bandaging them up. Then, assisted by my nurse, whose kindness and devotion to duty I shall be forever grateful, I was able to
shuffle a few shaky steps around my bed. Within a short space of time
I was able to walk up and down the ward, without a need to grasp at
each bed for support. I felt as free as a young fledgling about to leave
its nest.

Just to be able to feed myself, in spite of having both hands heavily bandaged, was to me a blessing after spending five long months
tied to a hospital bed, and having to be spoon fed. I was still dependant on the good services of the nurse, who each day washed my face
and tried, so gently, to remove a remnants of fuel oil clinging to my
hair, and carefully dressed my wounds.

Before allowing me to leave the ward, they gave me a suit of
regulation army blues, many sizes too large, the trousers having to be
rolled up at the bottom. A piece of string fastened around my waist
prevented them from falling down around my ankles, and the jacket
would have disgraced a scarecrow. Seeing me, the sister in charge
suppressed a desire to burst out laughing, and said, "You may take a
walk around the grounds if you wish, Mr Marshall."

"Why on earth do I have to be dressed in this manner?" I asked.
"Must we all wear this ridiculous garb?"

"Ah, that's in case you get lost," she joked.

"There's not much fear of that," I retorted. "Where on earth would
I get to, in this outfit?"

In accordance with the usual army regulations, all patients were obliged to wear hospital blues, until discharged. Now, it so happened as I wandered around the hospital, I was accosted by one of those regimental buffoons who took it for granted, I was part and parcel of His Majesty's forces and, in passing, was addressed as "Oi you" by this army wallah with three stripes on his arm. Answering him in like manner, I replied, "And what can I do for you, mate?"

Acting as if shell-shocked, he suddenly found his voice and gave me a right mouthful of his army repertoire, then, with a sneer, said, "First of all I'm not your mate, I'm your Sergeant Major, sonny. In future you'll address me as, sir."

"Oh, that's nice of you," I said, "but when were you knighted that I have to call you, sir?"

Fixing me with the sort of cold stare only a Sergeant Major can bestow on one of lower rank, he pointed to the three stripes surmounted by a crown on the sleeve of his uniform jacket, and said, "What the Hell do you think these are, sonny, Scotch mist?"

"Oh, they look very decorative, sir, Sergeant Major," I replied sarcastically. "But what am I supposed to do, salute them?"

Before he had time to recover from the shock of my caustic remark, I had taken to my heels and disappeared down a network of corridors inside the hospital, where I lost sight of him. As a result of this episode, I gathered all Regimental Sergeant Majors and N.C.O.'s as per rules and regulations were to be addressed as 'Sir,' by rank and file, and woe betide anyone who failed to do so. Likewise with their army number, each individual was obliged to repeat this when requested to by the above mentioned, before they had time to cough. Should they forget to include the word 'Sir' when answering an officer's question, it would be classed as an insult.

Taking my first steps outside the hospital since arriving some five months ago, I could not help but check my stride to take in a breath of fresh air, and admire the countryside's rugged scenery. Behind a backdrop of barren hills, white vapour trails were seen to criss-cross a clear blue sky, as Spitfires took off from their base at Luqua to engage the enemy. It was wonderful to, once again, feel soft green grass beneath my feet, with a freedom to move around unaided. Knowing but for the grace of God I would never have survived to savour this moment, I determined from now on, come what may, to enjoy whatever life offered.

Studying the island's wild terrain with its many vineyards dotted around hillsides like giant patchwork quilts, the morning stillness was rudely shattered, by the familiar sound of aircraft taking to the air. Accompanied by my two companions, who I learned were attached to the Royal Engineers, we strolled toward the outer perimeter of the hospital grounds, marked by a small stone wall. From our position on top of a hill, we had a bird's eye view of an area where the ground sloped gently away into a valley below, where a cluster of well-camouflaged huts and outbuildings lay adjacent to a small aerodrome.

Groups of men in uniform could be seen moving around and, even as we watched, fighter planes were taking off at short intervals to repel intruders heading our way. Fascinated by the speed with which these tiny aircraft took to the air and climbed with such consummate ease, I was oblivious to the hullaballo going on behind me. It was not until I noticed my companions had suddenly disappeared, I became aware of a Military Police Sergeant built like a Japanese sumo wrestler, bearing down on me.

"Oi, are you bloody deaf?" he hollered at me, in a voice that had given thousands of raw recruits, the screaming Abdabs.

"Are you shouting at me, mister?" I asked, feigning a look of mock surprise.

I watched tiny rivulets of perspiration roll down the ruddy face, as his upper lip, sporting an Errol Flynn moustache, began to twitch convulsively.

Pointing to a notice displayed nearby, he sneered, "The sign says out of bounds, sonny, and that means you. Can't you read or are you blind as well as bleeding deaf?"

"I am not as you so crudely remarked 'bleeding deaf,'" I retorted indignantly, when his tirade of abuse had subsided. "I don't know who you think you are and, furthermore, I resent being spoken to in such a manner," I replied.

Momentarily shocked that I should have the audacity to answer him back, he thrust a hand in his trouser's pocket, and produced a whistle. A series of shrill blasts was enough to bring a couple of his red-capped cronies rushing to his aid. Seizing hold of me in a vice-like grip, they frog-marched me to a wooden shed and shoved me inside. They left me there to sweat it out for what seemed an eternity in an oven-like temperature. I was on the verge of falling asleep, when a thickset fellow in army uniform with two stripes on his sleeve kicked the door in.

"You're wanted in there, mate," he gloated, jerking his thumb toward an adjacent building.

"I'm not your mate and don't wish to be," I replied. "Now where am I supposed to go?" I asked.

I was shown into a room, heavy with tobacco smoke, to face an immaculately dressed young officer sitting behind an ornately carved desk. He looked your typical old boy upper crust type, in a uniform fitting him like a glove. When I walked in on him, he was preoccupied with manicuring his nails, and took his time before deciding to look my way. Glancing through some paperwork the Sergeant Major handed him, he leaned back in his chair and, flicking an imaginary speck of dust from his sleeve, eyed me with suspicion.

Running his eye over my outfit of regulation hospital blues, as if I was something dragged in off the street, an expression of utter distaste spread across his face. In an impatience gesture, he put his hands together and tapped the tips of his fingers. Then in the usual authoritarian voice adopted by these jolly old army chaps, he declared, "Well, my man, you seem to have blotted your copy book. What have you got to say for yourself?"

His question caught me off guard so I simply shrugged my shoulders, and asked, "What would you like me to say, mister?"

He snapped back, "Now look here, my man, you have some serious charges laid against you by Sergeant Wilkins, standing here."

Picking up a copy of army rules and regulations off his desk, he read out a list of offences I was alleged to have committed. Refusing to obey an order and insulting behaviour to an N.C.O. were among many listed by the officer before pausing to catch his breath. Then he ask, "And what is your number?"

Without a second thought I gave him the first that came to mind, my home telephone number 3424952, which I rattled off.

During an enforced period of silence in the proceedings, I took note of my surroundings, as he wrote down the number I gave him. Meanwhile, Sergeant Wilkins stood to attention beside the desk with a smile on his face that would have done credit to a Cheshire cat, while waiting for the officer to pronounce sentence.

Instead, the young officer chose to glance up at me and ask, "What regiment are you attached to?"

Feigning surprise, I stammered, "Oh! I don't belong to any regiment. I'm in the Merchant Service," and waited for his response.

Sergeant Wilkins looked as if he'd been struck by lightning, his mouth dropped open and the sloppy grin disappeared from his face.

Turning to the Sergeant, the officer asked, "Why did you bring this man before me, without asking for his particulars?"

Caught with his pants down, so to speak, Sergeant Wilkins stuttered, "Well, sir, he's wearing hospital blues, so I took it for granted he was in the armed forces."

"Oh," said the young officer, a measure of sarcasm in his voice. "If a donkey is put into uniform it doesn't necessarily mean it's in the army, does it, Sergeant?"

"Er, no, sir," he muttered, standing to attention.

In a quick about turn, the young officer adopted a more courteous manner toward me, apologising for the abject stupidity of one of his subordinates. I made my peace with the officer, who apologized and, in typical gentlemanly fashion, shook me by the hand and blamed the episode on an error of judgement by one of his men. I took my leave of him. It was comforting to know I was rather more fortunate than a young soldier I had befriended some time earlier in the day, who having called the Matron a silly old fart (which in essence she no doubt was) earned him seven days in the glasshouse.

Lunch having been long overdue, I hurried back to my hospital ward in search of a morsel of food and almost collided with my old adversary, Sergeant Wilkins, whom I'd just had words with. Glowering at me, he hissed, "I'd love to get you in the army."

Without a moment's hesitation, I shouted, "Sod you and your army, mister, you can keep your bull shit."

Before he had time to reply, I'd taken to my heels, never to set eyes on his like again. Whether he'd been waylaid on some dark night by a soldier he'd been bullying, I'll never know or care. Suffice to say the authorities did not take kindly to my rebellious attitude against army rules or regulations. That eventually lead to my premature departure from the hospital. Some two days later, I was hurriedly transferred to a convalescent home, in the middle of nowhere, run by a couple of bible punchers.

Italian bombers over Malta.

One could say they put me out to grass on this barren hilltop retreat to teach me a lesson, where I endured a further month of boredom.

Unaccustomed to living the life of a nomad, I requested they move me nearer civilisation and, in doing so, faced many unexpected problems on the way. From the outset, I had no idea I'd be jumping out of the frying pan into the fire and eagerly accepted a move to the harbour area, when they promised me an early flight home. Taking up residence at the bug-ridden Bristol Hotel in a last ditch effort to get off this war-torn island was, without doubt, a tactless blunder on my part.

As night fell, the mournful sound of an air raid siren sent the population running for their lives to the nearest shelter. This only served to remind me of the foolish mistake I'd made.

Taking cover with the hotel residents, I followed them down an iron staircase leading to the bowels of the earth, where I stood shivering and cursing those responsible for luring me into this dump. For I now found myself trapped within the four walls of a sleazy hotel down in the harbour area of Valletta among the rubble of burnt-out buildings on this beleaguered island, where the sound of gunfire had become a way of life.

Above the sound of bombs bursting overhead and the chatter of anti-aircraft fire, Maltese families living in tiny rooms, hewn out of the rock, carried on with their daily lives, one hundred feet below ground level. How they managed to keep themselves warm in that air raid shelter is beyond me. The atmosphere was so cold and damp an old man standing beside me, waiting for the all clear signal, spent most of the time rubbing his frozen limbs, in an effort to restore the circulation.

"I bet it's some trigger happy army whallah that's set the air raid alarm off," he grumbled.

"Yes, it's probably another false alarm," said a by-stander, another one of the hotel residents waiting to hear the all clear.

The man was shabbily dressed and told me he'd been fitted out with cast off clothing, donated by some relief organization for distressed seamen, which no doubt was true, seeing that the canvas shoes he wore were long past their sell-by date. Like many survivors from the Pedestal convoy, I lost every stitch of clothing I possessed and arrived at Malta as naked as the day I was born.

My departure from hospital in khaki battledress was reason enough to pay a hurried visit to the naval tailors in the harbour area, to fit myself out in civilian clothes. Suitably dressed in grey flannel trousers and green checked hacking jacket with brown leather buttons, I had no wish to be mistaken for a member of His Majesty's forces, ever again.

Meanwhile, having now waited for hours on end in this damp bone-chilling air raid shelter beneath the Bristol Hotel, the distant wail of the all clear signal was music to my ears. It was shortly after one o'clock in the morning when I stretched cramped and frozen limbs to climb back up a winding staircase to my hotel room.

"Maybe, we'll get some sleep now," I said to the old man.

"Huh, you'll be lucky," he grimaced, rubbing his hands together once again. "You'll get no sleep in this flea pit, mark my word."

Bidding him goodnight, I closed the door of my room and ate what few grapes I'd managed to salvage from our evening meal, before slipping out of my clothes and into bed. Thoroughly exhausted, both mentally and physically after a long tiring day of travel, I lay between the lumps and bumps of a worn-out mattress, and listened for the moaning sound of an air-raid siren, until dozing off. Waking at intervals, I sought to free myself from the barbed end of springs poking out of the mattress puncturing my body, or to give myself a good old scratch. I was much too tired and weary to get up out of bed to discover the reason for my discomfort, so decided to wait until the pale light of dawn.

As morning sunlight filtered through the tattered remnants of an old lace curtain draped across my window, I'd had enough and carefully pried myself free from half a dozen springs holding me fast. Throwing back the bedclothes, I was shocked to find a squadron of fleas had been feasting throughout the night on blood I could ill afford to part with, and were now escaping in all directions.

At breakfast that morning, I complained to the hotel manager, a balding Maltese character with a pock-marked face and sad brown eyes, who listened impassively.

"Ah, so the little fellows get to bite you, mister," grinned the bald one. "You eat plenty garlic, my friend, they not touch you," he said.

As he spoke, I caught a whiff of his garlic laden breath, deciding it was not for me and sought to find some other remedy. Slipping aboard the *M.V. Melbourne Star* berthed in Valetta harbour, a word in the ear of the ship's friendly Chief Steward convinced him I was in desperate need of something to kill the pests. Leaving the ship armed with a quantity of D.D.T. powder, I planned to polish off the bloodsuckers before they bled me dry.

That night, I gave the bedsheets a liberal dusting of the magic powder to ensure I had a good night's sleep. Waking early next morning I pulled back the bedclothes to find a multitude of fleas laying motionless. I was now prepared to tolerate living in this flea pit for the time being with a regular supply of D.D.T. close at hand. Thankfully, my stay there was short lived.

Relief came, as darkness fell one evening in mid-December of 1942, when the authorities informed me I should get ready to leave the Island of Malta. So, having spent the last five months on this battle-scarred island, my enforced stay was coming to an end at last. It was almost midnight when I arrived at Luqua, one of Malta's heavily defended airfields, and waited until the early hours of the morning when I was allowed to board an American DC Douglas aircraft.

CHAPTER 19

AU REVOIR, MALTA

A smooth take-off saw us climbing above banks of heavy cloud, enabling our pilot to avoid contact with a formation of enemy fighters known to be in the vicinity. By dawn's early light, Gibraltar's lofty peak, at the western end of the Mediterranean, was seen to rise out of the morning mist, like some colossus. Outside the harbour area, dark grey silhouettes of naval vessels patrolling up and down were the only sign a war was raging in the vicinity.

Of strategic importance in safeguarding Allied interests in this theatre of war, the Rock, as Gibraltar is often referred to, was ceded to Great Britain by Spain in 1713. (Due to much pressure from the Spanish Government after hostilities had ceased, a referendum in 1967 for the return of this British Protectorate to Spain was ignored by the people of Gibraltar, who wished to remain a British Dependency.)

.   .   .

On a bright sunny morning, in early December of 1942, I stepped from the aircraft onto the tarmac at Gibraltar shortly after eight a.m. and breathed a sigh of relief. Our flight from the Island of Malta was no joy ride, as we played games of hide and seek with the enemy among the clouds. I was frozen stiff and delighted to have an opportunity to stretch my aching limbs, and feel the warmth of the morning sun on my back. Waiving aside the usual formalities one is accustomed to at airports, I along with many survivors from the ill-fated Pedestal convoy, were accommodated at the Winter Gardens Hotel situated high up on the Rock.

Leaving my hotel shortly after lunch that day, I set off to explore the main shopping area, some twenty minutes walking distance away. Here, in the City of Gibraltar, an abundance of duty-free goods unavailable in Britain were on display in many of the stores. Along its sidewalks, tables and chairs were set out in continental style inviting one to sample the many delicacies each café had to offer.

Around three o'clock each afternoon, the traditional cup of tea is taken by off-duty members of the armed forces stationed here, a favourite meeting place for local gossip. At a table on the sidewalk, I sat near a group of young servicemen waiting to be served.

Approaching my table, the waiter politely asked, "Can I take your order, sir?"

"I'd like a pot of tea and some cakes, please," I replied.

Within minutes, the table was laden with a fine pot of tea and a plate of the most delicious cream cakes that I had set eyes on for many a long day. Spellbound, I could only sit and admire the chocolate-covered eclairs with their fresh cream filling, and mouth-watering cream slices. With the pangs of hunger gnawing at my stomach, I was about to bite into one of them when I remembered seeing those poor young children on the streets of Malta, begging for food. Filled with a sense of guilt, I stayed my hand and wished the cakes would disappear, when a peal of laughter rang out from a nearby table.

Watching me hesitate to eat a mouth-watering cream cake, a young soldier sitting nearby laughed aloud, and said, "Don't look at them, hurry up and eat 'em, or you'll 'ave the bleeding rock apes pinching them. Go on, get 'em down yer," he urged, stuffing another chocolate eclair into his own mouth. With several of his pals watching, I devoured a cream slice. Resisting the temptation to eat another,

I rose from the table still hungry, and sauntered back to the hotel. Shortly after seven o'clock that evening, the chimes of the dinner gong sent me and my hungry fellow travellers, in a spirited dash for the dining-room.

Seated round a table laid out for dinner, our group of starving Merchant seamen waited patiently for the food to arrive. Knives and forks at the ready, we were Hell bent on devouring everything in sight. Having made short work of the soup, a main course of roast beef, fresh vegetables and the sauteed potatoes being served, the clatter of knives and forks suddenly ceased, stilled by the wailing of an air raid siren.

Within minutes, the huge dining-room doors were thrown open by a couple of army red caps who ordered residents to leave the hotel for some nearby air raid shelters. Protesting loudly, several seamen halfway through the evening meal refused to leave the dining room, until they'd had their fill. Warned they would be punished for refusing to obey orders, they took with them what little food was to be had from the table and, with some reluctance, followed their shipmates out of the hotel.

Night was upon us by the time the all-clear sounded and, with Gibraltar in total darkness, we stumbled along a well-worn footpath back to the hotel, to be politely informed the raid was a false alarm.

Nothing more than an exercise to keep us on our toes, one of the hotel guests grumbled. "Why there hasn't been an air raid on the rock for over six months," he said.

Nodding in agreement, the seamen made a beeline for the hotel dining-room, wasting little time devouring whatever food the waiter could put on the table, determined to enjoy their first decent meal for many a day.

Prior to my departure later that month, an influx of merchant seamen rescued from ships torpedoed out in the Atlantic were put ashore in Gibraltar. It was now mid-winter in the northern hemisphere with many among the survivors having been adrift in an open boat for days on end with nothing to eat, suffering untold deprivation. Few among us who'd seen and experienced the horrors of war had any desire to be repatriated to England in a hurry, knowing we'd have to face the same hazards again, once we were back at sea.

It is often said, nothing is forever, and having sampled the good life in this far-flung British outpost of Gibraltar, where the living is easy and food plentiful, it came as quite a shock to us all when the

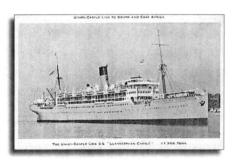

The Llanstephan Castle *arrives off England's southern coast.*

bubble burst. I was quite content to idle away the hours in peace and serenity with all the comforts of home, when, on a bright sunny morning some two days later, it all changed.

Seen as no more than a blot on the far horizon when the early morning mist had cleared, it posed no immediate threat. But as the dark grey shape drew closer, we discovered it was a large troop ship. Edging ever closer, like an angry black cloud preceding a storm, she turned sharply to port, and made ready to enter the harbour of Gibraltar. As she passed us by, the vessel's name, hardly distinguishable 'neath a layer of battleship gray, was later identified as the *M.V. Llanstephan Castle*, one of several passenger liners taken over by the government as a troop ship.

The vessel's arrival in Gibraltar set the scene for a period of feverish activity when some two to three hundred merchant seamen, staying in hotels around the peninsula, were put aboard. Sadly, many of these men had just recently arrived in Gibraltar after being rescued out in the north Atlantic in bitterly cold winter weather so were given little opportunity to sample the good life we had now become accustomed to. Some twenty-four hours later, we sailed from this land of plenty, under cover of darkness in the wake of a naval escort and, passing Gibraltar's submarine defence, set course for home.

.   .   .

Leaving our Mediterranean skies of blue with endless days of warm sunshine, we ran into the Bay of Biscay's stormy waters, whipped up by bone-chilling easterly winds. Back in winter's grip, the *Llanstephan Castle*, all twenty thousand tons of her, ducked and dived her way across mountainous seas.

Approaching home waters, extra lookouts from among three hundred survivors taking passage on board were placed at vantage points throughout the ship. Vigilance against surprise attacks by U-boats hunting in wolf packs around our shores had to be maintained at all times. Steaming down the English Channel at a speed of 16 knots, the *Llanstephan Castle* passed the blacked-out naval dockyard at Plymouth, as local fishing boats set sail on their nightly trawl.

Nearing Lands End, fingers of light from Eddystone Rock lighthouse, west of England's southern shores, pierced the night sky, flashing out its message of welcome, beckoning us home from the sea. Altering course abeam of the Isles of Scilly, we faced gale force westerly winds upon entering the Irish Sea.

Shadowed by our naval escort, the vessel zig-zagged her way through banks of fragmented sea mist, along Scotland's West Coast, to an anchorage at the Port of Gourock on the Firth of Clyde. The noise of our anchor cable, as it rattled down the hausepipe around midnight, was enough to waken the dead, shattering the peace and tranquillity of these silent waters, as it disappeared into the depths below.

Wakened at daybreak on the morning of December 20, 1942 by the cry of gulls on the wing, I stepped out on the deck of the *Llanstephan Castle* to survey this vast expanse of water swirling around me. As though it were yesterday, I recalled a night in July of 1942, when these same waters were host to a collection of merchant ships and men'o'war, setting out to do battle with the enemy.

Memories of that nightmare voyage that had its beginning here at the Port of Gourock in Scotland will forever haunt me. Our mission, to save the starving population of Malta, was undertaken at a heavy price. Many heroic crews manning those ships never returned.

There was a time during the height of the battle when, it seemed,

I had passed through the gates of Hell, as death's icy fingers brushed my cheek. Knowing, but for the grace of God, I would never have survived, I look back on this episode of the war to find there is nothing I care to remember other than the courage of our Merchant and Naval Forces, who took part in this mission against overwhelming odds. Also, the devotion to duty of a young Maltese nurse who attended my wounds, and the wonderful care provided by her and the hospital staff to the many of my wounded comrades remains with me.

I did, however, have the honour of meeting George 'Screwball' Beurling, said by many to have been Canada's greatest fighter pilot of World War II, during his tour of duty on the Island of Malta. We were introduced during a concert given by the R.A.F in aid of the children of Malta. It was said he flew upside down along Malta's main street as the oil tanker *Ohio* was being towed into Valletta harbour by naval escort vessels.

For my comrades who perished, their loved ones will have nothing but sad memories, while those among us lucky enough to have survived, will no doubt be reproached for being drunk while home on leave, trying to erase the memory of that horrendous voyage.

For the man in the street should try to imagine what it's like to be adrift on an open sea, in the middle of nowhere, burnt and beaten. Spare a thought for those in peril on the deep, and try not judge them too harshly.

If you should see them in the street
Rolling round on groggy feet,
Don't blame them for being on the spree,
Perchance you've never made a trip
On a dark and lonely ship,
Through submarine, or shark-infested sea.

CHAPTER 20

PUT OUT TO GRASS

On a damp grey morning in late December of 1942, I arrived at the Port of Gourock with three hundred and fifty British merchant seamen whose ships were destroyed by enemy action. It was shortly after midnight when we dropped anchor opposite the tiny Scottish holiday resort of Dunoon, on the Firth of Clyde.

From this very place some six months earlier a convoy set out to relieve the beleaguered Island of Malta. Now, all was still, as we lay in this quiet backwater of the Clyde, where nothing moved save for the ghostly grey shape of an escort vessel returning to base. Braving mist and rain, a group of Scottish survivors aboard waited out on the troop ship's open deck until daylight, for a glimpse of their native land.

A fragmented mist skirting the coastline slowly thickened while drizzling rain continued to fall incessantly, hiding what little there was to be seen of a bleak Scottish landscape. Returning to my cabin on B deck, all was peaceful and quiet as my comrades slept on, unaware the ship now lay at anchor back in home waters. Having brought with me little more than the clothes I stood up in, plus a couple of gifts I bought for my fiancée while in Gibraltar, I lay in my cabin waiting the call for breakfast.

When it came, it was loud enough to waken the dead. Cabin doors flew open and heads popped out in alarm, when a trumpeter playing reveille marched up and down the corridor of B deck.

"D'yer have to make such a bloody racket?" shouted an irate seaman from his cabin doorway. "We're not deaf!"

"I was told to make sure you were awake," said the Steward, holding a trumpet in his hand. "All survivors, taking passage, have to be off this ship by ten o'clock."

"Yes, we heard you, matey!" shouted Sullivan, a cocky young fellow from Liverpool. "Why don't you jerks leave us alone in peace?"

"Take your complaints to the Chief Steward. He gives the orders around here," said the trumpeter, as he hurried off.

A word in the ear of the Chief Steward at the breakfast table that morning made matters worse, "It's a wet nurse you fellows want?" he retorted. "Where the Hell do you think you are, on your Daddy's yacht?"

Around ten-thirty that morning, some two hundred survivors were ferried ashore, and taken to the seamen's mission. Arriving there, each man was issued with a railway warrant that would take them to a station nearest their home town, and given a lunch box to see them through the journey. With a party of thirty, I stepped aboard a waiting bus that whisked us away to the railway station at Gourock, a bleak and desolate place at this time of year, where we waited for our train to Liverpool.

In search of a little warmth and shelter from drizzling rain, I hurried inside a station waiting room to find graffiti-covered walls and dust-covered windows, allowing no more than a minimum of light in. Seats torn from their fastenings lay heaped together with old newspapers strewn all over the floor, amid a collection of cigarette ends, and a smell of urine that stung one's nostrils.

At first sight, I imagined the area had been hit by a bomb during an air raid, until remembering no enemy aircraft had at the time ventured this far. Pacing up and down the station platform, in an effort to keep myself from freezing to death, I popped into the ticket office on the pretext of having a conversation with the man in charge, in order to get a warm. So I asked, "What time is the next train for Liverpool?"

"In fifteen minutes, laddie," he replied, "and close the door on your way out," as he carried on reading his morning paper.

Beneath sullen skies of grey and drizzling rain that soaked me to the skin, I watched the approaching train belching plumes of black smoke from its squat chimney as it pulled into the station, and ground to a halt. No sooner had carriage doors opened allowing passengers to alight, my fellow travellers and I hurried into the nearest compartment, to rid ourselves of wet clothing sticking to our bodies. Whilst shedding our outer garments and hanging them on luggage racks to dry, little notice was taken of the two old ladies sitting in a corner of our compartment, chatting away.

"Did ye ever see the like o' that afore?" says one, pointing in our direction.

"Och, tak nae notice," said her companion, "what'll ye hae them do, lass, sit in their wet clothes? Shut your eyes, and ye'll see nothing."

Cold and hungry, my fellow travellers and I tore our luncheon boxes open to get at the food inside, as soon as the train took off. Not a word passed between us as we ate our cheese and ham sandwiches, provided by the good offices of some charitable institution. Approaching Glasgow's Central Station, the train for some unknown reason slowed to a snail's pace and the sound of children's voices were heard, out on the railway track. Half-eaten sandwiches were hurriedly put aside, as everyone scrambled to peer out of carriage windows.

With outstretched arms, several poorly-clad children begged for food, as they ran alongside our train, shouting, "Gie us a crust, mister!"

It was like a scene from Oliver Twist from the Dickensian era. Hard to believe such a thing could happen in this day and age.

In a spontaneous gesture, everyone in our carriage gave the children whatever food they had. Sandwiches, by the dozen, passed out of carriage windows were greeted with loud cries of 'Thanks, mister' from the hungry bairns. Shocked by the lack of clothing on one little girl, an elderly seaman gave her some dresses he'd brought home for his own grandchildren. With cries of thank you, several older children followed the train until we pulled into the station at Glasgow, to disappear just as suddenly as they arrived.

I bid farewell to my fellow travellers who accompanied me on the voyage from Gibraltar, and left them to make their own arrangements, while I continued on my journey south. At the ticket office, I was informed the train standing at platform four was due to leave for Liverpool in fifteen minutes, and advised to hurry on board. Leaving Glasgow Central Station, the train sped on past bleak highland hills and green valleys of Lanarkshire, then on into Dumfries, where we crossed the border into Cumberland, on England's northern border.

Passing Carlise, the train sped on through Westmorland into the County of Lancashire, to arrive at Liverpool's Lime Street station as night was falling. A waiting taxi took me through a maze of traffic in the town centre, to the Pier Head, where I was able to board a ferry and cross the River Mersey into the town of Birkenhead, in the County of Cheshire. Berthing at Woodside terminus, I caught a bus that dropped me off close to my lodgings in the village of Bebington, on the outskirts of town.

Arriving on her doorstep unannounced, Mrs Godfrey, my new landlady, welcomed me home. Widowed for many years, this kindly soul in her late fifties, managed to eke out a living running a boarding house in this tiny village. Pretty of face, the dark brown eyes were matched by the warmth of her smile. Taking off my coat and gloves, I went into the kitchen, where she waited with a cup of tea. Seeing my hands covered with bandages, she exclaimed, "My goodness, whatever happened to you, Rowland?"

Without going into detail, I told her my ship was destroyed by German dive-bombers on the voyage to Malta, and the injuries I received kept me in hospital for many months.

"I suppose you're going to be alright?" she said, a worried look on her face.

"That is for the Ministry of Pensions to decide, Mrs Godfrey," I replied, showing her a letter I had just received. "They have asked me to report to their office in Liverpool as soon as possible, which doesn't sound very encouraging."

"Will they send you to hospital?" she asked.

"Not if I can help it," I replied. "I've spent the last five months in a hospital ward in Malta."

"Thank goodness you arrived back in one piece," she replied. "So many of our young people have sacrificed their lives because of that awful fellow, Hitler."

"There'll be many more before this lot's over," I sighed. "It's going to be a long hard struggle."

Leaving the good lady to prepare the evening meal, I settled down to listen to the news from the B.B.C., having been out of touch with the latest war news for the past six months. It was most heartening to hear Allied Forces had invaded North Africa and the Eighth Army under the command of General Montgomery had Rommel's army in full retreat. This chain of events was followed by an announcement that the tide of war had turned against Germany's armies in Africa, and the Russian front. It was at this point, when I caught the aroma of our evening meal drifting in from the kitchen, that Mrs Godfrey announced supper was ready. At the table, I suggested I might slip over to Liverpool on the morrow, to pay a visit to the Ministry of Pensions.

Readily agreeing, Mrs Godfrey replied, "Well, I suppose it's best you should get it over and done with. Christmas will be upon us shortly, and they'll probably be closed for a couple of weeks."

Withdrawing the curtains of my bedroom window next morning, I was not in the least surprised to see shrubs and rose bushes in the garden appear like so many statues, shrouded in mantles of white. A layer of heavy frost covered the ground, a forerunner, one might say, of a hard winter to come. I shivered at the thought and, recalling those warm sunny days I'd spent beneath Mediterranean skies of blue, wished I were back there, not, however, under the same circumstances. As I sat there reminiscing, Mrs Godfrey's call for breakfast broke my train of thought.

"We have quite a covering of frost on the garden this morning, Rowland," she exclaimed, as I sat at table with her. "You'll have to wrap up well when you go out," she said. "Will you be visiting your fiancée later?"

"Why do you ask, Mrs Godfrey, is there anything wrong?" I replied.

"Oh, no, Rowland," she said. "It's just that your fiancée came round asking if I'd heard from you, a couple of weeks after you left. I haven't set eyes on her since. Although, I'm sure she'll be pleased to see you back safe and sound."

"Maybe I'll wait until after my interview with the Ministry of Pensions," I replied.

Glancing at the kitchen clock, I reminded the good lady it was time I was leaving for my appointment, and promised to be back for lunch. Wrapped up against biting winds on that cold frosty morning, I had to tread carefully along the road's icy surface and, reaching the terminus, waited for the bus to arrive. Boarding the vehicle as it skidded to a halt, I welcomed what little warmth and comfort the bus afforded my frozen limbs.

At Woodside terminus, I caught a ferry across the Mersey to the city of Liverpool. As I stepped ashore I saw the familiar green-encrusted twin towers of the Liver Buildings overlooking the waterfront, with the fabled Liver Birds perched on top. Close by, stands the Offices of the Mersey Docks and Harbour Company, a magnificent example of Gothic architecture.

Wandering through a maze of narrow back streets on the outskirts of the city, in search of the Ministry of Pensions Office, it was merely by chance I happened to find it behind a row of bomb-damaged dwelling houses. Smoke and sulphur fumes from chimneys of nearby factories had, with time, discoloured the white marble frontage, giving it a greyish appearance. Entering the building, I handed the letter to the young lady in the foyer, who directed me along a passage to a door marked, conference room. A murmur of voices from within the room ceased abruptly as I knocked on the door. A voice commanded, "Come in, please."

Three gentlemen seated round an oval table looked up as I entered the room. The eldest, a silver-haired gent in a smart grey suit, wore gold rimmed spectacles. Looking up from some papers he'd been studying, he politely asked, "Can I help you, young man?"

Handing my letter of introduction to him, I stammered, "I've been asked to report here."

A puzzled expression creased the gentleman's face as he took the letter, and studied it carefully. It must have suddenly crossed his mind he'd written to me, for he smiled, and said, "Why, of course, Mr Marshall, we've been expecting a visit from you for some time, having no idea when you would arrive back in this country." Then pointing to a chair, he requested I be seated opposite him.

Introducing himself and his colleagues as medical practitioners, he informed me they were acting on behalf of the Ministry of Pensions, in order to assess the extent of my war injuries. From a briefcase, he withdrew a sheaf of papers and studying me for a moment, said, "May I see the back of your hands, Mr Marshall?"

Carefully removing my gloves, I placed my hands on the table in front of him palms down, and heard his sharp intake of breath as he examined them. I watched, in dismay, as he shook his head, to say, "I'm afraid they are going to take a considerable time to heal, Mr Marshall. The skin still seems quite tender."

As he ran the tips of his fingers over my wounds, I gritted my teeth when a spasm of pain shot up my arms. Putting on a brave face, I smiled, knowing deep inside that my stomach was in revolt. I felt sick, and on the verge of regurgitating my breakfast.

Apologizing profusely, he told me the skin on the back of my hands was not taken from my body, but a new method of grafting known as tulle-gra. He then dampened my spirits further, for he went on to say, "I'm afraid we are, none of us, satisfied with the progress of your healing, as your present condition suggests."

It was then the elder of the trio, whose name I learned was Dr

McArdle, spoke of the ill-fated convoy codenamed Pedestal, and re-marked, "I must say, from what little information we were given concerning the fate of your convoy and its mercy mission to Malta, you are a lucky young man to come out of it alive. According to this report, you suffered third degree burns to both hands, restricting movement of your fingers. You will no doubt have great difficulty in using them effectively for some considerable time to come. I would recommend you see a physiotherapist, when your wounds have healed sufficiently."

It was at this point Dr. McArdle made the decision of his medical panel known, saying, "We are satisfied the damage to your hands may be irreversible." Pausing a moment to check some papers lying on his desk, he continued, in a more sombre tone, and said, "Due to the nature of your injuries, we are of the opinion you will not be fit to work for the foreseeable future, and have decided to award you a full disability pension."

I was stunned into silence by the Ministry's decision and sat there immobile, staring into space. I could not believe this was being said for my benefit. While I realized there was no way on earth I'd be fit to work for at least the next six months, I never dreamt I'd be thrown on the scrap heap, at the age of twenty-three. This was something I was not willing to accept. Without a word of protest, I left the conference room, with my sea career in the balance, and hurried out of the building.

Realizing the way ahead looked uncertain, there remained deep within me an irresistible desire to fulfil my boyhood dream. I was resolved that one day I might, against the odds, resume my career at sea. In pursuit of my goal, I determined there would be no lack of enthusiasm on my part to take up this challenge, should the opportunity arise. Meantime, I would seek the advice of my family doctor, to speed my recovery.

Wandering aimlessly along narrow streets, on the outskirts of a city littered with rubble, I somehow managed to find my way back to the Pier Head, on Liverpool's waterfront. Waiting to board a ferry that would take me back across the River Mersey, I watched several ocean-going ships arrive with much-needed war supplies. Vessels in dock along a seven-mile stretch of Liverpool's waterfront worked night and day to discharge their cargoes, while ships lying at anchor in the river waited their turn to berth. Within a matter of days, these same ships would be back at sea with the crews manning them, given little enough time ashore with their families.

Sailing to and fro across the North Atlantic, facing gale force winds, mountainous seas, and at times, bitterly cold weather, they would perchance arrive in America, if they were lucky enough to avoid the many enemy submarines lying in wait for them. Having survived, they would reload further supplies of war material and, once again, face the elements and surface raiders like the German battleship *Graf Spee* prowling the high seas in search of easy prey. Yet in spite of all the hazards one faces at sea, in time of war and peace, I would rather be outward bound aboard one of those ships, sailing off to God knows where.

For the time being however, I had other things on my mind as I waited for the local ferry. Along with some fifty or so would-be travellers at the pierhead, I waited for passengers on an incoming ferry to disembark, then hurried on board in search of shelter and warmth from a bitterly cold east wind. Through a window in the ship's lounge, I watched the vessel perform her acrobatic manoeuvres, as she fought against wind and tide. Ducking and diving on her way back across the river, I heaved a sigh of relief when we berthed at the Woodside terminus in Birkenhead.

Wasting little time, I hurried ashore and, hiring a taxi from several waiting there, set off for the village of Bebington.

As I entered the lounge, Mrs Godfrey looked up from the book she was reading and, smiling, said, "Can I offer you a cup of tea, Rowland?"

"That would be most welcome," I replied, and divesting the heavy overcoat I wore, remarked, "It's jolly cold out there."

Mrs Godfrey disappeared into the kitchen, returning a minute later to sit with me for a chit-chat, over a cup of tea.

"Well now, Rowland," she said, "tell me how was your day?"

"Not good at all, Mrs Godfrey," I replied.

"What do you mean?" she said, a look of concern on her face. "Did they say you'd have to go back to hospital for some sort of treatment?"

"It's of a more serious nature than that, Mrs Godfrey," I assured her. "They told me I would not be fit to work, for the foreseeable future. So it seems, I've been thrown on the scrap heap, if you please."

"But I thought they were short of men?" she insisted.

"Yes, Mrs Godfrey, every able-bodied seaman is needed at sea right now, I must agree with you, but try telling that to the Medical Officer at the Ministry of Pensions. Until they are satisfied my hands have healed, there is little I can do about it."

"Oh, I'm sure something can be done for you," she exclaimed. "Isn't there some treatment they could give you that would help with your recovery?"

"Maybe my family doctor could advise me," I suggested. "I'll make an appointment to see him as soon as possible."

"What about your fiancée, Rowland?" said Mrs Godfrey. "Don't you think you should see her and tell her what's happened? I'm sure she'll understand."

"Yes, I suppose I really should pay her a visit. I'll see her this evening," I countered, in an effort to change the subject.

"But she must be wondering where you are?" the good lady replied. "I think it best you see her."

"She'll probably want to know why I haven't written to her since I left," I replied. "Letters from abroad are censored, in an effort to stop vital information useful to the enemy being disclosed. Shipping companies are now forbidden to disclose movements of their vessels as they did in time of peace. Why this war has changed everything, Mrs Godfrey," I replied.

"Didn't you tell her your hands were injured while you were in hospital at Malta?" Mrs Godfrey asked. "Surely someone could have written a note for you, in your condition?"

"She hasn't received a letter from me since the day I left," I told the good lady, "so she's not likely to be overjoyed about that, I'm sure. I'll wait to see what happens when I visit her tonight."

"I hope she'll understand the awkward situation you are in, Rowland," Mrs Godfrey said with a sigh.

At six o'clock that evening, I switched on the radio and listened to the latest war information from the B.B.C. The announcer appeared to be in buoyant mood, as he read the evening news. I could almost feel the excitement mounting in his normally subdued voice, when he said, "Allied troops have continued their advance throughout North Africa and Admiral Darlan, Commander-In-Chief of Vichy French Naval forces, has been assassinated."

It now looked as if the tide of war had turned in favour of the Allies on both the Russian and North African fronts, easing tension in the Mediterranean. Ships were now supplying much needed food and medical supplies to the beleaguered Island of Malta, since the enemy's stranglehold on the island had been broken.

Switching the radio off as soon as the evening news had finished, I entered the dining-room where Mrs Godfrey had the table set out for two. "Tea is ready," she said, placing a dish of freshly cooked ham on the table, "so let's eat."

"How on earth did you manage to get food like this?" I asked, pointing to the ham.

Grinning good-humouredly, she remarked, "You know what they say about careless talk costing lives?"

Not wishing to pursue the matter further, knowing like everyone else in the country she was subject to rationing, I failed to understand how in times like this she managed to rustle up the most appetizing meals. Was her local butcher a close relative, I wondered?

As the meal ended, Mrs Godfrey asked, "How did you enjoy the meal, Rowland?"

"Most enjoyable," I replied, "just like those served up in many New York restaurants."

"Ah, yes, I'm going to miss the little luxuries you used to bring home from America. They were a great help. I really appreciated them," she said.

Agreeing with her, I replied tongue in cheek, "Who among us can tell what the future holds."

With that, I bid Mrs Godfrey goodnight and stepped out on a bitterly cold winter's night, to visit my fiancée, knowing the good lady would long be abed before I returned. Not a glimmer of light was to be seen in the darkened street outside, as I cautiously made my way along a tree lined avenue, dotted with icy patches.

Being an only child, my lady friend looked after her widowed mother in her detached bungalow, lying back off the main road.

The house itself lay some half a mile distant, on the outskirts of the village, in a secluded cul-de-sac, where no one would be up and about at this hour in the blackout, other than the local warden on his nightly round.

A pale moon, having risen above a thickly wooded copse, shed a beam of light on a row of small bungalows lying in total darkness, where no visible sign of life came from within. My knock on the door of number twenty-two brought an immediate response. The sound of heavy bolts being withdrawn must have roused the neighbours, as the door opened no more than a couple of inches and, a woman's voice, I recognized as that of my fiancée's mother, asked, "Who are you, and what do you want?"

"It's Rowland Marshall, Mrs Hulbert," I responded. "I've just arrived back home from sea."

I heard her sharp intake of breath and a half-strangled cry of, "Oh! Just a moment."

Safety chains attached to the door were released and, from inside a darkened doorway, she invited me in. Closing the door behind her, she drew the blackout curtain across, before switching on the light, illuminating the darkened hallway. I must have startled her for she looked pale and drawn as if she'd seen a ghost, and invited me into an adjoining room. From the foot of the stairs she called her daughter, who was busy in her bedroom, "Are you there, Marjorie?" she said.

There was a momentary pause, and in a faltering voice, Mrs Hulbert said, "Rowland is here to see you, dear."

I heard my fiancée's gasp of surprise, followed by the sound of her footsteps, as she hurried down stairs. From the hallway I heard snatches of conversation between Mother and daughter only to cease abruptly as the lounge door swung open. Ashen-faced she stared at me for a moment as though I were a ghost from the past, and shaking like a leaf, whispered, "Where on earth have you come from, Rowland? The War Office informed me you were missing in action, presumed dead."

"Good Lord, who gave you that information?" I asked.

From a drawer of her desk, she withdrew a large brown envelope and, handing it to me, said, "This arrived some months ago."

In bold black type on the envelope, the words O.H.M.S. leaped out at me. Inside was an official document from the War Office, which simply stated, "We regret to inform you, your fiancé, Mr Rowland Charles Marshall, has been reported missing in action, presumed dead."

There were no specific details to say what happened to me on that voyage to Malta, just a curt apology from some official at the War Office. I tried to explain to my fiancée why I had not written to her and how lucky I was to be alive, but she just sat there for minutes on end as though made of stone, refusing to look in my direction. When at last she turned my way, it was to stare at me, as if I were to blame for what had happened. I could see she was upset. Her pretty face flushed with anger, she said, "I'm sick of this damned war."

The rest of the sentence was cut short when her mother appeared from the kitchen carrying a tea tray, and said, "Why don't you take off your coat while you have tea with us, Rowland? It's a cold night, so you'll feel the benefit of it, when you leave."

As I slipped my coat and gloves off, my bandaged hands brought gasps of alarm from the pair of them.

"Whatever's happened to your hands?" Marjorie cried.

"I'm lucky to be here," I replied. "Most of my comrades perished on that voyage to Malta."

A trifle puzzled by my remark, she replied, "I don't know what you mean."

Briefly, I told her my ship was destroyed by enemy action during a voyage to Malta, and the injuries I sustained were by no means comparable to the loss of life suffered by most of the ship's company.

"You will be going back to sea, won't you?" she ventured.

"Not for a while I'm afraid. As of today, I am no longer fit for sea service, according to the Ministry of Pensions, who saw fit to award me a full disability pension," I replied. "It appears as if my career at sea is in the lap of the Gods."

A worried look creased her brow, for she asked, "Does that mean you'll not be going back to sea again?"

Uncertain if she were prepared to accept the situation I now found myself in, I replied, "Not for the foreseeable future, I'm afraid."

Her face suddenly paled with the shock and for a minute we stood facing each other in abject silence. When next she spoke, her voice sounded hollow, for she said, "I'm sorry, Rowland, there is no way I'll marry an invalid. Our engagement is off."

"Marjorie, I'm not a cripple," I protested. "In a matter of weeks I'll be back at work again."

"I'm not prepared to take that chance," she countered. "Mother and I are barely managing to survive on the meagre wage I earn and a pitiful allowance she receives from the government, as a widow's pension." She was quite adamant that anything I said would not alter her decision, it was obviously clear her mind was made up.

Rising from my chair, I stepped into the hall and took my overcoat and gloves from her mother who, waiting there, said with a sigh, "I'm sorry, Rowland, there is nothing I can do that will change her mind."

"Mrs Hulbert," I replied, "it's not your fault, I realize that."

At the front door I took my leave and, bidding her goodbye, stepped out into the dark of night. A waning moon shed its watery light on ice covered pavements, where none but the bravest would dare venture out on a night such as this. With careful step, I inched my way home and as expected Mrs Godfrey's house was in total darkness, showing not a glimmer of light. Inserting my key into the lock, the door slid open at a touch and as I stepped inside the house, a flow of warm air brushed my face. Closing the door behind me, I felt my way along the darkened hallway to the foot of the stairs, where I slipped my shoes off, and crept silently up to bed.

From Mrs Godfrey's bedroom, I heard the sound of her heavy breathing, a kind of buzzing noise, like that of a bee extracting honey from the flowers. There lies a happy soul at rest, I said to myself, would I be that fortunate? Closing the door of my bedroom, so as not to disturb the good lady from her melodious slumbers, I undressed, and slipped between the sheets. Unable to sleep, I lay there, tossing and turning for quite some time, wondering if there were some form of treatment available to me, one that would quickly heal my injured hands.

Should I seek my family doctor's advice, or read up about my injury at the local library, I kept asking myself as I lay there.

Wakened around eight-thirty next morning by the ringing of the telephone, I rubbed the sleep from my eyes and, slipping on my dressing gown, reached the lounge as the phone went dead. The aroma of freshly made toast lingered in the kitchen, but of my landlady, there was no sign. There was, however, a message on the kitchen table telling me she had to go out shopping, and would be back in time for lunch.

Having decided to pay a visit to my doctor who lived some distance away in town, I snatched a hurried breakfast, and made ready to leave the house. With overnight temperatures dropping below freezing, a downpour of hailstones in the early hours of the morning hid much of the landscape beneath a blanket of ice. Wrapped in a heavy winter overcoat, I stepped out into the chill morning air. My path to the nearest bus stop, some twenty yards away was, if anything, hazardous.

Finding little protection from a bitterly cold east wind, I made ready to board the bus as it slithered to a stop, spraying waiting passengers with a shower of hailstones. The bus slipping and sliding at frequent intervals on the icy road, some elderly passengers decided to leave the vehicle long before reaching their destinations, saying it was too dangerous to go any further. One irate passenger went so far as to accuse the man in charge of reckless driving, saying, "I could do better than that with my eyes closed. You're not safe to be left in charge of a pram."

Not wishing to get mixed up into what could have developed into a free-for-all, I slipped off the bus a couple of blocks further on and walked the rest of the way to the doctor's surgery, to keep my appointment. Giving my particulars to the receptionist, I sat in the waiting room until my name was called some twenty minutes later.

"Doctor will see you now, Mr Marshall," the young lady said, showing me into his consulting room.

Dr Richards, a man in his late fifties looking a lot younger than his years suggested, was well built with an abundance of hair, greying slightly at the temples. With the normal good manners a doctor affords his patients, he welcomed me in, and asked, "What can I do for you, Mr Marshall?"

"Is there any help or advice you can offer me to heal these hands of mine, doctor?" I asked. Then I explained, as best as I could, how I came to be injured on a ship destroyed by enemy action, carrying a cargo of high octane and explosives.

Examining my hands for a few minutes, he said, "The damage is not as serious as it seems. They can be healed with time and patience. I suggest you purchase a quantity of saline water and two sponges from the drug store. Bathe your hands in the solution, three times a day, using the sponges to exercise your fingers."

Thanking Dr Richards, I bid him goodbye and slipped into a nearby drug store for the medication I required.

"Ah, you're back in time for lunch, Rowland," my landlady said with a smile. "How did you get on at the doctor's, was he of any help to you?"

"A damn sight more helpful than that lot at the Ministry of Pensions," I replied. "He advised me to bathe my hands in warm saline water three times a day, and use these sponges to exercise my fingers," I replied, showing her them.

"Take this with you, it will do to bathe your hands in," she said after lunch, and handed me a small white bowl as I made to go upstairs to the bathroom.

Christmas was only a matter of days away and, with rationing as tight as ever, Mrs Godfrey was anxious to get her shopping in early. Luxuries such as tropical fruit and many other commodities imported from abroad before the war, would once again be missing from the dinner table during this festive season of 1942, with hostilities dragging on into a fourth year.

The Allied offensive at El Alamein in late October of 1942 saw Rommel's army in North Africa in full retreat. Since then, the bombing of our towns and cities having ceased, the tide of war in Europe had now swung in favour of the Allies.

Needless to say, our conversation at the dinner table that day centred on the advent of Christmas, with the good lady saying, "I suppose you'll be buying a Christmas present for your lady friend, Rowland. She must have been surprised to see you last night?"

"Shocked, would be more appropriate, Mrs Godfrey," I replied, showing her the letter my fiancée received from the War Office.

"Oh dear, how upsetting for her," said Mrs Godfrey, a look of concern on her face. "What did she have to say?"

"She's broken off our engagement," I replied.

"Why, has she found someone else?" the good lady asked.

"Not that I'm aware of, although it wouldn't surprise me if she had, seeing I haven't bothered to write her for the last six months. But as soon as she saw my hands covered in bandages, she said she's not prepared to marry an invalid."

"Then you're well rid of her, Rowland," she replied. "She has no feelings for you. There are far better fish in the sea than were ever pulled out," she remarked, trying to console me.

"If that's the case," I laughed, "maybe I've just rid myself of a shark!"

Changing the topic of our conversation, I spoke about the war and how it had affected our lives, more than we cared to admit. The post-war depression left the country suffering for over a decade with stagnation, poverty and mass unemployment during the 1920s and early 1930s. The country was just getting back on its feet in 1939, and we looked forward to a prosperous future. Then disaster struck as the chance slipped through our fingers, because of a power-crazed idiot named Hitler. We were right back where we started, at war once again with Germany, our old adversary.

Imports of foreign foodstuffs were now scarcer than ever and with food being rationed, the population tightened its belt another notch, while the country had to switch all its production from peace to war.

Even so, it seemed, nothing would deter the population enjoying the festive season of Christmas 1942, albeit with that tightening of the belt. Throughout this time, I carried on with my daily routine of bathing and exercising my fingers in a warm saline bath, which I found rather painful and difficult at first, especially when trying to clench my fists. Then, as the days and weeks slipped by, I felt the treatment was proving successful, for I could now bend my fingers with ease.

At the end of January 1943, a visit to Doctor Richards filled me with hope anew when he examined my hands, and suggested I dispose of the bandages covering them. "They have healed up nicely, Mr Marshall. You'll be back at work before you know it," he said with a grin, and added, "Massaging them each night with a medicated hand cream would be most beneficial."

Thanking Dr Richards for his help I left the surgery and felt the cold morning air chill me to the marrow, taking my breath away. Thrusting my hands deep inside the pockets of my overcoat to protect them from winter's icy blast, I headed for home. As ever, my dear old landlady was there to greet me when I stepped inside her front door, and asked, "How did you get on at the doctor's, and what did he have to say?"

Arms outstretched, I laughed like an excited school boy, and said, "Look, Mrs Godfrey, my hands are free of those unsightly bandages!"

"Oh! that's wonderful news. You must be delighted to be rid of them?"

"I most certainly am," I replied. "I feel as though I've been given a new lease of life."

With the passing of time, my hands improved beyond all expectations, even to withstanding winter's bitter weather. I now felt more at ease strolling through crowded city streets, without people staring at me, as if I had the plague. Plucking up courage, I decided to visit the Overseas Club in Liverpool, a place where seafarers from all corners of the globe met shipmates they'd sailed with in the past, to talk about old times. It was more like a social club, with library, games room and a large reception room where dances were held on Wednesday and Saturday nights. It was here by chance I met a wonderful young lady named Gladys Leswell, with whom I danced the night away, little realizing she would become my wife some eighteen months later.

Sharing many similar interests in life together, we arranged to meet whenever time permitted from her job at a nearby aircraft factory. Unlike my previous girl friend, who cast me aside because I was unable to work, this young lady was most understanding, and instrumental in helping me recover. In the days and weeks that followed, I was able to move my fingers more and more because of her help.

Prompted by her faith in me to succeed, I felt more at ease when applying for a job at the ship repair yard of Rollo Grayson and Clovers, where I managed to secure employment, once again, in the stores department.

Some weeks later, I received a reply to a letter I sent to an old shipmate of mine living in New Zealand, congratulating me on my speedy recovery. In replying, he gave me his home address, and said, "If you happen to get back to sea and find yourself in my part of the world, don't forget to visit my Mum in Wellington, she'll be real pleased to see you, sport."

By early spring of 1943, life took on a new meaning as the shadow of war receded and air raids, having been accepted as part of our daily lives, were no more than a memory one wished to forget. On Whit Sunday, May 12, the weather improved somewhat and with it came warm sunny days. Across the landscape the sun appeared to waken spring flowers from their earthbrown nurseries, to bask in its warmth.

On that particular morning, it was most noticeable that more people than usual were seen making their way to St Michael's, when church bells in the nearby village rang out, calling the faithful to prayer. While the dark clouds of war continued to threaten our neigh-bours in Europe, many in this green and pleasant land of England saw fit to offer a prayer for people who were still suffering at the hands of the enemy.

CHAPTER 21

THE INVASION OF ITALY

It was now early August of 1943 and for the past two months, I had been working seven days a week at the shipyard, with the continual clatter of the blacksmith's hammer and rivet guns pounding my ears. I soon found the job unsuitable and boring and realized that I was not cut out to waste my days languishing in this dust-laden atmosphere. I longed to be back at sea. Day after day I watched heavily-laden Merchant ships sail past my place of work, no more than a few hundred yards away. I grew restless, feeling I could not stay penned up here much longer. At night, I lay awake wondering how best to get away from the shipyard, without running into difficulties that forbid me to leave the job without permission.

By the end of August 1943, I became so unsettled with my work that I left without saying a word to anyone, and hopped aboard a train that took me across the River Mersey into the city of Liverpool.

Entering the Mercantile Marine shipping office in Canning Place, I requested an interview with the officer in charge, and asked to be given an opportunity to continue my career at sea. Because there was such a desperate shortage of seamen to man the ships, they were prepared to allow me to continue with my sea career, provided I received permission from the Ministry of Pensions. Not wishing to lose precious time, I wrote a letter to the Ministry, informing them I was now fit for duty, and wished to return to sea. As expected, they warned me any such action on my part would be at my own risk, resulting in the loss of my disability allowance.

Losing a pittance of a war injuries pension would, I decided, be no great loss so reported to the officer in charge at the shipping office, taking with me the letter I received from the Ministry of Pensions, and my discharge papers. Within forty-eight hours, I had signed on as Quartermaster and was back at sea aboard the troop ship *M.V. Monarch of Bermuda*, a former passenger liner of twenty-two thousand tons, with a top speed of twenty-one knots. Built in the early nineteen thirties for the Furness Withy Line as a cruise liner for their West Indies Service, she had been requisitioned by the Ministry of Transport at the outbreak of hostilities.

The sun had yet to rise on that summer's morning in August, as the *Monarch* left her berth at Gladstone Dock and headed out to Liverpool Bay, where the pilot was taken off in a launch allowing the vessel to rendezvous with her escorting destroyers. Steaming south at a speed of eighteen knots, word quickly spread through the ship we were heading for the Middle East, a rumour which was to prove correct, as the vessel altered course abeam of Southern Spain and passed through the Straits of Gibraltar.

When in sight of the Island of Malta, memories of that desperate do or die battle with the enemy some twelve months past, came back to haunt me. Once again, I recalled how I watched in horror as the bombs struck the vessel, igniting her cargo of high octane stowed on her foredeck, resulting in the loss of most of her crew, who were trapped in that cauldron of fire with no chance of escape. In passing the Island, I offered a prayer to my Maker for the many shipmates who perished on that fatal morning of August 13, 1942, that they may rest in peace.

The Allied invasion of Sicily, on July 10, 1943, which brought about the downfall of Mussolini and his ruling Fascist Party, was soon to follow with an assault on the Italian mainland. It therefore came as no surprise to any of us aboard the *Monarch*, to hear the vessel was heading for the Egyptian port of Alexandria.

With control of the Mediterranean firmly in Allied hands, our Middle East forces were set to invade the mainland of Italy itself by the time the *Monarch* arrived there. On the night of September 3, 1943, the vessel slipped from the harbour under cover of darkness, carrying a large contingent of troops from the Eighth Army, and headed out to sea.

By dawn's early light, an outline of the Italian coast was clearly visible on the horizon, while overhead enemy spotter planes kept a check on our every movement. Nearing our objective, enemy aircraft sneaking in to attack the vessel were chased off by Allied fighters, covering our entrance into the port of Taranto in southern Italy. Intermittent bursts of small arms fire could be heard from the shore as the *Monarch* entered the port, inching her way past sunken ships.

Amid scenes of wanton destruction, in the wake of Italy's retreating army, the vessel approached her berth with extreme caution, entering Taranto's picturesque harbour. Aided by a motor launch, we were able to get our mooring ropes ashore, securing the ship alongside a deserted wharf. With little enemy activity in and around the harbour area, other than a couple of sneak bomber raids causing negligible damage to the port's installations, troops on board the *Monarch* quickly disembarked and moved inshore.

Waiting until nightfall, our departure from the port of Taranto in the wake of two escorting naval minesweepers was undertaken as before, with safety first our watchword. The mastheads of sunken ships dotted around the harbour area were hardly visible to the naked eye on a moonless night such as this. Each one was marked by a pinpoint of red light that flickered in and out, warning passing ships of hidden dangers. From my vantage point, on the boat deck, I watched with bated breath as we followed in the wake of an escorting destroyer, zig-zagging through enemy minefields, until the ship was well out to sea.

.   .   .

In the weeks that followed, the *Monarch* returned, time and again, from Alexandria to Taranto, ferrying troops to the battle zone. Italy's surrender in early September 1943 saw British and American forces landing near Naples, to prevent the advancing German army, who were already in possession of the City of Rome, from overrunning the country.

At the end of October 1943, *M.V. Monarch of Bermuda* was withdrawn from the transport service and, leaving the Egyptian Port of Alexandria, set sail for Gibraltar. Pausing for a moment, once again, when passing Malta, I stood in silent prayer for my shipmates and ship, who had the heart ripped out of them by enemy dive-bombers.

Slipping through Gibraltar's narrow straits into the North Atlantic, the weather quickly changed from sunshine to skies of grey. Entering the Bay of Biscay, the vessel was tossed around like a child's plaything, by gale force winds and huge seas. There were times when the ship would roll around, like a drunken Polynesian hula-hula dancer, during the next twenty-four hours, doing everything except turn turtle. Diving ever deeper into huge troughs, she struggled to break surface, and at one point, I felt sure we were a goner when her lifeboats almost kissed the ocean. Such was the storm's ferocity that not until entering much calmer waters of the English Channel did the vessel regain some measure of stability, allowing the crew a few hours of respite after a horrendous passage through the Bay.

Off Lands End, an aircraft of Coastal Command intercepted the ship requesting we identify ourselves before allowing us to proceed, to our final destination. Heading in a northerly direction, our passage through an Irish Sea cloaked in a blanket of fog was fraught with danger. Coastwise vessels, criss-crossing our bows without warning during the hours of darkness, showed little regard for the safety of others. As expected, the area was a hive of activity, with the passage of ships on trade routes between Great Britain and Ireland clogging up the sea lanes. This in turn added to the hair-raising responsibility of crew members, stationed on the wing of the bridge, keeping a sharp lookout for wayward vessels in our path.

At first light on the morning of November 3, 1943, the *M.V.*

Monarch of Bermuda entered the wide reaches of the River Mersey. Looming up out of a mist-shrouded waterfront, attendant tugs took the vessel in tow, shepherding her into her berth at Gladstone dock. Already waiting at the dockside, a fleet of ambulances quickly transferred wounded servicemen to hospitals, in and around the city.

Along with members of the crew signing off the ship late that afternoon, I lost no time packing my bags and hurrying ashore, relieved my three-month stint of duty in the Middle East was over. Making my way back to my lodgings, I was welcomed, once again, by Mrs Godfrey.

"Thank goodness, your home," she exclaimed, as I set foot inside her front door. "Your lady friend phoned several times while you've been away, asking if I've heard from you, so will you let her know you have just arrived back home, Rowland?"

As soon as I'd finished unpacking, I dialled Gladys's number and heard her casual hello change to a cry of delight, when hearing my voice. "Rowland, where are you?" she asked, somewhat anxiously. "I've received no word from you since you went off to sea, and was worried lest something had happened to you."

"My ship arrived back home today," I replied. "I'm sorry to hear you haven't received my letters, dear, but as you are well aware, overseas mail is censored these days, so delivery could take forever."

"When will I see you?" she asked.

"Barring an earthquake, this evening," I laughed, and heard her sigh of relief, as I rang off. Mrs Godfrey calling from the kitchen, said tea was ready.

"Is everything alright?" the good lady asked, as I took my place at the table. She no doubt remembered the problem I faced with my previous girl friend, and, with this in mind, asked, "There's no bother I hope, Rowland?"

"Just a technical hitch, Mrs Godfrey," I assured her. "The letters I wrote to her while abroad have been delayed. She will, I'm sure, receive them in due course."

"Does she mind you being back at sea?" Mrs Godfrey asked.

"I have no choice to do otherwise while the war is on, but I've promised her I'll find a job ashore as soon as it's over. There are many openings I can explore," I replied.

Rain was falling in a steady drizzle that evening when I set off to meet Gladys. Wrapped up against a cold and damp November night, it was more by instinct my footsteps led me to the young lady's house, where not glimmer of light was to be seen. In answer to my knock on her door, I heard the note of caution in her voice as she held the door ajar, and asked, "Is that you, Rowland?"

"Yes, dear," I replied. "Can I come in, it's jolly cold out here?" Having just returned from daytime temperatures of one hundred degrees, the cold November night air gave me the shivers.

"Mind your step as you come in," she whispered, drawing a heavy blackout curtain to one side.

"It's as black as the ace of spades in here," I laughed, groping around in the dark. "I can't see a thing."

"Here, take my hand," she giggled.

Soft to the touch, her warm hand clasped mine, as she closed the front door, and switched on the hall light.

"Ooh, you're frozen," she gasped. "Come and warm yourself by the fire."

Together we moved down the lighted hallway where she paused to say, "Hold still a moment, I'll have to draw the blackout curtain across the door. If old man Philips, our A.R.P. warden, sees a chink of light, there'll be Hell to pay."

From an adjoining room, a shaft of light pierced the gloom and her mother's voice barely audible and a trifle nervous, asked, "Who's at the door, Gladys?"

"It's Rowland," her daughter replied. "He's just arrived back home and has come to visit us."

A woman in her early sixties, her mother left the comfortable chair by the fireside as we entered the lounge, and came to meet us. She was slightly built, with an abundance of jet black hair swept back off her forehead, fastened with a velvet ribbon at the nape of the neck, and her round face showed hardly a wrinkle. Life had, it seemed, treated the old lady kindly. Beckoning me to be seated in the warmth and comfort of her lounge, I sat chatting with my ladyfriend while her mother busied herself in the kitchen making a cup of tea. Tray in hand, she returned within minutes and, setting it down in front of us, said to her daughter, "Your father's not home yet, dear, and it's getting late."

"It's only seven o'clock, Mother," her daughter replied, glancing at a clock on the mantlepiece. "You know he always works late at the Insurance office on a Wednesday. He has to wait for his collectors to pay in," she reminded her.

With a mumbled apology, Mrs Leswell went back into her kitchen where she set to preparing her husband's dinner, singing, *Just a Song at Twilight*, an old favourite of hers.

Being a cheerful soul and like many women of her generation, she accepted being tied to the kitchen sink as her role in life, once married. So it was shortly after 8:30 p.m. and her husband arrived home, after a long tiring day at the office. Hearing his car crunching on the gravel driveway, she slipped into the lounge, just to make sure she'd remembered to put his slippers to warm by the fire.

Pallid of face and overweight through a lack of exercise, Mr Leswell, a man in his late fifties, spent long hours behind his office desk as manager. Coming from the south of England, he never quite settled among northerners and, as a stranger in the region, kept to himself, preferring to return to the south of England each year for his summer holidays, to visit relatives who lived in Southend on Sea, Essex.

Like many of his ilk, who treated their married partners as no more than servants, the emancipation of women might never have taken place, as far as he was concerned. A woman's place, he insisted, was at home, looking after their husband.

Assigned to the Royal Navy when called upon to serve his country during the First World War, he was far from happy. He criticized and mistrusted the Senior Service and certainly objected to his daughter courting a seaman. He did his best to turn her against the idea, saying, "Anyone who sails the seven seas as a career, was not to be trusted. You'll live to regret it. They've a girl in every port," he warned her.

But in spite her father's opposition to her associating with me, she refused to listen to his continual outbursts, and agreed we should get engaged. Since our time together was limited to a period of no more than two weeks' leave, Gladys likewise relied on the good graces of her employer at a nearby aircraft factory, allowing her time off work.

She did, however, insist we go ahead and make plans for our engagement, while enjoying every minute of our time together, exploring the ancient City of Chester. It is a delightful spot in the heart of the Cheshire countryside, situated at the head of the River Dee estuary. The City itself attracts crowds of tourists to the area during the summer months, eager to see its old Roman walls and quaint Tudor style timbered houses, in the centre of the town's shopping area. While there, my fiancée chose her engagement ring from a jeweller and together we celebrated the occasion with luncheon, at one of the area's top restaurants.

Some twenty-four hours before my leave was due to expire, a letter arrived with the morning mail, reminding me I had to report for duty and, for once in my life, lady luck was on my side. I was instructed to join the *M.V. Port Huon*, a twin screw vessel built in 1927 for the Port Line, trading between the U.K. and New Zealand. A vessel of approximately nine thousand tons dead weight, her top speed of thirteen knots was considered fast for a cargo vessel of that era, while many of our large passenger ships were barely capable of reaching twenty knots flat out. Undeterred by rumours she was bound for a Middle East war zone, I gambled on the outside chance she could be heading for New Zealand and signed on aboard the vessel, unaware she was due to sail the following day.

CHAPTER 22

NEW ZEALAND BOUND

I now faced the unenviable task of informing my ladyfriend I'd signed on a ship that afternoon and was due to sail within the next twenty-four hours. Before visiting her that evening, I purchased some flowers, and wondered how she would take the news of my sudden departure. When we met, her smile of welcome turned to one of dismay and, quite naturally, she was upset. A look of hurt and surprise spread across the lovely face as her arms reached out in a gesture of hopelessness. "My goodness, they haven't allowed you much time, Rowland," she protested.

For a minute or so she stood there in shock, not wishing to face the fact there was a war in progress. Then, with a shrug of her shoulders in a gesture of compliance, she sighed, "Well, I realize the choice is not yours and you have to go where you are told, Rowland, so I'm not blaming you."

Having surmounted that hurdle, I now had to face the usual barrage of questions from her father, when he arrived home from the office that evening.

"Huh, so you're off to sea, again," he remarked. "How long will you be away this time, six months? I don't know why you bother to come back here," he snapped, in his usual sarcastic manner.

While I sat listening to a tirade of nasty remarks tripping off his tongue, my fiancée could see I was getting upset and placed a finger to her lips, motioning me to keep quiet. I then realized there was no point in getting into an argument with him, as he only saw the gloomy side of life.

It was almost midnight when I rose to go, and before leaving, I told her not to expect a letter for at least four to six week. Having said our goodbyes, I set off home along blacked-out streets, treading furtively over ice-covered pavements, with the wind whistling round my ears. Reaching the street where I lived, I came across a couple of stray alley cats, fighting for the leftovers of an upturned garbage bin. Arching their backs as I passed them by, they snarled at me, as if daring me to touch it.

The house was in darkness so I carefully slid my key in the front door, and let myself in. I took off my shoes and slipped quietly upstairs to my room for some much needed sleep.

Waking at seven o'clock, I opened my bedroom curtains, and peered out on a cold grey November morning. A curtain of fog blotted out the landscape, reducing visibility to no more than a few hundred yards. It was enough to depress all but the hardiest of souls but, on this particular morning, I felt a glow of satisfaction deep within me, realizing I'd soon be basking in warm sunny weather in the South Atlantic. My immediate task however was to finish packing my bags for the long voyage ahead, then look among some personal papers for the address of Jack MacDonald, the old shipmate of mine from New Zealand.

Nicknamed 'Kiwi,' I found him to be a good sport with a sense of humour second to none and a favourite with the Sheilas, a term he used with reference to the girls. The man was a born practical joker, and a barrel of fun to be with. Oh, what swell times we had together, no matter what part of the globe we visited. It could be New York or Timbuctoo for that matter, he was always good for a laugh. I well remember his parting words when leaving the last ship on which we sailed together, "If you should by chance ever take a trip to New Zealand, don't forget to call and see my mum. She'd be glad to meet you, Rowland."

Rummaging among my papers, I finally unearthed his address, hastily scribbled on a sheet of Cunard White Star notepaper. Jack McDonald, 69, Kinghorn Road, Strathmore Park, Mirama, Wellington, New Zealand. Slipping the address in my wallet for safe keeping, I made ready to join the ship later that morning.

"There's a thick fog out there, Rowland," said Mrs Godfrey, when I came down for breakfast. "Will the ship sail without you if you're late?" she asked, rather nervously. "They won't take someone in your place, will they?"

"Time and tide wait for no man, Mrs Godfrey," I replied. "But never fear I'll be on board when she sails," I assured her, slipping upstairs to fetch my bags.

Nerves on edge she paced up and down the room, peering out the window from time to time. Then giving a sigh of relief, she cried, "Ah, this is your taxi," as it pulled into her driveway.

Leaving my luggage at the front door, I walked over to where she was standing, to say goodbye to the woman who treated me like a son. Drawing her to me as one would when bidding farewell to a loved one, I kissed her on the cheek, and whispered, "Thanks for everything, I'll write to you as soon as I can."

Saying goodbye to someone who has cared for you like your nearest and dearest, can at the best of times seem hard, so I dared not linger a moment longer. I noticed the look of sadness in her eyes and could not bear to witness the inevitable tears that were sure to follow, so thought it best not to tarry. Instead I hurried inside the waiting taxi and, catching a glimpse of her through the rear window, waved a final farewell.

She stood in the half-open doorway of her house, with a heavy shawl about her shoulders, a lonely figure, reluctant to say goodbye. But as my taxi pulled away, she slowly raised her right arm aloft and waved, in a brave attempt to bid me *au revoir*.

Overnight fog reduced visibility on the road that morning to no more than a few hundred feet, making driving difficult and delaying my arrival at the dockside, where the *M.V. Port Huon* was berthed. Newly-painted in battleship grey, she lay there, loaded down to her plimsoll mark and, as I stepped on board, I noted her hatches were battened down, ready for sea.

Not until late that afternoon when the tide was in full flow, were the ship's company ordered to standby stations, ready to leave port. Pacing up and down the bridge, the ship's pilot would look anxiously toward the river entrance, waiting for the incoming tide to level up with water in the dock. Then the huge lock gates swung open and a shrill blast on the Dock Master's whistle saw attendant tugs, fastened to the heavily laden vessel, take her in tow. Moving her stern first clear of the dock entrance, they proceeded to swing the ship round, to face the incoming tide.

As the ship gathered speed, the pilot dispensed with the services of his tugs and stepped aboard a launch waiting to take him ashore. As the ship's Captain moved the engine telegraph to full speed ahead, her twin screws thrashed the water as she headed down river, to join a convoy waiting at the River Estuary.

Reducing speed, we rendezvoused with several merchant ships gathered there, awaiting orders to proceed into the Irish Sea. Obscured in morning mist some distance away, one caught sight of the ghostly grey shapes of the convoy's naval escort circling the waiting ships and, like a mother hen fussing over her brood of chicks, forming a protective screen around them.

·   ·   ·

In fading light, an aldis lamp on the bridge of the leading escort vessel, flashed out a coded message to all ships requesting they form into columns of three, before proceeding south through the Irish Sea. Although U-boat patrols in and around the Western Approaches had produced scant returns of late, our naval escort remained with us until we were well out into the South Atlantic, before an order was given for all ships in convoy to break away and set course to their final destinations.

Seeking to distance himself from ships capable of steaming at no more than six to eight knots, the Captain of the *Port Huon,* acting on impulse, increased his speed to a maximum thirteen knots, and headed in a southerly direction. Within the hour, ships sailing in convoy with the *Port Huon* were seen as no more than a smudge on the far horizon. We were now sailing the South Atlantic on our own and the usual rumours one hears via the galley wireless regarding our final destination quickly spread round the vessel.

But as we all know, information concerning the movement of a ship or its destination in time of war is given to the Captain before leaving port, and classified as under sealed orders. Even so, word had already filtered among the crew the vessel was destined for Gibraltar, which proved to be unfounded, for I noticed we were heading in a south-westerly direction when I relieved the man at the helm.

Passing the Canary Islands, a former base used by Germany for refuelling their submarines, word leaked out we were heading for the naval base at Freetown, in the West African province of Sierra Leone. Entering the port as dawn was breaking, the *M.V. Port Huon* stayed only long enough to refuel and top up her fresh water tanks. Waiting until nightfall, the vessel left Freetown and, steering a south-westerly course we found ourselves en route for Panama, via the Windward Passage.

Steaming across the South Atlantic for days on end without another vessel in sight or a glimpse of a submarine's periscope to break the monotony, we zig-zagged, on and on, day after day, toward our destination. Each morning at daybreak, the tropical sun would raise its golden head above the far horizon when a lone albatross, our constant companion, would again join us. Dipping and swaying this way and that in time with the ship's foremast, the bird remained with us during the hours of daylight, as the ship scythed her way through the ocean's glassy surface.

Approaching Panama's Atlantic seaport of Colon, as dusk was falling, we encountered our first sign of life since leaving West Africa: a small fishing boat whose crew of two waved to us in passing. Panama, an isthmus no more than an narrow strip of land in Central America, connects the continents North and South. In 1903, it was handed over to the United States, by the then government of the day, for the purpose of building a canal. A feat of engineering, completed before the First World War, the canal, over eighty kilometres in length, allows ships of all nations passage from the Atlantic to the Pacific Ocean, and vice versa.

Built above sea level, with lock entrances at vantage points, the canal was opened to shipping in August 1914. As a gateway between oceans, the canal covers a distance of fifty-one miles, and varies between three hundred to one thousand feet wide, with a minimum depth of forty-one feet. Panama relies on the canal for the larger part of her economy, bolstered by exports of bananas, shrimp, coffee and copper. Against this, communications in the region, like those of their neighbours, are very poor.

Passing through the locks at Gatun on the Atlantic seaboard, the *M.V. Port Huon* sailed through an artificial lake, forty feet above sea level at Culebra Cut. Traversing a series of locks at Pedro Miguel and Miraflores, past mosquito-infested swamps with jungle on either side, we berthed at the Port of Balboa, our journey having taken a minimum of seven and a half hours from east to west, between the Atlantic and Pacific Oceans. Within the hour, we expected to be back out to sea again to begin the final leg of a long journey that lay ahead of us.

The journey across the Pacific from Balboa to New Zealand was delayed for several hours due to minor engine repairs, which gave the vessel ample time to finish refuelling and top up the fresh water tanks, that were rather low by now. In preparation for our journey across to Auckland, our first port of call, the Chief Steward ordered a quantity of fresh fruit and vegetables. It was late the following evening when the *M.V. Port Huon* made ready to leave Balboa and nosed her way out into the warm waters of the Pacific Ocean.

As soon as the vessel had drawn clear of Balboa's outer harbour, all lights on board were extinguished and extra lookouts were placed at vantage points around the vessel. As in home waters, our orders were to leave nothing to chance when venturing out of Balboa Harbour. The waters of the Pacific were said to be as dangerous as those of the Atlantic. According to reports, Japanese submarines, known to be scouring the Pacific in search of vessels sailing alone like their German counterparts roaming the high seas, sought to destroy any merchantmen they deemed easy prey.

.   .   .

Long after the harbour lights of Balboa disappeared astern of us, I stood on the ship's boat deck, and gazed in awe at the beauty of a tropical night sky, studded with stars brighter than flawless diamonds, all seemingly within my grasp. A warm southerly wind caressed my face as the vessel gathered speed, leaving in its wake a trail of white phosphorescent bubbles.

With Balboa's steamy jungle atmosphere far astern of us, the vessel carved her way through the silent waters of the Pacific when my body suddenly stiffened, and I let out a gasp of alarm.

Heading straight for the midship section on the vessel's starboardside, I watched in horror as a stream of white fluorescent bubbles homed in on us. Gripping the ship's rail for support, I welcomed the feel of cold steel, against my sweating palms. Then that familiar tightening of the stomach muscles one gets when going into action, had the perspiration trickling down my spine, as I waited for the inevitable explosion, I felt sure would follow.

"My God, I've had it this time," I muttered. Closing my eyes, I said a quick prayer and, bracing myself for whatever was to come, waited as the seconds ticked away, but nothing happened. Daring to open my eyes, I watched in stunned silence, as the trail of gleaming white bubbles suddenly veered away toward the bow. Releasing my grip on the rails, a surge of pent-up emotion escaped my lips as I sank to my knees muttering, "Oh, Hell, it's nothing more than a shoal of porpoise."

I felt a surge of relief and, hurrying below to my cabin, flopped on my bunk, thoroughly exhausted.

Waking as the sun glistened on the Pacific Ocean's glass-like waters, I left my cabin on an early morning stroll around the deck, for a breath of fresh air. As the ship sliced her way through the ocean's turquoise blue waters, flying fish aided by a light breeze, were seen to leap from beneath the ocean and scoot out of harm's way.

Out on deck, seamen busy with their daily chores, chipped away at rusty patches on bulwarks, wire brushing, painting or splicing eyes on new mooring ropes.

Leaving the steamy atmosphere of his galley for a breath of fresh air, the ship's cook wiped beads of perspiration from his forehead. Then placing a slightly soiled white linen hat on his balding head, he sat watching off-duty stokers playing cards, until it was time for him to serve lunch. Up on the bridge, the morning coffee came as a welcome break for the navigating officer, who had been plotting our course in the chart room, so I chanced to ask him what our position was.

The days passed peacefully enough without so much as a cry of 'ship ahoy' from the man on lookout scanning the ocean in search of enemy periscopes. There were times when the sight of an ugly-looking water spout appearing on the horizon helped break the monotony of our voyage across the Pacific, causing a ripple of excitement among the ship's company. Other than that, there were few, if any, other incidents worthy of mention during a most enjoyable crossing.

To pass the time of day, members of the crew spent much of their off-duty hours playing games of deck golf, keenly contested by all taking part. Times without number, many games won by Morgan, the ship's Chief Engineer, were viewed with a hint of suspicion by seaman 'Shifty' Walker, who accused the old fellow of cheating. Harsh words were exchanged between the pair of them with Walker deciding to take matters into his own hands, in an effort to get even with his old adversary.

It was common knowledge to all on board that old Morgan kept a chamber pot hidden beneath his bunk. "Let's pinch the old bugger's piss pot," Shifty suggested, to his mates.

"What the Hell are you going to do with it?" said Sandy Wilson. "Drink out of it?"

"Leave it to me," said Shifty, giving his shipmate a sly wink.

"The crafty devil's up to something," said young Peters, a third member of the gang, nodding in Shifty's direction.

At eight o'clock that evening, the vibrant tones of the dinner gong roused old Morgan from the settee in his cabin, where he'd been sleeping, to wander off to the dining saloon in search of something to eat. No sooner was he out of sight, a shadowy figure moved stealthily into the vacant cabin to seize the old man's chamber pot from beneath his bunk, and melt into the shadows.

Morning saw a ribbon of light spreading across the eastern horizon, heralding a new dawn. Rubbing the sleep from his eyes, McIntyre, the First Mate, left the warmth of his chartroom where he'd been pouring over his maps, and wandered out onto the open bridge to stretch his aching limbs. Glancing up at the foremast, he caught sight of a white object fastened to the starboard yard-arm, swaying back and forth with the movement of the ship. Taking a whistle from his trouser pocket, McIntyre gave a shrill blast alerting the seaman on standby duty, who hurried up to the bridge.

"What's that hanging up the foremast, Harris?" he asked the young seaman, who appeared on the bridge.

Taken by surprise, Harris glanced aloft and replied, "Dunno, sir, I ain't ever noticed it before."

"You must be walking round with your eyes closed, a blind man can see that," said the Mate. "Get it down and bring it up here to me," he ordered.

Protesting it was nothing to do with him, Harris left the bridge and sauntered along the foredeck where he released the yard-arm halyards, and gently lowered the heavy object down to the main deck. Bursting into a fit of uncontrollable laughter, he exclaimed, "Why it's old Morgan's piss pot," and, tucking it under his arm, hurried back up to the bridge. Grinning wildly, Harris took the *objet d'art* decorated with coloured ribbons into the chartroom, and handed it to Mr McIntyre. Suppressing a desire to laugh, he pointed to the large black let-tering on either side of the chamber pot that said, "The Morgan Cup for Deck Golf."

McIntyre turned to the young fellow and asked, "Is this the work of your crowd, Harris?"

"It wasn't me, mister," said the young seaman. "I don't know anything about it."

Doubled up in a fit of laughter, Limpy Roberts, the helmsman, let go of the wheel, allowing the ship to veer off course.

"Watch your steering, Roberts!" MacIntyre growled. "You're heading back to Panama."

"Sorry, Mr McIntyre," grinned Limpy. "I'd just like to see the look on old Morgan's face, when they hand him his piss pot for a golf trophy."

"So would a lot more like-minded people on this ship, Roberts," Mr McIntyre remarked, disappearing into the chartroom.

During a coffee break that morning, old Morgan's chamber pot festooned with brightly coloured ribbons was handed over to him by McIntyre.

"Here's your prize for deck golf, Chief," he grinned.

"And how did you get hold of it?" old Morgan asked.

"Found on deck this morning by one of my men," said McIntyre, "we've no idea where it came from."

"People should mind their own bloody business," old Morgan snarled. "I'll have a word with the Skipper over this," he warned, and shuffled away.

It was obvious the old devil failed to carry out his threat because the culprit was never brought to book. Morgan did however refuse to take part in another game of deck golf. Undeterred by his pettiness, games of deck golf and quoits continued to be keenly contested between seamen and stokers, to while away an otherwise boring journey.

It came as a pleasant surprise when, some two days later, a cry of land ahoy from the lookout man in the crow's nest saw the vessel arrive off the coast of New Zealand, a country made up of North and South islands separated by the Cook Straits.

Before the first light of dawn, on New Year's Day of 1944, the *M.V. Port Huon* sailed into Auckland harbour. Situated on the North Island, this thriving community has an extensive trade in shipping, exporting sugar, timber, glass and steel. Its climate, beautiful scenery and undulating hills, reminded me of my own County of Sussex, back in England.

All too soon our time with the friendly people who made our stay in Auckland so enjoyable, came to an end. While reluctant to say goodbye, I looked forward to our next port of call. The ship made ready to leave harbour, as night fell.

Dodging in and out of fragmented cloud, the moon played hide and seek with *M.V. Port Huon* until we reached the open sea, then a full moon beaming down on the ship made us a sitting target for any passing Japanese submarine. Keeping well within sight of the coast, we made our way south, checking our position against infrequent flashes of light from beacons stationed on shore. Dawn appeared as a reddish glow reflected off cumulus clouds, hanging over the port itself, as we sailed into the harbour at Wellington, lying at the southern end of North Island.

The City of Wellington, often referred to as 'Wet and Windy' by the seafaring fraternity, has much to be proud of with parks and gardens filled with fragrant magnolias, wisteria and countless tropical plants. A backdrop of stately pine forests encircle the city and it is here, in beautiful surroundings, one can sit and listen to the sound of bird song, or be content to watch multicoloured butterflies on the wing, flitting tirelessly over lily ponds. At vantage points in and around the park, Polynesian sculptures are placed in settings of rare beauty, creating an atmosphere of warmth.

It was midsummer in the Southern Hemisphere and, as expected, the weather tended to get hot and sticky, with the approach of midday. Even so, longshoremen toiled away down in the ship's holds, continuing throughout the day in spite of the heat, pausing only long enough to mop beads of perspiration from sweating brows. With the approach of evening these toil-worn workers slowly drifted home, and a stillness descended on the vessel, as cargo winches ceased their incessant clatter, and lay silent.

A pale yellow moon, popping in and out of the clouds, cast eerie shadows on a row of brownstone houses, as I passed down the tree-lined avenue of Kinghorn Road that evening. Knocking gently on the door of number forty-nine, I stood back and waited, fully expecting to meet Jack MacDonald, the old shipmate of mine. From inside the house, the strains of music ceased abruptly as the front door opened and a comely woman, in her late forties, stood before me. An abundance of black hair brushed back off the forehead, and hung over her shoulders. Traces of lissome beauty from days of her youth could still be seen, masking the sadness in her dark brown eyes.

Arms outstretched in welcome she somehow recognised me from photographs, sent some months earlier by her son Jack, as she greeted me.

"Why it's you, Rowland!" she cried with girlish delight. "How lovely to see you. Jack has written so much about you, please come in."

Ushered into a cosy lounge, I sat beside a large bay window draped with white lace curtains, overlooking a steep hill. Taking pride of place on her mantelpiece, I caught sight of a large photograph of Jack and I, on board the troop ship *Louis Pasteur*.

"When is Jack due home?" I asked, hoping I'd have an opportunity to meet him.

Her face suddenly paled and a look of anguish replaced the smile as she stood there, and instinctively I knew something was amiss.

Seconds ticked by before she spoke. Then in a voice barely audible she whispered, "He won't be coming back, Rowland."

"But why?" I asked. "Has something happened to him?"

Reaching into her desk she withdrew a buff-coloured envelope with the words O.H.M.S. printed on it, and handed it to me. I knew from past experience letters of this sort were never bearers of good tidings and an eerie silence hung over the room. I read the document. Nothing stirred, save for the ticking of a grandfather clock out in the hall, growing louder with each passing second.

The letter, addressed to Mrs Jean MacDonald from an Under Secretary at the War Office was dated February 1943, and simply stated, "We have reason to believe your son, Jack McDonald reported missing at sea, must now be presumed lost."

Handing the letter back to Mrs MacDonald, who looked sad and near to tears, I offered my condolences and, fearing I might have upset her, made ready to leave.

"There's no need for you to go, Rowland," she said. "Stay and have tea with me, maybe we can talk awhile."

I did not have the heart to refuse and although the hour was late, agreed to stay a little longer.

CHAPTER 23

A GENEROUS OFFER

In her spacious lounge at the rear of her house, Mrs MacDonald invited me to be seated, then disappeared into the kitchen, returning some minutes later with a tea tray. Having by this time recovered her poise, she now seemed anxious to talk and, pouring me a cup of tea, paused to ask, "How do you find New Zealand, Rowland? Rather like the old country, don't you think?"

"Yes, it reminds me so much of England," I replied, "more especially the County of Sussex where I was brought up."

"I was born in the fishing village of Yarmouth and left when just a young girl," she said, "and, as you must know, the place is quite famous for its kippered herrings. But I don't suppose you would have any on the ship would you, Rowland?" she said with shy smile.

"I'll ask the cook in the morning," I replied, "and if there are any on board you shall have some," I promised.

As Post Mistress in the little town of Mirama where she lived, the good lady was a much loved personality. Her tiny general store-come-post office, which she ran from day to day, kept her in touch with the local inhabitants.

Widowed early in her marriage, the loss of her seafaring husband

so early in life, came as a bitter blow. She somehow managed to struggle on, caring for her son Jack, until he reached adulthood. After her
husband's death, with help from her many good friends in the community and a little pinching and scraping here and there, she managed
to pick up the pieces of her life and carry on. Invites to social func-
tions such as the village fete, local dances or whist drives organized
by the church hall, gave her little time to brood over her loss.

Addressing me personally she said, "At times like this, we all
need a little help, Rowland. Even so, one can take comfort in the
knowledge that time is a great healer."

The room fell strangely silent as she finished the sentence, and
her voice trailed off into a whisper. No tears were shed as she sat there
motionless, hypnotized, saddened by the loss of her only son.

She sat for a while gazing into space as if trying to recall precious moments from the past, and the semblance of a smile, lit up her
face.

"Are you alright, Mrs MacDonald?" I asked, somewhat
anxiously.

Her face had paled considerably, and I feared she might pass out.
With an effort she pulled herself together, managing to hold back tears
that came perilously close to spilling over red-rimmed eyes. Gradu-
ally a little colour returned to the pallid cheeks, for it seemed the
past was haunting her, nudging her with memories she would rather
forget, like a ghost from the past that refused to go away. Assuring me
nothing was amiss, she gave a wan smile, saying, "I'm alright now,
Rowland, it's just this feeling of loneliness that tends to upset me
sometimes, but I'm so glad you came."

"I'm pleased to have met you, Mrs MacDonald," I replied. "This
is such a beautiful country you live in."

"You don't have to be so formal, Rowland," she insisted, "why
don't you call me, Jean, as all my friends do?"

She seemed noticeably more at ease now and brought out an old
family album to show me some photographs taken in happier times.
Pictures of them holidaying together during the boy's early childhood, portrayed them as a close-knit family. It came as no surprise

when her son Jack decided to follow in his father's footsteps, and took up a career at sea. Photographs taken of him during his early years aboard the sailing ship *Pamir* and many others were carefully placed in order.

There was also a picture, I had just given her of myself aboard the *Port Huon* during my visit to New Zealand, which had yet to find its place among her many souvenirs. With a sigh, she closed the album's well-thumbed pages and placed it aside, fighting with her inner self to hold back tears, that fell so easily these days.

"You have many lovely memories, Jean," I whispered, trying to soften the blow. "Jack did have a wonderful childhood, something I was never privileged to enjoy."

"Oh, I am sorry, Rowland, I had no idea," she murmured. "Why don't you tell me about it?"

"There's not much to really interest you, Jean," I warned her, "certainly nothing I'm proud of."

Apologizing, she went on. "I hope I'm not being tactless, Rowland, wanting to delve into your past like this?"

"No, not in the least," I assured her, "I've nothing to lose."

It was difficult for me to cast my mind back to a childhood of rejection and pain, especially when one is abandoned by their mother in infancy, and institutionalized. Never during my early years did I ever have any recollection of a loving parent, I told Jean, or if one ever existed. From as far back as I care to remember these so-called self-righteous nuns, in whose clutches orphan children were placed, showed no spark of love for unfortunate infants left in their care. Neither was any seen to manifest itself by these so called angels of mercy, who chose to hide behind an impenetrable cloak of religion. Strangely enough the outside world viewed them with reverence, totally unaware of what went on behind those convent walls.

Digging deep into the corners of my mind during our conversation that evening, I told Jean many things I hadn't dare mention to anyone before. Such as the emotional shock I experienced as a thirteen-year-old when the head teacher at my school said, "Your mother wants you to go home now, Ronald."

My school friends who knew me as an orphan named Ronald Brandon stood in shocked surprise. Then one remarked, "Hey, Brandy's got a mother."

I then explained to Jean that was the name given to me when I entered the convent as an infant.

There are many unhappy childhood memories secreted away in the furthest corners of my mind that refuse to fade with the passing of time, often surfacing to haunt me when least expected. Choosing to just listen attentively, Jean was shocked to hear of the suffering I myself and many others endured as children, both mentally and physically. Chatting well into the night, time was simply forgotten until I noticed the hour was late, and asked to be excused, saying, "I'll have to be getting back to my ship now, Jean," hoping I had not outstayed my welcome.

"But you will come and see me tomorrow, Rowland?" she pleaded, as I made ready to leave.

Seen from her house on the side of a hill, a panoramic view of the City of Wellington lay before me, while down in the harbour arc lights aboard vessels berthed there cast a luminous glow into the night sky. The clatter of the ship's steam winches echoed throughout the darkened night as longshoremen toiled away, discharging the vessel's general cargo. Bidding Jean goodnight, I retraced my steps from her house, back along the now darkened tree lined avenue, to my ship in the harbour below. Arriving on board, I closed the portholes in my cabin to shut out the noise, and turned in, leaving dock workers to pursue their nightly task.

Throughout the remainder of my stay in Wellington, every free moment of my time was spent in Jean's company, meeting her many friends who arranged sightseeing tours and picnics. Together we enjoyed the long summer evenings at various social gatherings. With so many places to visit, time, as always happens, slipped away all too quickly. Then quite unexpectedly during a farewell dinner on our last evening spent together, Jean, looking a little sad, took me by surprise when asking, "Would you consider staying in New Zealand with me, Rowland?"

Whilst my heart said yes, because I felt so sorry for her, my head instinctively said no. I had a fiancée waiting for me back home. There was also a sister whom I'd made several attempts to find. I'd had to abandon my search with the outbreak of World War II in September 1939. Certain in the belief that at sometime in the future my sister and I would meet, it seemed I must now wait until hostilities ceased before continuing my quest.

Thanking Jean for her hospitality, I said it was nice of her to invite me to stay in New Zealand, but I had an obligation to fulfil and felt honour bound to return home.

"Haven't you had enough of war, Rowland?" she sighed. "There's nothing for you to go back to England for. Besides, I could get you a nice comfortable job here at the Post Office."

"Maybe I should have told you at the outset, Jean," I replied. "I'm engaged to be married, and must continue the search for my sister."

I saw the look of sadness in her eyes and, placing an arm about her shoulder, drawing her to me, kissed her on the cheek.

"I'm sorry, Jean, but I must go home," I told her, "much as I would love to stay here with you."

Hiding her disappointment, she readily agreed with me the circumstances that prevailed required me to honour my promise, and thought it best I return home.

Down in the harbour next morning, a gathering of sail boats from the local Wellington yacht club set off for the open sea. Flags fluttering astern, I watched as each in turn raised its sails as though in some form of salute when leaving the harbour. Aboard my ship the *M.V. Port Huon*, the Blue Peter could be seen flying from her foremost yardarm. It was an established procedure required of all British merchant ships, signalling their intent to leave port within the next twenty-four hours.

By late afternoon the last slings of cargo had been dispatched down in the ship's holds, and all was made ready for the vessel to leave Wellington harbour. Then without warning, a number of cars were seen to arrive at the far end of the berth where we lay, and from out of them tumbled a group of young ladies. Amid shrieks of laughter they strolled down the quayside toward the *Port Huon*, carrying a collection of flags, rattles and coloured streamers. Leading them was my host and good friend, Jean MacDonald, determined to give me a good send off.

An order to let go the mooring ropes saw attendant tugs secured to the vessel fore and aft, easing the ship away from her berth, with our wellwishers on the quayside shouting goodluck, and *bon voyage*. As the last of the ship's mooring ropes were heaved inboard, the ladies burst into song. Crisp and clear the words of the Maori's Farewell *Now is the Hour* drifted across the harbour. This, I imagined, was Jean's way of saying a personal goodbye to me, as my ship sailed out of Wellington harbour, with emphasis on the words,

> *While you're away, oh please remember me.*
> *When you return, you'll find me waiting here.*

Reaching the open sea the pilot dispensed with the services of his tugs, and bidding us *bon voyage*, was himself transferred to a pilot launch and was gone. Ceasing to pace up and down his bridge, the Captain entered the wheel-house and hurriedly pushed the lever of the engine telegraph to full speed ahead. The *M.V. Port Huon* gave an involuntary shudder, as her twin screws thrashed the water, as though reluctant to obey the command, before springing into life. Then, like a hound straining at the leash, she knifed through the clear blue waters of the Pacific, and once again we found ourselves alone in a world of blue.

We were back out at sea, with nothing for company but the ocean, a sky of blue and clusters of cottonwool clouds drifting lazily overhead, on warm westerly trade winds. Since leaving Wellington, neither ship or tell-tale smudge on the horizon had been seen in this vast stretch of water to attract our attention.

With ample time to spare during off duty hours, there was little to occupy one's idle moments except games of Chinese Checkers, in which several members of the crew indulged. This was something of a novelty at the outset, but when played day after day with monotonous regularity, they soon became boring. As an alternative, many seamen eventually took up hobbies of their own. Sandy Wilson busied himself making rope mats, whilst Harris, who fancied himself as a modern day Van Gough, passed away the idle hours with his water colours, painting scenes from memory.

Shifty Walker, up to his old tricks as usual, renewed his long running feud with old Morgan. Like many an old sea dog before him, he loved nothing better than to sit out on deck, puffing away on his smelly old pipe. Shifty, in an effort to antagonize the old chap, would go out of his way in passing, to say, "Blimey, what yer smoking, Chief? Smell's like Camel dung."

Normally a placid sort of chap, old Morgan turned on his tormentor, "It's your underpants that stink, son," quipped the old man. "Why don't you put them in dry dock?"

Mouth agape, Shifty stood rooted to the spot for a moment, lost for words. Old Morgan sat there laughing at him having, at last, managed to turn the tables on his young adversary.

Before hurrying away to his quarters at the after end of the ship, Shifty muttered to himself, "The old fool, bloody old fool." Leaning on the stern rails, he joined forces with his mates, who had nothing better to do than spend time boasting of feminine conquests, one or the other made in various ports around the world.

We were now approximately halfway across the Pacific en route for Panama, when a cry of 'land ahoy' from the lookout put an end to the seamen's cozy tête-a-tête. Every man jack rushed to the ship's starboard side, to gaze longingly at our first sight of land since leaving New Zealand, some three thousand miles astern of us.

It was shortly after midday when we passed, within hailing distance of Pitcairn, an island measuring approximately two square miles. Discovered by Britain in 1767, the island was uninhabited until 1790, when mutineers from *H.M.S. Bounty*, under the command of the notorious Captain Bligh, deserted the ship and settled there. The island's population, of whom many are descendants of those mutineers, who subsist mainly on farming and fishing, are estimated to be no more than fifty-two in 1992. Some of her original crew who took possession of Pitcairn were said to have married the local Tahitian women, while others came from among the neighbouring islands of Henderson, Ducie and Oeno. These were islands of tropical beauty, with plentiful supplies of sweet potatoes, oranges, bananas and cocoa nuts.

With the wind on our starboard quarter, we made good progress, steaming at a steady thirteen knots toward the equator. But as the days grew hotter, worse was to come when the wind suddenly dropped altogether on entering the doldrums. Not a breath of air disturbed the ocean's stillness, other than that caused by the movement of the ship as it sliced through the Pacific's clear blue waters. But for this move-ment, there would have been scant relief from the day's choking heat, where temperatures in our cabins reached anywhere from eighty to ninety degrees, even with the assistance of an electric fan.

Relief from the intense heat did occur, from time to time, when formations of cloud, in varied hues, appeared on the far horizon, then without warning a violent wind would spring up, bringing rain in its path. As it approached the ship, you could see the squall coming. In the blink of an eye, formations of black cloud gathering out on the horizon kissed the sea, the heavens would open, then down came the rain. Like pennies from heaven, it splattered over the ship's deck in great big blobs, sweeping all before it. Then just as quickly, the wind would drop and the rain subside, leaving everything fresh and clean.

On leaving the doldrums, winds coming from the southeast would suddenly spring up to near gale force, a rare treat after the scorching heat we had to endure of late. It was also amazing to see schools of silvery blue flying fish, measuring eight to twelve inches in length, leap from the ocean. Skimming a few feet above the water, they'd travel on for maybe a quarter of a mile, before disappearing below the surface. Like the last time I saw them, many caught by an updraught of air were unfortunate to land on deck, only to be hauled away by the ship's cat. If nothing else, this helped ease the sheer monotony of our long journey of over six thousand miles across the Pacific Ocean to Panama.

Once night had fallen in this vast expanse of the Pacific, it was so black, one's eyes had first to grow accustomed to the dark. Only then, was it possible to see the Southern Cross, surrounded by a galaxy of stars, as it lay upside down. As the wind increased, it created an illusion, giving one the impression the ship appeared to be hurtling through the dark of night like an express train, leaving in its wake a phosphorescent stream of fluffy bubbles.

On one crisp clear morning I left my cabin to snatch a breath of fresh air. A cry of 'land ahoy' saw the duty officer hurrying from the chartroom to the starboard wing of the bridge with his binoculars. Our first sight of land for many a long day was seen to rise up in the distance.

We were fast approaching the Galapagos Islands, a wildlife sanctuary lying off the North-West Coast of Ecuador, home to colonies of seagulls, cormorants and many aquatic creatures.

Guano, an excrement of sea birds found in large quantities on the island, is exported from these shores for its use as a valuable fertilising agent, being rich in phosphate and ammonia. Among the many land animals on these islands are the giant tortoise, some weighing as much as five hundred pounds. To this day, these beautiful islands are protected by the Government of Ecuador, and remain mostly unspoilt by the ravages of entrepreneurs from the outside world of commerce. They are also a modern day Garden of Eden, to any nature lover.

Cooled by ocean breezes, we bid farewell to the Galapagos Islands basking in their tropical splendour, and continued towards Panama. Some three days later, the *M.V. Port Huon* entered Balboa harbour from the opposite direction. Within an hour of berthing, we once again endured sweltering temperatures in excess of one hundred and twenty degrees, being careful not to fry our feet on the ship's steel deck.

Shifty Walker and his shipmates took advantage of the vessel's overnight stay to refuel and top up our fresh water tanks. Slipping ashore for a night out, they caught sight of old Morgan standing by the ship's gangway in conversation with Quiggley, the Chief Steward. To ribald cheers from his mates, Shifty teased old Morgan as he left the ship, shouting, "We're going ashore for a leg up, Chief, why don't you join us?"

"It'll take that kink out of yer back," laughed Limpy Roberts, "you look like an S-hook."

"Have you nothing better to do than dash off to the brothel?" sneered Quiggley, who in the absence of a doctor, was responsible for handing out medicine to members of the crew on board the ship.

"Don't bother coming to me with a sore dick, because you'll get nothing," he told them.

As young Harris was about to step ashore, Morgan pulled him to one side, and said to the lad, "Now you don't want to follow their example, son, they'll only get you in trouble. They've got no sense," said the old engineer.

"That's because their brains are in their dicks," said Quiggley.

Harris ignored old Morgan's good advice and marched boldly down the gangway, to join the rest of his pals at Dirty Doris's bar in the red light district up town.

Come the morning, a ribbon of silver etched along the far horizon heralded a new dawn, and from the shore wisps of grey smoke were seen to rise steadily into the air above a cluster of whitewashed dwellings. Below deck on the *M.V. Port Huon*, a chorus of protests from irate crew members was silenced by the Bo'sun's urgent call, "Show a leg there!"

Receiving no response, he again urged his men to hurry out on deck, and hollered, "C'mon, me lads, let's be avin yer, we've got to get away from this stinking heat."

"Aw Hell, I can't move," moaned Shifty Walker. "Me bloody back's killing me."

"Serves yer right for dipping yer wick last night," the Bo'sun sneered. "We don't all have money to waste on ladies of easy virtue."

"Yer mean whores, don't yer?" laughed Limpy Roberts.

With great reluctance, they left their quarters and trudged silently along to the fo'c'sle head, where they set about hauling in the ship's mooring ropes. At a signal from the pilot, the *Port Huon* moved smoothly away from her berth at Balboa, then proceeded on her journey through the locks at Miraflores and Pedro Miguel, into the Culebra Cut. Sailing across Gatun's artificial lake, we passed through a system of locks that literally took us over a mountain, before our descent to ocean level at Cristobal, where we journeyed on. As dusk was falling the *Port Huon* arrived at the Port of Colon on Panama's Atlantic coast, where we stayed overnight to replenish our provisions and fresh water.

AGAIN

Never one to miss the chance of a night on the tiles, Shifty Walker and his motley crew slipped ashore and headed for the nearest bar. Drinking their fill of the local fire water, they sought the company of maidens of ill-repute, who having long since lost their cherries, were only too willing to lavish their favours on drunken seamen. Pie-eyed and legless, they remained ashore throughout the night in the arms of their chosen companions.

Morning brought an unpleasant reminder of the price they would have to pay for their folly. As the first light of dawn etched the eastern horizon, a bedraggled group of seamen with Shifty in the lead crept stealthily along the wharf, hoping to slip aboard the ship unnoticed. But an early riser in the shape of old Morgan was watching them closely, as Shifty and company staggered up the gangway. Then, with perfect timing, old Morgan stepped from his cabin nearby to intercept them. With a wry smile he said, "Been for a night's drift have you, lads?"

"Yes and we've all got sore bloody heads, so what's it to you?" demanded Shifty.

A chuckle of sheer delight escaped old Morgan's lips, "It's not your heads you should worry about, boy-os, it's your dicks!" the old Chief jeered, in his lilting Welsh drawl. "I suppose it's like they say is it?" he quipped. "Any port in a storm."

A wall of silence met the old man's final caustic remark, so for the time being at least he had the upper hand.

It was almost midday when Carruthers, a tall sunburnt individual who acted as the company's agent ashore, clambered slowly up the ship's gangway. His pale blue open-necked shirt, bleached white by a tropical sun, stuck to his sweat-soaked back like a limpet. Removing a huge sombrero protecting his bald head, he mopped his perspiring brow with a spotted handkerchief as he stepped on deck, and hurried toward the Purser's Office.

Placing a heavy package on the desk in front of him containing the ship's papers and a sizeable amount of mail for the crew, he slumped down into a nearby chair. Then taking a multicoloured handkerchief from his trouser's pocket, he wiped his sweating palms.

"Phew, that damned heat is enough to kill you," he moaned. "Is there a drink handy?" he asked Stevens, the Purser.

Motioning his assistant Purkiss to fetch a drink, Stevens then handed it to the scruffily-attired individual.

"Is there nothing stronger?" Carruthers enquired, with a look of distaste at the glass of iced water.

"Sorry, old chap, we're clean out of booze at the moment," came the apologetic reply, from Stevens, who, watching the fellow shift uncomfortably in his chair, felt no sympathy for him as beads of perspiration continued to roll down his face. An ardent teetotaller, Stevens was reluctant to waste the company's good liquor on scroungers in the shape of company reps, from whatever quarter they came.

Placing his half-finished glass on the table beside him, Carruthers struggled to his feet. "I'd better be going then," he said tersely.

Without so much as a backward glance at either of the two men, Carruthers sauntered off down the gangway, hurrying back to his office ashore.

Sifting among the mail he'd brought on board, I came across a letter from Gladys, enclosing news of the family. As expected, there was no mention of the war back home, just tidbits of local news saying Mrs Murphy's cat had been run over and old Mother Mason next door had an argument with the A.R.P. man.

Of many whispered plans we heard mentioned in connection with the invasion of Europe while in New Zealand, nothing seemed to have materialized since our departure from England, some five months earlier. But reading my fiancée's letter, I realized I'd made the right decision in refusing Jean MacDonald's generous offer to stay with her in Wellington. I was now free to resume my search for my sister Caroline when the opportunity presented itself.

With the setting sun seen as a mere ribbon of yellow fused with shades of red and gold as it slipped below the far horizon, the *Port Huon* made ready to leave Panama. Shrouded in semi-darkness, we sailed unobtrusively out of Colon harbour into a South Atlantic sea swell, for the final leg of our journey home. With the sinking of the German battleship *Scharnhorst* in December 1943, the last vestige of enemy surface raiders was removed from Allied shipping lanes. It was now apparent that the U-boat menace had also eased somewhat, although the utmost vigilance was essential.

Maintaining a steady speed of thirteen knots, our progress across the South Atlantic during the first week passed without incident. Warm southerly trade winds blowing from astern seemed to give the vessel fresh impetus as she sliced her way through a sea as smooth as glass. Sighting ships no more than a mere smudge on the horizon since leaving Panama, now four thousand miles astern, it was something of a novelty seeing so many vessels moving to and fro on our approach to home waters.

Abeam of St George's Channel, a Sunderland Flying Boat, patrolling home waters, swept over the ship several times. Then from inside the huge body of the aircraft, an aldis lamp flickered, requesting the vessel's name and destination. Satisfied our credentials were in order, they bid us safe passage and allowed the *M.V. Port Huon* to proceed on her journey north. Entering the Irish Sea, a brisk southwesterly wind met the ship head on, tossing her around as these winds like to do.

Daybreak saw frequent showers of hail and rain lash the vessel, as the weather turned nasty in sight of the Bar Lightship, marking the entrance to the Mersey itself. It is here one catches sight of a line of demarkation between the Irish Sea and River Mersey, formed by a change in sea colour where the two waters meet. Picking up our pilot, we sailed up river to the port of Liverpool, passing familiar landmarks of home. Before long we were in the thick of sea-borne traffic making slow and steady progress behind a line of ships, heading toward their respective berths.

Glancing up river, the navigation officer pointed to the fabled Liver Birds atop the Liver Buildings, saying, "It won't be long now, we've had a good passage."

"Yes, and some good luck, too," I replied.

Seamen who are strangers to the port will no doubt pass away a few hours in the local pub, and who can blame them trying to blot out the memory of a horrendous trip. The local boys will head home.

Traditionally used to handling much of the country's imported raw cotton, Liverpool receives cargoes of sugar, grain, oilseed, minerals and crude petroleum from abroad. During the Industrial Revolution this port was the main outlet for exports from Lancashire and West Yorkshire, with manufactured goods being dispatched world wide. The City's present Town Hall, built in 1676, was reconstructed by James Wyatt, after it had been severely damaged by fire. Over the entrance to the building the original coat of arms, dating back to 1797, shows Neptune and Triton standing beside a Liver Bird. Inscribed is the motto, *Deus Nobis Haec Otia Fecit*. Translated it reads, 'God has given us these blessings.'

Waiting for high water, the *M.V. Port Huon* was ordered to anchor abreast of Princes Pier, referred to as a centre piece of the City of Liverpool's seven-mile system of docks. The *Port Huon* then received orders from the Dockmasters' Office to heave up anchor, and proceed to our allotted berth. Aided by attendant tugs, the vessel eased her way through the lock gates into her berth at Huskisson Dock, a fitting end to a truly enjoyable voyage.

Among the many memorable occasions, with the most friendly people one could wish to meet, I will long remember the kindness shown me, by Jean MacDonald. Had I taken advantage of the generous offer to stay with her in New Zealand, my life would have changed completely.

CHAPTER 24

THE INVASION OF EUROPE

S oon after my ship arrived back in England, rumours from an unidentified source hinted that plans were already under way for the invasion of Europe. So, even having been out of touch with news of the war, while away on the other side of the world, it came as no surprise when signing off the ship we were told there was every possibility our leave could be cancelled, at a moment's notice. With this in mind, I rushed through the formalities of clearing customs and, saying goodbye to shipmates I'd sailed with over the past months, hurried ashore. Without a backward glance at the ship, I took a waiting taxi to Liverpool's Pier Head, where I boarded a ferry across the River Mersey to Birkenhead.

It was from here that Benedictine Monks, of the Birchen Head Priory, operated the first ferry across the River in 1330, when Edward III granted them passage to Liverpool. Untouched by the ravages of the Industrial Revolution in Liverpool and other North Western Cities, and distanced by the River Mersey, Birkenhead remained an agricultural area until the advent of a steam ferry service in 1820. With access to the City of Liverpool via road and rail opening up, Birkenhead's rapid growth as an industrial centre began to material-ize. The town's vast ship building yard of Cammel Laird employed thousands of local men who played a vital role throughout the Second World War, repairing Naval and Merchant vessels.

Delighted to welcome me back home, my dear Mrs Godfrey fussed around like a mother guarding her only son. "How long are you home for, dear, and did you have a good trip?" were the first questions she asked.

When I told her my leave might be cut short because of the impending invasion of Europe, she seemed quite upset. "But why do you have to go back so soon," she said, "when you've only just come home?"

"All able-bodied men are liable to be dragged into this second front, Mrs Godfrey," I replied. "They'll need every ship they can lay their hands on, plus the seamen to man them. Just think of all the people who are suffering in Europe, waiting for the Allies to drive the Nazi invaders out," I replied.

"Yes, I suppose it is hard for them," she said with a sigh, and left me to finish unpacking my bags. Visiting my fiancée later that evening, we discussed the present situation concerning my recall for duty to take part in the invasion of Europe, and decided to bring forward plans for our forthcoming marriage. After choosing her birthday on May 1, no more than a week away, we were told we would need to obtain a special licence.

Leaving my fiancée's family to take care of arrangements for her wedding dress and those of the bridesmaids, I attended to other important matters such as the church service, ordering flowers and booking the hotel reception. In a flurry of excitement, all was ready when the day of our wedding arrived and, with the weather relenting on this special occasion, we were blessed with ample sunshine and a cloudless sky of blue.

Nerves a little on edge that morning, I made ready for the marriage service set to take place at the village church. Mrs Godfrey, who was generous to a fault, did her best to calm my ruffled nerves, and said, "Why don't you try a drop of whiskey to steady you up, Rowland?"

My wonderful new bride Gladys and myself on our wedding day.

Refusing the good lady's offer of a drink, I arrived at the church for the ceremony some ten minutes before it was due to take place. Now very nervous, I hurried past a crowd of well wishers, and taking my place at the head of a small congregation of friends and family of the bride, I shifted uneasily from one foot to the other, waiting for my future wife to appear. It was then I felt the butterflies cartwheeling around inside my stomach. Hearing a murmur from the rear of the church, I cast a hurried glance over my shoulder.

Seeing my bride proudly walking up the aisle eased the tension building up inside me. Her smile of encouragement, when our eyes met, assured me all was well. The wedding went off without a hitch.

Waiting to greet us, on leaving the church, several members of the family and a few friends showered us with rice for good luck, as our carriage sped away to the Central Hotel for our wedding breakfast.

Not until late that afternoon, did we managed to slip away unnoticed from the wedding reception. Gathering our luggage, we drove off to Llandudno, a quiet seaside resort on the coast of North Wales. Overlooking the beach, our hotel nestled in the shadow of rugged mountains and green valleys, an ideal place to spend a honeymoon. These gifts of nature were ours to enjoy, on this our first week of married bliss. During walks along the shore, we thrilled to the raucous cry of sea birds as they swooped down to feed on shoals of whitebait coming in with the tide. Wandering down quiet country lanes, we listened to snatches of song from the blackbird, as it foraged under hedgerows, surrounded by lush green meadows.

In the sky above, a skylark joined its feathered friends in welcoming the day with a joyful tune and, all around, the peace and tranquillity of our time together remained undisturbed. Then, all too soon, a call to duty midway through the second week of our honeymoon turned our world upside down. On May 10, 1944, the spectre of war once again raised its ugly head in the form of a telephone message from my father-in-law that sent us hurrying back home.

A letter bearing the familiar government stamp O.H.M.S, and marked urgent, lay on the hall table waiting for my return. Brief and to the point, it requested I report back for duty immediately, with all necessary documents, plus my lifeboat efficiency certificate.

We were halfway into the month of May when I bid goodbye to my beautiful young wife of just a few days, and took passage on a ferry to cross the Mersey's busy waters. Alighting at Princes Landing Stage, I walked past the burnt-out remnants of our old Shipping Office at Canning Place, destroyed during the blitz of 1941.

Beside a disused Customs office, adjacent to a row of bonded warehouses at Canning Dock, I found what appeared to be the Shipping Office's makeshift headquarters. Waiting outside, groups of young men huddled together in animated conversation, cast questioning glances in my direction as I entered the building. The place was cold and uninviting, with paint peeling off its dust-coated walls, adding to an atmosphere of doom and gloom pervading the office.

In one corner of the room, old Repp, the shipping clerk with whom I'd crossed swords with in the past, sat behind a large oak desk, dressed in a blue serge suit that had seen better days. Seeing me he gave a sardonic grin. "So, we've roped you in again," he leered, as I handed my credentials to him.

As directed, I entered a door marked conference room, where I joined a group of men waiting to receive their orders from a young naval officer. In a calm voice he addressed the gathering with the following, "You have been chosen to undertake special training in preparation for the Liberation of Europe, and on leaving, you will be assigned to one of several hospital ships fitted out for the task." Then, bidding us safe journey and Godspeed, the officer said we should all meet at 10 a.m. the following morning at Lime Street Station.

Next morning I boarded a train with the rest of my group, and promptly left en route for the Scottish town of Inveraray, at the head of Loch Fyne. Soon after arriving at our destination, we were put through a period of training, using water ambulance launches from the *S.S. Naushon*, a hospital ship stationed in the area. Constructed of stout five-ply timber, with an overall length of thirty feet, these specially designed boats were to be used to ferry wounded Allied soldiers from the battlefront, to a waiting hospital ship. Powered by six cylinder Chrysler Marine engines and a fifty gallons supply of fuel, these sturdy craft were capable of transporting twenty-one injured personnel from the beachhead.

As soon as our period of training was completed, I left Inveraray to join a hospital ship berthed at a repair yard in South Shields, situated at the mouth of the River Tyne. A close-knit community of people living in tiny houses adjacent to the shipyard, South Shields was one of many ports around Britain's coast allowed to fall into decline during the recession of the twenties and early thirties, its usefulness having long since ceased to exist. The reopening of the shipyard at the start of hostilities gave badly needed employment to many families of this hard-pressed community that was only just beginning to recover from years of neglect.

.   .   .

On the afternoon of May 29, 1944, I arrived at South Shields with a twelve strong complement of specially-trained merchant seamen prepared for battle, and boarded the *S.S. Prague* in the dockyard's fitting out basin. The vessel was requisitioned by the Ministry of Transport at the outbreak of World War II. Her peace time role as a cross channel ferry, *Prague* had undergone a complete transformation. Along with her original crew, she was now ready to serve as a hospital ship on the Invasion of Europe, with our group of merchant seamen to operate her four ambulance launches.

Like a thing of beauty etched on an artist's canvas, her gleaming white painted hull and brilliant red cross on the funnel symbolized hope anew to the area's unemployed and the ship repair yard.

The month of June, normally associated with endless hours of sunshine, burst on the scene with gale force easterly winds that buffeted the *S.S. Prague* about as she left the dock. Entering the North Sea as dawn was breaking on the morning of June 2, mountainous seas and storm force winds tossed the vessel about, as if it were a piece of cork. But, like an acrobat, she skipped over the crest of many giant waves and then, courting disaster, would plunge headlong into a deep trough, taking forever to surface. Keeping within sight of land on our journey down Britain's east coast, we sailed on, heading in the direction of the English Channel to a destination unknown.

Abreast of Dover's White Cliffs as dusk fell, the ship's navigation lights were switched on when, without warning, the unmistakable sound of gunfire echoed from across the channel. Intermittent flashes of light were seen coming from the direction of Calais, and a fusillade of shells whined overhead, as German shore batteries opened up on us. Anxious to get away from the danger zone, the ship's Captain ordered all lights extinguished, and asked the engineer on duty down in the engine room for every ounce of speed her engines could muster. The old tub shuddered as her twin screws churned the windswept waters of the North Sea and, with a sudden lurch forward, she raced for the safety of England's southern shores.

Arriving off the Isle of Wight at first light on the morning of June 3, the *S.S. Prague* entered Southampton's extensive system of docks, to lay alongside several hospital ships berthed in the port. Anchored some distance away in the Solent, a vast armada of ships carrying men of the Allied forces waited for zero hour, ready to play their part in the Invasion of Europe as soon as the weather abated. On the morning of June 5, the gale force winds and rough seas that hampered operations slowly subsided, allowing over six thousand ships in the invasion fleet to set sail.

Protected by an escort of battleships, cruisers and destroyers, the invasion fleet moved en masse from ports along England's southern coast toward the beaches of France. Following astern of the main body were the hospital ships S.S. *Duke of Argyle* and S.S. *Duchess of Argyle,* accompanied by the S.S. *Prague.*

Throughout that first day, we inched toward the French coast in the direction of Normandy, a movement both conspicuous and daring. Yet amazingly in this age of communication by radar and reconnaissance planes, our approach went unnoticed by the enemy across the channel. That night an overcast sky afforded the convoy ample cover, until a break in the cloud around two a.m. saw a full moon light up this vast armada of ships. Silhouetted against an angry dark gray sea, we were sitting ducks for any submarine or E-boat in the vicinity, but luck had its way and there was no attempt by the enemy to intercept us. Could it have been because the weather was so bad the enemy thought they were safe from invading forces across the English Channel and, in doing so, were caught napping? The largest convoy of ships the world had ever seen sailed from England's shores, without let or hindrance from the enemy until reaching their objectives.

CHAPTER 25

THE BATTLE FOR OMAHA

The night's angry black sky disintegrated into uneven patterns of grey by dawn's early light on the morning of June 6, 1944, nominated as the day of deliverance for the oppressed peoples of Europe. Preparing to meet the enemy head on, the Allied Invasion Fleet moved ever closer to its objective, the beaches of occupied France. It was almost unbelievable that a huge armada of ships, such as this, was allowed to sail from England unhindered, right under the noses of the German High Command. If just one Nazi patrol boat had been in the vicinity of the English Channel at that particular time, it could have given the enemy ample warning, but it was not to be.

. . .

Before the first assault waves of British and Canadian forces hit the beaches at 6.25 a.m., Allied warships lying off the French coast went into action. Salvo after salvo from their sixteen-inch guns pounded German coastal batteries, the noise echoing across the windswept waters of the English Channel. Soon the sound of approaching aircraft developed into a deafening roar, as squadrons of Spitfire, Mustang

US GIs huddle behind the landing craft's protective front ramp as they approach Omaha Beach.

and Thunderbolt fighter-bombers passed overhead. Painted beneath the wings and fuselage of every Allied aircraft were distinguishing marks of broad white stripes, setting them apart from the enemy.

In a never-ending stream, they flew toward the coast of France to destroy enemy positions overlooking the beaches of Normandy, where the German High Command were said to have amassed batteries of 155-millimeter guns. Abreast of beaches codenamed 'Juno' and 'Gold,' a section of the invasion force carrying British and Canadian troops left the main body. Following up astern, the hospital ships *Duke* and *Duchess of Argyle* dropped anchor some half a mile off shore, as the first invading party landed opposite the town of Caen.

Battling against gale force winds showing little sign of abating, the remainder of the Allied invasion force moved on, in the direction of Cherbourg. In seas that at times threatened to swamp us, the hos-

The first assault is met by a hail of German machine gun fire. Within minutes, the troops are leaderless.

pital ship *S.S. Prague* dropped anchor half a mile from the shore, opposite the Omaha beachhead. It was here at first light on the morning of June 6 that American forces fought what was described as the bloodiest and most desperate battle of D-Day. Facing them on cliff-tops 100 feet high, the enemy had sighted their weapons at either end of the Omaha beachhead, with every inch covered. Protected by concrete walls three foot thick, the enemy waited for the first American assault force to arrive, 75 and 88-mm high-velocity guns ready to sweep the entire beach with a fusillade of fire.

Near Omaha Beach, smoke pours from a U. S. Landing Craft after German bullets ignited a smoke grenade carried by one of the GIs.

Before the first landing craft touched down on this mist-shrouded beach at 6:30 that morning, young GIs heard a tattoo of machine-gun bullets hammering on the ramps of their LCTs. Within ten minutes of hitting the beach, their assault force was leaderless, every officer and sergeant either killed or wounded. The enemy, in a commanding position on the cliff-tops, opened up with 88-millimeter howitzers, heavy mortars and machine guns, pinning down what little remained of the assault force behind a protecting sea wall. Further units of invading GIs, following on the heels of the first wave ashore, found an enemy ready and waiting to decimate them before they set foot ashore.

It seemed obvious a pre-emptive strike by Allied bombers on enemy positions covering the Omaha beachhead some hours earlier was unsuccessful. Hampered by low cloud, bad visibility, and fearing they might hit American troops in the landing area below, Allied aircraft sent to strafe the enemy were forced to eject their bombs further inland. In so doing, they allowed enemy positions along

British Landing Craft with tethered balloons to make it difficult for German aircraft to get close for strafing.

the cliff-tops overlooking the Omaha beachhead to cause havoc among invading Allied forces.

The situation looked desperate indeed, for it appeared every attempt by American assault forces to land on the beach was being fore-

Injured American soldiers huddle behind a sea wall, awaiting transfer to the Hospital Ships.

stalled by the enemy. Fortunately for many GIs trapped on the beach, a miracle was about to happen in the shape of the U.S. destroyer *Frankford*. Seeing the plight of the assault force, her Captain moved his ship as close to the shore as he dared in an effort to help them. Reducing the distance between himself and the enemy who had control of the beachhead, gave his gunnery officer a clear view of their adversary on the cliff-tops. Using telescopic sights, the gunnery officer aboard the destroyer *U.S.S. Frankford* blasted away at enemy pillboxes, machine gun nests and heavy mortar batteries.

Seeing the *Frankford* in action encouraged other vessels in the squadron to move closer to the beachhead and join in. Before long, enemy fortifications on this section along the cliff-tops began to fall apart, forcing German troops to come out with their hands up, surrendering to the advancing Americans. Around 9:30 a.m. that morning, low cloud hanging over enemy positions on the cliff-top lifted somewhat, and in the sky to our right, bursts of anti-aircraft fire were seen to puncture the air, in the direction of the Cherbourg Peninsula.

Then, as if prearranged by the gods of war, the weather relented, and out came the sun. Aided by a strong south-westerly wind, sunshine pierced a heavy smoke screen and as the dust of battle settled, one viewed a scene of mayhem in the aftermath of the first American assault. Dead and wounded bodies of GIs lay strewn along the beachhead. From the boat deck of the hospital ship *S.S. Prague* I watched with bated breath as Allied fighter bombers returned to the scene of carnage, and moved in en masse on the enemy. Now with a clear view of German fortifications along the cliff-tops of Omaha, Allied bombers zoomed in to attack enemy mortar and artillery positions holding up an American assault force. In support of Allied aircraft pounding enemy targets, U.S. battleships *Arkansas* and *Texas,* lying offshore, fired salvo after salvo from their fourteen-inch guns.

Within a short space of time, all resistance within enemy fortifications were silenced, and with the exception of the odd sniper yet to be winkled out, enemy opposition ceased to exist.

Around 10 a.m. that morning, American assault troops of the Sixteenth Infantry Regiment swept ashore in their hundreds. Scaling steep one hundred foot high cliffs, they overran the remnants of German shore batteries, and although the price paid was high, the hand of fate had perchance prevented what might have been a large massacre.

As a result of the pulverising attack by Allied sea and air power along the cliff-top, a column of black smoke from the rubble was seen to rise heavenward. The smell of cordite from exploding shells drifted towards the hospital ship lying offshore. This merciless assault on enemy positions no doubt effectively turned the tide of war, from possible defeat into a measure of success for the advancing American forces on the beach at Omaha. When failure at this stage could have jeopardized the entire invasion, it was miraculously averted.

By day three of the invasion, the fierce storms that caused so much confusion from the outset had abated somewhat, but a heavy sea swell and boiling surf pounding the beaches prevented the hospital ship from using her ambulance launches. We therefore found it necessary to rely on the services of American water transport to transfer wounded soldiers from first aid stations ashore out to the ship. With the weather improving considerably during the next day or so, the hospital ship *S.S. Prague* was able to move closer inshore, allowing ambulance crews to use their launches, sheltered from the wind.

With a sea swell buffeting us about, we managed to lower three of our craft into the water on the leeward side of the vessel. Leaving the hospital ship in line astern, our launches set off with all possible speed toward the Omaha beachhead where we faced the task of ferrying wounded GIs from first aid stations back to the ship.

On reaching the beach, I gazed in horror at a scene of utter carnage. It seemed we had entered Hell itself. Columns of dense smoke from burnt-out vehicles formed a choking black curtain across the landscape, hampering our vision. There was also a chance our ambulance launches might be left high and dry on the beach if we were not careful, due to fast-receding tides in the area.

We therefore decided to move quickly inshore to look for any sign of life among a collection of wrecked tank landing craft bobbing around like corks in the sea swell, and found none. All were apparently abandoned by their recent occupants to drift back and forth in the sea with the turn of the tide. Several assault craft among their number had engaged in fierce combat with enemy shore batteries, and now were useless hulks of twisted metal, stranded on the beach.

Disabled tanks caught fast in the sand had spewed out oil that somehow caught fire, and were left burning furiously. Further along the beach we came across the burnt-out remnants of supply trucks, bulldozers, jeeps and half tracks littering the shore. In the water nearby, equipment belonging to young GIs caught in a fusillade of machine-gun fire from enemy batteries on the cliff-tops, drifted back and forth in the surf. Some soldiers, having reached the water's edge of Omaha Beach, lay chopped to pieces beside the burnt-out debris of their vehicles, mutilated beyond recognition. Others, cut down before ever touching the shore, floated back and forth in the foaming surf, a pinkish hue colouring sections of the beach. The sea itself was littered with the bodies of young GIs who, in making the ultimate sacrifice, breathed their last so far from home.

Oblivious to the roar of distant gunfire on the cliff-tops above them, several crews of burnt-out tanks who'd managed to survive the initial onslaught lay on the beach badly wounded. The tide of war having immobilized them it might well have been light years away, for they would remember little of what took place on this day. Having received medical attention they sat gazing among the debris of battle at fallen comrades with sightless eyes bobbing about on the incoming tide. Horrific scenes such as this were nothing new to the battle-hardened seamen among our ambulance crews; they'd seen it all before. So it was not without some misgiving and a feeling of revulsion for the horrors of war that they'd volunteered to take part in this Invasion of Europe when asked to do so, knowing many of their number might never return.

Fully aware the road ahead was fraught with danger when having to reckon with magnetic mines and sunken objects obstructing their way ashore, ambulance crews from the hospital ship stuck to their task, giving aid to friend and foe alike. Throughout the days and nights that followed, in a never-ending stream hundreds of wounded GIs were transferred from the beachhead to the hospital ship lying off shore. Drawing on every ounce of energy, overworked ambulance crews carried on regardless of sneak enemy air raids, ferrying wounded GIs to safety.

While the toughest fighting was undoubtedly on Omaha's beachhead, an American assault force at Utah to our west was making good progress. Reinforcements of the American XIX and V Corps had joined forces to overrun enemy defences in and around the important port of Cherbourg. A few pockets of spirited enemy resistance on the part of the garrison held up the capture of the harbour for a time, its possession being of great importance to the Allied cause.

Although the D-Day invasion on June 6 had started disastrously, the big breakthrough came after much bitter fighting. On June 18, forces under the command of General Joe Collins's VII Corps cut off the Cherbourg Peninsula from the mainland, and seized the important fortress port from its German Commander, Lieutenant General Karl von Schlieben. The ultimate surrender of the port provided a landfall for Operation Pluto, an undersea pipeline used to supply millions of gallons of fuel oil to Allied armies.

In securing the peninsula, the Allies slammed the door shut on any hope the Nazis had of driving the Allies back into the sea. Mopping up operations in the area continued for a time, with GIs having to winkle out a few German diehards lying hidden in underground bunkers.

Following on the heels of the American advance, a force of Liberator and Flying Fortress bombers was sent to the town of Saint-Lo, where a concerted air bombardment by the Allies at the end of July resulted in entire German defence systems being wiped out. The breaching of enemy lines provided an opening for columns of American tanks to surge through gaps in their defence, causing total confusion among dispirited bands of fleeing German soldiers.

Picking up casualties from the battlefront had now become part and parcel of the daily lives of ambulance crews on board hospital ships. Hampered at times by the weather and enemy air raids, they continued to sail back and forth across the English Channel from the Normandy beachhead, to Netley Hospital in Southampton.

It was whilst the hospital ship *S.S. Prague* waited her turn to leave the port of Cherbourg, that I stood on the boatdeck watching several American supply ships approach the harbour with a contingent of troops and war supplies aboard. Packed together like sardines, young GIs sat astride a collection of tanks secured to the deck of each vessel, ready to join their comrades at the battlefront.

The leading vessel was less than half a mile from the harbour entrance when a huge explosion rent the air, tearing the ship apart and setting her on fire. Within minutes, a pall of black smoke billowing skyward was all that remained of the stricken vessel, as it sank quickly. Seeing the American supply ship disappear, the hospital ship *S.S. Prague* immediately made ready to leave harbour in search of survivors.

Speeding toward the wreckage-strewn area, there appeared to be no sign of life among a sea of mangled bodies, floating aimlessly about in oil-covered waters. Ambulance launches were quickly lowered from the hospital ship, as her crew set about the grim task of picking up corpses, mutilated beyond recognition, and shipping them back to the U.K. for internment.

Within a matter of minutes, a force of naval minesweepers arrived on the scene to sweep the area clean of enemy mines, before ships lying at anchor could safely enter the port of Cherbourg. Meanwhile, news coming through confirmed earlier reports that enemy minelaying submarines, slipping through the port's defence system during the hours of darkness, had managed to drop magnetic mines in the path of vessels entering and leaving the harbour. There was little doubt they were responsible for the loss of many an unsuspecting ship or landing craft, and their crews.

Seeing the lifeless bodies of these young men lining the deck of the hospital ship as an unnecessary waste of life, sent a cold shudder through me. Turning my back on this grim spectacle, I offered a silent prayer for them and recalled my day in August of 1942, when I too might have perished. Pausing a moment, I sought to remind myself once again, 'But for the Grace of God there go I.'

Clearing up the wreckage of sunken ships and other debris cluttering the harbour of Cherbourg and its approaches was quickly undertaken, allowing supply ships to efficiently use the port's berthing facilities. This in turn saw hospital ships sailing in and out of Cherbourg non-stop, ferrying thousands of badly-wounded service men from the front line to hospitals in the U.K. The tide of battle was now in favour of the Allies, who by the month of August, were rampaging through France at will. Ocean-going ships were now free to move in and out of captured French ports along the channel coast.

Although the D-Day landing at Utah was hailed as the greatest success story of the invasion, it was no easy task for the GIs who had to fight every inch of the way on the blood-soaked beach of Omaha. It was an operation that almost ended in disaster for, as General Omar Bradley said, "Theirs was no cake-walk."

CHAPTER 26

A SHORT RESPITE,
THEN BACK IN THE FRAY

Having fulfilled our purpose for the initial D-Day assault on Normandy's beaches, the hospital ships, such as the *S.S. Prague* with their merchant seamen crews, were recalled to the U.K. So, by the end of August 1944, I found myself reporting back to the shipping office in Liverpool, from whence I started out and where, for me, the Invasion of Europe had its beginnings.

Arriving home, I was welcomed by my wife who agreed it would be an opportune time for the two of us to travel south, in search of my mother. Never having set eyes on her since leaving home for my first trip to sea in March of 1936, I'd been forced by the outbreak of World War II to postpone my quest.

Well aware of the danger we faced from buzz bombs when passing through the City of London, I was determined to visit Mother's last known address in the Surrey area of Morden, in the slim hope of finding her. Since she was the only person who knew the whereabouts of my sister Caroline, it was imperative I should find her.

The train for London slowed to a crawl on its approach to Liverpool's Lime Street Station. Travelling south with us were a group of young servicemen returning to barracks after a spell of leave. They seemed none too eager to hurry on board the train, burdened as they were with kitbags, haversacks and rifles. With a loud snort, the train jerked forward, as if glad to get away from this bomb-scarred city of Liverpool where shattered buildings stood out at odd angles against the grey of a morning sky.

Rumbling on at breakneck speed, we passed the ancient city of Chester with its old Roman walls amid the tranquil waters of the River Dee. Moving into the delightful Cheshire countryside, we viewed its many charming villages and thatched cottages. Some miles on, we stopped at the town of Crewe, a major railway junction and important manufacturing centre for Rolls Royce and Bentley cars.

It was here in 1904 that a Mr Henry Royce, the son of a local miller and a well established engineer at the Manchester-based firm of F.H. Royce & Co., met the Hon Charles S. Rolls, son of a wealthy landowner. Together they built the factory on a green field site owned by a railway company in 1842, to produce the first Rolls Royce, a motorcar way ahead of its time, with a silver lady as its mascot. Its marketing was based on an observation of the worldly-wise Mr Royce that, 'The quality remains, long after the price is forgotten.'

Leaving Crewe, we crossed the Cheshire border into neighbouring Staffordshire, an area rich in deposits of iron and coal, known as the Black Country. Surrounded by tall factory chimneys spewing out industrial waste, we viewed the town of Stafford, famed the world over for its delicate china and ceramics.

A pall of smoke from blackened kilns hung over the town's dingy back-to-back terraced houses of pottery workers. In the background, slag heaps blotted the landscape. At the railway station, a group of servicemen were seen squatting down on the platform apprehensively, as if it were a roulette wheel about to decide their fate. Others stared disconsolately at the train as it slid to a halt.

Were it not for the uniforms they wore, one could excuse them for their lack of concern over a war that had gone on, for five long years. No sooner had passengers boarded the train, an order from their N.C.O. saw the waiting soldiers jump to attention. With a great deal of reluctance, they gathered up their equipment and shuffled onto the train. Then, with a sudden hiss of steam from beneath its belly, the giant locomotive let out grunt and, with a jerk, she was on her way south again.

The train gathered speed and headed toward the City of Lichfield, birthplace of Dr Samuel Johnson. In passing, one catches a glimpse of Lichfield cathedral, its spires gleaming in the late autumn sunlight. Crossing the boarder of Staffordshire, we entered the County of Warwickshire, birthplace of William Shakespeare, and the castles of Kenilworth and Warwick, where the River Avon flows through the town. By-passing the industrial cities of Birmingham and Coventry, we arrived at the market town of Rugby where, in addition to its well known Public School, a thriving electrical engineering industry and aircraft pattern works flourishes.

A timely delay at the station gave me a chance to slip from the train to purchase two penny bars of chocolate from a red painted machine on the platform. When on my way back to the train, I passed an elderly railway porter holding a green flag who glanced up at the station clock and advised me to hurry aboard. From the carriage window I looked on as he withdrew a watch and chain from his waistcoat pocket. He appeared to be checking the time of day when a shrill blast on the stationmaster's whistle at the far end of the platform injected some life into him. Hoisting his green flag aloft to signal all was clear, he sauntered off towards the ticket office.

As the train gathered speed, one viewed posters advertising Bisto Gravy, Gold Flake Cigarettes and Andrews Liver Salts displayed at intervals along the station platform. From Warwickshire, our journey south took us through Northamptonshire where one glimpsed quaint little villages and old world cottages nestling in the countryside.

Passing through the town of Northampton, through which the River Nene flows, we noted the site of its shoe manufacturing industry for which the town is famous. An unscheduled stop at St Albans in Hertforshire delayed our arrival at London's Victoria Station until late that afternoon. Puffing out clouds of black smoke, the train ground to a halt beneath the station's glass-covered roof as the last rays of autumn sunlight struggled to filter through gaps in the dust-laden glass.

Stepping from the train, Gladys and I followed passengers heading for the station exit, where our tickets were snatched from us by a frustrated railway official. Out in the city, the shopping area was as busy as ever, in spite of being threatened by the enemy's latest instrument of war, the V-2 rocket, or 'flying bomb.'

Outlined against a backdrop of the sun's reddish evening glow, one could not help but notice the remnants of burnt-out buildings, standing at crazy angles. This was the result of buzz bombs leaving widespread paths of death and destruction in their wake, while striking fear in the hearts of many a poor soul in the city. Not since the blitz, in the early forties, had Londoners suffered such disruption to their daily lives, due to the enemy's indiscriminate bombing of their homes.

Waiting to fleece the unwary traveller arriving at London's Victoria Station, touts and spivs on the lookout for a soft touch were to be seen hanging around outside. One seedy-looking individual, wearing a faded blue suit sporting dinner stains of yesteryear down the front, sought to accost my wife and I. Standing directly in our path, he whinged, "D'yer wanna cab, lady?"

Sidling up to me, he pointed to a rust-laden car standing at the curbside. "'Ere yah, mister, we'll take yer wherever yer wanna go," he grinned, showing rows of tobacco-stained molars.

Crouched behind the steering wheel sat an unkempt-looking individual wearing dark glasses, his face half-hidden in the turned-up collar of his overcoat, not wishing to reveal himself.

With a polite, "No thanks, we'll take the train," we moved swiftly out of earshot, leaving the disgruntled spiv issuing a torrent of curses in our wake. The threat of flying bombs saw us hurrying to Victoria Underground Station where we caught our train to Wimbledon, famed the world over as the mecca of lawn tennis. Its playing courts lay but a short distance from where Mother once lived.

Looking for suitable accommodation in the area was a problem we quickly solved with help from the local constabulary, who obliged us with a list of boarding houses offering bed and breakfast to the weary traveller. Choosing an establishment run by a Mrs Clarkson, we decided to retire early that night, after an exhausting day's travel. We planned to rise early next morning, in a last ditch effort to find my mother, if humanly possible, before my leave expired.

Before dawn, a rumbling noise normally associated with the approach of a thunderstorm woke me with a start. Sitting bolt upright up in bed, I waited for the inevitable downpour of rain I felt certain would follow, lashing against the bedroom window. For a moment there was an eerie silence, then I heard the unmistakeable sound of exploding bombs, shattering the morning stillness. Was this another one of those V-2 rocket attacks on the city, I wondered, well aware the City of London had seen more than their fair share of them since the D-Day landings in June? Careful lest I disturb my wife who lay sleeping, I left the bed, and stood by the window. Through a chink in the bedroom curtains I watched a tiny orange glow spread like wildfire along the distant horizon.

Fingers of light stabbed the semi-darkness as searchlight batteries swept the sky, and anti-aircraft batteries opened up. Working in unison, they sought to destroy any pilotless missiles homing in on the city, before another projectile found its target.

Looking in the direction of the nation's capital, I watched as a series of blue lights flickered in and out, like jets on a gas burner, setting light to everything in their path. With each successive attack, fires raged out of control to form an iridescent display of colour where the missiles landed. Not until the raid had ended at dawn, did I dare go back to bed, thanking my lucky stars I decided not to stay overnight in London.

Down the hall, a grandfather clock chimed the hour of eight and, somewhere in the vicinity, one heard church bells, calling the faithful to morning prayer. Hearing their urgent peals, I shook my sleeping wife gently by the shoulder, and whispered, "It's eight o'clock, and time we were up."

Opening her eyes she looked at her strange surroundings, and murmured, "Where are we, dear?"

My response was interrupted by the melodious sound of a gong, calling boarders to breakfast. From the kitchen below, an aroma of toast drifting through our bedroom door attacked the nostrils, encouraging me to hurry with my morning ablutions.

Breakfast was served each morning from eight-thirty until ten o'clock by Mrs Clarkson, an amply-proportioned woman in her late forties who, since losing her husband at Dunkirk, eked out a living taking in boarders. Seeing my wife and I, she smiled, and as we sat at table, said, "Good morning. Did you sleep well?"

"Yes," I replied. "That is until the buzz bombs started to fall on the City. I'm afraid some poor devils caught a packet."

Nothing more was said, as we sat down to a breakfast of cereals, fresh milk and new laid eggs from a nearby farm, with generous helpings of toast and marmalade. As the meal ended, Mrs Clarkson seemed eager to resume her conversation, and said, "Your wife tells me you once lived in this neighbourhood, Mr Marshall. I do hope you'll enjoy your visit."

"Oh, I'm sure we will," my wife replied, and begged to be excused from the table. Neither of us wished to divulge the nature of our visit.

In order to make an early start in our search for my mother, Gladys and I left Mrs Clarkson's soon after breakfast, telling the good lady we would not be back until late that evening. Hand in hand, we arrived at the bus stop and waited patiently as a Green Line coach slithered to a halt in front of us, scattering red and gold autumn leaves in all directions. The vehicle's destination to Sutton via Merton quickly brought to mind the times I travelled this same route with Mother, on weekend shopping trips.

Alighting from the bus at the village of Morden, deep in the Surrey countryside, the spicy scent of new mown grass reached my nostrils. I caught sight of the house where Mother once lived, partly hidden by horse chestnut trees, lying back off the road among a row of recently-painted dwellings. Seeing it after all these years took me back in time to a bitterly cold morning in March of 1936, when I left on my first voyage to sea as a seventeen-year-old – a journey that was to take me around the world during the next two years.

Saying our goodbyes, I remember seeing the look of sadness on Mother's face turn to alarm when I pleaded with her, "Why won't you give me my sister's address?" The hurt I felt inside when she refused my request was nothing compared to the awful shock awaiting me when I arrived back home from sea, and found she'd left without a word of goodbye.

"Is this where you used to live, Rowland?" my wife asked, a hint of sadness in her voice.

A nod of the head was all I could do in response, as my mind drifted back in time, and the hurt of yesteryear returned. I was trapped between reality and what might have been, when I felt a hand tugging at my sleeve. I turned to face my wife, who understood how I must have felt.

"Let's go home, dear," she said. "We've nothing to gain by staying here."

Without a backward glance at the only home I'd known as a boy, I took my wife by the hand, and we set off in the opposite direction. Despite this setback, I was as determined as ever to continue the search for my sister and decided to pay a visit to the local Council Offices, where Mother paid her rent. The office lay in the shadow of a railway bridge spanning the main road and appeared much smaller now than it did in those far-off days. Why, it seemed like only yesterday that I played beneath its huge archway, as a young school boy.

Entering the office, I found the staff's response very courteous. Sadly, what little information they offered was of no help in tracing her whereabouts. Thanking them for their concern, I left the office to make a few discreet enquiries among local shopkeepers in the village of Rose Hill, where she was well known, but once again drew a blank. It was at this point, I mentioned an aunt of mine living in the village of Downham, Kent, and suggested we visit the place. But my wife simply shook her head, to say, "Ah! But that was such a long time ago, dear, and the person you are seeking could be long gone, for all we know."

I had to agree with her – too much water had flown under the bridge, so to speak, making our task hopeless. I realized any chance I had of finding my mother after all these years had faded with the passing of time. Having failed, once again, in this search for my mother, any hope of finding my sister Caroline looked slim indeed. As I was clearly crestfallen, and on the verge of tears, my wife reached out to comfort me. Placing an arm around my shoulder, she whispered, "There's nothing more we can do here. Let's go home, dear."

CHAPTER 27

VICTORY IN EUROPE

It was early September 1944 when enemy resistance began to crumble, as Allied forces swept across Belgium and Holland at will, allowing our armies to take the fight onto German soil. Desperate to stem the tide of war that had suddenly turned against him, Hitler had retaliated by unleashing V-2 rockets on the City of London, with indiscriminate attacks on innocent civilians. Elsewhere, Allied forces were advancing on several fronts, including mainland Greece, where they occupied the strategic city of Athens.

The speed with which the Allies advanced across Europe led to an urgent request to the United States for further shipments of war supplies, in support of our frontline troops. With increased naval patrols in and around the western approaches, control of the waters around Europe had now passed into Allied hands and, as a result, the U-boat menace slowly diminished. Although it was now considered unnecessary to shepherd large convoys across the Atlantic, all ocean-going ships were still given a sea and air escort for two days, which was deemed sufficient.

Returning home from the south of England following an unsuccessful search for my mother, I found a letter from the Ministry of

Shipping waiting for me. My shore leave having expired some two days earlier, they requested I report for duty immediately. As usual, my luck ran out when I was sent to join the *S.S. Benbury*, an old tramp steamer I'd sailed on a few years earlier. A relic of yesteryear, it had offered little comfort to those who sailed in her on that never-to-be-forgotten voyage across the North Atlantic in the winter of 1940.

Running head on into hurricane force winds and battered by mountainous seas threatening to swamp us, we'd had to fight for our very existence to stay afloat. At the height of the storm the vessel's lifeboats disintegrated and, like so much matchwood, were swept away. At one stage she stood on her beam ends, and almost capsized. Her maximum speed of six knots, in calm seas, was of little use against the fury of a North Atlantic storm in mid-winter. Despite the odds of survival stacked against her, that rusting heap of scrap iron performed more moves than a limbo dancer, gallantly staggering on. We eventually managed to limp into our home port of Liverpool having left the Canadian Port of Halifax some twenty-eight days earlier.

Thus it was with a feeling of trepidation that I set foot aboard that heap of junk once again, although why I chose to do so, the Lord only knows. Suffice to say, old Creswell, the ship's Bo'sun, whom I'd sailed with on this same vessel in 1940, encouraged me to stay, saying, "Stick with her, son, she's a stout old lady. She'll see you through, you mark my word."

Taking the old sea dog's advice, I took passage in the *Benbury* for the next six months, along with the cockroaches and weevils who'd made it their home. During a period from late October 1944 until early May 1945, the old tub carried thousands of tons of much-needed war supplies from the U.S. to various ports along Europe's western seaboard. Approaching home waters in early May 1945, we were overjoyed upon hearing Germany had capitulated. Their humiliated and demoralized army was forced to surrender on May 18, 1945, thus bringing an end to World War II.

Peace, officially declared at one minute after the hour of midnight on that day, sent a feeling of jubilation throughout the vessel. For me, however, the celebrations were short-lived, as I paused for thought

Briefly, I remembered my comrades aboard the *M.V. Waimarama* who made the supreme sacrifice for a starving population on the beseiged Island of Malta. This, it was said, marked the turning point on which hinged the success or failure, on the outcome of the war.

Though not wishing to spoil the festive spirit, the Captain chose to remind all on board the cessation of hostilities did not come into force until after midnight. Therefore, not one of us at this point in time could afford to relax. Vigilance was necessary, he insisted, if we were to come through unscathed. Late that evening, I spoke with Cowdrey, the navigation officer, who reckoned we'd make landfall within forty-eight hours.

"I guess, it's the last voyage this old tub will make," he grinned sardonically. "She's destined to return from whence she came, the scrap yard."

"What will old Creswell do now?" I asked. "This heap of junk is his home."

"Yeah, I guess the old fellow's part and parcel of the blooming ship," laughed Cowdrey. "He'll have to be cut away from her."

It was now the end of May and summer had, it seemed, come rather early to England's northern hemisphere, with a spell of warm weather. Our first sight of land as we sailed into Liverpool Bay was the Blackpool Tower. Then, bobbing about in tidal waters marking the entrance to the Mersey, we passed the all familiar Bar Lightship.

Behind a backdrop of blue sky, the City of Liverpool's cathedral spire appeared on the horizon, bathed in bright morning sunshine, as if to welcome us back home.

Given advanced warning of our arrival, a pilot boarded the *S.S. Benbury* as she entered the River Mersey and, sailing up river, we passed many familiar landmarks. Still standing after five years of war, the offices of the Mersey Docks and Harbour Company facing the city's waterfront and the domes and twin spires of the Liver Buildings had come through unscathed, after the blitz on the City.

Now a blackened ruin, the Cotton Exchange, having been the target of an earlier bombing raid, stood empty and forlorn, a burnt-out shell. Like many fine old buildings in the area, it had been torn apart during enemy air raids. Sailing past the seven miles of docks, one noted idle cranes and empty warehouses as a result of heavy losses suffered by our Merchant Fleet. Thankfully, the shadow of war hanging over our country for the past five years, with its trail of wanton death and destruction, had now been lifted. With this in mind, I made ready to leave this rusting hulk that had been my home for the past six months, to spend a brief period of well-earned leave with my wife.

Saying goodbye to my shipmates aboard the *S.S. Benbury*, I made a point of seeing old Creswell, whom I found sitting in his cabin, staring into space. Rising from his chair, he shook me warmly by the hand and said, "Well, son, the old girl made it, just as I predicted."

With that far away look in his eyes, the tough old sea dog, who many said joined the vessel when her keel was laid, just shrugged his shoulders when I put the question to him, "What will you do, when the old tub is sent to the breaker's yard?"

Leaving him with his thoughts, I hurried off the ship into a waiting taxi that took me along country roads with fields of ripening corn to the place I called home, where my wife waited to welcome me.

Sandwiched between the rivers Mersey and Dee, the village of Oxton lies on the Wirral Peninsula, accessible by way of the Mersey Tunnel and Ferry or by the underground railway, with trains running from Liverpool to Birkenhead. As an alternative route to the area from outlying places on Merseyside and Cheshire, many motorists prefer to use the M.53 Motorway, running north and south along the peninsula.

During spells of leave, my wife and I would often drive along the motorway past the ancient City of Chester, lying deep in the Cheshire countryside, en route to nearby beauty spots in North Wales. It was a journey taking little over an hour by car.

But for peoples in the Pacific and on the continent of Asia, the dark clouds of war had continued to threaten their very existence, since the invasion of Pearl Harbour by Japanese forces in 1941.

We were now halfway into the month of July 1945, and my period of leave had hardly expired when I found myself back at the shipping office in Liverpool, reporting for duty. Putting pen to paper,

I joined the troop ship *M.V. Worcestershire*, a twin-screw vessel of eleven thousand tons, with a top speed of thirteen and a half knots. By noon of the following day, a contingent of troops had boarded the vessel and I was back out to sea, once again under sealed orders, and rumoured heading for the Middle East.

A smooth passage through the Bay of Biscay saw the vessel pass the Straits of Gibraltar, where all was peaceful and calm, as ships of all nations once again were free to enter the waters of the Mediterranean, without let or hindrance. In passing the Island of Malta I recalled, once again, a convoy codenamed Pedestal, where my ship was blown from beneath me, with the loss of so many of my shipmates. August 13,1942. It has never ceased to haunt me and will continue to do so, for the rest of my life.

Facing a stiff easterly breeze, we were now some five miles from the entrance to the Suez Canal and, as usual, an aroma of camel dung sullied one's nostrils. Built in 1869 by Firdinand de Lesseps, a French engineer, the canal has an overall measurement of 101 statute miles long and 186 feet wide, connecting the Mediterranean to the Red Sea. Freedom to navigate through the canal was granted to ships of all nations in time of peace or war under the Convention of 1888, thus shortening the time taken for the passage of ships from east to west. The canal saved shipping companies, with trade routes to India and all points east, much time and money.

Prior to entering the Port of Said, a pilot was assigned to the *M.V. Worcestershire*, ensuring her safe passage through the canal until reaching Port Taufiq, at the eastern entrance to the Red Sea. Our arrival at Port of Said set the scene for a motley collection of local ne'er-do-wells to gather in force on the quayside, waiting to pick the ship clean, if given a chance. Ropes hanging over the vessel's side were quickly hauled inboard before the locals, who could climb a coconut tree faster than a monkey, had a free hand to roam about the ship to plunder at will.

It was almost midday when we sailed out into the Red Sea on our way to God knows where, and what little breeze we enjoyed from the movement of the ship suddenly disappeared. Our cabins were hotter than a ship's stokehold, as the temperature climbed higher and higher until even breathing became difficult. Not until the setting of the sun that evening did the temperature in my cabin slowly recede, allowing myself and the rest of the ship's company a measure of respite from the burning heat of day.

CHAPTER 28

JAPAN SURRENDERS

As dawn was breaking on the morning of August 9, 1945, the *M.V. Worcestershire* was midway across the Indian Ocean, where the sight of a waterspout on the horizon was as natural as watching rain falling during the monsoon season. As expected, rumours from the galley wireless, a most unreliable source of information at best when secrecy is the watchword, gave our ultimate destination as Singapore. Having a quiet word with our navigation officer during my stint of duty at the helm, I asked him what our ultimate destination was. He simply shrugged his shoulders and replied, "Your guess is as good as mine."

It was then I noted the vessel was heading in an east-south-east direction, which would no doubt put us on course for Singapore. So, for once, I assumed the rumours from the galley wireless might, after all, be true.

Shortly before ten o'clock on that bright summer's morning, a series of loud explosions from the after end of the ship shattered the morning stillness, forcing the entire ship's company to hurry out onto the open deck. This was followed by a volley of parachute flares and rockets, being fired into the air, accompanied by a bout of cheering.

This led me to believe the guns crew on the afterdeck had, maybe, sunk a Japanese submarine, one of many reported to be operating in the Indian Ocean. It was not long before news spread around the ship like wildfire, that at precisely 9:44 a.m. that morning, an American B-29 bomber dropped an atomic bomb on Nagasaki, forcing Japan to surrender. At this point in time the *M.V. Worcestershire* was midway between Ceylon and Burma. Soon she received a message ordering the vessel to proceed to Rangoon. Arriving there, we discharged our complement of troops and supplies, and were told to await further orders.

After an anguished waiting period of two weeks, with nothing to do but watch sampans loaded with sightseers by day, and a contingent of rats on the quayside playing leapfrog at night, we made ready to receive our British prisoners of war who'd been languishing in Japanese labour camps. Around noon the following day, a train arrived alongside the ship and out staggered men who were nothing more than living skeletons. It was like Belsen, all over again.

Many of these men were so weak and undernourished they had to be helped up the ship's gangway, while others were carried aboard on stretchers. It was indeed a pitiful sight to see these young men, whose eyes were alive, but whose bodies suffered untold agony with tropical diseases such as Malaria, Dysentry and Hook Worms. Some two days later, I was glad to see the last of the City of Rangoon, as we sailed off down the Irrawaddy River to the open sea, en route for England and home.

M.V. Worcestershire *shown before the war with signal flags flying.*

Early in September the *M.V. Worcestershire* arrived back in home waters and sailed blithely up the River Mersey, berthing at the Princes Landing Stage in Liverpool. As soon as the ship was made fast, a number of buses bearing the insignia of the Red Cross drew alongside the vessel, taking our repatriated prisoners of war to nearby hospitals. Knowing the world by all accounts was now at peace, while packing my bags ready to leave the ship, I decided this would be an opportune time for me to swallow the anchor, so to speak. Signing off the ship later that day, I was given two weeks leave, and ordered to report back at the shipping office when it expired. We were officially still under the jurisdiction of the British Government, even though peace had been declared, so I still had to obey orders.

Sunset was inclined to be early toward the end of summer, and evening shadows had slowly crept in by the time I arrived home. Having received no warning of my home-coming, my wife was overjoyed to see me. Throwing her arms around me, she whispered, "The war is over now, so we can make plans for the future, dear."

She was rather upset when I told her I had to report back at the end of my leave, as she'd been unaware merchant ships and the men who sailed in them were still under the government's jurisdiction until further notice. There was, she agreed, little we could do about it for the present, and should try to make the best of it. There were, of course, the usual sarcastic remarks from her father, when he saw me later that evening. He said, "Back again, are you? So how long is it for this time? The war's over now, so why don't you look for a job ashore?"

He needn't have worried himself. My tentative inquiries at the offices of the Mersey Docks and Harbour Company, with a view to seeking employment, were paying off. Some two days later, I received word from the Harbour Master's Office that I was to get in touch with him as soon I returned home from sea. Although the weather tended to cool off toward the end of summer, we were blessed with plenty of sunshine throughout the rest of my leave. In fact the time, as usual, flew by all too quickly and here I was, back on the doorstep of the shipping office, wondering what they had cooked up for me this trip.

Hardly had I placed a foot inside the door when I was spotted by none other than my old sparing partner, Mr Repp, the inscrutable old devil, sitting behind his worm-eaten desk. Seeing me, he gave a sickly grin and, lifting a claw-like hand, beckoned me to him. I somehow guessed he had a surprise up his sleeve waiting for me, so I asked him, "What have you got for me this time, Mr Ripp, the same old garbage, I suppose?"

What little blood he had, in that skinny frame of his, rushed to his face, as he turned the colour of beetroot, and spluttered, "It's Mr Repp to you, sonny. Here's a ship I've had waiting for you."

Handing me a green slip of paper which, I knew from past experience, was a travel warrant, he gave a chuckle and said, "You'll have to go down to London to join the ship. How will that suit you?"

The M.V. Highland Monarch *was a Royal Mail steamer before being commandeered for the war effort.*

The old devil reached inside a desk, from which woodworm were trying to escape, and withdrew a sheaf of papers. Handing a single sheet to me, he said, "Those are your orders, I'll catch up with you when you come back."

Looking him in the eye, I quipped, "Not if I can help it, you silly old fart," and took to my heels, before he could open his mouth.

According to my instructions, I was to travel to London, where I was to join a ship there on a special assignment. Arriving at London's Tilbury dock late that afternoon, I was taken on board the Royal Mail steamer *M.V. Highland Monarch*, a vessel of about fifteen thousand tons, with a top speed of sixteen knots. Capable of accommodating several hundred passengers in time of peace, she had, throughout the war years, been commandeered by the government as a troop ship.

Among the many rumours running rife on board the ship, her ultimate destination, according to the galley wireless, was said to be the Middle East. Having spent some of my time at sea, in this theatre of war in convoy to the Island of Malta and, taking part in the invasion of Italy, I had no desire to renew my acquaintance with Egypt's pyramids, much less inhale a thousand and one obnoxious odours from wandering tribes of nomads and camel droppings, left to ferment along its shores. So it was with much foreboding I prepared myself, for whatever challenges lay ahead.

The day dawned bright and sunny, although a slight breeze tended to ruffle the murky waters of the River Thames, as the *M.V. Highland Monarch* left her berth. Entering the river on that late summer morning, her final destination veiled in secrecy was the main topic of conversation among the crew. Among many familiar sights missing along the Thames were the large silver barrage balloons that protected our ships from low-flying enemy bombers.

On our way to the Estuary we passed Southend-on-Sea where holiday makers, sunning themselves on the pier, looked on in silence as we sailed by. Rounding the North Foreland lightship into the North Sea, we set course for the English Channel. Steaming at a steady fifteen knots in calm weather, it was heartening to see Dover's White Cliffs looming up on our starboard hand. Tall and majestic they rose up from the sea, like some statue larger than life itself, guarding the entrance to the Straits.

In a never-ending stream, ocean-going freighters and coastwise vessels, having sailed in convoy throughout the war years, were now free to ply their trade without let or hindrance around British waters. As night fell along England's channel coast, a rare sight presented itself: illuminations on pleasure beaches that had been blacked-out for so long, lit up the night sky. Passing the Isles of Scilly at daybreak, the *Highland Monarch* altered course toward Ushant, on the French coast, northernmost point of the Bay of Biscay. Seeing the Red Ensign fluttering from the vessel's stern, crews of French trawlers waved excitedly. Free after five years of German occupation, their gratitude came to the fore, with cries of Vive Angleterre.

Renowned for its inclement weather, the Bay of Biscay lay as calm as a millpond, encouraging off duty members of the crew to bask in the warm sunshine. Abreast of Cape Finistere, my worst fears were realized when the vessel continued to hug the coast along the western seaboard of Spain and Portugal, apparently heading for the Straits of Gibraltar. Throughout the night, hurried changes to the ship's course were carried out by the officer on watch, in order to avoid fouling the nets of inshore fishing fleets, an exercise he could well have done without.

Within hailing distance of Gibraltar at daybreak, silhouettes of three naval vessels patrolling the area appeared on the far horizon. Picking up his binoculars, Fullbright, the duty officer, stepped out onto the wing of the bridge and studied them closely.

"Oh, it's just a few of our naval craft returning to the Rock," was his nonchalant comment, receiving no more than a grunt from the Captain in response.

Passing through Gibraltar's Straits into the Mediterranean later that morning, one viewed the Rock in all its glory, a formidable obstacle for an enemy to overcome. Overshadowing the landscape for miles around, Gibraltar's massive Rock dwarfs the City of Gibraltar and the Spanish border town of La Linea. This giant of nature, attached to the mainland by a narrow sandy isthmus, stands as the acknowledged guardian of the Western entrance to the Mediterranean Sea.

We continued steaming along at a comfortable speed of fifteen knots while the sun grew hotter by the hour, with temperatures soaring over one hundred degrees at midday. Approaching the Island of Malta, strong southerly winds blowing across the Libyan Desert into the Mediterranean caused no more than a ripple on the sea's glassy surface, as the vessel continued her steady progress toward Port Said. This island fortress of Malta, strategically placed between Gibraltar to the west and the Egyptian port of Alexandria to the east, was a thorn in the side of would-be German invaders throughout five long years of World War II. When Malta is no more than a dark smudge on the horizon, one is aware of being in close proximity to the Suez Canal, long before catching sight of this gateway to the east. Suddenly a pungent aroma of Oriental spices and camel dung tends to savage the nostrils.

No sooner had we berthed at Port Said, an advance party of West Indian troops stationed in and around the Suez Canal Zone boarded the ship. Before nightfall, a further complement of fifteen hundred of their number boarded the *M.V. Highland Monarch* and, within the hour, we were back out to sea.

Was this the special assignment we had been chosen to carry out, I wondered, and was there really any need for all the secrecy in performing a cloak and dagger exercise?

Our hasty departure from London was, indeed, to transport West Indian troops back to their homeland from the Middle East, and this turned out to be a most enjoyable experience.

As darkness fell each night, we had nothing more to contend with than listening to a harmonizing of native voices as they sang of home, accompanied by the rhythm of bongo music. So much easier on the ears than the horrific rumble of explosions, as ships were torpedoed and sunk on a daily basis throughout five years of war. Our leisurely sojourn around these sun-kissed tropical islands lasted but three weeks. In that time, batches of West Indian soldiers were discharged ashore to their homelands in Barbados, Trinidad, Bahamas, Antigua and St. Lucia.

CHAPTER 29

THE MYSTERY DEEPENS

At Belize, the capital of British Honduras in Central America, our main contingent of troops disembarked and, believing our mission had been accomplished, I took it for granted we were about to return to England. Instead a wave of disappointment swept throughout the ship when we received orders to proceed south to Buenos Aires, the capital of Argentina. Suffice to say, once again, an air of mystery surrounded this latest order. Why should we be visiting a country who stabbed us in the back when aiding and abetting the Nazis at the outbreak of World War II when things looked black?

Arriving at Rio de la Plata, the estuary between Argentina and Uruguay, silhouettes of two large naval vessels were seen cruising up and down on the far horizon. Anxious to discover their nationality, Vicary, the ship's Third Officer, clapped a telescope to his eye, and studied them for a moment. Lowering the eyeglass, he turned to Captain Richards standing nearby, and remarked, "Looks like the Argentine Navy is having a day out."

Making no response, the Captain left the duty officer on the port wing of the bridge and entered the chart room. Taking a map from a pigeon hole above the desk, he spread it out on the table in front of him, studying it intensely. Entering the estuary, we picked up a pilot and continued our journey up river, berthing close to the shopping centre in Buenos Aires. Within a matter of minutes, rolls of heavy wire netting and lengths of stout timbers arrived on board and were placed at various points around the ship's deck. Shortly after midday carpenters arrived and began to fence off sections of the vessel around the second class passenger accommodation. At this point the question on everyone's lips was, "What on earth is going on?"

Rumours aboard the *Highland Monarch* were now at fever pitch, ranging from the sublime, to the ridiculous. At sunrise the following morning, the sight of a Royal Navy destroyer arriving at the port, caused more confusion to a puzzled ship's crew. The plot deepened

The Graf Spee *terrorized Allied convoys in the South Atlantic before being cornered by the Royal Navy.*

when a complement of Royal Marines was seen to leave the naval vessel and board our ship.

As is the custom in Latin countries, the local populace were enjoying a midday siesta when several coaches, escorted by a contingent of the local gendarmerie, arrived alongside the ship. Under the watchful eye of these gun-toting *señors*, the occupants of the coaches were quickly shepherded aboard our vessel. Members of the crew wondered who these people could be as the *Highland Monarch* made ready to leave port.

Under cover of darkness we slipped out of Buenos Aires harbour that evening, with our destroyer escort following close astern.

Outside international waters, we rendezvoused with the Royal Navy cruisers *Ajax* and *Achilles*, who played such an important part in the sinking of the notorious German battleship *Admiral Graf Spee*. As for our mysterious passengers, confined to wire cages on the second class deck, many of the crew had reason to believe they were illegal immigrants from the U.K. The mystery however was solved some hours later when the *Highland Monarch* was well out to sea and we were informed they were the crew of the *Admiral Graf Spee*.

With nowhere to run or hide, after being cornered by the British Navy on the thirteenth of December 1939 during the Battle of the River Plate, the battleship *Graf Spee* was scuttled, on orders from Hitler. It was, therefore, a fitting tribute to the Royal Navy's light cruisers *Ajax* and *Achilles* who along with the *Exeter* were responsible for trapping the *Graf Spee*, to be given the task of escorting the battleship's crew back from whence they came.

Faced with a fuel shortage, it was decided the *Highland Monarch* would set course for Freetown, Sierra Leone, to replenish her oil supply. Our arrival was seen to attract a gathering of natives to the ship anxious to sell their bananas, oranges and limes. Refuelling the ship took place well into the hours of darkness when the swarms of mosquitoes and nocturnal creatures, attracted by the vessel's arc lights, descended on us like a plague of locusts.

Before the light of dawn had streaked across the far horizon to herald a new day, the *Highland Monarch* and her escorting destroyers were well out to sea. Sierra Leone's palm fringed coastline of jungle green had all but faded from view when the morning sun suddenly appeared as an orange ball of fire to peep above the ocean on its heavenward climb. With little wind, other than that produced by the speed of the ship itself, on a sea of glass, the sweltering heat of an equatorial day became unbearable. Regular sluicing of the vessel's wooden decks had to be maintained in an effort to cool fast-melting seams of tar, while on the African coast.

From behind a barrier of chain link fencing separating them from the rest of ship's company, Germans looked on sullen-faced, as seamen hosed the vessel down. Weather-wise, the temperature had cooled off considerably by the time the ship was due to arrive in Lisbon, the Portuguese capital. Our next port of call being a short distance away, Conroy, a young seaman barely out of his teens, rubbed his hands together gleefully, and gave old Dobson, the ship's Bo'sun, a knowing wink.

"I guess we're okay for a leg up ashore tonight?" he grinned.

Dobson smiled sardonically. "Don't count on it, son, we might only be here for a short while," he replied.

"Oh! C'mon, boss, don't be a spoil sport," Conroy chided. "I suppose the lead has run out of your pencil," he teased.

"It's a pity you don't use up your energy scrubbing the decks," Dobson sneered, turning his back on the cocky young fellow.

A call for all hands, to standby stations as we entered port, put paid to a heated argument between the two, as they went to their separate stations, fore and aft. At the mouth of the Tagus, a river spiralling from east to west across Portugal, we picked up a pilot, who took the ship into the harbour, where we dropped anchor. This was a set back for several of the ship's company hoping for a spell of shore leave, in particular Seamen Conroy. He expected the ship to berth alongside the wharf and cursed his luck when his well-laid plans went up in smoke. There would be no opportunity for him to spend a night ashore in the arms of some amorous Portuguese maiden, in the city's red light district. For him, it would be no more than a pipe dream.

Cursing the ship's Captain, Conroy slipped away to his quarters on the after-deck and, lying on his bunk, gazed longingly toward the shore. Through the open porthole of his cabin he could see people moving about on the shore, and let off a stream of abuse. He blamed the pilot and ship's Captain for his misfortune in having to remain on board and eventually fell asleep, to dream of what might have been.

Midway through an imaginary *tête-à-tête* with a young *señorita*, he was rudely awakened by the Bo'sun bellowing in his ear, "C'mon me, lad, let's be having you!"

Rubbing the sleep from his eyes, Conroy crawled out of his bunk. Shading his face from the glare of the afternoon sun as he stepped out on the open deck, he was greeted by Dobson, the ship's Bo'sun, who waited for him to appear. Grinning from ear to ear, Dobson placed a friendly arm around Conroy's shoulder and, teasing him, said, "There'll be no dipping yer wick tonight, son. Our passengers have just arrived and, as soon as they've embarked, we'll be on our way."

Turning a deaf ears to Bo'son's remark, Conroy took hold of a mooring rope they passed up to him from a launch that had arrived alongside the ship, and secured it to a nearby bollard. Sullen-faced, he stood watching members of the German Legation, stationed in Lisbon who were being repatriated, struggle up the vessel's accommodation ladder with their luggage. Cursing them under his breath, he refused to help them on board and sauntered off to his quarters.

No sooner had the last of our German deportees clambered aboard, the *Highland Monarch* slipped from the harbour, to rendez-vous with her escorting destroyer out at sea. Heading in a northerly direction, the vessel was forced to alter course several times during the hours of darkness, to avoid the nets of Portuguese sardine fisher-men strung out in never-ending lines along the coast. Passing Cape Finisterre, on a warm sunny morning in late July, we entered the Bay of Biscay, with hardly a ripple on its surface.

Some twenty-four hours were to pass before we sighted the is-land of Ushant, on the French coast, where the vessel altered course to enter the English Channel. Threading our way along England's southern coast, past ships of all shapes and sizes, something we were not accustomed to seeing for the last five years, as we set course for Dover.

Abeam of Dover's White Cliffs, the ship altered course to port, and entered the North Sea. We were now on the final leg of our spe-cial assignment, bound for the Elbe Estuary and the City of Hamburg, or what remained of it following months of sustained air raids by Allied Forces.

At the mouth of the Elbe, the vessel slowed down to pick up a pilot, then proceeded on her way up river. On either side of the ship's deck, the erstwhile crew of the *Admiral Graff Spee* looked on in alarm at unbelievable scenes of destruction to their homeland.

Steaming up river toward the port of Hamburg, the *Highland Monarch* wove her way in and out of sunken vessels lying in her path, along the eighty-five mile stretch. With uncanny skill and good seamanship on the part of the pilot in avoiding these obstacles, our arrival at the port of Hamburg was greeted by a wall of silence. Un-like the glory days when Hitler ruled the roost, there were no brass bands or cheering crowds to welcome the crew of the German battleship back home. Crestfallen, they gazed at the ruins of their once great city of Hamburg, unwilling to believe this could have happened to the fatherland. In the city's bomb-scarred streets people wandered aimlessly about, looking for food.

Seeing such utter desolation staring you in the face, you could not help feeling sorry for ill-clad children, attempting to sneak on board the *Highland Monarch*, looking for scraps of food from the ship's garbage bins. I was more than relieved to leave this shattered city of rubble and desolation, choosing to remember a once proud city of Hamburg.

As soon as the last of our disillusioned German prisoners disembarked and having completed her mission, the *Highland Monarch* once again faced the unenviable task of manoeuvring past sunken vessels along the river Elbe. Entering the North Sea, we set sail for England where, as in those far off days before the outbreak of World War II, there were scenes of non-stop activity. Fleets of fishing trawlers from Hull and Grimsby on England's eastern seaboard could be heard over the air waves, exchanging greetings with colliers sailing out of the Tyne. Ocean-going freighters and passenger liners once again sailed the seven seas as before, free to come and go, unhindered and without fear of being torn asunder by enemy U-boats and dive-bombers.

Counting myself one of the luckiest among my seafaring comrades to have survived those dark days of war, a prayer of thanks escaped my lips as the vessel sailed up the broad reaches of the River Mersey. Abreast of Gladstone Dock lying at the northern end of the city's dock system, the *Highland Monarch* was taken in tow by tugs from the Alexander Towing Company, and shepherded into her berth. Having made up my mind this would be my last voyage to sea, now the war was over, I was anxious to sign off the ship and be on my way home.

With the berthing of the ship completed, I wasted little time collecting my few belongings and headed for home.

"Oh, Rowland," Gladys whispered, as we embraced, "it's wonderful to have you home again."

"Hopefully, it will be for good, this time," I replied. "I've no intention of going back to sea, if I can help it."

"Oh, that will be lovely, dear!" she cried, as she held me tight. "What will you do?"

"Let's go in the house," I said, taking her by the hand. "Then I'll tell you what I have in mind."

Over a cup of tea, I told her I'd been looking for a job with the Mersey Docks and Harbour Company prior to leaving on my last voyage. The gentleman who interviewed me at the Harbour Company's Office said I should see him when I came home.

"But what about your leave, dear," my wife asked. "You have a couple of weeks due to you?"

"If I'm offered the job, I'm quite prepared to accept it, and sacrifice whatever leave is due," I told her.

CHAPTER 30

ASHORE AT LAST

At the end of August 1948, I received my discharge papers from the Merchant Service and took them with me to the Harbour Office where I was informed a vacancy existed at Huskisson Dock, at the North End of Liverpool. Although I lived some distance from the area, I told the Harbour Master I was quite prepared to travel, if offered the job. A week later, I signed an agreement to abide by the Company's rules and regulations and was told to report for duty at the Dockmaster's office at Huskisson Dock, at eight o'clock on Monday morning. To all intents and purposes, I was now a land lubber or, should I with tongue in cheek simply say, a dryland sailor.

Hurrying home, I gave the good news to Gladys who was over-joyed to hear I'd given up my career at sea. When my initial two-week period of training was finished, I took to my new job like a duck takes to water and soon learned to operate the hydraulic machinery used to open and close the lock gates. Shallow drafted vessels, such as barges and coasters, were able to sail in and out of the system, according to the state of the tide, four hours before and four hours after high water.

Ocean-going freighters and passenger liners moved in and out of the dock system according to the ship's draft, after which time the lock gates were closed until the next tide. Periods on duty were of eight hours duration, similar to those worked on ships at sea. Uniform clothing supplied by the company on a yearly basis, consisted of a suit, shirt, tie, boots or shoes, an overcoat, and a suit of oilskins for use in wet weather. Employees were expected to report for duty wearing their uniform, looking neat and tidy at all times.

So engrossed was I in my work I hardly noticed the passing of 5 years of time until I received a message from the Harbour Master's Office asking if I would like a transfer nearer home, to the company's Alfred Dock System across the River Mersey at Birkenhead. Needless to say I jumped at the opportunity to be near my home. Having to say goodbye to many friends one has worked with over the years, is never easy.

As a newcomer at the Alfred Dock, my first week on duty was spent on the night shift, in late November of 1953. With a cold easterly wind whistling around my ears and rain coming down by the bucketful, I trudged up and down a lock adjacent to the river entrance in an effort to keep myself warm. During my next twenty years at the Alfred Dock System, I spent many a cold winter's night chilled to the marrow.

Having settled into my new surroundings, as an established member of the Harbour Company, I now found time to renew the search for my mother. With time to spare, my wife and I agreed to spend part of our vacation each year searching for her, well aware we were looking for a needle in a haystack.

I was driven on by a desire to meet my sister Caroline. As elusive as ever, Mother must have taken great pains to cover her tracks, leaving no trace of her movements. Houdini himself could not have done better. We kept looking for her, fruitless though it seemed, until my daughter Susan was born in 1955.

Determined, I decided to try another route in a last ditch effort to trace this will-o'-the-wisp mother of mine and placed an advert in the *Empire News*, an established Sunday newspaper, hoping someone on this tiny island of ours might happen to read it, and get in touch with me. Time without number failure had stared me in the face, yet time itself could not extinguish a spark of hope that burned within me, that I might one day meet my sister. Knowing little about her other than she was younger than me, I would often think of her, and wonder where she was. Had she managed to survive the perils of World War II, and was she like me, happily married? Absorbed in my day to day work passing ships in and out of the port, I was left with little time to dwell on the pain and heartache caused by my mother, for whatever reason she had, in wanting to keep my sister and I apart. There were of course times when I allowed myself to drift off into my world of make-believe, and a thousand and one thoughts would flash through my mind. Day-dreaming, I would picture my sister Caroline standing before me, a perfect resemblance of her mother who, when young, was very beautiful. Then as dreams often do, those precious moments slowly melt away and I find myself back to stark reality.

Midway through my twenty-fifth year of service with the Harbour Company, I was promoted to Marine Supervisor, a position carrying a great deal of responsibility. Throughout the next ten years, many changes occurred whereby Harbour Company employees nearing retirement were offered early release, with a pension and the golden handshake. This was a sum of money given to an individual for his years of loyal service.

A step up the promotion ladder was within my grasp, when an old war injury put paid to my career. Seeing one of my men struggling to heave a ship's mooring rope ashore, I ran to assist him and felt a searing pain in the lower part of my back. I was unable to walk and had to be taken home in an ambulance. My family doctor examined me the following day, but could do little more than prescribe a course of painkillers and arrange for me to visit a specialist. In his report to my employer, the specialist informed them I was suffering from a damaged vertebrae in the lower half of my back and would be unfit for work, for the foreseeable future.

Visiting the local hospital for physio treatment which lasted several weeks, I was fitted with a corset by a therapist, enabling me to move about without the aid of a stick. No sooner was I back on my

feet, I received a letter from the Harbour Office in Liverpool, requesting I attend an interview with a company representative. Concerned
for my future welfare, the company felt it best that I be placed on the
retirement list and granted me a handsome amount in severance pay
for my years of service with them, plus a monthly pension.

My employment with the company, the Harbour Master informed
me, would be terminated as of June 30, 1976. Signing the necessary
documents severing my ties with the company, I thanked him and
hurried home to give my wife the news. A couple of days later, I
returned to the dock office to clear my locker and pick up a few personal belongings, before saying goodbye to my many friends, and
then left, without a backward glance.

So here I was, at the age of fifty-seven, being put out to grass, so
to speak, because of a war injury I received in 1942, when enemy dive
bombers blew my ship apart. In the months following my retirement,
I received a further course of physiotherapy, enabling me to move
with greater freedom. Far from allowing the grass to grow under my
feet, I carried out minor repairs to the lovely home I shared with my
wife, in the Cheshire countryside. Soon I was fit enough to travel
wherever I pleased, and made arrangements for the two of us to spend
a winter holiday basking in Mediterranean sunshine, on the beautiful
Spanish Island of Majorca.

On a bitterly cold morning in January of 1979, my wife and I
boarded a plane at Manchester Airport, and flew off to our island in
the sun. Winging our way over the snow-capped mountains of the
Pyrenees, separating France from the Iberian Peninsula, we touched
down some two hours later at Palma, the island's capital, bathed in
sunshine. Leaving the aircraft, we divested our heavy overcoats and,
boarding a coach, were whisked away to our hotel, the Rio Bravo,
little more than a stone's throw from the beach. The accommodation
was first class with everything we needed, including air-conditioned
rooms with balcony facing the sea and an indoor swimming pool,
with restaurant close by.

Buffet style meals were served for breakfast from eight to ten
a.m., and dinner from seven to nine p.m., allowing guests time to

explore the island throughout the day. Taking full advantage of this opportunity to go sightseeing, Gladys and I visited many wonderful sites, such as the pearl and leather factories, and the Caves of Drac. Between trips around the island, much of our time was spent down by the shore, where foam-laced Atlantic rollers caressed the island's sun-kissed beaches.

 All too soon it was time to leave this sun-drenched island paradise and return to Manchester's wet and wind. Having enjoyed ourselves so much, we returned to sample the good life on the nearby islands of Ibiza and Minorca, taking my daughter's family with us for their summer holidays. Then, as a special treat for my wife, whose one wish was to visit America, my daughter arranged for the family to spend our next holiday at Fort Lauderdale in Florida for her birthday, on the first of May.

On a day heavy with rain, we boarded a Laker Airways flight at Manchester Airport and took off into the wide blue yonder as the sun tried in vain to find a way past banks of ominous black cloud. Arriving at Miami Airport as dusk was falling, we hurried from our aircraft into an air conditioned arrivals lounge, to escape the heat of a tropical night. Clearing customs and immigration at the airport, we boarded a coach and were taken to Stouffer's beach side hotel in Fort Lauderdale. Shortly after settling in, we visited one of many car hire companies in the area and booked a vehicle that would carry five of us in comfort to Florida's Walt Disney World.

Shortly after sunrise next morning, we took breakfast at a nearby restaurant, then drove at a leisurely pace along the motorway to Orlando. From a list of holiday apartments supplied by the tourists' board, we booked into Larson's Lodge, a well-run motel with swimming pool and sauna, offering residents a free breakfast. Having settled in for the next four days we set off for Walt Disney World, just a short step away.

Boarding a paddle steamer with hundreds of tourists visiting the Magic Kingdom, my wife sat there starry-eyed, listening to the haunting melody of *When You Wish Upon a Star*, as we sailed around the theme park. It seemed as if she were back in her childhood days, reliving scenes one reads about in story books, knowing her dream of a lifetime was, at last, coming to fruition. This truly was an unforgettable moment in her life and a very emotional one, surging back and forth through her sylphlike figure. It was by chance I saw a tear roll down her cheek, and nudging my daughter sitting beside me, I whispered, "Your mother's on cloud nine, dear, she's in a world of her own."

It was a wise man who once said nothing is forever, and no truer words were spoken for it was soon time to return home, taking with us the memory of a holiday we were to enjoy many times over, recalling it in the years to come. Arriving at Manchester Airport where, believe it or not, the sun was cracking the flagstones, so to speak, we picked up our car and headed home, with nothing to do except make plans for our next winter holiday in the sun.

Sadly, during a holiday on the Spanish island of Majorca in the winter of 1988, my wife was taken ill, so I decided it was best we return home. I felt she would be far better off under the care of her family doctor, who was familiar with her case history. Arriving back home, my wife paid a visit to Doctor Richards who, on examining her, referred her to a specialist at the local hospital. This came as quite a shock to us both, more especially when he informed her she was suffering from an irritable colon. For a time, the medication prescribed helped ease the pain she suffered, allowing us to continue holidaying on the Spanish Islands of Majorca and Ibiza, with alternative jaunts to Florida in the U.S.A.

Shortly before we were due to take off for the Canary Islands on a winter's morning in March of 1990, her condition suddenly worsened. Our holiday was cancelled and Gladys was admitted to the local hospital. Throughout a period of five weeks, she was given a series of tests. Sitting at her bedside, I looked on as the white-coated figure of the hospital's resident doctor passed down the ward and stopped to talk to several patients, hoping he would say to my wife, "you can go home now, Mrs Marshall," but it was not to be.

As he approached my wife's bed, she asked, "Have my results come through, Doctor?"

He stood in silence for what seemed an eternity, then in a voice barely audible, replied, "I'm sorry, Mrs Marshall. There is nothing we can do for you."

Outwardly calm, my wife bravely asked, "How long do I have, Doctor?"

Somewhat reluctant to answer her question, he shrugged his shoulders in a gesture of hopelessness, and said, "It's in the hands of the Lord, Mrs Marshall. It could be days, weeks or even months."

I sat there, in abject silence, listening to the doctor's report on the state of my wife's health, as the strength drained from my body and tears, I fought so hard to control, ran down my cheeks. There was nothing I could do. Unaware the doctor had already left my wife's bedside, I sat, as if in a trance staring into space, until I felt a hand on my shoulder, and turned to face the young nurse attending my wife. I detected a note of compassion in her voice, when she said, "Doctor would like to see you in his office, Mr Marshall. Would you please come with me?"

Leaving my wife's bedside, I followed the nurse from the ward. Motioning me to be seated, the doctor finished wrapping a small package, and handing it to me, said, "This is your wife's medication. Please make sure she takes it each day, as directed. I have also arranged for her to receive frequent visits from a member of the McMillan Nursing Order, who will attend to all her needs."

Stemming a flood of tears threatening to spill over, I managed to put on a brave face while inside my stomach turned cartwheels. Thanking the doctor for his kindness, I left his office and returned to the ward, where my wife waited for me to take her home. For a time this change of environment worked wonders for her. In fact, there appeared to be a vast improvement in her state of health the moment she left hospital. Whether this was due to the homely atmosphere or the medication, I could not be sure. Suffice to say, within a few days, she seemed to be her old self again, enjoying life as before. The transformation in her well-being was so remarkable, I kept asking myself, could a wrong diagnosis have been made by the specialist at the hospital?

Her condition continued to improve with each passing day, until eventually she was well enough to accompany me on shopping trips.

Spring arrived a little earlier than usual that year. Forsythia, encouraged by the sun's warmth to leave its winter retreat, blossomed with a flourish of brilliant yellow. In parks and gardens, crocus, snowdrops and daffodils peeped from earth brown nurseries, to exhibit a riot of colour.

The first half of the month of April simply flew by and, Easter, a special time of the year for Gladys and me, was almost upon us. Weatherwise, we were treated to our usual spell of sunshine and intermittent showers. Easter Sunday we would always remember as that of our first meeting way back in 1943, during a time of war. Since that time we had aged, yet when I looked at the love of my life, she was to me just as beautiful as she was on our first date all those many years ago, when I presented her with a bouquet of yellow tulips. The march of time had no doubt treated her kindly for when we first met she was such a dainty young thing, slim of build with auburn hair and a pair of laughing brown eyes the image of which will remain with me forever.

Our friendship blossomed into romance soon after our first meeting and, eventually, led to our being married a year later with the wedding taking place on her birthday, the first of May. That we might suddenly be torn apart came as a terrible blow, for she was my shoulder to lean on, my confident and a wonderful wife, mother, and friend. I could not bear the thought of losing her. Yet somehow I sensed there was no escape from the illness, now ravaging her body. With the time available to us all too short, I was not prepared to face the inevitable when it came.

With the passing days, my wife's internal condition worsened, for it was now clear the disease was beginning to take its toll. I too felt the pain of her suffering, for her face had now paled and she looked worn out. Soon, tiny furrows appeared on her forehead, but as ever, the laughing brown eyes never wavered. Her indomitable spirit would as always come to the fore, in that she refused to succumb to her incurable illness.

In the short space of time since leaving hospital, she'd made a remarkable recovery, but was now slipping away. With no more than a shrug of the shoulders, she would brush aside problems that we mere mortals grapple with throughout our lives, for she had no fear of tomorrow's unknown. She was simply accepting with dignity whatever lay ahead.

She was now at peace with herself and living life to the full, but the radiant smile and outward calm emanating from her person, gave little sign, if any, our time together would be so short-lived.

CHAPTER 31

A TIME OF SORROW

For whatever length of time the good Lord chose to allow us, we sought to enjoy each precious moment and set off to our caravan home to the beautiful Isle of Anglesey. Driving along the North Wales coast road, en route to our enchanted hideaway, one passes villages and white-washed cottages, nestled amid the green hills of North Wales. From the Welsh mainland, we drove over Telford's suspension bridge across the Menai Straits, to the Isle of Anglesey. A short distance from the town of Beaumaris, we arrived at our holiday home near the village of Penmon.

The Isle of Anglesey has long been recognized as a former stronghold of the Druids, whose cult was stamped out by the Romans in A.D. 61. To this day a stark reminder of the Roman presence can be seen in the island's seaport town of Holyhead, where the remains of a high-walled Roman fort runs through the town's centre. Ships sailing from the harbour run a local passenger service to the United Kingdom, Ireland, and the Isle of Man throughout the summer months, attracting many thousands of tourists who choose to roam at will around this beautiful island.

The island's rugged coastline of mile after mile of sheer cliffs and dangerous reefs has claimed hundreds of ships that foundered there in south-westerly gales during the hard winter months. Elsewhere, the island is largely given over to heathland and rough pasture, where smallholders are content to rear pigs, black cattle and geese. During the winter, the sturdily-built whitewashed farmhouses of rough-hewn stone in which the local people live, are often buffeted unmercifully by howling gales sweeping in from the Irish Sea.

From the Coastguard Station at Black Point, one has a bird's eye view of Puffin Island lying less than a mile from the shore. As we strolled along a deserted beach that evening, a gathering of sea birds wheeling around in the clear blue sky overhead caught our attention. They seemed intent on shadowing large shoals of mackerel who in turn were pursuing schools of whitebait on the incoming tide. For several minutes they watched and waited as the mackerel circled around in a frenzy, gorging themselves on their smaller prey. Then suddenly the hunters became the hunted, as flocks of herring gulls swooped in for the kill.

As with most towns and villages in North Wales, Sunday is strictly a day of observance, with both young and old in this ancient town of Beaumaris attending chapel. Although not of the same denomination as the local people who are for the most part Welsh Methodist, my wife, being an ardent churchgoer, insisted on attending Sunday morning service with them. Since in many communities throughout the area, the church is, and always has been apart from anything else, a storehouse of information and local gossip, I felt a reluctance to enter its hallowed portals.

Within this independent and close-knit community, outsiders arriving in town are tolerated with a certain amount of caution. Therefore, our entrance into their holy of holies was cause enough for the tiny congregation to turn their heads as one, and gaze with suspicion at the strangers in their midst. Nevertheless, one could forgive them for their peculiar behaviour and off-hand attitude to new arrivals, when one chanced to hear the voices of their church choir raised in song. Echoing throughout the hills and valleys of the Welsh countryside, their lilting refrains would charm the birds from the tree tops.

Around the nearby village of Penmon, an abundance of early spring colour had no sooner faded from view, before summer's wild flowers appeared, covering banks and hedgerows throughout country lanes. A stranger, passing through the village itself, will often pause to catch the heady perfume of roses in the morning air, or maybe stop to admire gardens with neatly-clipped lawns surrounded by beds of geraniums, edged with blue and white lobelia. And in the distance, one views Holyhead Mountain, the island's highest point rising to a height of 720 feet above a landscape of green and summer-gold.

Wandering hand-in-hand along the island's country lanes and sandy beaches enjoying days of endless sunshine, we also spent time combing its rocky shoreline. Here, quite by chance, we discovered tiny coves echoing to the sound of the in-rushing tide, as it swept over banks of sea-washed shingle.

Then changing direction, we sought to wander through dense woods to suddenly come within sight of elegant old Tudor-style houses on Anglesey's southern shore, where the Menai Straits separates the island from the Welsh mainland.

Nearing the end of our second month on this wild and beautiful island, I noted a gradual change in my wife's health. Although tanned by the sun, her face appeared pale and drawn. It was, however, her loss of appetite that caused me the greatest concern, more especially since I was helpless to alleviate the awful pain and suffering she endured, other than give her medication. Yet through it all, she steadfastly refused to allow me to take her home. Sadly the day arrived when my wife was overcome with fatigue during one of our daily walks along the shore, and our time together on this charming island had to be cut short.

This sudden decline, in her state of health, worried me so much I simply had to take her back to our caravan home, where she collapsed exhausted on the settee. I was so concerned for her well-being, I made ready to leave the island without delay, and return home. Crossing the Menai Bridge onto the Welsh mainland, our journey through the town of Bangor during the midday rush hour was an absolute nightmare. Studying a road map I took an alternative route to avoid traffic jams in and around the seaside towns of Conway, Colwyn Bay, and Llandudno, arriving at the Cheshire village of Oxton as night was falling, where my daughter waited to meet us.

"Is Mother alright?" she asked, as I stepped from the car.

I could see the worried look on her face, and replied, "Mother's very ill, dear." Holding the car door open, I said, "You'll have to help me into the house with her, she's hardly able to walk."

Gladys was weakened by this illness and thoroughly exhausted after such a long journey. With my daughter's help, we carried her gently upstairs to bed. Making her as comfortable as possible I waited at her bedside until she dozed off, then left her sleeping peacefully to return down stairs. In the lounge, I sat talking with my daughter for a while before deciding there was little we could do at this late hour of the day, doctor's surgery having finished some hours earlier.

"Try not to worry, Dad," my daughter whispered, and taking her leave of me, said, "Give me a call, if you need me."

I heard the front door close behind her and watched from the lounge window, as she disappeared from view. I felt so tired and distraught. It seemed as if I had suddenly been transported from sunlight, to a place of eternal darkness. The long journey home, having drained me mentally and physically, I managed to creep quietly upstairs, before some much-needed sleep caught up with me.

Careful, lest I disturb my wife who now slept soundly, I slipped into an adjoining room, leaving the door slightly ajar. Seizing this opportunity to close my eyes and snatch a few hours rest, I undressed, and literally fell into bed. But sleep would not come, for I just lay there listening to the sound of my wife's laboured breathing in the next room. Tossing and turning well into the small hours, I finally dropped off into a fitful sleep.

Waking long after the sun had risen high in the morning sky, I withdrew my bedroom curtains and peered out. It was a beautiful summer's day and from the garden below the scent of orange blossom drifted up, filling the morning air. From the branches of a nearby horse chestnut tree, the trill of a blackbird flowed through the open window of my room and, as if in answer to its tuneful song, the bells in the village church struck the hour of eight. Worried the noise might disturb my wife who lay fast asleep in the next room, I closed my bedroom window.

Her poor state of health and heavy breathing worried me greatly, as I stood at the bedside of the woman I loved, with a longing to help her in her hour of need. Helpless to do so, I became angry and reproached myself for being so useless and, tip-toeing quietly down stairs to the kitchen, I closed the door behind me and busied myself preparing breakfast.

A sudden cry of pain from the bedroom saw me hurrying to my wife's aid. Fearing the worst, I dashed up stairs and, to my horror, saw her lying in a crumpled heap on the bathroom floor, unconscious. My first thought was to gather her up in my arms but, fearing complications might set in, I hesitated to do so. Instead, I placed a pillow beneath her head and, covering her with a blanket to keep her warm, rang the family doctor, seeking whatever help he was able to provide.

Within minutes of the doctor arriving, he examined my wife and said, "I'm afraid she'll have to go to hospital, immediately."

With a helping hand from the doctor we managed to lift her from the bathroom floor into the bedroom, where she slowly regained conscious. Pale and drawn she gazed up at me through pain-filled eyes and whispered, "Don't worry, dear, I'm going to be alright."

Sitting beside her I could not but admire the courageous manner with which she made light of her life-threatening disease.

"Dear Lord," I murmured to myself, "if only what she said were true."

The mournful sound of an ambulance siren could be heard long before the vehicle arrived at the house. With amazing speed and efficiency, they quickly transferred my wife to the local hospital. Unable to take my eyes off the vehicle until it was out of sight, I sat by the window surrounded by a sea of loneliness. Then falling to my knees I offered a prayer to the Almighty for her safekeeping.

"Was this to be the end?" I kept asking myself. "Did the good Lord spare me from certain death those many years ago, that I should suffer a catastrophe such as this? Had He deserted me in my hour of need?" I wondered.

Swirling emotions careened subconsciously through my mind, leaving me in a state of utter confusion. Tears I'd forcibly withheld for so long fell unashamedly when, in the midst of prayer, an outward feeling of calm descended upon me. Its purpose: to leave me at peace with the world once again. Rising unsteadily from the bedside where my wife had lain, I returned downstairs to the lounge, and telephoned my daughter.

At the sound of her hello, I drew a deep breath, and said, "Your mother was taken to Arrowe Park Hospital a short time ago, dear."

A note of alarm in her voice, she gasped, "Why, what has happened to her, Dad?"

Briefly, I told her. "Don't worry, dear, she's in good hands, now," I said. "Shall I come and pick you up as soon as I'm ready, then we can call at the hospital to see her?" to which she agreed.

I drove to my daughter's and, before I'd set foot in her driveway, the front door opened and my granddaughter Stacey ran out to meet me.

"Oh, Grandad, is my Nana alright? She's not going to die, is she?" the child asked.

Holding back an avalanche of tears, I held her hand whilst trying to comfort her. Knowing my answer would be far from the truth, I did what I could to allay her fears, saying, "Nana's going to be alright, my dear."

Willing myself to believe what I said to the child were true, I knew in my heart of hearts the end was near. But as a drowning person clutches at a straw, deep within me that tiny spark of hope still burned that my wife might somehow recover. Refusing to believe otherwise, I was in all honesty afraid to face the truth myself, when my daughter and I set off for the hospital.

Although the day was bright and sunny it could have been midwinter for all I cared, as we sped along the motorway. My thoughts were for the woman I loved.

The hospital lay hidden away in a far corner of the local park amid a sea of green, a more cold and uninviting place one could not imagine. As I stepped inside the huge swing doors, an overpowering smell of disinfectant stung my nostrils.

"Could I see Mrs Marshall?" I asked the young nurse who came to meet me.

"She is under sedation and sleeping at the moment, but you may go in," said the nurse. "You'll find her down the corridor in ward two."

With faltering step, we made our way to a far corner of the hospital ward and sat in silence at her bedside. The curtains, having been partly drawn to keep out the morning sun, added to the sombre appearance of this cold and dismal place.

Unable to comfort her, we looked on helplessly and watched the pale face twitch spasmodically every time the pain surged through her weakened body. As I took her hand in mine, her eyelids fluttered and she looked up at the ceiling misty-eyed.

Turning to look at my daughter and I sitting at her bedside, a smile of recognition spread across the once beautiful face, now gaunt and bony, ravaged by pain. For an instant, her eyes remained focused on the two of us, then slowly closed as she surrendered to the effects of a pain-killing sedative. We were numb with grief.

"There is nothing more we can do, dear," I whispered. "Let's go home."

Rising from the chair to stretch her aching limbs, my daughter placed an arm around my shoulder to comfort me. Together we left the hospital, and stepped out into the morning sunshine. Gripped by a sudden bout of fear bordering on panic, I walked unsteadily to my car, feeling as if part of me had been torn away. Although the day was hot, I began to shiver and found it hard to concentrate on the road ahead as we left the hospital.

Arriving at my daughter's house some twenty minutes later my granddaughter ran out and, throwing her arms around me, asked, "Is my Nana alright, Grandad?"

On the verge of tears threatening to cascade down my cheeks, I whispered, "The Lord is watching over her, dear."

Taking leave of my daughter later that morning, I noted the sky had suddenly darkened, as storm clouds rolled in. Then flashes of lightning swept across the darkened sky and peals of distant thunder drew ever closer, bringing rain in its wake. The downpour lashed against the windscreen of my car as I drove along the motorway, forcing the wipers to work overtime. As the storm progressed, the wind increased in intensity, to make driving difficult. No sooner had I reached my house and stepped inside the front door, the telephone started ringing.

Lifting the receiver from its cradle, my hurried, "Hello" was answered by a young lady, who asked, "May I speak with Mr Marshall?" There was something in the tone of her voice that caused my body to stiffen.

"Yes, this is Mr Marshall speaking," I replied rather hurriedly. "What can I do for you?"

"This is Arrowe Park Hospital calling you, sir," was her response, which startled me.

Fearing the worst I interrupted her in mid-sentence, to ask, "Is there anything wrong?"

"It's your wife, sir," she went on. "I'm afraid there is nothing more we can do for her here. We have just transferred her to a hospice at Clatterbridge, where they are better able to give her the special care she needs."

Her message sent my mind awhirl, and shivers down my spine as a bout of dizziness threatened to overtake me. Then the young lady, whose voice now seemed rather distant, went on to ask, "Do you have transport to take you to the hospice, sir?"

A sandpaper dryness clutching my throat prevented me from answering her question, until I managed a hurried reply, saying, "Yes, I have a car. I'll get there as soon as I can, and thank you."

In response, she said, "Your wife will be well taken care of while at the hospice, Mr Marshall. On behalf of the hospital staff at Arrowe Park, may I say we are sorry."

There followed a brief period of silence before the line went dead. I put the receiver back on its cradle and quickly made ready to visit my wife. Putting aside a need to stop for lunch I called at the local florists and bought some flowers to brighten her day. Then I drove as fast as I dared along the motorway in the direction of Clatterbridge village.

Arriving at the hospice, I was shown into a spacious ward curtained off into small sections, a far cry in many respects from the dismal Arrowe Park Hospital. Wards at the hospice, tastefully decorated in pastel shades, lent an air of peace and serenity for those who suffered from incurable diseases.

Reaching my wife's bedside, I placed the flowers on her table. Although she had appeared fast asleep, she sensed my presence as soon as I sat near her, for she opened her eyes. Her smile of welcome could not, however, disguise the terrible pain from which she suffered, in spite of her determination to put on a brave face. Hunched up among the pillows, she looked a mere shadow of her former self.

Deep furrows lined the pale face, indicating how months of pain and suffering had taken their toll. Her breathing, slow and ponderous at times, gave way every now and then to slight convulsions. I feared the end was quite near for the love of my life. Realizing I was going to lose her, I broke down and cried. There was nothing I could do to stop a river of tears rolling down my face.

With great difficulty, she reached out to me and, as her hand closed on mine, she whispered, "You have your life to live, dear, so please don't grieve for me. There is someone out there waiting for you."

Exhausted by this effort, she lay back on her pillow and closed her eyes, her every move dictated by what little strength was left in the frail body. Was this the ramblings of a sick person, I asked myself as I sat and listened or could she, a devout Christian, have been granted some supernatural vision by the good Lord? A power enabling her before she passed on, to predict some happening that would come to pass in the future? Before leaving her bedside, I stood for a while gazing down at the woman I loved. A feeling of great sorrow came over me as I turned to leave, for I knew there was little I could do to help her.

At the doorway leading from the hospice, a young nurse approached me, and asked, "May we have your telephone number, Mr Marshall?"

"Yes, of course," I replied, reaching in my pocket for a notebook I carried with me. Tearing a page out, I wrote my phone number down and handed it to her.

"We'll call you if there's any change in her condition," she said. Bidding me goodnight, she added, "Try to get some rest, sir."

Thanking her, I left the hospice, then headed back home along the motorway.

Night had fallen by the time I arrived. Pinned to the front door was a note from my daughter, asking to call her as soon as possible.

Picking up the phone from the hall table I dialled her number, and waited for some response. Before the sound of her "Hello" had faded, she stammered, "Dad, where have you been? I've called you several times. I was getting quite worried that something had happened to you."

"Oh, I'm alright, dear, it's your mother. They've had to move her from the hospital to a hospice in Clatterbridge," I replied, somewhat nervously.

I heard her quick intake of breath, as she said, "Oh, Dad," and fearing her children were listening, whispered, "Is it serious?"

"I'm afraid so," I replied. "They've asked for my telephone number and said if there is an emergency they will call me, so all we can do is wait and pray. Meantime try not to worry, dear, I'll call you in the morning." As an afterthought, I added, "Please don't let the children know, it will only upset them. Goodnight, dear, and once again please don't worry. It's in the hands of the Lord."

I replaced the receiver back on its cradle and wandered back into the kitchen in search of something to eat. It was only then I felt this gnawing pain in my midriff, reminding me I'd eaten nothing since early morning. Realizing that to keep mind and body alert I had to eat, I set to cooking myself a meal.

Having eaten, I felt exhausted by the day's events and wasted no time climbing the stairs to give myself a lick and a promise of a wash, before tumbling into bed. But sleep seemed as far away as ever, my mind was in a whirl, fearing what a new day would bring. I simply lay there tossing and turning, well into the small hours, before sleep finally caught up with me.

The rat-a-tat of raindrops on the bedroom window was enough to waken me, with a start. Through red-rimmed eyes, I peered at the clock on the bedside table, and heaved a sigh of relief. It was eight-thirty in the morning and the night had apparently gone well, for I'd slept like a log. Slipping downstairs, I put the kettle on for my morning cup of tea and, withdrawing the lounge curtains, looked out on a new day with hope in my heart.

Beneath a formation of dark cloud I watched an angry morning sky splashed with streaks of red and gold, spread across the far horizon. Back in the kitchen, the eerie silence was broken by the ringing of my telephone sitting on the hall table. Picking it up, my "Hello" was answered by a softly spoken young lady, saying, "This is Clatterbridge Hospice calling you, Mr Marshall."

Then pausing a moment, she said, "We regret to inform you that your wife passed away early this morning." She then added, "May we offer you our deepest sympathy?"

Her carefully chosen words hit me like a hammer blow. I felt the strength ebbing from my body and in that instant, a part of me died. Gripping the telephone table for support, I slumped down in a nearby chair. In stunned silence, I sat there immobile, staring at the receiver in my hand, totally unaware someone at the hospice was still on the line.

Through a mist of tears, I heard a garbled noise coming from the telephone in my hand. Placing the receiver to my ear once again I heard the young lady ask, "Are you alright, Mr Marshall?"

While in the process of trying to release my tongue, which appeared to have stuck fast in the roof of my mouth, I swallowed hard, then managed to say, "Yes, I'm alright now, thank you," knowing it was far from the truth.

There was a momentary pause, then the young lady spoke again to ask, "Will you be coming to the hospice, Mr Marshall?"

I suddenly found my voice, and with a measured degree of urgency, hurriedly answered, "I'll come as soon as possible, and thank you very much."

"That's quite alright, sir," she replied. "We'll await your arrival."

For the first time in forty-six years, I knew the meaning of loneliness. It seemed unfair, so unreal. Gladys, my lovely wife, dead. How could I go on living without her, I asked myself, over and over again. What was I to do?

I saw no need to press the panic button, and simply reasoned with my inner self. For, in spite of it all, life must go on. With a supreme effort, I pulled myself together, and picked up the telephone to ring my daughter.

Her answering "Hello" at the other end of the line forced me to hesitate a moment, before I summoned up enough courage to say, "The hospice has just informed me that Mother passed away early this morning, dear."

I heard her sharp intake of breath, as she sobbed, "Oh no, Dad!"

Allowing a little time for her tears to subside, I asked if she would come to the hospice with me after breakfast. Within the hour, I drew up outside her house and, as she'd seen her children off to school, we were free to make our way to the hospice at Clatterbridge. Little, if anything, was said between us during our journey, the shock of losing a loved one left each of us with our own silent thoughts.

At the hospice we were ushered into the room where my wife lay and, as I stood there gazing down at her still form, I realized it was just an empty shell. Though I'd seen death in various guises many times before, I was not prepared for this. There was nothing attractive about it, for the suddenness of death simply appeared as it really was. A shrunken white face with sagging jaw and hands, hanging limp and lifeless. I sat at the bedside and took in every little detail, knowing it would be imprinted on my mind. Another moment I would forever remember.

Close to an emotional display of tears, I rose unsteadily from the bedside and, taking my daughter's arm in mine, we left the ward together. Lingering would have served no useful purpose, now death

had placed an insurmountable barrier between us. Paying a silent tribute to a loving wife and mother, we tried to comfort each other as we
walked back along a silent corridor. Our footsteps beat a tattoo on the
cold marble floor until we reached the hospice exit.

The funeral, a simple affair with members of the family and a few
close friends in attendance, took place in the early days of September,
in a tiny chapel within the cemetery grounds. There, I listened to a
moving epitaph from the young vicar who conducted the service, his
voice gentle and moving.

Seated in close proximity to the coffin, a feeling of spiritual to-
getherness overwhelmed me. Even as the purple drapes closed to separate the two of us, I still felt her presence. This feeling of nearness
with my departed appeared to linger as I moved out of the chapel into
the churchyard beyond, and remained long after the hearse had left.

Only then did our many friends attending the service stop to offer
their condolences before slipping away, allowing my family to return
home.

Having survived many periods of great emotional stress and ex-
ceptional disappointments during my life, none affected me more
profoundly than the loss of a loving wife. But where does one find
comfort and hope, when an incurable illness invades one's personal
life to claim a loved one? My wife's passing left a void I found impossible to fill, for there were times when it seemed life itself had no
meaning.

Wandering around with unseeing eyes and on unsteady legs, I
simply had no idea in what direction I was going. With faltering step
I placed one foot in front of the other as though in a dream, groping in
the dark in an effort to pick up the threads of my life. But through it
all, this awful feeling of emptiness deep within me persisted, making
everyday living seem unreal. Although deeply shocked with a loss I
found hard to accept, my faith never wavered in the Lord who had
come to my aid during many critical moments throughout my life.
In His own time, I somehow felt He would surely intervene on my
behalf, easing the pain and deep sorrow a bereavement causes.

Overcome with grief I found hard to hide, little did I realize at the time, my life would be filled with unbounded joy and happiness, in the days to come. Meantime, I had to set about the task of pulling myself together and coming to terms with things as they really were, preparing to face the future without the love of my life.

CHAPTER 32

AN UNEXPECTED SURPRISE

The house in which my wife and I shared so many happy memories lay empty, but I dare not venture over its threshold, lest I break down in tears. Since the day of the funeral, I had been living at my daughter's, refusing to step outside her house. Then the day arrived in the latter part of November 1990, almost two months after losing my nearest and dearest, when Susan succeeded in coaxing me to venture into town, saying, "You can't spend the rest of your life cooped up here, Dad. Mother wouldn't have wanted that. Let's go and check your house, just to make sure it's safe. Then we'll carry on into town."

Now in every neighbourhood, there are friends willing to keep an eye on the house whilst you are away on holiday. Or on special occasions when, for one reason or another, you have business to attend.

There are also in many communities busybodies who love nothing better than to seize the first opportunity available to pry into other people's business. In this respect, the tiny village of Oxton in Cheshire was no exception. Returning home after a prolonged absence, my arrival was witnessed by several pairs of inquisitive eyes peering from behind lace curtains, wondering what I had been up to all this time.

Making discreet inquiries around the village during my absence was Mother Mason, my next door neighbour, an elderly widow of immense proportion, square of jaw with protruding teeth, sharp beady eyes, and deaf as a post. Her husband, an inoffensive little weed of a man whom, many say, married her to win a bet, had passed on some years previously. The cause of death, described by the coroner as heart failure was, many of her critics believed, due to her unnatural demands on him.

As the local busybody, it was only natural she was anxious to know what I'd been doing for the past months. As usual she waited until I'd stepped from the car, before opening her front door. Then acting as if taken her by surprise, she hollered, "Why, hello, Rowland, I haven't seen you for some time, is everything alright?"

In neighbourly fashion I acknowledged her friendly gesture to say, "I'm just fine, thank you, Mrs Mason," and made as if to enter my house.

She, however, was determined to prolong our discussion and tried to squeeze a little more information from me, adding, "Is there anything I can do for you?"

"No, thank you, Mrs Mason," I replied, endeavouring to be rid of her. At the same time I was muttering under my breath, "I wish she'd mind her own damned business."

Hurrying inside the house to avoid further questions, I was faced with the job of sorting out a huge collection of mail that Susan had picked up off the vestibule floor and placed on the hall table. Then joining her in the kitchen for a cup of tea, I remarked, "Mother Mason is such an old busybody, she's like a vulture waiting to pick the bones of its prey. Why can't she mind her own business?"

Breaking into a fit of laughter, my daughter sought to pacify me, saying, "She's only trying to help, Dad. There's been a few burglaries in the area so it's just as well she's keeping an eye on things."

Not to be put off, I replied, "There are too many pairs of eyes watching us right now, that's the trouble, dear. The house is fitted with a burglar alarm system, so why do I need their help? They are too damned nosey for my liking."

Gathering my mail, I placed it on the dining-room table, where it remained until an inspection of the house had been completed. Meanwhile, my daughter checked each room on the ground floor, opening windows to let in a breath of fresh air. That left me to see to bedrooms and bathroom where nothing had, apparently, been disturbed during my absence, although the air was somewhat stale and needed circulation.

Among a collection of mail accumulating over the past month or so, much of which could only be described as 'bum fodder,' were three buff-coloured envelopes. Printed on the front, in large black type were the words, ON HER MAJESTY'S SERVICE. All seemed to be written in the same hand, requesting the return of my wife's pension book which I had previously forwarded to them. So I was left with the task of sorting out begging letters, adverts, and a heap of junk mail mixed up with the undertaker's bill, which I placed aside, disposing of the rest with the household garbage.

November, normally a mild but damp sort of month, turned quite cold as it petered out. With night temperatures dropping below zero, a blanket of frost was seen to cover the ground each morning. Because of this sudden change in the weather, I found it necessary to leave the central heating system on in the house day and night, to prevent water pipes from freezing up. By raising the temperature to a minimum of fifty-five degrees, I felt this would suffice, should the weather worsen. Then, gathering up my mail and a few personal papers, I joined my daughter in the lounge.

"Why, it's lunch time, Dad," she exclaimed, looking at the clock.

"Let's eat out. I don't feel like cooking," she said. "It will do you good to get out and about again."

Seated at a table in one corner of a restaurant in town, I took in the spectacle before me. The place was packed with lunch time customers deep in idle gossip, the hum of voices barely audible above the clatter of knives and forks. This atmosphere of warmth and friendliness within the establishment certainly helped dispel a fit of depression I'd allowed myself to fall into since my wife passed on.

By the time our lunch arrived, I somehow felt more at ease, having just exchanged greetings with one or two old friends at a nearby table. It was at this point, our conversation turned to old Mother Mason, my next door neighbour, nicknamed 'The News of the World.'

Catching me unaware, my daughter asked, "Will you live in your house when things have settled down, Dad?"

To which I replied, "After this morning's performance from her next door, would you expect me to? The house is much too big for one person to manage, and furthermore I don't need four bedrooms. Besides, there are far too many memories and how could I avoid being pestered to death by her next door, the old windbag wants to know all my business. No, dear, my mind is made up, the property will be put up for sale."

In deciding to sell the house, I now had to find a smaller place in which to live. Meantime, my daughter suggested I stay with her until I'd found a place of my own. As the month of November drew to a close, I phoned the estate office of Messrs Jones & Chapman, with a view to putting the property on the market. Taking my name and address, a representative called later that week and took down details of alterations I had carried out to modernize a property constructed back in the nineteen hundreds.

Built of red-glazed brick and mortar that tended to crumble with age, the house was at the time I purchased it in a bad state of repair, requiring large areas of the outside walls to be repointed. I undertook to do this myself, some two years earlier. Since that time, a course of weatherproof silicone had been injected into the brickwork around the foundations of the house to keep out the damp. No dampcourse having previously been used when the property was built.

Due to extensive war damage, the slate-covered roof supported by oak beams had over the years sagged beneath its weight, causing considerable leakage to bedroom ceilings in the house. The whole structure was eventually taken down and replaced with Marley tiles, with a guarantee of twenty years. Wooden joists beneath the house had over a period of time succumbed to wet rot due to rising damp, so it was therefore necessary to replace the flooring throughout the lower part of the house. For added warmth, draughty shuttered-type windows tending to rattle in the wind were replaced with double glazed units, and a central heating system installed.

Satisfied the property was in good saleable condition, the estate agent telephoned me later that week to inform me the house had been placed on their list for sale. At the same time he advised me not to expect the house to be sold right away because the market was inclined to be rather slow at that time of the year. He added, "One never knows in this business. You could get a surprise caller any day."

It was now early December of 1990 and a worsening in the winter weather brought morning frost and bitterly cold easterly winds. With a forecast of the worse to come, I hurried home to check the temperature in my house that had lain unoccupied since my wife passed away at the end of August. Careful lest Mother Mason next door saw me entering the property, I waited until nightfall before slipping into a darkened house to draw the curtains and switch on the lights. Checking the heating system was high enough to prevent the water pipes from freezing, I switched off the lights and withdrew the lounge curtains before leaving.

Seeing my car parked in front of the house, Mother Mason opened her front door and stood there gossiping with a lady friend about the approaching festive season of Christmas. I was about to leave when she caught sight of me and screeched, "Hello, Rowland, I see you've a 'for sale' sign up there. Are you leaving the area?"

"I'm afraid so," I replied. "The house is too big for me to manage on my own," and begging to be excused, said, "I'm sorry I can't stop to talk with you, I have some urgent business to attend to," and breathing a sigh of relief, drove off.

It was just four days before Christmas when the estate agents Jones & Chapman phoned to say they had received a call from a prospective buyer, wishing to view the house. Would I be kind enough to make myself available at three p.m. that day, to show the person around the property?

Arriving outside my house around ten minutes to three, I stepped from my car and noticed a slight movement behind the lace curtains of my next door neighbour. There was little doubt my every move was being closely watched. Not wishing to be delayed, I was in such a hurry to get in my house that I tripped over a heap of mail lying on the floor of the vestibule.

Among the correspondence, a brown envelope with O.H.M.S. printed in large black letters on the front caught my eye. Ah! Here's another of those damned official questionnaires, I thought. I was about to throw it in the waste basket when the front door bell rang, so I slipped the letter in my back pocket. Opening the door, a neatly dressed young man smiled at me and held out his hand in greeting. "I've come to view the property, may I come in?" he asked.

"Yes, please do," I answered and, stepping aside, bade him enter. I ushered him into the lounge. From our conversation I learned he was a doctor from South America attached to the Liverpool School of Tropical Medicine. Looking around the property he made a particular note of the four bedrooms and suggested the smaller one at the rear of the house would be suitable for his study. He was obviously pleased with the property and asked, "But why do you want to sell? It's a lovely house."

"Yes, I have to agree with you," I replied, "but having lost my wife some three months ago, I have no further use for it."

Apologizing profusely, the young man took his leave, promising to return at a later date. From the lounge window I watched as he disappeared from view then sat down on the settee to collect my thoughts. It was at this point in time I felt the bulky package I'd thrust into my back pocket and, studying the post mark, noted it was from Newcastle-On-Tyne. Now, why would someone from that God-forsaken place be writing to me, I asked myself. My curiosity aroused, I slit the envelope open and from inside withdrew a letter and a heavily-sealed white envelope, bearing my name.

The letter dated December 17, 1990 was from the Social Services Investigation Department in Newcastle. Now what on earth had I done to get caught up in an investigation such as this, I wondered and carried on reading the letter, which said, "Dear Sir, we have been requested to forward this sealed envelope to you. The contents of which we are entirely unaware, are of a personal nature."

The signature scribbled across the bottom of the page was illegible which led me to believe the letter might have been sent as nothing more than a practical joke. I sat there for a minute or two staring at the sealed envelope bearing my name, wondering what dark secrets lay within, that someone would choose to write to me in this manner. To the best of my knowledge, I had done nothing that would warrant an invasion of my privacy by the Social Services Investigation Department, especially at a time when I mourned the loss of my wife.

For several minutes, I held the envelope in my hand, wondering whether I should take a chance and open it, or simply tear it up. Nothing more than idle curiosity saw me rip the envelope open, unaware the information inside would leave me in a state of deep emotional shock, and thereafter change the course of my life.

Inside was a letter from the Salvation Army Social Services Investigation Department in London, which read,

Dear Mr Marshall,

You will perhaps be aware of the Salvation Army's work in the realms of family relationships, especially in circumstances where for some reason there has been a loss of contact. We are attaching details relating to one of our current inquiries, and are writing to you in the hope that you may be the person sought. If you believe that the information given refers to you, we would be most grateful to have your reaction to this inquiry, and to know whether you might wish to be put in touch with the inquirer. If you have any hesitation about disclosing your present whereabouts, may we suggest that we invite the inquirer to write a letter which we could then forward to you – provided, of course, that you supply us with your address. We would give you our assurance that this will not be divulged to anyone else, without your prior consent. If for any reason contact is not desired, please inform us accordingly, in order that we need not trouble you again. If this

communication has reached you in error, kindly accept our
apology for any inconvenience which may have been caused.
Our reply-paid envelope is enclosed for your response, and
we look forward to hearing from you.
Yours sincerely,
J.Beech, for Colin Fairclough
Major, Investigation Secretary

A type-written note pinned to the back of the letter left me speechless, for it read,

"Your sister, Caroline Marshall,
wishes to get in touch with you."

The message set my pulses racing and my mind in a whirl.

Was this the person my wife spoke of before she passed on, when saying, "Don't grieve for me, dear. There is someone out there waiting for you?"

I was so overcome with excitement, I felt the room spin around like a ferris wheel. In the blink of an eye, I was swallowed up in a sea of emotion. Following the loss of my nearest and dearest, this startling news, like a bolt from the blue, proved too much of a shock for me to grasp what was happening. I simply collapsed on the settee and passed out. Drifting back and forth from reality into the mists of time, I recalled days of my childhood when convent life for an orphan was full of ups and downs. Then, as a shocked and bewildered boy of thirteen, the Mother Superior appeared before me to say, "Your mother wants you to go home."

Stepping off the train at London's Victoria station, I had visions of Mother running toward me, arms outstretched. Lost in the warmth of her embrace, I hardly noticed her tears caressing my cheeks. Then again as though it were only yesterday, Grandmother sought to appear and whispered 'Caroline is your sister,' then the picture slowly faded. Weightless, I found myself floating aimlessly into space, gripped by a spiritual force beyond my control wrapping itself around me.

Rudely awakened by the incessant ringing of the telephone, I fumbled around in the now-darkened room, and lifted the phone from its cradle.

My hurried "Hello" was answered by my daughter who somewhat anxiously asked, "What on earth has happened? You've been at the house an awful long time. Are you alright, Dad?"

"Oh, I must have dropped off to sleep, dear. I'm a little overtired with all the running around," I replied.

"Did the gentleman come to view the property?" she asked. "And what did he have to say?"

"Yes, he looked the house over," I replied. "I'll be on my way home now, so I'll tell you about it when I arrive."

My sister Caroline
as a young woman.

"Alright, Dad," she replied, "but you will be careful, won't you? It's quite dark out now. Bye bye."

A little confused, I placed the telephone back on its cradle and sat for a while, trying to recall what had happened that would have caused me to pass out. Somewhat vaguely I remembered reading a letter from the Salvation Army, with reference to my sister Caroline. It might have been that I was dreaming it all, but I couldn't say for sure until I drew the curtains across the window of the darkened room, and switched on a reading lamp.

My attention was instantly drawn to a piece of paper, no more than six inches square, lying on the floor with a typewritten message, which simply said, "Your sister, Caroline Marshall, wishes to get in touch with you." Its effect was to set my pulses racing when I realized I hadn't been dreaming after all.

I read the message again and again until the words grew so large, they appeared to leap from the paper to touch me. But when I looked for the letter that came with the message, it was nowhere to be found. It has to be somewhere in the room, I said to myself and threw the cushions off the settee onto the floor, in a frantic search for the missing letter.

Conscious of a sense of overwhelming joy, I gave a sigh of relief when seeing the letter lying there. I was as happy as a young schoolboy who'd found a treasure trove, for there was no doubt in my mind the letter was genuine. It had been written on notepaper, bearing the Salvation Army crest, with the telephone number of their London Office, requesting I speak to a Miss C. MacDowell, should I wish to call them.

So how on earth had the Salvation Army managed to find my sister Caroline after all these years when I had searched for her so many times in the past, and failed? The truth is, I knew little about my sister at the time other than her name, and that she was much younger than me. Were it not for Mother taking me to visit my grandmother, who told me I had a sister named Caroline, I would never had known she existed.

Once again, lady luck had come to my aid, as she had done many times in the past, when danger threatened. This, however, was a joyous occasion, a time for celebration and to give thanks to the Salvation Army, without whose help my sister and I might never have met.

Night had closed in by the time I left the house and slipped behind the wheel of my car. With a song in my heart, I set off to visit my daughter. Having tucked the letter I received from the Salvation Army in my pocket for safe keeping, my hand would subconsciously touch it to make sure it was there during the drive.

"Where on earth have you been all this time, Dad?" Susan asked, as I stepped from the car. "I expected you home hours ago."

"I'll explain in a moment," I answered. Placing an arm around her shoulder, I hurried us inside a brightly-lit lounge, where I flopped into a comfortable chair to relax.

"My goodness, what on earth's happened to you?" my daughter

gasped, as I sat down. "Your face is quite pale, you look as if you've seen a ghost."

Taking the letter I received from the Salvation Army from my pocket, I handed it to her, saying, "Read this, dear. I'm afraid it will shock you."

Her face showed no trace of emotion while reading the letter until she saw the note, pinned to the back. Then, in the blink of an eye, the colour drained from her face, her eyes opened wide in disbelief, and a strangled cry escaped her lips. "Oh, Dad, I can't believe it!" she gasped. "Can this really be true? How on earth has your sister managed to find you among the millions of people living in this country after you and Mother had searched for her over these many years without success?"

"That is something I cannot be sure of until I hear from the Salvation Army on Monday morning," I replied.

"But who else knew you had a sister?" she asked.

"Only your mother," I replied. "Sadly she is no longer with us – she would have enjoyed this moment."

Nothing ever prepares one for the unexpected, and this was one of those occasions. It was now Friday evening so I had to wait until nine a.m. on Monday morning to get in touch with them.

Throughout the long week-end, I became restless and looked for something to occupy my mind. How I managed to pass the time away during such an anxious and nerve-wracking period is beyond me, for I barely ate enough to keep a mouse alive. Each night I would slip the letter from the Salvation Army under my pillow, and hardly sleep a wink thinking about it.

By the time Monday morning arrived, my nerves were on edge and I felt like the wreck of the *Hesperus*. Waking long before the first light of dawn streaked across a sullen morning sky, my hand slid beneath the pillow to satisfy myself the letter was still there. As my fingers touched its paper-silk surface, my heart skipped a beat. Never in my wildest dreams did I ever imagine I would receive a message from my sister. I had lost all hope of ever finding her. How long had she been aware of my existence, I wondered. Had she lived with Mother after I went away to sea?

There was nothing I could do to quell the excitement coursing through my body that morning, as I slipped into the bathroom to hurry through my ablutions, and creep quietly downstairs to the kitchen. Breakfast consisted of nothing more than a cup of tea and a slice of toast, which I forced myself to eat before leaving my daughter's house on that cold December morning of 1990. Not wishing to burden her with further expense to her household bills, I decided to telephone the Salvation Army's London office from my home.

Giving myself ample time to make the journey, I drove at a leisurely pace along the motorway to Oxton. It was shortly after eight fifteen when I parked the car in the driveway and hurried inside. The air was heavy with the scent of pot-pourri, almost to the point of being overbearing and stuffy. Without attracting too much attention from neighbours, I opened a window in every room for a much-needed breath of fresh air, and flopped down in my favourite armchair to try to relax.

Keeping an eye on the clock as the minutes ticked slowly by, I sat there wondering how on earth my sister succeeded in locating me, after so much water had flown under the bridge, so to speak. But where had I gone wrong in my search for her all those years ago, and where was she now?

As the hands of the clock moved toward the hour of nine, I picked up the phone, and dialled the Salvation Army's Headquarters in London. Pen and paper ready to jot down my sister's address, my heart beat ten to the dozen when a young lady answering my call said, "This is the Salvation Army. Can we help you?"

My mouth opened, but I couldn't tell the lady my name. Tongue-tied I sat there like something made of stone, as the seconds ticked away. With a supreme effort I forced myself to say, "This is Rowland Marshall speaking. I received a letter from your office on Friday, December 22, informing me my sister Caroline Marshall wished to get in touch with me."

Almost breathless I rambled on, "The letter requested I ask for a Miss C. MacDowell. Could I speak to her please?"

There was a short pause, then, "One moment, please, Mr Marshall. I'll go and fetch her."

My whole being trembled with excitement. At the other end of the line I could hear the rustle of papers, and the chatter of female voices. The young lady seemed to take forever answering my call, but it was actually no more than half a minute.

I thought they might have forgotten I was on the other end of line until a voice broke the silence to say, "Hello, Mr Marshall. Sorry to keep you waiting." Pausing a moment, she said, "This is Miss MacDowell speaking. I have your sister's letter to hand. Would you like us to get in touch with her, on your behalf?"

"Er, no thank you, miss," I spluttered, nervously. "If you would oblige me with her address, I'll write to her today."

"Just as you wish, Mr Marshall," she replied good-humouredly. "If you have a pen handy, I'll read it out for you."

My eyes misted over and tears of unbounded joy fell in great big blobs on my notepad, as the young lady read out my sister's name and address. Nothing could check the tide of emotion sweeping over me until a voice at the other end of the line, hearing my stifled sobs, paused to ask, "Are you feeling alright, Mr Marshall?"

"Er, yes, miss," I spluttered, wiping my eyes.

"I understand how you feel, sir, so please take your time," said the young lady. "There is no hurry."

"I'm alright now, miss," I replied, wiping the notepaper with my handkerchief. I wrote down the rest of my sister's address as the young lady read it out.

Pausing a moment, she asked, "Do you have that down now, sir?"

"Yes, thank you, miss!" I answered, breathless with excitement.

"Very well, Mr Marshall," she replied. "Good luck and may God bless you both." Then the line went dead.

As if in a trance, I held on to the receiver for some minutes before placing it back on its cradle and gazing at the tear-stained notepaper with my sister's address on. A feeling of elation such as I had never before experienced swept through my whole being with electrifying speed. Reading it over and over again, I suddenly realized she was not as I expected, living in England, but thousands of miles away in the far reaches of Western Canada.

What on earth was she doing on the other side of the world, I wondered. Had she, like many children in the aftermath of the First World War, been shipped out to the colonies without her parents' knowledge?

My mind in a whirl, I could do little to stop myself collapsing on the settee, where I passed out again. The occasion had, it seemed, proved too much for me.

Waking to the sound of the phone, I heard, "Did you telephone the Salvation Army, Dad, and have they given you your sister's address?"

"They most certainly did," I replied excitedly, and read it out for her.

"She's in Canada. That's on the other side of the world, Dad!" Susan replied. Then as an after-thought, she said, "That's no problem, you can reach her by phone."

"There's an eight hour difference in time between ourselves and Western Canada," I replied, "so we'd need to be sure not to wake her in the middle of the night." I laughed. Then as if to remind myself, I said, "There's only a few days left before Christmas so I'll slip into town right away and send a greetings card. That should surprise her. I know it's late, but better late than never!"

"Very well, Dad," my daughter replied. "I'll see you later. Cheer-io for now."

With the stores in town packed with shoppers looking for Christmas bargains, I had no trouble choosing the best card I could find from what little was left in the store. Then slipping into one of the many restaurants in town, I found a quiet corner where I was able to sit down and write a letter to my sister.

CHAPTER 33

WINGING MY WAY TO CANADA

Pen in hand, I sat there wondering what to say until some inner instinct bade me hurry. So, without further ado, I wrote:

My Dear Caroline,
I cannot describe the feeling of joy and sheer delight I
experienced when receiving your message, through the good
services of the Salvation Army.
It is however nothing short of a miracle, you were able
to get in touch with me in the twilight of our lives. How you
managed to do this is beyond my wildest dreams. In clos-
ing, may I wish you every happiness for the festive season
and hope and pray after all the painful years of waiting, we
shall meet in the near future.
Your brother,
Rowland.

As the old year drew to a close, a change in the weather saw banks of ominous black cloud scurrying across the sky, forming an impenetrable curtain of grey across the landscape. Bitterly cold winds sweeping in from the east caused temperatures to drop quite dramatically, bringing our first snowfall of the winter. Down it came in huge white flakes swirling around like mounds of foam in a boiling sea, covering the ground in a thick white carpet. Swirling around the rooftops, it continued to fall until well into the New Year.

Not until the second week of January did the weather choose to abate, allowing our postman who we'd seen little of during this period, to resume his daily round. From my lounge window, I watched as he trudged through the snow. Reaching my front door, he popped an envelope through the letter box. As it fluttered gently to the floor, I rushed to pick it up, tore open the envelope, and let out a whoop of delight. My face wreathed in a smile, I read the opening lines of the first letter I'd ever received from my sister Caroline. Dated December 28, it read:

> *My dear Rowland,*
> *When I received your lovely Christmas card and letter today my first thoughts were, who do I know in Liverpool? I just cannot believe this miracle that has happened, making it possible for us to finally contact each other after so many lost years. Our thanks must surely go to the Salvation Army for a task well done, despite searching a trail that had long gone cold. Although I received no indication the Salvation Army was prepared to carry out a search for you I was, of course, only able to give them your barest details. Such as where you were born, and the date. Yet in spite of this, they managed to track you down.*
> *How they ever found you among so many millions of people living in Britain is amazing, beyond comprehension. Strange as it may seem, I was totally unaware of your existence until October of this year [1990] when David Wright, a researcher in the County of Kent, found details of your birth when searching the records at St. Catherine's House in London and sent me your birth certificate.*
> *In finding you at last, sadness creeps into one's very*

heart, realizing we were deprived of a childhood together.
That in itself is distressing. But, it is the time we have lost
in knowing and growing up together in a family life, that
is so devastating. We have both missed so much. The urge
within me now, compulsive as it may seem, is the need for
us to meet before more years pass us by. I simply don't have
another forty-six years to spare. This, Rowland, is the time it
has taken me to search for Mother.

According to our birth certificates, we were born in the
London area, so what happened to you, and where were you
brought up? I have so many questions to ask and I sincerely
hope you will be able to answer most of them for me. When
you next write, will you give me all the news of your life and
where you spent it. I do hope, Rowland, you will come to
Canada. Spend some time with me, I'll spoil you!

Welcome to the family, and let us meet soon. My best
wishes to you and your family for a good Christmas and
New Year.
I send you my love and affection,
Caroline.

Only now could I feel at peace with my inner self, knowing I
am no more than a telephone call away from my sister, realizing a
boyhood dream of mine will come true. Throughout many years I
searched for her without success, but that tiny spark of hope burning within me refused to die. I somehow had a feeling the day would
come when we would meet. Even as I waited to put in a call to my
sister living a world apart in Western Canada, I found it hard to believe this is really happening.

It was now mid-winter and, with the light of day fast receding,
evening shadows slowly crept in. As the grandfather clock in the hall
struck the hour of six, I lifted the telephone from its cradle, and dialled my sister's number. A buzzing at the other end of the line ceased
abruptly. Hearing a woman's voice say hello set my pulses racing
and my heart beating like a trip-hammer. For in that instant, I experi-

enced sensations of varying degrees from emotion to ecstasy coursing through my body, realizing the voice at the other end of the line
belonged to my sister Caroline. A feeling of warmth and belonging
came over me and I wanted so much to speak to her, but the tension
proved too much for me. The notes I had carefully prepared beforehand slipped from my grasp onto the floor, leaving me tongue-tied.

I had to somehow quickly respond to her hello at the other end
of the line and, fearing I might be cut off, forced myself to stam-
mer, "Hello, Caroline. This is your brother Rowland calling you,"
and waited.

A startled gasp of excitement from the other end of the line was
followed by an excited cry of, "Rowland, my dear, what a lovely surprise! Tell me this really is you, and I'm not dreaming?"

Pausing long enough to catch her breath, she asked, "Where have
you been all these years, and what have you done with your life,
please tell me?"

"I have so much to tell you," I replied, and gave her a brief run
down of my life as an infant, cared for by Franciscan nuns at a convent in Littlehampton, Sussex. Then told her I was thirteen years of
age when the Mother Superior called me into her office and said,
"your mother wants you to go home."

"You lived with Mother!" she cried aloud. "But where were you,
Rowland?"

"In Morden, Surrey," I replied. "Are you familiar with the area,
Caroline?"

"Why, of course," she said, "I know it well."

Not wishing to upset my sister, I decided to say nothing for the
time being, and asked, "How did you manage to find me, after facing
so many disappointments?"

"Strange as it may seem," she replied, "it came about after I decided to retire in 1987 and moved from Ontario to British Columbia.
While browsing through books in the genealogy section of the local
library, I came across a book entitled, *Searching for Your British and
Irish Roots*, written by author Angus Baxter living in Ontario."

After writing to him about the obstacles she faced in an effort to find her family over a period of forty years, he kindly offered to help. She then went on to say that Angus Baxter put her in touch with Mr. Rudall, a researcher attached to St Catherine's House in London, where records of births, deaths and marriages are kept. In response to Mr Baxter's request on my sister's behalf, Mr Rudall agreed to carry out a ten-year family research for a nominal fee. Mr Baxter urged her to agree to this sum, if she was to get all the information she desperately needed. The only details she could give Mr Rudall was her parents' name. Nothing was heard from the researcher for over a month. Then on July 16, 1988, to her immense relief, she received a letter from him enclosing the marriage and birth certificates of her parents.

It was at this point that Mr Baxter advised that, because she now had acquired all the documents from Mr Rudall, there was little more he could do to help. Caroline realized it was necessary to make another trip to England, specifically to check the church's records of her father's birthplace to learn where other members of the family were borne and bred.

Upon arriving in Lydd, Kent, her first impulse was to go to All Saints Church to check the records of the Marshall family who had for generations lived in the area. The Parochial secretary, Dorothy Beck, was exceptionally kind in going out of her way to help track the Marshall family listed in the church records, giving her a detailed list of births, marriages and deaths. Dorothy Beck also advised that if she wanted further help with family history to contact David Wright, a researcher living in Whitstable, Kent.

In April 1989, my sister corresponded with Joan Savage, someone she met while searching the family records at All Saints Church. During a conversation, Caroline told Joan she was in touch with David Wright who, when checking further into the records of her family at St. Catherine's House in London, discovered details of a brother born in 1919. He sent her a birth certificate of a brother she'd never met! It was then Joan Savage suggested she contact the Salvation Army in London who were instrumental in putting missing families in touch with each other, and ask for their help. And it simply snowballed on from there.

"You never finished explaining, what happened to you over the years, Rowland?" asked Caroline. "I'm dying to know what you have done with your life."

Not wishing to go into detail on the phone, I promised I'd write her in the next day or so, with a brief account of my life thus far.

"I'll look forward to that," she said. "I'm anxious to know all about you." Pausing a moment, she asked, "Do you have a photograph of Mother?"

"I'm awfully sorry, Caroline. I lost the only one I had," I replied.

"Oh, what a pity," she sighed. "But it's been wonderful just to be able to talk with you. Goodbye, Rowland, I'll look forward to your letter."

Long after the line went dead, I sat as if in a dream, with the telephone receiver pressed to my ear. It was the operator who brought me back to reality, reminding me my caller had rung off. Having spoken with my sister for the first time in my life and, realizing she lived a world apart from me in the far reaches of Western Canada, I wished I had wings so I could fly to her. We were like a couple of excited school children, chatting away for over an hour, swapping news and views about our lives.

When a letter dated January 15, 1991 arrived from Caroline, it fair took the wind out of my sails. For it read,

My Dear Rowland,
With this letter, I have enclosed certificates of Mother's marriage in 1915 to our father E. R. Marshall, together with his divorce papers in 1926.

It is, therefore, not surprising that after forty years of agonizing search for family, I am still trying to unravel some of the mysteries Mother left behind. Many of which I doubt I ever will. No, I don't suppose in your wildest dreams you ever imagined when finding you, I would throw you into such turmoil, which sadly I regret doing. But I thank God you are an understanding man, and did not choose to turn your back on me. Finding you, Rowland, has made all the heartache, pain and suffering worthwhile. I wish you and your family every happiness for the coming year.

In closing, my sister asked,

"Do you have a baptismal certificate? If not, write to the administrator at St George's Cathedral. There is every possibility you were baptized there, as it was the nearest Catholic church to where Mother lived. Summing up the situation we find ourselves in, I must admit, Rowland, the many names Mother used at times to hide her true identity becomes more bizarre the deeper we delve into our family history. Of one thing however we can be certain, she left us in a terrible mess.
My Love to You,
Caroline.

I had to be baptized before entering St Joseph's convent in the seaside town of Littlehampton, Sussex, but had no idea where. Taking my sister's advice, I wrote to St George's Cathedral for a copy of my baptismal certificate, giving my date of birth and the name of Rowland C. Marshall. In reply I was informed by the administrator, they had no record for such a person. Undaunted, I applied for a baptismal certifcate for Ronald Brandon, the name given to me when entering St Joseph's convent, and my date of birth. Some four days later, I received a letter from St. George's Cathedral with the much sought after certificate enclosed, with details that shocked and saddened me.

There is little doubt the information on this baptismal certificate was false. My name on the certificate was given as Ronald Brandon, born January 29, 1919, father John Brandon, mother Caroline Brandon, nee Hinks.

Sifting through the marriage and birth certificates my sister sent me, I was now faced with the unenviable task of trying to piece together details of Mother's life, following the break up of her marriage to my father E. R. Marshall in 1926. According to records I secured, he was a Petty Officer in the Royal Navy at the time of his marriage to my mother in 1915.

Baptism certificate of Ronald Brandon with mother listed as Caroline Brandon nee Hinks, one of Mother's aliases.

A certificate issued at that time shows I was born on January 1919, father Edgar Rowland Marshall, mother Caroline Elizabeth Marshall nee Ashby. I also have information supplied by the Greater London Record Office and History Library at Norhampton Row, London, regarding the whereabouts of my father shortly after my birth. This lists him as being stationed in Salonika on a two-year draft, aboard *H.M.S Wildfire*. My father was now a Warrant Officer, and my mother's address at the time was given as 182 Westmorland Road, London.

I was two years of age when, on February of 1921, my father was sent abroad and stationed in the Dardanells for a period of two years. Apparently, Mother was not prepared to wait two years for my father to return and, in July of that year, formed a relationship with John Brandon, a naval stoker, and eloped with him on November 6. I was now obviously a burden to my mother who took me to St George's Cathedral in London, and had me baptised into the Catholic faith. On December 6, I was taken by a person unknown to the seaside town of Littlehampton and handed over to nuns at St Joseph's Convent, where I remained until aged thirteen.

Feeling all too vividly the loss of growing up together that my sister and I endured throughout our childhood, I found it hard to forgive

Mother for depriving us of our birthright. Yet in spite of this, my sister and I made a special journey to visit her grave at Margate Cemetery in the County of Kent, on a bitterly cold day in March of 1994. There was no headstone to say it was my mother, just a small metal plate with a number stamped on it. This saddened me to think she had three sons from her third and last marriage, who could not find the time to give her a decent burial.

Arriving home, I put away the many family documents and marriage certificates I received from my sister, that had taken her a lifetime to collect. Among them were many names Mother used to hide her true identity, such as Hinks and Brandon. Satisfied I had put the finishing touches to the ups and downs of Mother's tattered life, I kept a copy of her marriage certificate, and a document with the details of her divorce from my father, putting them aside for future reference.

Then in early May of 1990, I received a letter from my sister in Canada, requesting the following,

> *My Dear Rowland,*
> *Once again I write asking a favour, hoping all is well with*
> *you and the family. I am enclosing a copy of Grandfather's*
> *death certificate signed by his son, Uncle Ernest, whom*
> *you met when visiting Grandmother when just a boy. Would*
> *you, Rowland, please secure the services of David Wright, a*
> *researcher living in the County of Kent, England, who was*
> *instrumental in sending your birth certificate to me, and ask*
> *him if he would trace Uncle Ernest, or his survivors? This I*
> *hope will finalize a long drawn-out search, undertaken over*
> *the last forty-five years, in an effort to find our family.*
>
> *In your last letter, you mentioned the property market*
> *was at a standstill. I do hope things will pick up, now that*
> *Spring has arrived. So do try and come over as soon as*
> *your house is sold. You will love Canada. More especially*
> *the beautiful areas of British Columbia where I live, with its*
> *sub-tropical climate. The city of Victoria and the impressive*
> *Empress Hotel overlooking the harbour are, no more than*

a short journey by car, from my home by the sea. I wish you
every success with the sale of your property and in your
efforts to trace Uncle Ernest, so take care, dear, and do give
my love to the family,
Loving you as always,
Your sister Caroline.

When I contacted David Wright by telephone he agreed to carry out a search for Uncle Ernest Ashby, for a nominal fee. Accepting his offer, I forwarded the necessary death certificate, and waited for his response. Some three weeks passed before I received a letter from him, saying:

Dear Mr Marshall,
On receipt of your letter I carried out a thorough search for
your missing uncle but without success. I will however give
you a telephone number to ring, that I feel would certainly be
to your advantage.
Wishing you luck in your latest endeavour.
Yours sincerely,
David Wright, Family Researcher.

With little to work with other than a telephone number, I waited until evening before deciding to pick up the phone and dial the number I was given. My call was answered by a gentleman who asked me to hold the line, and passed the receiver to his wife.

"Can I help you?" she asked.

"I hope so," I replied. "I am trying to trace my Uncle Ernest, whom I have reason to believe may have lived in the area."

"Yes, he did," she said. "We purchased the bungalow we now live in from his wife, a Mrs Phyllis Ashby, a couple of years ago. I believe she has since past on but, if it's any help, I'll give you the phone number of her niece."

Thanking her for the information, I rang off and waited a few minutes before dialling the number she had given me. My call was answered by an elderly woman who seemed rather agitated when I asked her if she knew of my aunt Phyllis. She said, "Who are you, and what do you want with her?"

"My name is Rowland Charles Marshall," I replied. "I am trying to trace any living relative of my uncle, Ernest Ashby."

"Oh well, I don't think I can help you," she muttered. "Let me have your telephone number. Maybe someone will call you," she said rather hastily, and rang off.

Uncle Ernest Ashby.

Some two hours later while typing a letter to my sister, I received a call from a lady who asked, "Are you Mr Rowland Charles Marshall?"

Her question puzzled me, so I answered, "Yes, I am that person, what can I do for you?"

"Can you tell me the name of your mother, and anyone else in your family?" she went on.

This is a funny sort of question for a stranger to ask, I said to myself. Who on earth can this person be who wants to know my family history? After hesitating a moment, I decided to tell her, replying, "My mother's name was Caroline Elizabeth Marshall - nee Ashby, and my Uncle Ernest lived in Downham, Kent."

The lady's response went through me like an electric shock when she said, "Yes, I remember you coming to my house as a young boy in short pants." And giving a chuckle, she added, "I am your first cousin, Elizabeth Markham. Your mother and mine were inseparable."

"Yes, I remember that visit!" I replied excitedly, and pleaded with her, "Do you have a photograph of my mother? I have a sister in Canada who would love one."

"Why, of course," she replied. "I have photographs of the whole family. I'll post them to you if you give me your address."

There followed a brief period of silence, and when next she spoke it left me speechless, for she said, "You know, Rowland, you are not your mother's first born."

Startled, I simply gasped, "What do you mean, Elizabeth?"

She then told me that Mother married a man named Antonio Capolongo in 1910.

"Antonio Capolongo," I replied. "Oh! I've often wondered why she would sing *Oh! Oh!! Antonio, he's gone away*, and my stepfather would moan, 'Do you have to sing that rubbish?'."

Elizabeth broke into a fit of laughter and said, "Yes, that's just like your mother, Rowland, always full of fun."

"My goodness, how many more times has she been married?" I asked.

Then on a more serious note, she told me, Mother had a little girl named Marie Capolongo on September 6, 1911. Sadly the mite suffered with bronchial pneumonia and passed away some sixteen months later at Queen Mary's Hospital in Carshalton, Surrey. We chatted on for some considerable time until Elizabeth said she had to go and, promising to send me some family photographs and keep in touch, said, "My, it was quite a surprise hearing from you, Rowland. Give my regards to your family and, until next time, goodbye and good luck."

Wasting little time, I telephoned my sister in Canada and told her I had been in touch with a first cousin of ours living in Sussex, who promised to provide us with a photograph of Mother. She was over the moon to hear the good news and cried, "Oh, thank you so much, Rowland, you've done a wonderful job. I can't wait to see this picture of Mother!"

Meanwhile, correspondence between my sister and I continued apace across the Atlantic throughout the month of May and on into June, a month usually associated with days of endless sunshine. On this particular year, however, the month of June was rather cool and somewhat damp at the outset so it was not until the middle of the month, traditionally accepted as the Summer Solstice, that we felt the sun's warmth. This sudden change in the weather sent prospective house hunters flocking to estate agents offices, looking for bargains. With the housing market having sunk to an all time low, there were many to be had. As time moved on I despaired of ever ridding myself of this property I'd offered for sale.

Come what may, I had to be rid of a house that was nothing more than a millstone round my neck before I could arrange my flight to Canada, even if it meant lowering the price. Then, when all seemed lost, out of the blue a telephone call from my estate agent caught me by surprise. They informed me the South American doctor who was interested in purchasing the property back in December of 1990 had made a new offer, nearer the original asking price.

"Would you be willing to sell now, sir?" the gentleman asked.

Seeing this as a golden opportunity to be rid of the house I'd lost interest in since my wife passed away, I instructed the agent to go ahead with the sale. By the end of July, documents transferring the property to the new owner were duly signed by both parties, leaving the way clear for me to arrange a long-awaited trip to Canada.

CHAPTER 34

OUR FIRST MEETING

With the holiday season in full swing, travel agents were inundated with people seeking to book flights to the more popular Mediterranean resorts of Majorca and Ibiza. I did, however, manage to raise a few eyebrows when asking the young lady at the office of Pickford's Travel, "Would you book me a flight to British Columbia?"

"Ah, let me see now," she said, taking a reference book from the drawer of her desk. She seemed at a loss to find the destination I had requested and not wishing to upset her unduly, I offered, "It's in Western Canada, miss."

"Which part of British Columbia would you like to book your flight to, and how long will you be staying, sir?" she asked.

"To Vancouver Island, as soon as possible, for a period of three months," I replied.

"Ah, you'll need a ticket to Vancouver Island International Airport," she said with a smile. There and then, I booked a flight with British Airways due to leave for Canada the following afternoon and telephoned my sister, informing her of my time of arrival. It was almost mid-day when I left the travel agent's office and having eaten precious little since early that morning, I slipped into a nearby restaurant for lunch. Having eaten my fill, I wandered around town and purchased a few odds and ends I might need during my three month stay in Canada.

Late that evening, I arrived at my daughter's house, where I'd been staying since the sale of my property, and sat talking with her over a cup of tea. Then slipping up to my bedroom, I was packing away some presents ready for my journey on the morrow, when a wave of excitement surged within me. I sat on my bed, and allowed my mind to run riot. For a brief moment, I imagined I was about to take flight on a magic carpet no less, knowing, within a few short hours, I would be meeting my sister.

It was past the hour of midnight before my head touched the pillow but sleep would not come. I simply lay in that darkened room and listened to the beating of my heart. Eventually the tide of pent-up emotion waiting to burst slowly dispersed, as sleep caught up with me. I awoke to find darkness had turned to dawn's early light and, through a chink in the bedroom curtains, I lay watching the sun as it rose majestically toward the heavens.

Morning had broken on this memorable day of July 31, 1991 and my immediate thoughts were of my sister, as I had been doing constantly since receiving news of her from Canada. Having spoken with her on the telephone she gave only the barest details of her struggle to survive during the early years of her adult life, and I wondered how she had fared since that time. I was soon to find out, but first I had to fly halfway around the world to meet her.

Rising early, I carried out the usual morning ablutions. Dressing at a leisurely pace, I slipped downstairs to the kitchen and cooked myself some breakfast.

It was around 11:30 a.m. by the time I had tidied up in the kitchen. Looking around the house to make sure everything was in order, I hopped into my car and took off into town. There was no need for me to hurry, since my flight was not due to take off for Canada until late that afternoon. Therefore I took my time over lunch and arrived home shortly after two p.m. Changing into some loose-fitting clothes for travelling. I slipped on my coat and after checking I had my passport and flight ticket, I picked up my luggage and carried it downstairs to the front door.

My daughter arrived home from school with the children at around three o'clock and suggested we should leave early. So, without further ado, I put my luggage in her car and we took off.

As if in a dream I watched the English countryside slip away as we sped along the motorway in the direction of Manchester Airport. As usual the place was a hive of activity, with excited crowds of would-be travellers about to depart for foreign shores.

Accompanied by my daughter and grandchildren who had come to see me off, I eased my way past the maddening crowd to reach passport control. Then, with my family bidding me a safe journey and Godspeed, I hurried into the departure lounge from where I boarded my flight for Vancouver. Even at this late stage, I still had to ensure myself this was not a dream and, within a few short hours I would meet the sister I had thought was lost forever.

Seated at the window of a British Airways 747 on that summer evening, I held my breath as we taxied along the runway to take off to a new world. There followed a thunderous roar as the engines burst into life. The aircraft gathered speed to take to the air, a prayer escaping my lips. Within minutes an eerie feeling of weightlessness claimed me as I sat there enthralled, watching the cold grey waters of the Atlantic Ocean receding beneath me.

Reaching an altitude of twenty thousand feet, the aircraft tended to level out as the roar of her giant engines faded to a gentle hum, hardly audible above the sound of excited passengers' voices. As we sped off into the wide blue yonder, one heard a clicking of seat belts being unfastened and all was momentarily stilled when the lights dimmed, and the cinema screen came to life. Covering myself with a blanket provided by a flight attendant, I curled up in my seat, seizing the opportunity to catch up on some much-needed shut-eye.

Sunlight streamed through the window of the aircraft when I finally awoke somewhat bleary-eyed, for night had now turned into day. A fellow traveller advised, "You had better fasten your seat belt, we're due to land shortly."

Struggling into a sitting position, I noticed an empty food tray in front of me and gave my fellow traveller a questioning look, to which he replied, "You were having such a good old snore, it seemed a shame to wake you. Now, I couldn't let the grub go to waste and I guess you weren't hungry, Buddy, or you'd have surfaced."

"Oh, I'm not really hungry," I lied. But all the while my stomach craved for sustenance, to stop it turning somersaults.

Having slept since leaving Manchester's International Airport, I woke up as to we approached Canada's heartland, the wheat growing provinces of Manitoba, Saskatchewan and Alberta.

Ahead lay the Rocky Mountains, their snow-capped peaks extending along Canada's West Coast, from Alaska into the U.S.A. and on to Mexico. Soon we were en route across the Province of British Columbia where panoramic scenes of unspoiled natural beauty left me spellbound. It was a spectacle I shall never forget.

Shortly after midday the aircraft began its descent and I looked on spellbound as the huge air flaps slid out, checking our approach to Vancouver Airport. With engines throbbing in reverse we touched down ever so gently on the tarmac to taxi along the runway, and shudder to a halt outside the arrival's lounge. I cleared customs and immigration, then telephoned my sister on Vancouver Island.

"Where are you, Rowland?" she cried, her voice bubbling over with excitement.

"I've just landed at Vancouver Airport and I am about to catch the next plane to Victoria," I replied.

My telephone call was cut short by an announcement on the airport tannoy system, requesting would-be passengers to Vancouver Island be prepared to board. With so little time available to get from a crowded terminal to catch my flight, I was rather fortunate in having been advised to book my luggage through to Victoria, before leaving Manchester Airport in the U.K. Hurrying past waiting crowds and traversing many lifts I managed to board my plane, with little time to spare.

Caroline and Rowland, sister and brother, are finally united in Canada after over 40 years of searching for each other.

Within minutes, the aircraft took off and rose steadily into a cloudless sky of blue. Then, banking sharply as if in some form of salute, the tiny plane left the mainland far behind. Winging off in a westerly direction, she skimmed low over sheltered bays and inlets with yachts bobbing gracefully up and down at their moorings, on our approach to Vancouver Island.

Catching sight of Victoria's International Airport I heaved a sigh of relief, thankful my long journey had ended. With little more than a slight bump, our tiny aircraft touched the tarmac and taxied to a halt outside the arrivals lounge. A tremendous feeling of excitement gripped me as I left the plane and watched the doors to the arrivals lounge slide open, realizing a boyhood dream had come true. Among the crowd waiting inside, I recognized my sister instantly. She was standing near a small group of people waiting to meet their loved

LUCK WAS MY COMPANION   409

ones and, recognizing me from a recent photograph I sent her, she ran to greet me. Her welcoming smile, just like our mother's, took me completely by surprise, for I could have sworn it was my mother who had come to meet me, instead of my sister Caroline.

Her likeness to Mother was perfect in every detail and, for an instant I remained rooted to the spot, afraid to move. But as we embraced no words of mine could describe this feeling of joy I experienced. Overcome with emotion on this, our first-ever meeting, for once in my life I was speechless. There was so much I'd planned to say to her on this wonderful occasion but, try as I may, words of welcome I'd rehearsed so often failed me.

Oblivious to those watching, we remained in a loving embrace for some minutes, reluctant to break the spell of this magic moment. Then, gathering my luggage from the carousel, we left the arrivals lounge arm in arm. At the curbside we hailed a taxi and, stepping inside, sat holding hands, as we drove off. Our journey took us along winding country roads edged with stately pine forests sweeping down to the sea, where the clear blue waters of the Pacific Ocean were seen to tumble over the island's sandy beaches.

Dotted here and there among dense green foliage, one glimpsed rows of brightly painted dwelling houses, set back off the road. Then as suddenly as it began, my journey ended, when our taxi pulled into the driveway of a neatly painted ranch-style bungalow in a quiet cul-de-sac. Retrieving my luggage from the taxi driver, I followed Caroline into the house where she lived, less than a stone's throw from the town's shopping centre.

Inside, everything was neatly set out, with an eye for beauty and comfort. In a bedroom she'd made ready for my arrival, I unpacked my clothes, putting them away inside a closet and chest of drawers. As soon as I'd finished, Caroline invited me to join her for a cup of tea. Ushering me into a tastefully furnished lounge, she suggested I take a seat. Sitting beside her I could see a perfect likeness between my sister and the mother she never knew, even to Mother's facial expressions and the infectious smile I remembered so well from my boyhood.

Reluctant to break the spell of this magic moment, I simply sat there and repeatedly asked myself, "Is this for real or, is it just a dream?"

Looking back on life, I must say I've been lucky to come this far, having been abandoned at the age of three, and suffering untold hardships throughout my childhood at the hands of nuns. Reaching adulthood I chose a sea-going career and on my first trip to Africa caught the white man's bogey, Malaria, from which I suffered bouts of this dreaded disease for the next six years. I travelled the globe and visited countries around the world many would never see in their lifetimes. I survived the horrors of five long years of war. I did not however come away scot-free, for I still carry the scars of third degree burns on my hands, the result of a dive-bombing attack on my ship during a relief convoy to the Island of Malta, in August 1942. The scars are a stark reminder of a brush with death that haunts me to this day.

Today as I near the ripe old age of eighty-nine, I have no regrets for I now reside in a country that cares for its senior citizens like no other, and honours its war veterans. Canada, in my humble opinion, is the finest country in the world, and I'm proud to now call myself a Canadian citizen.

ROWLAND C. MARSHALL

Rowland C. Marshall was born in London, England, in the aftermath of the First World War. Completing his education at St. Joseph's College in Blackheath, London, he trained as a radio operator and joined the Merchant Service in March 1936, at the age of seventeen.

A sea career spanning thirteen years enabled him to travel extensively to many countries throughout the world, until leaving the Merchant Service in 1948. He then joined the Mersey Docks and Harbour Company in Liverpool and, after many years service, was promoted to the position of Marine Supervisor. In 1976, an old war injury forced him to retire from the company at the age of fifty-seven.

He was married in 1944 to Gladys Leswell; she passed away at the end of August 1990. Rowland now lives in Victoria, Canada with his sister Caroline.

Lightning Source UK Ltd.
Milton Keynes UK
09 November 2009

146007UK00002B/20/P